STATISTICAL THINKING

Improving Business Performance

STATISTICAL THINKING

Improving Business Performance

Michail Dimov Todorov

Kruger Brentt
Publishers
2025

Kruger Brentt Publishers UK. LTD.
Company Number 9728962

Regd. Office: 68 St Margarets Road, Edgware, Middlesex HA8 9UU

ISBN: 978-1-78715-397-4

For information on all our publications visit our website at http://krugerbrentt.com/

PREFACE

"Statistical Thinking: Improving Business Performance" offers a comprehensive exploration into the principles, methodologies, and applications of statistical thinking in the context of business operations and decision-making. This book serves as an essential resource for business professionals, managers, analysts, and anyone interested in harnessing the power of statistical thinking to drive organizational success and performance improvement.

In today's data-driven world, businesses face increasing complexity and uncertainty, making it essential to adopt a systematic and evidence-based approach to decision-making. Statistical thinking provides a framework for understanding variability, identifying patterns, and making informed decisions based on data and evidence. By applying statistical principles and techniques, businesses can improve processes, optimize performance, and achieve competitive advantage in a rapidly changing environment.

As editors of this volume, we have endeavored to compile a diverse array of perspectives, methodologies, and case studies from leading experts and practitioners in the field of statistical thinking. Through a blend of theoretical foundations, practical insights, and real-world examples, this book covers a wide range of topics, including data collection and analysis, statistical methods for quality improvement, predictive analytics, and decision-making under uncertainty.

Our overarching goal in presenting this book is to provide readers with a comprehensive understanding of the principles and applications of statistical thinking in business settings. By offering insights into the latest advancements, best practices, and emerging trends in statistical thinking, we aim to empower business professionals to make data-driven decisions, identify opportunities for improvement, and drive business performance and success.

We extend our sincere gratitude to all the contributors who have generously shared their expertise, experiences, and insights in the field of statistical thinking. It is our hope that this book will serve as a valuable reference and guide for business professionals, managers, analysts, and students as they strive to leverage statistical thinking to improve business performance and achieve their organizational goals.

Michail Dimov Todorov

CONTENTS

Chapter 1 INTRODUCTION: BASIC CONCEPTS OF STATISTICS

1.1 INTRODUCTION: AN OVERVIEW

This chapter presents the fundamental principles of statistics. The first half of this book focuses on graphical and quantitative statistical methods for describing data (descriptive statistics) and the mathematical theory of probability, which allows statisticians to make inferences from data. These concepts receive special emphasis. The course utilizes the popular open-source programming environment for statistical analysis, called R. This chapter will cover the installation of the program and introduce the fundamental aspects of the system.

1.2 THE IMPORTANCE OF LEARNING STATISTICS

You may be pondering the inquiry, "In what circumstances and locations will I apply statistics?" If you engage in activities such as reading newspapers, watching television, or using the Internet, you will come across statistical information. Statistics are available for crime, sports, education, politics, and real estate. Usually, when you peruse a newspaper article or tune into a news show on television, you are presented with illustrative material. Based on this information, you can assess the accuracy of a statement, claim, or "fact". Statistical methods can assist in making a highly informed estimation. Given that you will inevitably encounter statistical information at some stage in your life, it is imperative that you acquire the skills to interpret such information in a thoughtful manner. Consider the prospect of purchasing a property or effectively overseeing a budget. Reflect upon your selected vocation. Professions such as economics, business, psychology, education, biology, law, computer science, police science, and early childhood development necessitate the completion of a statistics course. This chapter encompasses the fundamental concepts and terminology of probability and statistics. As you progress through the initial and subsequent sections of the book, you will come to comprehend the interplay between statistics and probability.

1.3 STATISTICS

Statistics is the scientific field that focuses on gathering, analyzing, interpreting, and presenting data. Data is a ubiquitous and integral part of our daily existence. Proficiency in data utilization is crucial for several occupations and is highly advantageous for personal advancement.

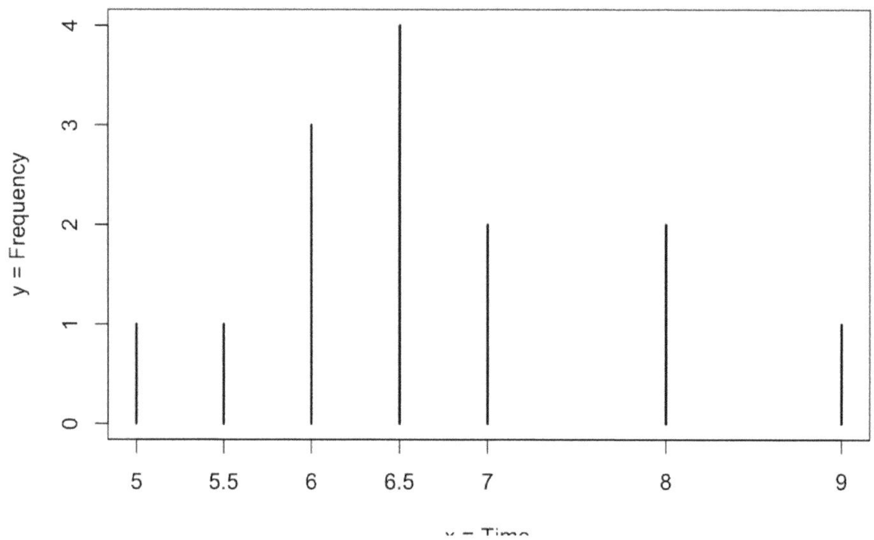

Figure 1.1: Frequency of Average Time (In Hours) Spent Sleeping Per Night

For example, assume the average time (in hours, to the nearest half-hour) a group of people sleep per night has been recorded. Consider the following data:

5,5.5,6,6,6,6.5,6.5,6.5,6.5,7,7,8,8,9.

In Figure 1.1 this data is presented in a graphical form (called a bar plot). A bar plot consists of a number axis (the xx-axis) and bars (vertical lines) positioned above the number axis. The length of each bar corresponds to the number of data points that obtain the given numerical value. In the given plot the frequency of average time (in hours) spent sleeping per night is presented with hours of sleep on the horizontal x-axis and frequency on vertical y-axis.

Think of the following questions:

- Would the bar plot constructed from data collected from a different group of people look the same as or different from the example? Why?
- If one would have carried the same example in a different group with the same size and age as the one used for the example, do you think the results would be the same? Why or why not?
- Where does the data appear to cluster? How could you interpret the clustering?

The questions above ask you to analyze and interpret your data. With this example, you have begun your study of statistics.

This course will teach you the techniques for organizing and summarizing data. Descriptive statistics refers to the process of arranging and condensing data. There are two methods for summarizing data: graphing and numerical analysis, such as calculating an average. The latter portion of the book will also provide instruction on utilizing formal methodologies to derive logical inferences from reliable data. Inferential statistics refers to the formal approaches used in statistical analysis. Statistical inference employs probabilistic principles to assess the reliability of drawn findings. The successful interpretation of data relies on the implementation of sound data production techniques and careful analysis of the data. While acquiring the skill of data interpretation, you are likely to come across an abundance of mathematical formulas that describe these operations. Nevertheless, it is crucial to bear in mind that the objective of statistics is not merely to carry out several computations using formulas, but rather to get a comprehensive comprehension of your data. The computations can be performed utilizing either a calculator or a computer. The comprehension must originate from within oneself. Having a comprehensive understanding of the fundamentals of statistics enables you to make more assured decisions in several aspects of life.

1.4 PROBABILITY

Probability is the mathematical theory used to study uncertainty. It provides tools for the formalization and quantification of the notion of uncertainty. In particular, it deals with the chance of an event occurring. For example, if the different potential outcomes of an experiment are equally likely to occur then the probability of each outcome is taken to be one divided by the number of potential outcomes. As an illustration, consider tossing a fair coin. There are two possible outcomes – a head or a tail – and the probability of each outcome is 1/2.

If you toss a fair coin 4 times, the outcomes may not necessarily be 2 heads and 2 tails. However, if you toss the same coin 4,000 times, the outcomes will be close to 2,000 heads and 2,000 tails. It is very unlikely to obtain more than 2,060 tails and it is similarly unlikely to obtain less than 1,940 tails. This is consistent with the expected theoretical probability of heads in any one toss. Even though the outcomes of a few repetitions are uncertain, there is a regular pattern of outcomes when the number of repetitions is large. Statistics exploits this pattern regularity in order to make extrapolations from the observed sample to the entire population.

The theory of probability began with the study of games of chance such as poker. Today, probability is used to predict the likelihood of an earthquake, of rain, or whether you will get an "A" in this course. Doctors use probability to determine the chance of a vaccination causing the disease the vaccination is supposed to prevent. A stockbroker uses probability to determine the rate of return on a client's investments. You might use probability to decide to buy a lottery ticket or not.

Although probability is instrumental for the development of the theory of statistics, in this introductory course we will not develop the mathematical theory of probability. Instead, we will concentrate on the philosophical aspects of the theory and use computerized simulations in order to demonstrate probabilistic computations that are applied in statistical inference.

1.5 KEY TERMS

In statistics, we generally want to study a population. You can think of a population as an entire collection of persons, things, or objects under study. To study the larger population, we select a sample. The idea of sampling is to select a portion (or subset) of the larger population and study that portion (the sample) to gain information about the population. Data are the result of sampling from a population.

Because it takes a lot of time and money to examine an entire population, sampling is a very practical technique. If you wished to compute the overall grade point average at your school, it would make sense to select a sample of students who attend the school. The data collected from the sample would be the students' grade point averages. In presidential elections, opinion poll samples of 1,000 to 2,000 people are taken. The opinion poll is supposed to represent the views of the people in the entire country. Manufacturers of canned carbonated drinks take samples to determine if the manufactured 16 ounce containers does indeed contain 16 ounces of the drink.

From the sample data, we can calculate a *statistic*. A statistic is a number that is a property of the sample. For example, if we consider one math class to be a sample of the population of all math classes, then the average number of points earned by students in that one math class at the end of the term is an example of a statistic. The statistic can be used as an estimate of a population *parameter*. A parameter is a number that is a property of the population. Since we considered all math classes to be the population, then the average number of points earned per student over all the math classes is an example of a parameter.

One of the main concerns in the field of statistics is how accurately a statistic estimates a parameter. The accuracy really depends on how well the sample represents the population. The sample must contain the characteristics of the population in order to be a representative sample.

Two words that come up often in statistics are *average* and *proportion*. If you were to take three exams in your math classes and obtained scores of 86, 75, and 92, you calculate your average score by adding the three exam scores and dividing by three (your average score would be 84.3 to one decimal place). If, in your math class, there are 40 students and 22 are men and 18 are women, then the proportion of men students is 22/40 and the proportion of women students is 18/40. Average and proportion are discussed in more detail in later chapters.

1.6 THE R PROGRAMMING ENVIRONMENT

The R Programming Environment is a widely used open source system for statistical analysis and statistical programming. It includes thousands of functions for the implementation of both standard and exotic statistical methods and it is probably the most popular system in the academic world for the development of new statistical tools. We will use R in order to apply the statistical methods that will be discussed in the book to some example data sets and in order to demonstrate, via simulations, concepts associated with probability and its application in statistics.

The demonstrations in the book involve very basic R programming skills and the applications are implemented using, in most cases, simple and natural code. A detailed explanation will accompany the code that is used.

Learning R, like the learning of any other programming language, can be achieved only through practice. Hence, we strongly recommend that you not only read the code presented in the book but also run it yourself, in parallel to the reading of the provided explanations. Moreover, you are encouraged to play with the code: introduce changes in the code and in the data and see how the output changes as a result. One should not be afraid to experiment. At worst, the computer may crash or freeze. In both cases, restarting the computer will solve the problem ...

You may download R from the R project home page https://www.r-project.org and install it on the computer that you are using.

In addition to installing R we recommend that you also install RStudio https://www.rstudio.com. RStudio is an integrated development environment (IDE) for R. It includes a console, syntax-highlighting editor that supports direct code execution, as well as tools for plotting, history, debugging and workspace management.

Figure 1.2: The RStudio interface

The screenshot in Figure 1.2 shows the RStudio interface. There are four panels. The top-left panel is the editor, the bottom-left panel shows the R-Console. The two right panels show the R-environment, history, file browser, plot panel and help viewer among others.

1.6.1 Some Basic R Commands

R is an object-oriented programming system. During the session you may create and manipulate objects by the use of functions that are part of the basic installation. You may also use the R programming language. Most of the functions that are part of the system are themselves written in the R language and one may easily write new functions or modify existing functions to suit specific needs.

Let us start by opening RStudio. It is good practice to have a separate folder for each project where you will store your data and R-code. We have a folder called IntroStat. When starting a R or RStudio-session it is good practice to set the current working directory to your project directory using the "`setwd'" function for example like this:

```
setwd("~/IntroStat")
```

Now we are ready to run our first R-command. Type in the R-Console panel, immediately after the ">" prompt, the expression "1+2" and then hit the Return key. (Do not include the double quotation in the expression that you type!):

```
1 + 2
```

```
## [1] 3
```

The prompt ">" indicates that the system is ready to receive commands. Writing an expression, such as "1+2", and hitting the Return key sends the expression to be executed. The execution of the expression may produce an object, in this case an object that is composed of a single number, the number "3".

Whenever required, the R system takes an action. If no other specifications are given regarding the required action then the system will apply the pre-programmed action. This action is called the *default* action. In the case of hitting the Return key after the expression that we wrote the default is to display the produced object on the screen.

Next, let us demonstrate R in a more meaningful way by using it in order to produce the bar-plot of Figure 1.1. First we have to input the data. We will produce a sequence of numbers that form the data[1]. For that we will use the function "c" that combines its arguments and produces a sequence with the arguments as the components of the sequence. Write the expression:

```
c(5,5.5,6,6,6,6.5,6.5,6.5,6.5,7,7,8,8,9)
```

at the prompt and hit return. The result should look like this:

```
## [1] 5.0 5.5 6.0 6.0 6.0 6.5 6.5 6.5 6.5 7.0 7.0 8.0 8.0 9.0
```

The function "c" is an example of an R function. A function has a name, "c" in this case, that is followed by brackets that include the input to the function. We call the components of the input the *arguments* of the function. Arguments are separated by commas. A function produces an output, which is typically an R object. In the current example an object of the form of a sequence was created and, according to the default application of the system, was sent to the screen and not saved.

If we want to create an object for further manipulation then we should save it and give it a name. For example, it we want to save the vector of data under the name "X" we may write the following expression at the prompt (and then hit return):

```
X <- c(5,5.5,6,6,6,6.5,6.5,6.5,6.5,7,7,8,8,9)
```

The arrow that appears after the "X" is produced by typing the less than key "<" followed by the minus key "-". This arrow is the assignment operator.

Observe that you may save typing by calling and editing lines of code that were processes in an earlier part of the session. One may browse through the lines using the up and down arrows on the right-hand side of the keyboard and use the right and left arrows to move along the line presented at the prompt. For example, the last expression may be produced by finding first the line that used the function "c" with the up and down arrow and then moving to the beginning of the line with the left arrow. At the beginning of the line all one has to do is type "X <-" and hit the Return key.

Notice that no output was sent to the screen. Instead, the output from the "c" function was assigned to an object that has the name "X". A new object by the given name was formed and it is now available for further analysis. In order to verify this you may write "X" at the prompt and hit return:

```
X
```

```
## [1] 5.0 5.5 6.0 6.0 6.0 6.5 6.5 6.5 6.5 7.0 7.0 8.0 8.0 9.0
```

The content of the object "X" is sent to the screen, which is the default output. Notice that we have not changed the given object, which is still in the memory.

The object "X" is in the memory, but it is not saved on the hard disk. With the end of the session the objects created in the session are erased unless specifically saved.

You can save objects with the "save" function

```
save(X, file = "X.RData")
```

To see whether this worked, delete the object X' from your environment using the function "rm"", load your saved object using the""load" function, and print it contents to check whether we successfully restored it:

```
rm(X)
load("X.RData")
X
```

We used a capital letter to name the object. We could have used a small letter just as well or practically any combination of letters. However, you should note that R distinguishes between capital and small letter. Hence, typing "x" in the console window and hitting return will produce an error message:

```
x
```

```
## Error in eval(expr, envir, enclos): object 'x' not found
```

An object named "x" does not exist in the R system and we have not created such object. The object "X", on the other hand, does exist.

Names of functions that are part of the system are fixed but you are free to choose a name to objects that you create. For example, if one wants to create an object by the name "my.vector" that contains the numbers 3, 7, 3, 3, and -5 then one may write the expression "my.vector <- c(3,7,3,3,-5)" at the prompt and hit the Return key.

If we want to produce a table that contains a count of the frequency of the different values in our data we can apply the function “table” to the object “X” (which is the object that contains our data):

```
table(X)
```

```
## X
##   5 5.5   6 6.5   7   8   9
##   1   1   3   4   2   2   1
```

Notice that the output of the function “table” is a table of the different levels of the input vector and the frequency of each level. This output is yet another type of an object.

The bar-plot of Figure 1.1 can be produced by the application of the function “plot” to the object that is produced as an output of the function “table”:

```
plot(table(X))
```

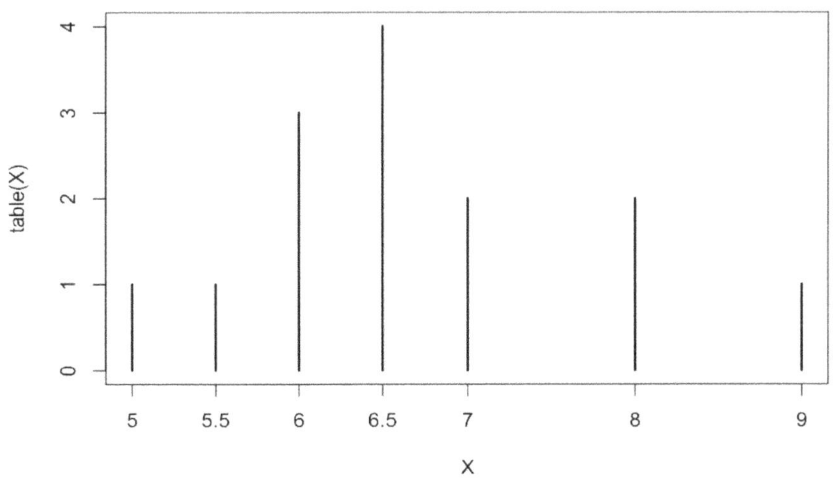

This plot is practically identical to the plot in Figure 1.1. The only difference is in the names given to the access. These names were changed in Figure 1.1 for clarity.

Clearly, if one wants to produce a bar-plot to other numerical data all one has to do is replace in the expression plot(table(X)) the object X by an object that contains the other data. For example, to plot the data in my.vector you may use plot(table(my.vector)).

1.7 EXERCISES

Exercise 1.1 A potential candidate for a political position in some state is interested to know what are her chances to win the primaries of her party and be selected as parties candidate for the position. In order to examine the opinions of her party voters she hires the services of a polling agency. The polling is conducted among 500 registered voters of the party. One of the questions that the pollsters refers to the willingness of the voters to vote for a female candidate for the job. Forty two percent of the people asked said that they prefer to have a women running for the job. Thirty eight percent said that the candidate's gender is irrelevant. The rest prefers a male candidate. Which of the following is (i) a population (ii) a sample (iii) a parameter and (iv) a statistic:

1. The 500 registered voters.
2. The percentage, among all registered voters of the given party, of those that prefer a male candidate.
3. The number 42% that corresponds to the percentage of those that prefer a female candidate.
4. The voters in the state that are registered to the given party.

Exercise 1.2 The number of customers that wait in front of a coffee shop at the opening was reported during 25 days. The results were:

4,2,1,1,0,2,1,2,4,2,5,3,1,5,1,5,1,2,1,1,3,4,2,4,3

1. Identify the number of days in which 5 costumers where waiting.
2. The number of waiting costumers that occurred the largest number of times.
3. The number of waiting costumers that occurred the least number of times.

1.8 CONCISE SUMMARY

Glossary

Data:A set of observations taken on a sample from a population.

Statistic: A numerical characteristic of the data. A statistic estimates the corresponding population parameter. For example, the average number of contribution to the course's forum for this term is an estimate for the average number of contributions in all future terms (parameter).

Statistics The science that deals with processing, presentation and inference from data.

Probability: A mathematical field that models and investigates the notion of randomness.

R functions introduced in this chapter

- setwd(dir) is used to set the working directory to dir.
- c() is a generic function which combines its arguments.
- save(..., file) writes R objects to the specified file.
- load() reloads datasets written with the function save.
- rm() can be used to remove objects.
- table() constructs a table of counts of the different values.
- plot() is a generic function for plotting of R objects.

2 Chapter — SAMPLING AND DATA STRUCTURES

2.1 INTRODUCTION: AN OVERVIEW

This chapter focuses on the challenges related to the data acquired from a sample. The emphasis is placed on the variability of this data, and critical thinking is encouraged regarding the validity of the data. This chapter presents a proposed method for importing data from an external source into *R*, together with a description of the data types utilized by *R* for storage.

2.2 THE SAMPLED DATA

The objective in statistics is to acquire knowledge about the attributes of a population by analyzing a sample that has been chosen from that group. A crucial aspect of this analysis entails the examination of the variability present in the data.

2.2.1 Variation in Data

Statistics assigns a significant importance to variation. The statistician's primary focus is to measure variation and quantify its impact on uncertainty while forming inferences.

Variation is present in any set of data. For example, 16-ounce cans of beverage may contain more or less than 16 ounces of liquid. In one study, eight 16 ounce cans were measured and produced the following amount (in ounces) of beverage:

15.8,16.1,15.2,14.8,15.8,15.9,16.0,15.5

The measurements of the beverage quantity in a 16-ounce can may differ due to variations in the measurement conditions or because the cans were not filled precisely with the intended amount of 16 ounces of liquid. Manufacturers frequently conduct testing to ascertain whether the quantity of liquid in a 16-ounce can is within the desired range.

2.2.2 Variation in Samples

Two independent samples drawn from the same population, although they may exhibit similarities to the population, will inevitably display differences between each other. Assume that Doreen and Jung have chosen to investigate the mean duration of sleep per night among all students at their college, using the entire student population as their sample. Doreen may opt to randomly select a sample of 50 students from the whole population of college students. Jung further gathers a haphazard sample of 50 students. The variability in the sampling process will lead to Doreen's sample comprising different students compared to Jung's sample. Consequently, there will be distinct variations in sleeping patterns solely due to sampling variation, rather than errors in measuring sleep for individual students.

Both samples, nevertheless, will exhibit similarities to the population. By increasing the sample size, Doreen and Jung would obtain samples that are more representative of the actual population. Consequently, the properties of their samples, such as the average amount of time a student sleeps, would be more accurate. However, it is quite likely that their samples would differ from one another.

The size of a sample (often called the number of observations) plays a key role in determining the uncertainty regarding what we can learn from our data about the population. The examples you have seen in this book so far have been small for convenience, but are usually too small to learn something with relative certainty about a population. Samples of only a few hundred observations, or even smaller, can however be sufficient. In polling, samples that are from 1200 to 1500 observations are considered large enough and good enough if the survey is random and is well done. The theory of statistical inference, that is the subject matter of the second part of this book, provides justification for these claims as well as techniques to quantify the uncertainty arising from random sampling and make decisions about sample sizes.

Finally, for the reasons outlined above, if an investigator collects data they will often vary somewhat from the data someone else is taking for the same purpose. However, if two investigators or more, are taking data from the same source and get very different results, it is time for them to reevaluate their data-collection methods and data recording accuracy.

2.2.3 Frequency

The basic method for summarizing the variability of data is through the use of a frequency distribution. Let's examine one example. Twenty students were asked how many hours they worked per day. Their responses, in hours, are listed below:

5,6,3,3,2,4,7,5,2,3,5,6,5,4,4,3,5,2,5,3

Let us create an R object by the name "work.hours" that contains these data:

```
work.hours <- c(5,6,3,3,2,4,7,5,2,3,5,6,5,4,4,3,5,2,5,3)
```

Next, let us create a table that summarizes the different values of working hours and the frequency in which these values appear in the data:

```
table(work.hours)
```

```
## work.hours
## 2 3 4 5 6 7
## 3 5 3 6 2 1
```

Recall that the function "table" takes as input a sequence of data and produces as output the frequencies of the different values.

We may have a clearer understanding of the meaning of the output of the function "table" if we presented outcome as a frequency listing the different data values in ascending order and their frequencies. For that end we may apply the function "data.frame" to the output of the "table" function and obtain:

```
data.frame(table(work.hours))
```

```
##   work.hours Freq
## 1          2    3
## 2          3    5
## 3          4    3
## 4          5    6
## 5          6    2
## 6          7    1
```

A frequency is the number of times a given datum occurs in a data set. According to the table above, there are three students who work 2 hours, five students who work 3 hours, etc. The total of the frequency column, 20, represents the total number of students included in the sample.

The function "data.frame" transforms its input into a data frame, which is the standard way of storing statistical data. We will introduce data frames in more detail in Section 2.3 below.

A relative frequency is the fraction of times a value occurs. To find the relative frequencies, divide each frequency by the total number of students in the sample - 20 in this case. Relative frequencies can be written as fractions, percents, or decimals.

As an illustration let us compute the relative frequencies in our data:

```
freq <- table(work.hours)
freq

## work.hours
## 2 3 4 5 6 7
## 3 5 3 6 2 1

sum(freq)

## [1] 20

freq/sum(freq)

## work.hours
##    2    3    4    5    6    7
## 0.15 0.25 0.15 0.30 0.10 0.05
```

We stored the frequencies in an object called "freq". The content of the object are the frequencies 3, 5, 3, 6, 2 and 1. The function "sum" sums the components of its input. The sum of the frequencies is the sample size, the total number of students that responded to the survey, which is 20. Hence, when we apply the function "sum" to the object "freq" we get 20 as an output.

The outcome of dividing an object by a number is a division of each element in the object by the given number. Therefore, when we divide "freq" by "sum(freq)" (the number 20) we get a sequence of relative frequencies. The first entry to this sequence is 3/20=0.15, the second entry is 5/20=0.25, and the last entry is 1/20=0.05. The sum of the relative frequencies should always be equal to 1:

```
sum(freq/sum(freq))

## [1] 1
```

The cumulative relative frequency is the accumulation of previous relative frequencies. To find the cumulative relative frequencies, add all the previous relative frequencies to the relative frequency of the current value. Alternatively, we may apply the function "cumsum" to the sequence of relative frequencies:

```
cumsum(freq/sum(freq))

##    2    3    4    5    6    7
## 0.15 0.40 0.55 0.85 0.95 1.00
```

Observe that the cumulative relative frequency of the smallest value 2 is the frequency of that value (0.15). The cumulative relative frequency of the second value 3 is the sum of the relative frequency of the smaller value (0.15) and the relative frequency of the current value (0.25), which produces a total of

0.15+0.25=0.40. Likewise, for the third value 4 we get a cumulative relative frequency of 0.15+0.25+0.15=0.55. The last entry of the cumulative relative frequency column is one, indicating that one hundred percent of the data has been accumulated.

The calculation of the cumulative relative frequency was performed using the "cumsum" function. This function accepts a number series as an input and returns a numerical sequence of the same length, where each component is the cumulative sum of the corresponding component in the input sequence.

2.2.4 Critical Evaluation

Improper techniques for sampling and data collecting can result in samples that do not accurately represent the intended population. An uncritical application of statistical analysis to such data may lead to deceptive findings. Therefore, it is crucial to carefully assess the statistical analyses we come across before adopting the results derived from them. Notable issues that can arise in data that one should be mindful of include:

- **Problems with Samples:** A sample should be representative of the population. A sample that is not representative of the population is biased. Biased samples may produce results that are inaccurate and not valid.
- **Data Quality:** Avoidable errors may be introduced to the data via inaccurate handling of forms, mistakes in the input of data, etc. Data should be cleaned from such errors as much as possible.
- **Self-Selected Samples:** Responses only by people who choose to respond, such as call-in surveys, that are often biased.
- **Sample Size Issues:** Samples that are too small may be unreliable. Larger samples, when possible, are better. In some situations, small samples are unavoidable and can still be used to draw conclusions. Examples: Crash testing cars, medical testing for rare conditions.
- **Undue Influence:** Collecting data or asking questions in a way that influences the response.
- **Causality:** A relationship between two variables does not mean that one causes the other to occur. They may both be related (correlated) because of their relationship to a third variable.
- **Self-Funded or Self-Interest Studies:** A study performed by a person or organization in order to support their claim. Is the study impartial? Read the study carefully to evaluate the work. Do not automatically assume that the study is good but do not automatically assume the study is bad either. Evaluate it on its merits and the work done.

- **Misleading Use of Data:** Improperly displayed graphs and incomplete data.
- **Confounding:** Confounding in this context means confusing. When the effects of multiple factors on a response cannot be separated. Confounding makes it difficult or impossible to draw valid conclusions about the effect of each factor.

2.3 READING EXTERNAL DATA INTO R

In the examples so far the size of the data set was very small and we were able to input the data directly into R with the use of the function "c". In more practical settings the data sets to be analyzed are much larger and it is very inefficient to enter them manually. In this section we learn how to read data from a file in the Comma Separated Values (CSV) format.

The file "ex1.csv" contains data on the sex and height of 100 individuals. This file is given in the CSV format. The file can be found on the internet at http://pluto.huji.ac.il/~msby/StatThink/Datasets/ex1.csv. We will discuss the process of reading data from a file into R and use this file as an illustration.

2.3.1 Saving the File and Setting the Working Directory

Prior to reading the file into R, it is necessary to acquire a duplicate of the file and save it in a certain directory on the computer. Then, the file can be read from that directory. We suggest establishing a dedicated directory to store all the course-related materials. In the following discussions, we make the assumption that the directory where the file is placed is named "IntroStat".

CSV files are text files. They can be generated either manually or by transforming data stored in a different format into this specific format. A prevalent method for generating, navigating, and modifying CSV files is through the utilization of conventional electronic spreadsheet software, such as Excel or Calc. The Excel spreadsheet is a component of Microsoft's Office suite. The Calc spreadsheet is a component of the costless LibreOffice suite. It is important to note that you should never directly modify raw data files. Store them in a distinct folder and avoid replacing them with any modifications. Ensure that any modifications made to the data are traceable and well-documented using R-scripts. Additionally, save the modified data under a distinct name.

Opening a CSV file by a spreadsheet program displays a spreadsheet with the content of the file. Values in the cells of the spreadsheet may be modified directly. (However, when saving, one should pay attention to save the file in the CVS format.) Similarly, new CSV files may be created by the entering of the data in an empty spreadsheet. The first row should include the name of the variable, preferably as a single character string with no empty spaces. The following rows may contain the data values associated with this variable. When saving, the spreadsheet should be saved in the CSV format by the use of the "" dialog and choosing there the option of CSV in the "Save by Type" selection.

After saving a file with the data in a directory, R should be notified where the file is located in order to be able to read it. A simple way of doing so is by setting the directory with the file as R's *working directory*. The working directory is the first place R is searching for files. Files produced by R are saved in that directory. In RStudio one may set the working directory of the active R session to be some target directory in the "Files" panel The dialog is opened by clicking on "More" on the left hand side of the toolbar on the top of the Files panel. In the menu that opens selecting the option of "Set As Working Directory" will start the dialog. (See Figure 2.1.) Browsing via this dialog window to the directory of choice, selecting it, and approving the selection by clicking the "OK" bottom in the dialog window will set the directory of choice as the working directory of R.

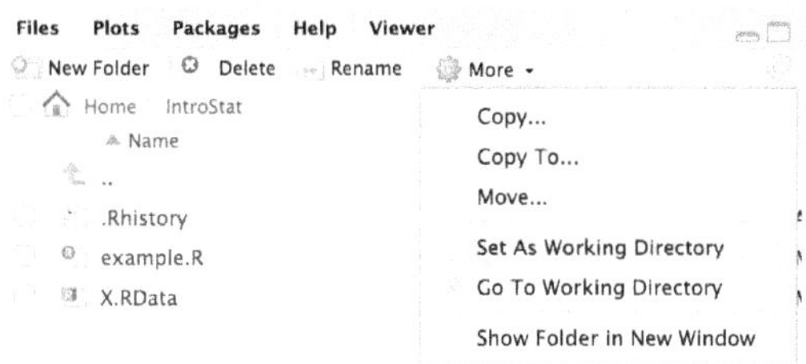

Figure 2.1: Changing the Working Directory

A full statistical ananlysis will typically involve a non-negligible number of steps. Retracing these steps in retrospect is often difficult without proper documentation. So while working from the R-console is a good way to develop (steps) in an analysis, you will need a way to document your work in order for your the analysis to be reproducible. Rather than to work only from the R-console (and change the working directory every time that R is opened manually), it is better to organize your R-code in so-called scripts. R-scripts are plain text files which contain the R-commands that perform your analysis. Executing these scripts will perform your full analysis and thereby make your work reproducible.

Figure 2.2 shows how to create an R-script in RStudio. This is done by clicking on the first button on the main toolbar in RStudio. This will popup a menu where you can click on R-script. RStudio will then create a new empty R-script in the editing panel as shown in Figure 2.3. Here you can add the R-commands that will perform your analysis. Make sure to save your new script. Finally note that you can select one or several lines in your R-script and click on the `Run' button in the toolbar to execute them in the R-console.

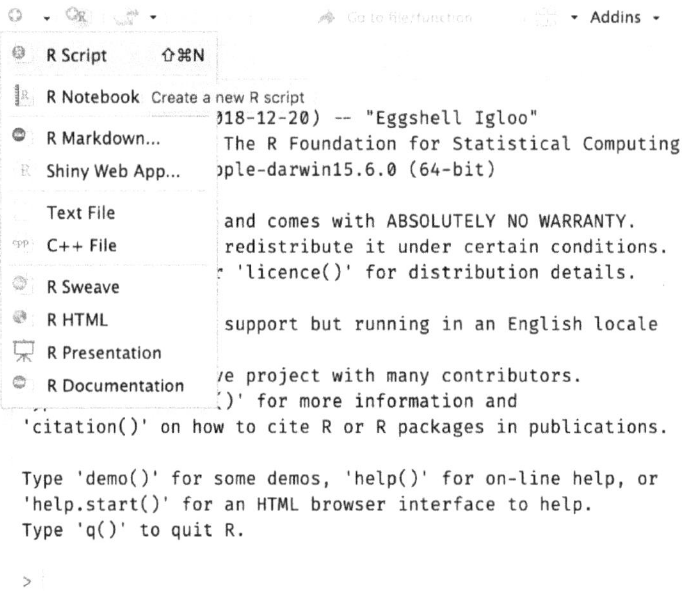

Figure 2.2: Creating an R-script

Figure 2.3: Editing an R-script

In the rest of this book we assume that a designated directory is set as R's working directory and that all external files that need to be read into R, such as "ex1.csv" for example, are saved in that working directory. Once a working directory has been set then the history of subsequent R sessions is stored in that directory. Hence, if you choose to save the image of the session when you end the session then objects created in the session will be uploaded the next time the R Console is opened.

2.3.2 Reading a CSV File into R

Now that a copy of the file "ex1.csv" is placed in the working directory we would like to read its content into R. Reading of files in the CSV format can be carried out with the R function "read.csv". To read the file of the example we run the following line of code in the R Console panel:

```
ex.1 <- read.csv("_data/ex1.csv")
```

The function "read.csv" takes as an input argument the address of a CSV file and produces as output a *data frame* object with the content of the file. Notice that the address is placed between double-quotes. If the file is located in the working directory then giving the name of the file as an address is sufficient.

Consider the content of that R object "ex.1" that was created by the previous expression, by inspecting the first part using the function "head()":

```
head(ex.1)
```

```
##        id    sex height
## 1 5696379 FEMALE    182
## 2 3019088   MALE    168
## 3 2038883   MALE    172
## 4 1920587 FEMALE    154
## 5 6006813   MALE    174
## 6 4055945 FEMALE    176
```

The object "ex.1", the output of the function "read.csv" is a *data frame*. Data frames are the standard tabular format of storing statistical data. The columns of the table are called *variables* and correspond to measurements. In this example the three variables are:

id: A 7 digits number that serves as a unique identifier of the subject.

sex: The sex of each subject. The values are either "MALE" or "FEMALE".

height: The height (in centimeter) of each subject. A numerical value.

When the values of the variable are numerical we say that it is a *quantitative variable* or a *numeric variable*. On the other hand, if the variable has qualitative or level values we say that it is a *factor*. In the given example, sex is a factor and height is a numeric variable.

The rows of the table are called *observations* and correspond to the subjects. In this data set there are 100 subjects, with subject number 1, for example, being a female of height 182 cm and identifying number 5696379. Subject number 98, on the other hand, is a male of height 195 cm and identifying number 9383288.

2.3.3 Data Types

The columns of R data frames represent variables, i.e. measurements recorded for each of the subjects in the sample. R associates with each variable a type that characterizes the content of the variable. The two major types are

- Factors, or Qualitative Data. The type is "factor".
- Quantitative Data. The type is "numeric".

Factors are the result of categorizing or describing attributes of a population. Hair color, blood type, ethnic group, the car a person drives, and the street a person lives on are examples of qualitative data. Qualitative data are generally described by words or letters. For instance, hair color might be black, dark brown, light brown, blonde, gray, or red. Blood type might be AB+, O-, or B+. Qualitative data are not as widely used as quantitative data because many numerical techniques do not apply to the qualitative data. For example, it does not make sense to find an average hair color or blood type.

Quantitative data are always numbers and are usually the data of choice because there are many methods available for analyzing such data. Quantitative data are the result of counting or measuring attributes of a population. Amount of money, pulse rate, weight, number of people living in your town, and the number of students who take statistics are examples of quantitative data.

Quantitative data may be either discrete or continuous. All data that are the result of counting are called quantitative discrete data. These data take on only certain numerical values. If you count the number of phone calls you receive for each day of the week, you may get results such as 0, 1, 2, 3, etc. On the other hand, data that are the result of measuring on a continuous scale are quantitative continuous data, assuming that we can measure accurately. Measuring angles in radians may result in the numbers $\frac{\pi}{6}, \frac{\pi}{3}, \frac{\pi}{2}, \pi, \frac{3\pi}{4}$, etc. If you and your friends carry backpacks with books in them to school, the numbers of books in the backpacks are discrete data and the weights of the backpacks are continuous data.

The data are the number of books students carry in their backpacks. You sample five students. Two students carry 3 books, one student carries 4 books, one student carries 2 books, and one student carries 1 book. The numbers of books (3, 4, 2, and 1) are the quantitative discrete data.

The data are the weights of the backpacks with the books in it. You sample the same five students. The weights (in pounds) of their backpacks are 6.2, 7, 6.8, 9.1, 4.3. Notice that backpacks carrying three books can have different weights. Weights are quantitative continuous data because weights are measured.

The data are the colors of backpacks. Again, you sample the same five students. One student has a red backpack, two students have black backpacks, one student has a green backpack, and one student has a gray backpack. The colors red, black, black, green, and gray are qualitative data.

The differentiation between continuous and discrete numeric data is typically not taken into account in the statistical methods used to examine the data. Indeed, R does not differentiate between these two sorts of numeric data and stores them both as "numeric". Therefore, we shall disregard the precise classification of numerical data and consider them as a unified entity. However, the focus will be on distinguishing between numeric and factor data.

Data can be collected in numerical form and then reported in a categorical manner. As an illustration, the quiz scores for every student are documented for the duration of the semester. At the conclusion of the term, the quiz scores are recorded and categorized as A, B, C, D, or F. Alternatively, it is possible to assign numerical values to categories of qualitative data and then present those values. However, it is important to consider the produced data as a significant variable. By default, R stores variables with non-numeric values as factors. Alternatively, the variables are stored as numerical values. The variable type is crucial as distinct statistical approaches are employed for different data kinds. Therefore, it is essential to ensure that the variables being evaluated possess the correct type. Factors that use numbers to represent the levels are specifically referred to as numerical factors. Otherwise, R will interpret them as numerical data.

2.4 EXERCISES

Exercise 2.1 Consider the following relative frequency table on hurricanes that have made direct hits on the U.S. between 1851 and 2004 (http://www.nhc.noaa.gov/gifs/table5.gif). Hurricanes are given a strength category rating based on the minimum wind speed generated by the storm. Some of the entries to the table are missing.

Table 2.1: Frequency of Hurricane Direct Hits

Category	# Direct Hits	Relative Freq.	Cum. Relative Freq.
1	109		
2	72	0.2637	0.6630
3		0.2601	
4	18		0.9890
5	3	0.0110	1.0000

1. What is the relative frequency of direct hits of category 1?
2. What is the relative frequency of direct hits of category 4 or more?

Exercise 2.2 The number of calves that were born to some cows during their productive years was recorded. The data was entered into an R object by the name "calves". Refer to the following R code:

```
freq <- table(calves)
cumsum(freq)
```

```
##  1  2  3  4  5  6  7
##  4  7 18 28 32 38 45
```

1. How many cows were involved in this study?
2. How many cows gave birth to a total of 4 calves?
3. What is the relative frequency of cows that gave birth to at least 4 calves?

3 Chapter

DESCRIPTIVE STATISTICS

3.1 INTRODUCTION: AN OVERVIEW

This chapter focuses on the quantitative and visual methods used to describe and present data. The field of statistics that deals with summarizing and describing data is referred to as descriptive statistics. You will acquire the skills to compute and analyze these metrics and charts.

3.2 DISPLAYING DATA

Upon gathering data, what actions will you take with it? Data can be characterized and displayed in several formats. Suppose you have a specific interest in purchasing a house in a particular locality. If you are unaware of the current house pricing, you might request your real estate agent to provide you with a sample dataset containing price information. Examining the various prices in the sample might be somewhat overwhelming. An alternative approach would be to examine the median price and the range of prices. Describing data involves learning about the median and variation, which are two distinct methods. Your representative may also furnish you with a graphical representation of the data. A statistical graph is a visual instrument that facilitates the understanding of the distribution pattern of a sample. Graphs are a superior method of data presentation compared to a large set of numbers because they allow us to visually identify data clusters and areas with limited data values. Newspapers and the Internet utilize graphs as a means to present trends and facilitate rapid comparison of data and figures for readers. Statisticians frequently initiate the study by visually representing the data using graphs, aiming to obtain a comprehensive overview of the information. Subsequently, further formal instruments can be utilized. In the preceding chapters, we employed the bar plot, which involves placing bars over the values to represent the frequencies of those values in the data. This chapter will focus on histograms and box plots, which are additional forms of graphs. Other commonly utilized types of graphs, such as the stem-and-leaf plot, the frequency polygon (a variant of the broken line graph), and the pie charts, will not be covered in this book. The mentioned plots and the excluded plots are closely connected to the concept of data frequency established in Chapter 2, aiming to visually depict this concept.

3.2.1 Histograms

The histogram is a commonly employed technique for illustrating the distribution of continuous numerical data. One benefit of using a histogram is its ability to effectively present extensive data sets. An empirical guideline is to employ a histogram when the dataset comprises 100 or more variables. To generate a histogram in R, one can use the "hist" function on a sequence of numerical data. Import the data frame "ex.1" into R, which includes information on sex and height. Generate a histogram to visualize the distribution of heights.

```
ex.1 <- read.csv("_data/ex1.csv")
hist(ex.1$height)
```

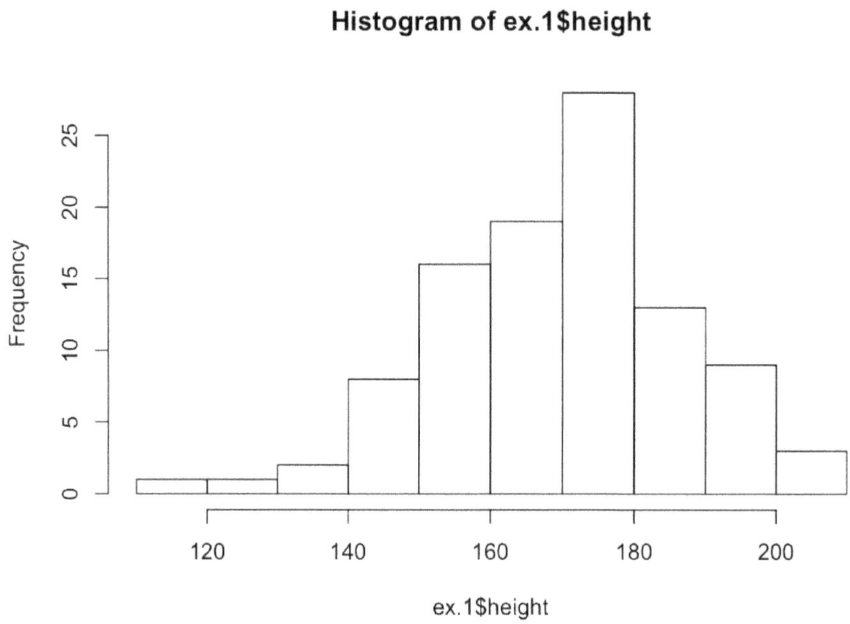

Figure 3.1: Histogram of Height

The data set, which is the content of the CSV file "ex1.csv", was used in Chapter 2 in order to demonstrate the reading of data that is stored in a external file into R. The first line of the above script reads in the data from "ex1.csv" into a data frame object named "ex.1" that maintains the data internally in R. The second line of the script produces the histogram. We will discuss below the code associated with this second line.

A histogram consists of contiguous boxes. It has both a horizontal axis and a vertical axis. The horizontal axis is labeled with what the data represents (the height, in this example). The vertical axis presents frequencies and is labeled "Frequency". By the examination of the histogram one can appreciate the shape of the data, the center, and the spread of the data.

The histogram is constructed by dividing the range of the data (the x-axis) into equal intervals, which are the bases for the boxes. The height of each box represents the count of the number of observations that fall within the interval. For example, consider the box with the base between 160 and 170. There is a total of 19 subjects with height larger that 160 but no more than 170 (that is, 160<height≤170160<height≤170). Consequently, the height of that box[1] is 19.

The input to the function "hist" should be a sequence of numerical values. In principle, one may use the function "c" to produce a sequence of data and apply the histogram plotting function to the output of the sequence producing function. However, in the current case we have already the data stored in the data frame "ex.1", all we need to learn is how to extract that data so it can be used as input to the function "hist" that plots the histogram.

Notice the structure of the input that we have used in order to construct the histogram of the variable "height" in the "ex.1" data frame. One may address the variable "variable.name" in the data frame "dataframe.name" using the format: "dataframe.name$variable.name". Indeed, when we type the expression "ex.1$height" we get as an output the values of the variable "height" from the given data frame:

```
ex.1$height
```

```
##   [1] 182 168 172 154 174 176 193 156 157 186 143 182 194 187 171 178 157
##  [18] 156 172 157 171 164 142 140 202 176 165 176 175 170 169 153 169 158
##  [35] 208 185 157 147 160 173 164 182 175 165 194 178 178 186 165 180 174
##  [52] 169 173 199 163 160 172 177 165 205 193 158 180 167 165 183 171 191
##  [69] 191 152 148 176 155 156 177 180 186 167 174 171 148 153 136 199 161
##  [86] 150 181 166 147 168 188 170 189 117 174 187 141 195 129 172
```

This is a numeric sequence and can serve as the input to a function that expects a numeric sequence as input, a function such as "hist". (But also other functions, for example, "sum" and "cumsum".)

There are 100 observations in the variable "ex.1$height". So many observations cannot be displayed on the screen on one line. Consequently, the sequence of the data is wrapped and displayed over several lines. Notice that the square brackets on the left hand side of each line indicate the position in the sequence of the first value on that line. Hence, the number on the first line is "[1]". The number on the second line is "[16]", since the second line starts with the 16th observation in the display given in the book. Notice, that numbers in the square brackets on your R Console window may be different, depending on the setting of the display on your computer.

3.2.2 Box Plots

The box plot, also known as the box-whisker plot, provides a concise visual representation of the data's concentration. Additionally, it demonstrates the extent to which the extreme values deviate from the majority of the data. The box plot is generatedusingfivevalues:theminimumvalue,thefirstquartile,themedian,thethird quartile,andthemaximumvalue.Thispartwillcoverthemedian,thefirstquartile,and the third quartile. These concepts will also be reviewed again in the following section. The median is a numerical measure used to determine the central value of a dataset. The median can be conceptualized as the central value, even if it is not necessarily one of the values observed. A median is a numerical value that divides ordered data into two equal halves. The median divides the values into two equal parts, with half of the values being equal to or smaller than it, and the other half being equal to or bigger than it. For example, consider the following data that contains 14 values:

1,11.5,6,7.2,4,8,9,10,6.8,8.3,2,2,10,1

Ordered, from smallest to largest, we get:

1,1,2,2,4,6,6.8,7.2,8,8.3,9,10,10,11.5

The median is between the 7th value, 6.8, and the 8th value 7.2. To find the median, add the two values together and divide by 2:

$$\frac{6.8 + 7.2}{2} = 7$$

The median is 7. Half of the values are smaller than 7 and half of the values are larger than 7.

Quartiles are numbers that separate the data into quarters. Quartiles may or may not be part of the data. To find the quartiles, first find the median or second quartile. The first quartile is the middle value of the lower half of the data and the third quartile is the middle value of the upper half of the data. For illustration consider the same data set from above:

1,1,2,2,4,6,6.8,7.2,8,8.3,9,10,10,11.5

The median or second quartile is 7. The lower half of the data is:

1,1,2,2,4,6,6.8

The middle value of the lower half is 2. The number 2, which is part of the data in this case, is the first quartile which is denoted Q1. One-fourth of the values are the same or less than 2 and three-fourths of the values are more than 2.

The upper half of the data is:

7.2,8,8.3,9,10,10,11.5

The middle value of the upper half is 9. The number 9 is the third quartile which is denoted Q3. Three-fourths of the values are less than 9 and one-fourth of the values[4] are more than 9.

Outliers are values that do not fit with the rest of the data and lie outside of the normal range. Data points with values that are much too large or much too small in comparison to the vast majority of the observations will be identified as outliers. In the context of the construction of a box plot we identify potential outliers with the help of the *inter-quartile range* (IQR). The inter-quartile range is the distance between the third quartile (Q3) and the first quartile (Q1), i.e., IQR=Q3-Q1. A data point that is larger than the third quartile plus 1.5 times the inter-quartile range will be marked as a potential outlier. Likewise, a data point smaller than the first quartile minus 1.5 times the inter-quartile range will also be so marked. Outliers may have a substantial effect on the outcome of statistical analysis, therefore it is important that one is alerted to the presence of outliers.

In the running example we obtained an inter-quartile range of size 9-2=7. The upper threshold for defining an outlier is 9+1.5×7=19.59+1.5×7=19.5 and the lower threshold is 2−1.5×7=-8.52−1.5×7=-8.5. All data points are within the two thresholds, hence there are no outliers in this data.

In the construction of a box plot one uses a vertical rectangular box and two vertical "whiskers" that extend from the ends of the box to the smallest and largest data values that are not outliers. Outlier values, if any exist, are marked as points above or blow the endpoints of the whiskers. The smallest and largest non-outlier data values label the endpoints of the axis. The first quartile marks one end of the box and the third quartile marks the other end of the box. The central 50% of the data fall within the box.

One may produce a box plot with the aid of the function "boxplot". The input to the function is a sequence of numerical values and the output is a plot. As an example, let us produce the box plot of the 14 data points that were used as an illustration:

```
boxplot(c(1,11.5,6,7.2,4,8,9,10,6.8,8.3,2,2,10,1))
```

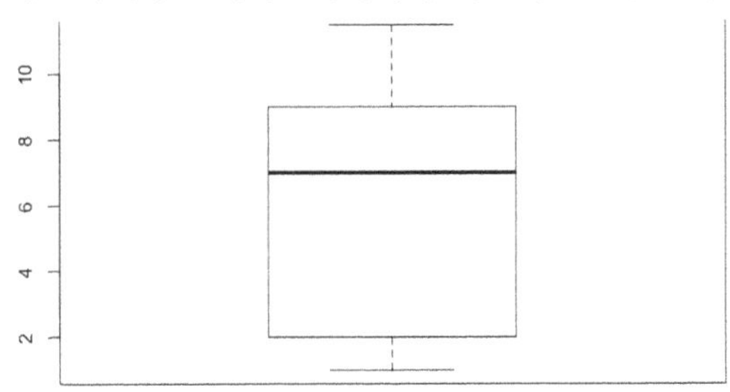

Observe that the end points of the whiskers are 1, for the minimal value, and 11.5 for the largest value. The end values of the box are 9 for the third quartile and 2 for the first quartile. The median 7 is marked inside the box.

Next, let us examine the box plot for the height data:

```
boxplot(ex.1$height)
```

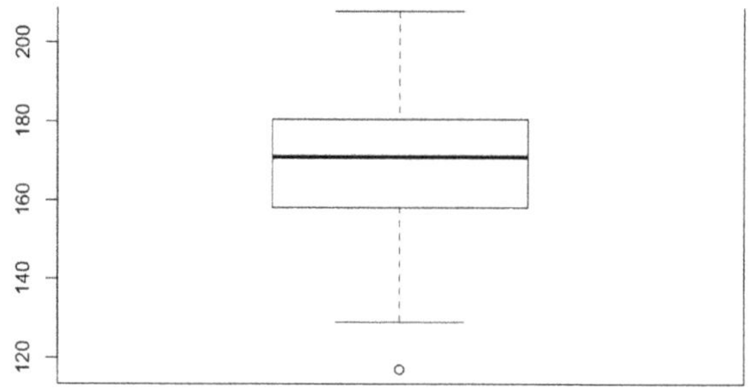

In order to assess the plot let us compute quartiles of the variable:

```
summary(ex.1$height)

##    Min. 1st Qu.  Median    Mean 3rd Qu.    Max.
##   117.0   158.0   171.0   170.1   180.2   208.0
```

The function "summary", when applied to a numerical sequence, produce the minimal and maximal entries, as well the first, second and third quartiles (the second is the Median). It also computes the average of the numbers (the Mean), which will be discussed in the next section.

Let us compare the results with the box plot for the height data. Observe that the median 171 coincides with the thick horizontal line inside the box and that the lower end of the box coincides with first quartile 158.0 and the upper end with 180.2, which is the third quartile. The inter-quartile range is 180.2-158.0=22.2. The upper threshold is 180.2+1.5×22.2=213.5. This threshold is larger than the largest observation (208.0). Hence, the largest observation is not an outlier and it marks the end of the upper whisker. The lower threshold is 158.0−1.5×22.2=124.7. The minimal observation (117.0) is less than this threshold. Hence it is an outlier and it is marked as a point below the end of the lower whisker. The second smallest observation is 129. It lies above the lower threshold and it marks the end point of the lower whisker.

3.3 MEASURES OF THE CENTER OF DATA

The mean (average) and the median are the two most commonly employed methods for determining the central location of data. To determine the average weight of 50 individuals, one must sum up the weights of all 50 individuals and then divide the total by 50. In order to determine the median weight of the 50 individuals, one can arrange the data in ascending order and identify the value that divides the data into two equal halves. The median is a more reliable measure of central tendency in the presence of extreme values or outliers, as it is unaffected by the specific numerical values of these outliers. However, the mean is the most frequently utilized measure of central tendency.

We shall use small Latin letters such as x to mark the sequence of data. In such a case we may mark the sample mean by placing a bar over the x: $\bar{x}$ (pronounced "x bar").

The mean can be computed by taking the average of the data points or by using the relative frequencies of the values in the data. In the latter scenario, one would calculate the product of each unique value and its corresponding relative frequency, and then total up these products for all values. To see that both ways of calculating the mean are the same, consider the data:

$$1,1,1,2,2,3,4,4,4,4,4$$

In the first way of calculating the mean we get:

$$\bar{x} = \frac{1+1+1+2+2+3+4+4+4+4+4}{11} = 2.7\ .$$

Alternatively, we may note that the distinct values in the sample are 1, 2, 3, and 4 with relative frequencies of 3/11, 2/11, 1/11 and 5/11, respectively. The alternative method of computation produces:

$$\bar{x} = 1 \times \frac{3}{11} + 2 \times \frac{2}{11} + 3 \times \frac{1}{11} + 4 \times \frac{5}{11} = 2.7\ .$$

3.3.1 Skewness, the Mean and the Median

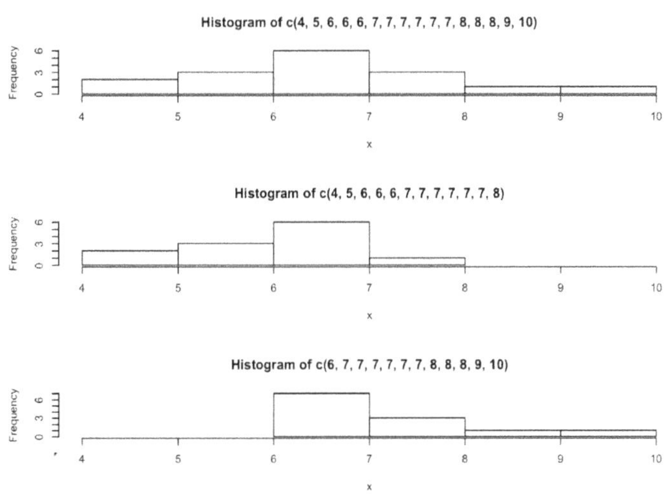

Figure 3.2: Three Histograms

Consider the following data set:

4,5,6,6,6,7,7,7,7,7,7,8,8,8,9,10

This data generates the highest histogram in Figure 3.2. Each interval has a width of one unit, and each value is positioned at the midpoint of the interval. The histogram exhibits a distribution of data that is symmetrical. A distribution is considered symmetrical if it exhibits a property where a vertical line can be drawn on the histogram in such a way that the shapes on both sides of the line are exact mirror images of each other.

Let us compute the mean and the median of this data:

```
x <- c(4,5,6,6,6,7,7,7,7,7,7,8,8,8,9,10)
mean(x)
```

```
## [1] 7
```

```
median(x)
```

```
## [1] 7
```

The mean and the median are each 7 for these data. In a perfectly symmetrical distribution, the mean and the median are the same[3].

The functions "mean" and "median" were used in order to compute the mean and median. Both functions expect a numeric sequence as an input and produce the appropriate measure of centrality of the sequence as an output.

The histogram for the data:

4,5,6,6,6,7,7,7,7,7,7,8

is not symmetrical and is displayed in the middle of Figure 3.2. The right-hand side seems "chopped off" compared to the left side. The shape of the distribution is called skewed to the left because it is pulled out towards the left.

Let us compute the mean and the median for this data:

```
x <- c(4,5,6,6,6,7,7,7,7,7,7,8)
mean(x)
```

```
## [1] 6.416667
```

```
median(x)
```

```
## [1] 7
```

(Notice that the original data is replaced by the new data when object x is reassigned.) The median is still 7, but the mean is less than 7. The relation between the mean and the median reflects the skewing.

Consider yet another set of data:

6,7,7,7,7,7,7,8,8,8,9,10

The histogram for the data is also not symmetrical and is displayed at the bottom of Figure 3.2. Notice that it is skewed to the right. Compute the mean and the median:

```
x <- c(6,7,7,7,7,7,7,8,8,8,9,10)
mean(x)

## [1] 7.583333

median(x)

## [1] 7
```

The median is yet again equal to 7, but this time the mean is greater than 7. Again, the mean reflects the skewing.

In summary, if the distribution of data is skewed to the left then the mean is less than the median. If the distribution of data is skewed to the right then the median is less than the mean.

Examine the data on the height in "ex.1":

```
mean(ex.1$height)

## [1] 170.11

median(ex.1$height)

## [1] 171
```

Observe that the histogram of the height (Figure 3.1) is skewed to the left. This is consistent with the fact that the mean is less than the median.

3.4 MEASURES OF THE SPREAD OF DATA

The inter-quartile range, which was presented in the context of the box plot, is a measure of the spread of the data. Nevertheless, the standard deviation is the most crucial indicator of dispersion.

Before dealing with the standard deviation let us discuss the calculation of the variance. If xix_i is a data value for subject ii and ¯x$\bar{x}$ is the sample mean, then xi-¯x$x_i-\bar{x}$ is called the deviation of subject ii from the mean, or simply the deviation. In a data set, there are as many deviations as there are data values. The variance is in principle the average of the squares of the deviations.

Consider the following example: In a fifth grade class, the teacher was interested in the average age and the standard deviation of the ages of her students. Here are the ages of her students to the nearest half a year:

9,9.5,9.5,10,10,10,10,10.5,10.5,10.5,10.5,11,11,11,11,11,11,11.5,11.5,11.5.

In order to explain the computation of the variance of these data let us create an object x that contains the data:

```
x <- c(9,9.5,9.5,10,10,10,10,10.5,10.5,10.5,10.5,11,11,11,11,11,11,11.5,11.5,11.5)
length(x)

## [1] 20
```

Pay attention to the fact that we did not write the "+" at the beginning of the second line. That symbol was produced by R when moving to the next line to indicate that the expression is not complete yet and will not be executed. Only after inputting the right bracket and the hitting of the Return key does R carry out the command and creates the object "x". When you execute this example yourself on your own computer make sure not to copy the "+" sign. Instead, if you hit the return key after the last comma on the first line, the plus sign will be produced by R as a new prompt and you can go on typing in the rest of the numbers.

The function "length" returns the length of the input sequence. Notice that we have a total of 20 data points.

The next step involves the computation of the deviations:

```
x.bar <- mean(x)
x.bar

## [1] 10.525

x - x.bar

##  [1] -1.525 -1.025 -1.025 -0.525 -0.525 -0.525 -0.525 -0.025 -0.025 -0.025
## [11] -0.025  0.475  0.475  0.475  0.475  0.475  0.475  0.975  0.975  0.975
```

The average of the observations is equal to 10.525 and when we delete this number from each of the components of the sequence x we obtain the deviations. For example, the first deviation is obtained as 9 - 10.525 = -1.525, the second deviation is 9.5 - 10.525 = -1.025, and so forth. The 20th deviation is 11.5 - 10.525 = 0.975, and this is the last number that is presented in the output.

From a more technical point of view observe that the expression that computed the deviations, "x - x.bar", involved the deletion of a single value (x.bar) from a sequence with 20 values (x). The expression resulted in the deletion of the value from each component of the sequence. This is an example of the general way by which R operates on sequences. The typical behavior of R is to apply an operation to each component of the sequence.

As yet another illustration of this property consider the computation of the squares of the deviations:

```
(x - x.bar)^2
```

```
## [1] 2.325625 1.050625 1.050625 0.275625 0.275625 0.275625 0.275625
## [8] 0.000625 0.000625 0.000625 0.000625 0.225625 0.225625 0.225625
## [15] 0.225625 0.225625 0.225625 0.950625 0.950625 0.950625
```

Recall that "x - x.bar" is a sequence of length 20. We apply the square function to this sequence. This function is applied to each of the components of the sequence. Indeed, for the first component we have that (-1.525)2=2.325625(-1.525)2=2.32 5625, for the second component (-1.025)2=1.050625, and for the last component $(0.975)^2=0.950625$.

For the variance we sum the square of the deviations and divide by the total number of data values minus one (n−1n−1). The standard deviation is obtained by taking the square root of the variance:

```
sum((x - x.bar)^2)/(length(x)-1)
```

```
## [1] 0.5125
```

```
sqrt(sum((x - x.bar)^2)/(length(x)-1))
```

If the variance is produced as a result of dividing the sum of squares by the number of observations minus one then the variance is called the *sample variance.*

The function "var" computes the sample variance and the function "sd" computes the standard deviations. The input to both functions is the sequence of data values and the outputs are the sample variance and the standard deviation, respectively:

```
var(x)

## [1] 0.5125

sd(x)

## [1] 0.7158911
```

In the computation of the variance we divide the sum of squared deviations by the number of deviations minus one and not by the number of deviations. The reason for that stems from the theory of statistical inference that will be discussed in Part II of this book. Unless the size of the data is small, dividing by nn or by n−1$n-1$ does not introduce much of a difference.

The variance is a squared measure and does not have the same units as the data. Taking the square root solves the problem. The standard deviation measures the spread in the same units as the data.

The sample standard deviation, ss, is either zero or is larger than zero. When s=0$s=0$, there is no spread and the data values are equal to each other. When ss is a lot larger than zero, the data values are very spread out about the mean. Outliers can make ss very large.

The standard deviation is a number that measures how far data values are from their mean. For example, if the data contains the value 7 and if the mean of the data is 5 and the standard deviation is 2, then the value 7 is one standard deviation from its mean because $5+1\times2=7$. We say, then, that 7 is one standard deviation larger than the mean 5 (or also say "to the right of 5"). If the value 1 was also part of the data set, then 1 is two standard deviations smaller than the mean (or two standard deviations to the left of 5) because $5-2\times2=1$.

The initial presentation of the standard deviation may be challenging to interpret. By plotting your data on a graph, you can gain a more intuitive understanding of the variations and the measure of dispersion known as the standard deviation. In symmetrical distributions, the standard deviation is a valuable measure, whereas in skewed distributions, its usefulness is diminished. The skewed distribution has differing spreads on its two sides. When analyzing a skewed distribution, it is advisable to examine the first quartile, median, third quartile, minimum value, and maximum value.

3.5 EXERCISES

Exercise 3.1 Three sequences of data were saved in 3 R objects named “x_1”, “x_2” and “x_3”, respectively. The application of the function “summary” to each of these objects is presented below:

```
> summary(x1)
   Min. 1st Qu.  Median    Mean 3rd Qu.    Max.
  0.000   2.498   3.218   3.081   3.840   4.871
> summary(x2)
     Min.   1st Qu.    Median      Mean   3rd Qu.      Max.
0.0001083 0.5772000 1.5070000 1.8420000 2.9050000 4.9880000
> summary(x3)
   Min. 1st Qu.  Median    Mean 3rd Qu.    Max.
  2.200   3.391   4.020   4.077   4.690   6.414
```

In Figure 3.3 one may find the histograms of these three data sequences, given in a random order. In Figure 3.4 one may find the box plots of the same data, given in yet a different order.

1. Match the summary result with the appropriate histogram and the appropriate box plot.
2. Is the value 0.000 in the sequence “x_1” an outlier?
3. Is the value 6.414 in the sequence “x_3” an outlier?

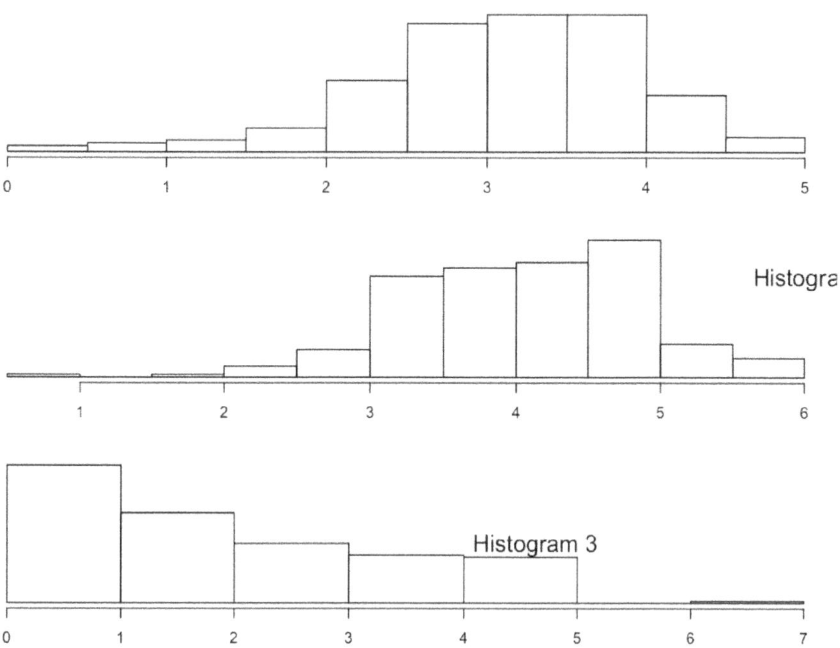

Figure 3.3: Three Histograms

Exercise 3.2 The number of toilet facilities in 30 buildings were counted. The results are recorded in an R object by the name "x". The frequency table of the data "x" is:

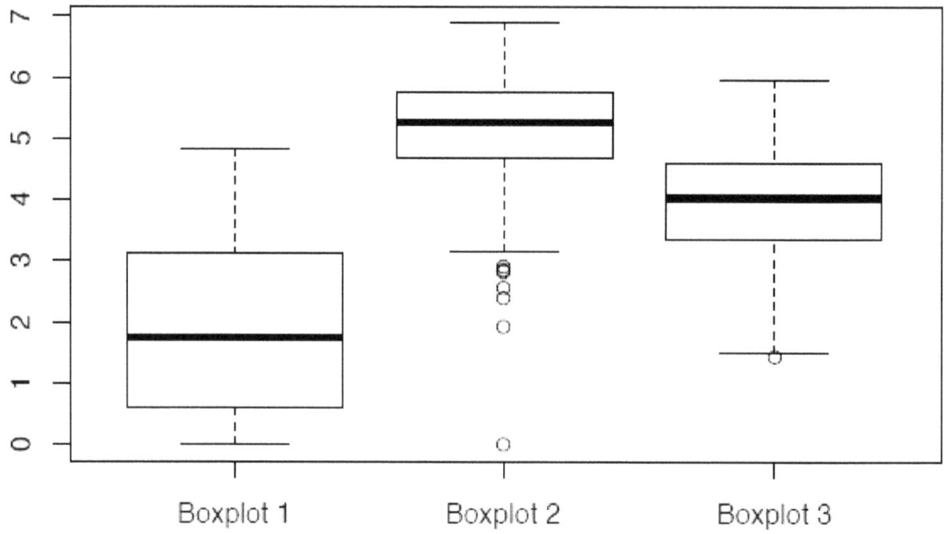

Figure 3.4 Three Box Plots

```
> table(x)
x
 2  4  6  8 10
10  6 10  2  2
```

1. What is the mean (¯xx¯) of the data?
2. What is the sample standard deviation of the data?
3. What is the median of the data?
4. What is the inter-quartile range (IQR) of the data?
5. How many standard deviations away from the mean is the value 10?

4 Chapter

PROBABILITY

4.1 INTRODUCTION: AN OVERVIEW

This section expands upon the concept of variability, which was previously introduced in the context of data, and applies it to additional scenarios. The discussion revolves around the variability of the entire population and the notion of a random variable. These principles are fundamental for the advancement and understanding of statistical inference.

4.2 DIFFERENT FORMS OF VARIABILITY

In the preceding chapters, we analyzed the diversity in the data. In the statistical context, data is acquired by sampling a subset from the target population and measuring the relevant variables for the individuals inside the sample. Varied participants within the sample may yield distinct measurements, resulting in data variability. This variability can be summarized using a frequency table, a table displaying relative frequencies, or by using cumulative relative frequencies. One can visually represent the variety in the data using the bar plot, histogram, or box plot. Numerical summaries can be calculated to describe the primary characteristics of variability. We employed the mean and the median to ascertain the central tendency of the distribution. The sample variance, or more precisely the sample standard deviation, together with the inter-quartile range, were all referred to as measures to assess the overall dispersion of the data. The purpose of these graphical representations and numerical summaries is to examine the variability of the data. The purpose of this chapter is to present two additional types of variability that are not directly related to the observed data. The initial form of variability is known as population variability. Another form of variability is the variability exhibited by a random variable. The concepts of variability that will be introduced are abstract and not directly derived from observed data. They possess a mathematical-theoretical nature. Initially, these abstract concepts may appear to be a futile use of your time and may seem disconnected from the course's content. The inverse is accurate. At the heart of statistical reasoning lies the connection between observed data and theoretical and abstract models of a phenomenon.

Through this comparison, and by utilizing the statistical inference tools outlined in the latter portion of the book, statisticians are able to derive insights or assert statements about the phenomena based on the observed data. The abstract concepts of variability introduced in this chapter, and further developed in the succeeding chapters until the completion of this section of the book, form the fundamental basis for the application of statistics. The initial concept of variability refers to the variability that is linked to the population. It shares the same characteristics as the variability of the data. The distinction between these two forms of variability lies in the fact that the former pertains to the variation of the amount of interest over the entire population, encompassing all individuals, rather than solely those that were chosen for the sample. In Chapters 2 and 3, we analyzed the data set "ex.1" that included information about the gender and height of a sample of 100 observations. This chapter will examine the gender and height of all individuals in the population from whom the sample was chosen. The size of the target population is 100,000, which includes the 100 people that were part of the sample. Upon analyzing the height statistics across the overall population, it becomes evident that individuals may possess varying heights. The variation in heights represents the variability of the population. The variability of a random variable is a mathematical term that represents another sort of abstract variability. The purpose of this concept is to represent the idea of unpredictability in measurements or the lack of certainty about the result of a measurement. Specifically, we will first examine the variability of a random variable while choosing a person at random from the population. Consider a population with a magnitude of 100,000, from which we are about to randomly select a single participant. Our objective is to determine the height of the chosen subject. Before the selection and measurement, the value of height that will be achieved is uncertain. The concept of variability is often linked to uncertainty. When selecting different subjects, the evaluations of the measurement may vary, and we cannot predict in advance which subject will be chosen. The resulting variability refers to the variation exhibited by a random variable. Random variables can be specified in contexts that are more conceptual or theoretical. Their objective is to offer models that represent randomness and uncertainty in measurements. This chapter will present straightforward instances of abstract random variables. Additional illustrations will be included in the following chapters. Abstract examples of random variables may not necessarily need to be linked to a particular population. However, the definitions that are used for the example of a random variable that arises from sampling a single individual from a population will also be applicable to the more abstract structures. Graphical tools and numerical summaries can be used to illustrate and describe all forms of variability, including the variability of the data we previously worked with, as well as the other two types of variability. The same style of charts and numerical summaries, with potential alterations, can and will be utilized. It is important to note that the variability of the data is directly related to a specific set of data values that are provided to us. Unlike the variability of the data, other types of variability are not linked to quantities that we directly observe. We have access to the data for the sample, but not for the entire population. However, we may still analyze the variability of a population, even if we don't have access to the complete set of observations for the entire population. The population example provided in this chapter was deliberately created and is used solely for illustrative purposes. In the statistical context, measures are not obtained from the entire population, but rather from a sample of participants. The topic of variability in this context is purely speculative. However, this theoretical debate is crucial for comprehending statistics.

4.3 A POPULATION

This section aims to elucidate the variability of a population and provide numerical summaries that accurately depict this variability. Prior to proceeding, let us examine, using an illustrative example, some of the statistical summaries that were employed to describe the variability of the data.

Recall the file "ex1.csv" that contains data on the height and sex of 100 subjects. (The data file can be obtained from http://pluto.huji.ac.il/~msby/StatThink/Datasets/ex1.csv.) We read the content of the file into a data frame by the name "ex.1" and apply the function "summary" to the data frame:

```
ex.1 <- read.csv("_data/ex1.csv")
summary(ex.1)
```

```
##        id               sex          height     
##  Min.   :1538611   FEMALE:54   Min.   :117.0  
##  1st Qu.:3339583   MALE  :46   1st Qu.:158.0  
##  Median :5105620               Median :171.0  
##  Mean   :5412367               Mean   :170.1  
##  3rd Qu.:7622236               3rd Qu.:180.2  
##  Max.   :9878130               Max.   :208.0  
```

We saw in the previous chapter that, when applied to a numeric sequence, the function "summary" produces the smallest and largest values in the sequence, the three quartiles (including the median) and the mean. If the input of the same function is a factor then the outcome is the frequency in the data of each of the levels of the factor. Here "sex" is a factor with two levels. From the summary we can see that 54 of the subjects in the sample are female and 46 are male.

Notice that when the input to the function "summary" is a data frame, as is the case in this example, then the output is a summary of each of the variables of the data frame. In this example two of the variables are numeric ("id" and "height") and one variable is a factor ("sex").

Recall that the mean is the arithmetic average of the data which is computed by summing all the values of the variable and dividing the result by the number of observations. Hence, if *nn* is the number of observations (n=100 in this example) and x_i is the value of the variable for subject i, then one may write the mean in a formula form as

$$\bar{x} = \frac{\text{Sum of all values in the data}}{\text{Number of values in the data}} = \frac{\sum_{i=1}^{n} x_i}{n},$$

where $\bar{x}$ corresponds to the mean of the data and the symbol "$\sum_{i=1}^{n} x_i$" corresponds to the sum of all values in the data.

The median is computed by ordering the data values and selecting a value that splits the ordered data into two equal parts. The first and third quartile are obtained by further splitting each of the halves into two quarters.

Let us discuss the variability associated with an entire target population. The file "pop1.csv" that contains the population data can be found on the internet (http://pluto.huji.ac.il/~msby/StatThink/Datasets/pop1.csv). It is a CSV file that contains the information on sex and height of an entire adult population of some imaginary city. (The data in "ex.1" corresponds to a sample from this city.) Read the population data into R and examine it:

```
pop.1 <- read.csv(file="_data/pop1.csv")
summary(pop.1)
```

```
##         id              sex            height
##  Min.   :1000082   FEMALE:48888   Min.   :117
##  1st Qu.:3254220   MALE  :51112   1st Qu.:162
##  Median :5502618                  Median :170
##  Mean   :5502428                  Mean   :170
##  3rd Qu.:7757518                  3rd Qu.:178
##  Max.   :9999937                  Max.   :217
```

The object "pop.1" is a data frame of the same structure as the data frame "ex.1". It contains three variables: a unique identifier of each subject (id), the sex of the subject (sex), and its height (height). Applying the function "summary" to the data frame produces the summary of the variables that it contains. In particular, for the variable "sex", which is a factor, it produces the frequency of its two categories – 48,888 female and 51,112 – a total of 100,000 subjects. For the variable "height", which is a numeric variable, it produces the extreme values, the quartiles, and the mean.

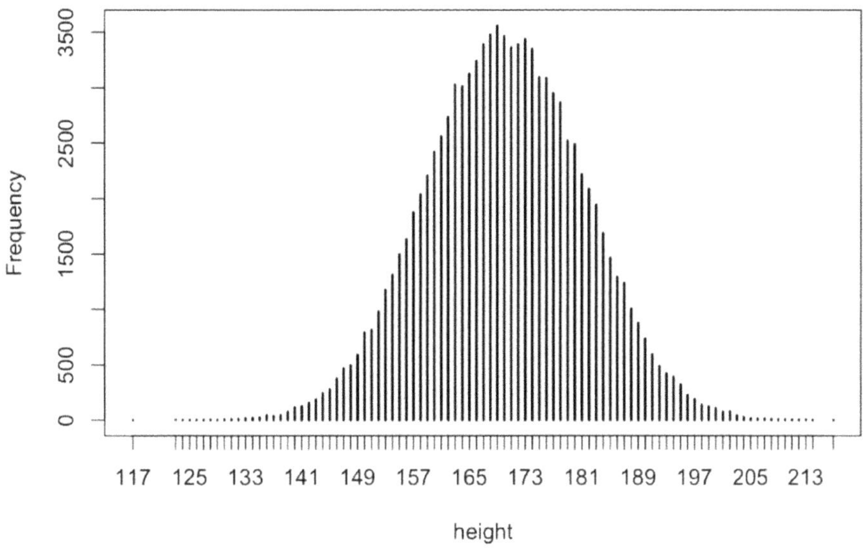

Figure 4.1: Bar Plot of Height

Let us concentrate on the variable "height". A bar plot of the distribution of the heights in the entire population is given in Figure 4.1 [1]. Recall that a vertical bar is placed above each value of height that appears in the population, with the height of the bar representing the frequency of the value in the population. One may read out of the graph or obtain from the numerical summaries that the variable takes integer values in the range between 117 and 217 (heights are rounded to the nearest centimeter). The distribution is centered at 170 centimeter, with the central 50% of the values spreading between 162 and 178 centimeters.

The mean of the height in the entire population is equal to 170 centimeter. This mean, just like the mean for the distribution of data, is obtained by the summation of all the heights in the population divided by the population size. Let us denote the size of the entire population by N. In this example N=100,000. (The size of the sample for the data was called nn and was equal to n=100 in the parallel example that deals with the data of a sample.) The mean of an entire population is denoted by the Greek letter μμ and is read "*mew*". (The average for the data was denoted $\bar{x}$). The formula of the population mean is:

$$\mu = \frac{\text{Sum of all values in the population}}{\text{Number of values in the population}} = \frac{\sum_{i=1}^{N} x_i}{N} .$$

Observe the similarity between the definition of the mean for the data and the definition of the mean for the population. In both cases the arithmetic average is computed. The only difference is that in the case of the mean of the data the computation is with respect to the values that appear in the sample whereas for the population all the values in the population participate in the computation.

In actual life, we will not have all the values of a variable in the entire population. Hence, we will not be able to compute the actual value of the population mean. However, it is still meaningful to talk about the population mean because this number exists, even though we do not know what its value is. As a matter of fact, one of the issues in statistics is to try to estimate this unknown quantity on the basis of the data we do have in the sample.

A characteristic of the distribution of an entire population is called a *parameter*. Hence, μμ, the population average, is a parameter. Other examples of parameters are the population median and the population quartiles. These parameters are defined exactly like their data counterparts, but with respect to the values of the entire population instead of the observations in the sample alone.

Another example of a parameter is the population variance. Recall that the sample variance was defined with the aid of the deviations $x_i - \bar{x}$, where x_i is the value of the measurement for the ith subject and $\bar{x}$ is the mean for the data. In order to compute the sample variance these deviations were squared to produce the squared deviations. The squares were summed up and then divided by the sample size minus one (n-1). The sample variance, computed from the data, was denoted s^2.

The population variance is defined in a similar way. First, the deviations from the population mean xi-μx_i-μ are considered for each of the members of the population. These deviations are squared and the average of the squares is computed. We denote this parameter by σ2σ^2 (read "*sigma square*"). A minor difference between the sample variance and the population variance is that for the latter we should divide the sum of squared deviations by the population size (N) and not by the population size minus one (N-1):

$$\begin{aligned}\sigma^2 &= \text{The average square deviation in the population} \\ &= \frac{\text{Sum of the squares of the deviations in the population}}{\text{Number of values in the population}} \\ &= \frac{\sum_{i=1}^{N}(x_i - \mu)^2}{N} .\end{aligned}$$

The standard deviation of the population, yet another parameter, is denoted by $\sigma\sigma$ and is equal to the square root of the variance. The standard deviation summarizes the overall variability of the measurement across the population. Again, the typical situation is that we do not know what the actual value of the standard deviation of the population is. Yet, we may refer to it as a quantity and we may try to estimate its value based on the data we do have from the sample.

For the height of the subjects in our imaginary city we get that the variance is equal to σ2=126.1576 σ^2=126.1576. The standard deviation is equal to $\sigma = \sqrt{126.1576} =$ 11.23199. These quantities can be computed in this example from the data frame "pop.1" with the aid of the functions "var" and "sd", respectively[2].

4.4 RANDOM VARIABLES

In the previous section we dealt with the variability of the population. Next we consider the variability of a random variable. As an example, consider taking a sample of size n=1 from the population (a single person) and measuring his/her height.

The object pop.1$height is a sequence with 100,000 entries. Think of it as a population. We will apply the function "sample" to this sequence:

```
sample(pop.1$height,1)
```

```
## [1] 162
```

The first entry to the function is the given sequence of heights. When we set the second argument to 1 then the function selects one of the entries of the sequence at random, with each entry having the same likelihood of being selected. Specifically, in this example an entry that contains the value 162 was selected. Let us run the function again:

```
sample(pop.1$height,1)
```

```
## [1] 160
```

In this instance an entry with a different value was selected. Try to run the command several times yourself and see what you get. Would you necessarily obtain a different value in each run?

Now let us enter the same command without pressing the return key:

```
sample(pop.1$height,1)
```

Can you tell, before pressing the key, what value will you get?

The answer to this question is of course *"No"*. There are 100,000 entries with a total of 94 distinct values. In principle, any of the values may be selected and there is no way of telling in advance which of the values will turn out as an outcome.

A random variable is the future outcome of a measurement, **before** the measurement is taken. It does not have a specific value, but rather a collection of potential values with a distribution over these values. After the measurement is taken and the specific value is revealed then the random variable ceases to be a random variable! Instead, it becomes data.

Although one is not able to say what the outcome of a random variable will turn out to be. Still, one may identify patterns in this potential outcome. For example, knowing that the distribution of heights in the population ranges between 117 and 217 centimeter one may say in advance that the outcome of the measurement must also be in that interval. Moreover, since there is a total of 3,476 subjects with height equal to 168 centimeter and since the likelihood of each subject to be selected is equal then the likelihood of selecting a subject of this height is 3,476/100,000 = 0.03476. In the context of random variables we call this likelihood *probability*. In the same vain, the frequency of subjects with hight 192 centimeter is 488, and therefore the probability of measuring such a height is 0.00488. The frequency of subjects with height 200 centimeter or above is 393, hence the probability of obtaining a measurement in the range between 200 and 217 centimeter is 0.00393.

4.4.1 Sample Space and Distribution

Now, let's refer to the precise definition of a random variable: A random variable is a numerical value that represents the outcome of an observation, measurement, or function.

A random variable is characterized via the collection of potential values it may obtain, known as the *sample space* and the likelihood of obtaining each of the values in the sample space (namely, the probability of the value). In the given example, the sample space contains the 94 integer values that are marked in Figure 4.1. The probability of each value is the height of the bar above the value, divided by the total frequency of 100,000 (namely, the relative frequency in the population).

We will denote random variables with capital Latin letters such as XX, YY, and ZZ. Values they may obtain will be marked by small Latin letters such as xx, yy, zz. For the probability of values we will use the letter "\Prob\Prob". Hence, if we denote by XX the measurement of height of a random individual that is sampled from the given population then:

$$\mathrm{P}(X = 168) = 0.03476$$

and

$$\mathrm{P}(X \geq 200) = 0.00393 \,.$$

Consider, as yet another example, the probability that the height of a random person sampled from the population differs from 170 centimeter by no more than 10 centimeters. (In other words, that the height is between 160 and 180 centimeters.) Denote by XX the height of that random person. We are interested in the probability P ($|X-170|\leq 10$).[3]

The random person can be any of the subjects of the population with equal probability. Thus, the sequence of the heights of the 100,000 subjects represents the distribution of the random variable X:

```
pop.1 <- read.csv(file="_data/pop1.csv")
X <- pop.1$height
```

Notice that the object "X" is a sequence of lenght 100,000 that stores all the heights of the population. The probability we seek is the relative frequency in this sequency of values between 160 and 180. First we compute the probability and then explain the method of computation:

```
mean(abs(X-170) <= 10)

## [1] 0.64541
```

We get that the height of a person randomly sampled from the population is between 160 and 180 centimeters with probability 0.64541.

Let us produce a small example that will help us explain the computation of the probability. We start by forming a sequence with 10 numbers:

```
Y <- c(6.3, 6.9, 6.6, 3.4, 5.5, 4.3, 6.5, 4.7, 6.1, 5.3)
```

The goal is to compute the proportion of numbers that are in the range [4,6] [4,6] (or, equivalently, $\{|Y-5|\leq 1\}$).

The function "abs" computes the absolute number of its input argument. When the function is applied to the sequence "Y-5" it produces a sequence of the same length with the distances between the components of "Y" and the number 5:

```
abs(Y-5)

## [1] 1.3 1.9 1.6 1.6 0.5 0.7 1.5 0.3 1.1 0.3
```

Compare the resulting output to the original sequence. The first value in the input sequence is 6.3. Its distance from 5 is indeed 1.3. The fourth value in the input sequence is 3.4. The difference 3.4 - 5 is equal to -1.6, and when the absolute value is taken we get a distance of 1.6.

The function "<=" expects an argument to the right and an argument to the left. It compares each component to the left with the parallel component to the right and returns a logical value, "TRUE" or "FALSE", depending on whether the relation that is tested holds or not:

```
abs(Y - 5) <= 1
```

```
## [1] FALSE FALSE FALSE FALSE  TRUE  TRUE FALSE  TRUE FALSE  TRUE
```

Observe the in this example the function "<=" produced 10 logical values, one for each of the elements of the sequence to the left of it. The first input in the sequence "Y" is 6.3, which is more than one unit away from 5. Hence, the first output of the logical expression is "FALSE". On the other hand, the last input in the sequence "Y" is 5.3, which is within the range. Therefore, the last output of the logical expression is "TRUE".

Next, we compute the proportion of "TRUE" values in the sequence:

```
mean(abs(Y - 5) <= 1)
```

```
## [1] 0.4
```

When a sequence with logical values is entered into the function "mean" then the function replaces the TRUE's by 1 and the FALSE's by 0. The average produces then the relative frequency of TRUE's in the sequence as required. Specifically, in this example there are 4 TRUE's and 6 FALSE's. Consequently, the output of the final expression is 4/10=0.4.

The computation of the probability that the sampled height falls within 10 centimeter of 170 is based on the same code. The only differences are that the input sequence "Y" is replaced by the sequence of population heights "X" as input. the number "5" is replaced by the number "170" and the number "1" is replaced by the number "10". In both cases the result of the computation is the relative proportion of the times that the values of the input sequence fall within a given range of the indicated number.

The probability function of a random variable is defined for any value that the random variable may obtain and produces the *distribution* of the random variable. The probability function may emerge as a relative frequency as in the given example or it may be a result of theoretical modeling. Examples of theoretical random variables are presented mainly in the next two chapters.

Consider an example of a random variable. The sample space and the probability function specify the distribution of the random variable. For example, assume it is known that a random variable X may obtain the values 0, 1, 2, or 3. Moreover, imagine that it is known that PX=1)=0.25, P(X=2)=0.15, and P(X=3)=0.10. What is P (X=0), the probability that X is equal to 0?

The sample space, the collection of possible values that the random variable may obtain is the collection {0,1,2,3}. Observe that the sum over the positive values is:

$$P(X > 0) = P(X = 1) + P(X = 2) + P(X = 3) = 0.25 + 0.15 + 0.10 = 0.50 .$$

It follows, since the sum of probabilities over the entire sample space is equal to 1, that P (X=0)=1−0.5=0.5.

Table 4.1 summarizes the distribution of the random variable X*X*. Observe the similarity between the probability function and the notion of relative frequency that was discussed in Chapter 2. Both quantities describe distribution. Both are non-negative and sum to 1. Likewise, notice that one may define the cumulative probability the same way cumulative relative frequency is defined: Ordering the values of the random variable from smallest to largest, the cumulative probability at a given value is the sum of probabilities for values less or equal to the given value.

Table 4.1: The Distribution of *X*

Value	Probability	Cum.Prob
0	0.50	0.50
1	0.25	0.75
2	0.15	0.90
3	0.10	1.00

Knowledge of the probabilities of a random variable (or the cumulative probabilities) enables the computation of other probabilities that are associated with the random variable. For example, considering the random variable *X* of Table 4.1, we may calculate the probability of X*X* falling in the interval [0.5,2.3]. Observe that the given range contains two values from the sample space, 1 and 2, therefore:

$$P(0.5 \leq X \leq 2.3) = P(X = 1) + P(X = 2) = 0.25 + 0.15 = 0.40 .$$

Likewise, we may produce the probability of X*X* obtaining an odd value:

$$P(X = \text{odd}) = P(X = 1) + P(X = 3) = 0.25 + 0.10 = 0.35 .$$

Observe that both {0.5≤X≤2.3} and {*X*=odd} refer to subsets of values of the sample space. Such subsets are denoted *events*. In both examples the probability of the event was computed by the summation of the probabilities associated with values that belong to the event.

4.4.2 Expectation and Standard Deviation

The center of a distribution of a random variable and the spread of the distribution can be described using methods similar to those used for characterizing the distribution of data and a population.

The *expectation* marks the center of the distribution of a random variable. It is equivalent to the data average ¯xx¯ and the population average μμ, which was used in order to mark the location of the distribution of the data and the population, respectively.

Recall from Chapter 3 that the average of the data can be computed as the weighted average of the values that are present in the data, with weights given by the relative frequency. Specifically, we saw for the data

1,1,1,2,2,3,4,4,4,4,4

that

$$\frac{1+1+1+2+2+3+4+4+4+4+4}{11} = 1\times\frac{3}{11} + 2\times\frac{2}{11} + 3\times\frac{1}{11} + 4\times\frac{5}{11},$$

producing the value of $\bar{x} = 2.727$ in both representations. Using a formula, the equality between the two ways of computing the mean is given in terms of the equation:

$$\bar{x} = \frac{\sum_{i=1}^{n} x_i}{n} = \sum_{x} (x \times (f_x/n)) .$$

In the first representation of the arithmetic mean, the average is computed by the summation of all data points and dividing the sum by the sample size. In the second representation, that uses a weighted sum, the sum extends over all the unique values that appear in the data. For each unique value the value is multiplied by the relative frequency of the value in the data. These multiplications are summed up to produce the mean.

The expectation of a random variable is computed in the spirit of the second formulation. The expectation of a random variable is marked with the letter "\Expec\Expec" and is define via the equation:

$$\mathrm{E}(X) = \sum_{x} (x \times \mathrm{P}(x)) .$$

In this definition all the unique values of the sample space are considered. For each value a product of the value and the probability of the value is taken. The expectation is obtained by the summation of all these products. In this definition the probability P(x) replaces the relative frequency $f_{\square}/n$ but otherwise, the definition of the expectation and the second formulation of the mean are identical to each other.

Consider the random variable XX with distribution that is described in Table 4.1. In order to obtain its expectation we multiply each value in the sample space by the probability of the value. Summation of the products produces the expectation (see Table 4.1:

$$\mathrm{E}(X) = 0 \times 0.5 + 1 \times 0.25 + 2 \times 0.15 + 3 \times 0.10 = 0.85 \;.$$

```
## Expectation = sum(Value*Probability) =  0.85
```

Table 4.2: The Expectation of *X*

Value	Probability	Value * Probability
0	0.50	0.00
1	0.25	0.25
2	0.15	0.30
3	0.10	0.30

In the example of height we get that the expectation is equal to 170.035 centimeter. Notice that this expectation is equal to μμ, the mean of the population[9]. This is no accident. The expectation of a potential measurement of a randomly selected subject from a population is equal to the average of the measurement across all subjects.

The sample variance (s^2) is obtained as the sum of the squared deviations from the average, divided by the sample size (n) minus 1:

$$s^2 = \frac{\sum_{i=1}^{n}(x_i - \bar{x})^2}{n-1} \;.$$

A second formulation for the computation of the same quantity is via the use of relative frequencies. The formula for the sample variance takes the form

$$s^2 = \frac{n}{n-1}\sum_{x}\left((x-\bar{x})^2 \times (f_x/n)\right) .$$

In this formulation one considers each of the unique value that are present in the data. For each value the deviation between the value and the average is computed. These deviations are then squared and multiplied by the relative frequency. The products are summed up. Finally, the sum is multiplied by the ratio between the sample size nn and n-1n-1 in order to correct for the fact that in the sample variance the sum of squared deviations is divided by the sample size minus 1 and not by the sample size.

In a similar way, the variance of a random variable may be defined via the probability of the values that make the sample space. For each such value one computes the deviation from the expectation. This deviation is then squared and multiplied by the probability of the value. The multiplications are summed up in order to produce the variance:

$$\mathbf{V}(X) = \sum_x \left((x - \mathbf{E}(X))^2 \times \mathbf{P}(x)\right).$$

Notice that the formula for the computation of the variance of a random variable is very similar to the second formulation for the computation of the sample variance. Essentially, the mean of the data is replaced by the expectation of the random variable and the relative frequency of a value is replaced by the probability of the value. Another difference is that the correction factor is not used for the variance of a random variable.

```
## Var = sum(p*(x-sum(p*x))^2) =  1.0275
```

Table 4.3: The Variance of *X*

x	$P(X=x)$	$x - E [X] $	$ (x - E[X]^2$)	$P(X=x)* (x - E [X]^2$)
0	0.50	-0.85	0.7225	0.361250
1	0.25	0.15	0.0225	0.005625
2	0.15	1.15	1.3225	0.198375
3	0.10	2.15	4.6225	0.462250

As an example consider the variance of the random variable *X*. The computation of the variance of this random variable is carried out in Table 4.3. The sample space, the values that the random variable may obtain, are given in the first column and the probabilities of the values are given in the second column. In the third column the deviation of the value from the expectation E(X) = 0.85 is computed for each value. The 4th column contains the square of these deviations and the 5th and last column involves the product of the square deviations and the probabilities. The variance is obtained by summing up the products in the last column. In the given example:

$$\begin{aligned}\mathbf{V}(X) =& (0 - 0.85)^2 \times 0.5 + (1 - 0.85)^2 \times 0.25 \\ &+ (2 - 0.85)^2 \times 0.15 + (3 - 0.85)^2 \times 0.10 = 1.0275 .\end{aligned}$$

The standard deviation of a random variable is the square root of the variance. The standard deviation of *X* is $\sqrt{\mathbf{V}(X)} = \sqrt{1.0275} = 1.013657$.

In the example that involves the height of a subject selected from the population at random we obtain that the variance is 126.1576, equal to the population variance, and the standard deviation is 11.23199, the square root of the variance.

Other characterization of the distribution that were computed for data, such as the median, the quartiles, etc., may also be defined for random variables.

4.5 PROBABILITY AND STATISTICS

Modern science is distinguished by its methodical gathering of actual measurements and its endeavor to formulate laws of nature using mathematical terminology. The desire to get improved measurements prompted the creation of measurement equipment that are both more precise and more responsive. However, it became evident that measurements may not be completely reproducible, and any repeated measurement of the same events will usually result in fluctuation in the outcomes. Furthermore, scientists have discovered that there exist universal principles that regulate the variety in repetitions. For instance, it has been found that the mean of multiple independent repetitions of the measurement exhibits lower variability and greater reproducibility compared to each individual measurement. The concept of probability was initially developed as a mathematical field to study the uncertainty and unpredictability inherent in gambling and games of chance. In the early 19th century, probability started being employed to represent the diversity in measurements. This utilization of probability proved to be highly effective. One significant accomplishment of probability is the formulation of a mathematical theory that elucidates the phenomenon of decreased variability when averages are employed instead of individual measurements. Chapter 7 focuses on the final outcomes and deductions derived from this theory. Statistics is a study method that involves making inferences based on data. Probability is the fundamental mathematical basis for the construction of statistical theory. This chapter presented the probabilistic notion of a random variable. Understanding this concept is crucial for comprehending statistics. In the remaining portion of Part I of this book, we delve into the probability theory that is employed for statistical reasoning. The book delves into the topic of statistical inference in Part II.

4.6 EXERCISES

Exercise 4.1 Table 4.4 presents the probabilities of the random variable Y.

Table 4.4: The Distribution of Y

Value	Probability
0	1p
1	2p
2	3p
3	4p
4	5p
5	6p

These probabilities are a function of the number p, the probability of the value "0". Answer the following questions:

1. What is the value of p?
2. $P(Y<3) = ?$
3. $P(Y=\text{odd}) = ?$
4. $P(1 \leq Y < 4) = ?$
5. $P(|Y-3|<1.5) = ?$
6. $E(Y) = ?$
7. $V(Y) = ?$
8. What is the standard deviation of Y.

Exercise 4.2 One invests $2 to participate in a game of chance. In this game a coin is tossed three times. If all tosses end up "Head" then the player wins $10. Otherwise, the player losses the investment.

1. What is the probability of winning the game?
2. What is the probability of loosing the game?
3. What is the expected gain for the player that plays this game?

(Notice that the expectation can obtain a negative value.)

5 Chapter

RANDOM VARIABLES

5.1 INTRODUCTION: AN OVERVIEW

This section introduces some important examples of random variables. The distributions of these random variables emerge as mathematical models of real-life settings. In two of the examples the sample space is composed of integers. In the other two examples the sample space is made of continuum of values. For random variables of the latter type one may use the density, which is a type of a histogram, in order to describe the distribution.

5.2 DISCRETE RANDOM VARIABLES

In the preceding chapter, we presented the concept of a random variable. A random variable represents the result of an observation or measurement that occurs before the actual measurement is made. In this context, one might refer to all the possible values that the measurement may potentially acquire. The sample space refers to this collection of variables.

Each value in the sample space can be assigned a corresponding probability. Probabilities can be understood as the ratios of occurrences of an event compared to the total number of possible outcomes. All probabilities in a sample space are non-negative, and the total sum of these probability is equal to one. A random variable is characterized by its sample space and the probabilities assigned to the values in the sample space. To analyze each sort of random variable, we will initially determine the sample space, which refers to the possible values it might take. Subsequently, we will proceed to define the probabilities associated with each of these values. Illustrations of scenarios where each category of random variable can be utilized as a representation of a measurement will be presented. The R system has functions for calculating probability related to specific categories of random variables. In subsequent chapters, we will utilize these functions to do calculations related to the random variables and to graphically represent their distributions. Numerical summaries can be used to characterize the distribution of a random variable, similar to how they are used to characterize the distribution of data. We utilized summary statistics, specifically the mean, sample variance, and standard deviation. The mean is employed to denote the center tendency of the distribution, while the variance and standard deviation are utilized to represent the overall dispersion. Parallel summaries are employed to analyze random variables. For a random variable, the term "expectation" refers to the center location of the distribution. The "variance" and "standard deviation" (which is the square root of the variation) are used to summarize the extent of the spread. For all instances of random variables, we will determine the expected value and the variance (and consequently, the standard deviation as well). Random variables serve as probabilistic models for measurements. Theoretical considerations are frequently employed to establish the definitions of random variables and their corresponding distributions. A discrete random variable refers to a random variable in which the values in the sample space are distinct and separated from each other. For instance, if the values are integers, it means that there are no intermediate values between them. This section presents two significant random variables that take integer values: The Binomial and the Poisson random variables. These stochastic variables may arise as mathematical representations in situations where the measurement requires quantifying the frequency of certain events or phenomena. There are other alternative models available for discrete random variables, in addition to the Binomial and Poisson distributions. In Section 5.4, we will examine the Negative-Binomial model as an illustration of such a model. When dealing with measures that have particular values, one can choose either the Binomial, Poisson, or another model to approximate the distribution of the data in a theoretical manner.

5.2.1 The Binomial Random Variable

The Binomial random variable is used in settings in which a trial that has two possible outcomes is repeated several times. Let us designate one of the outcomes as "Success" and the other as "Failure". Assume that the probability of success in each trial is given by some number pp that is larger than 0 and smaller than 1. Given a number nn of repeats of the trial and given the probability of success, the actual number of trials that will produce "Success" as their outcome is a random variable. We call such random variable *Binomial*. The fact that a random variable XX has such a distribution is marked by the expression: "$X \sim$Binomial(n,p)".

As an example consider tossing 10 coins. Designate "Head" as success and "Tail" as failure. For fair coins the probability of "Head" is 1/2. Consequently, if X is the total number of "Heads" then $X \sim$Binomial(10,0.5), where n=10 is the number of trials and p=0.5 is the probability of success in each trial.

It may happen that all 10 coins turn up "Tail". In this case X is equal to 0. It may also be the case that one of the coins turns up "Head" and the others turn up "Tail". The random variable X will obtain the value 1 in such a case. Likewise, for any integer between 0 and 10 it may be the case that the number of "Heads" that turn up is equal to that integer with the other coins turning up "Tail". Hence, the sample space of X is the set of integers {0,1,2,...,10}. The probability of each outcome may be computed by an appropriate mathematical formula that will not be discussed here[1].

The probabilities of the various possible values of a Binomial random variable may be computed with the aid of the R function "dbinom" (that uses the mathematical formula for the computation). The input to this function is a sequence of values, the value of n, and the value of pp. The output is the sequence of probabilities associated with each of the values in the first input.

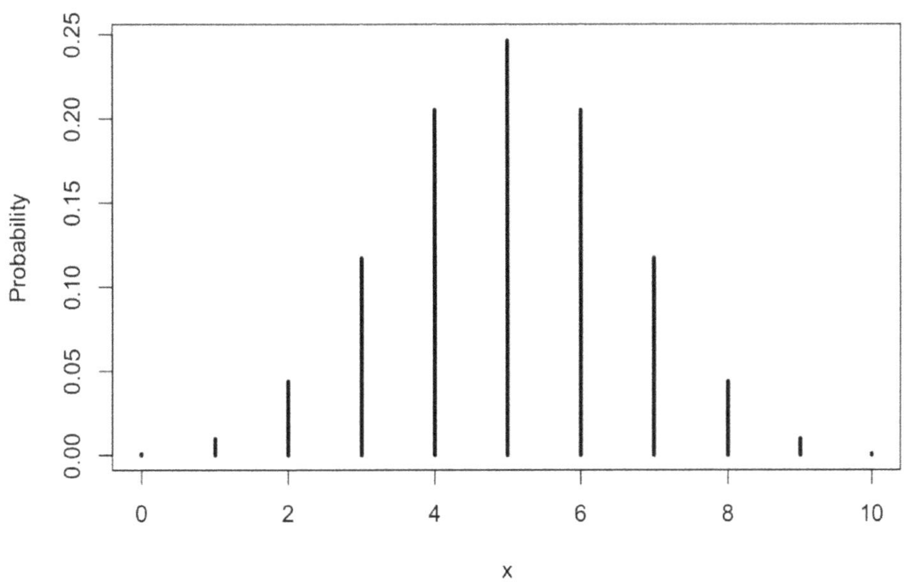

Figure 5.1: The Binomial(10,0.5) Distribution

For example, let us use the function in order to compute the probability that the given Binomial obtains an odd value. A sequence that contains the odd values in the Binomial sample space can be created with the expression "c(1,3,5,7,9)". This sequence can serve as the input in the first argument of the function "dbinom". The other arguments are "10" and "0.5", respectively:

```
dbinom(c(1,3,5,7,9),10,0.5)
```

```
## [1] 0.009765625 0.117187500 0.246093750 0.117187500 0.009765625
```

Observe that the output of the function is a sequence of the same length as the first argument. This output contains the Binomial probabilities of the values in the first argument. In order to obtain the probability of the event {X is odd}{X is odd} we should sum up these probabilities, which we can do by applying the function "sum" to the output of the function that computes the Binomial probabilities:

```
sum(dbinom(c(1,3,5,7,9),10,0.5))

## [1] 0.5
```

Observe that the probability of obtaining an odd value in this specific case is equal to one half.

Another example is to compute all the probabilities of all the potential values of a Binomial(10,0.5) random variable:

```
x <- 0:10
dbinom(x,10,0.5)

##  [1] 0.0009765625 0.0097656250 0.0439453125 0.1171875000 0.2050781250
##  [6] 0.2460937500 0.2050781250 0.1171875000 0.0439453125 0.0097656250
## [11] 0.0009765625
```

The expression "start.value:end.value" produces a sequence of numbers that initiate with the number "start.value" and proceeds in jumps of size one until reaching the number "end.value". In this example, "0:10" produces the sequence of integers between 0 and 10, which is the sample space of the current Binomial example. Entering this sequence as the first argument to the function "dbinom" produces the probabilities of all the values in the sample space.

One may display the distribution of a discrete random variable with a bar plot similar to the one used to describe the distribution of data. In this plot a vertical bar representing the probability is placed above each value of the sample space. The hight of the bar is equal to the probability. A bar plot of the Binomial(10,0.5) distribution is provided in Figure 5.1.

Another useful function is "pbinom", which produces the cumulative probability of the Binomial:

```
pbinom(x,10,0.5)

##  [1] 0.0009765625 0.0107421875 0.0546875000 0.1718750000 0.3769531250
##  [6] 0.6230468750 0.8281250000 0.9453125000 0.9892578125 0.9990234375
## [11] 1.0000000000

cumsum(dbinom(x,10,0.5))

##  [1] 0.0009765625 0.0107421875 0.0546875000 0.1718750000 0.3769531250
##  [6] 0.6230468750 0.8281250000 0.9453125000 0.9892578125 0.9990234375
## [11] 1.0000000000
```

The output of the function "pbinom" is the cumulative probability P $(X \le x)$ that the random variable is less than or equal to the input value. Observe that this cumulative probability is obtained by summing all the probabilities associated with values that are less than or equal to the input value. Specifically, the cumulative probability at x=3x=3 is obtained by the summation of the probabilities at x=0, x=1, x=2, and x=3:

$$P(X \leq 3) = 0.0009765625 + 0.009765625 + 0.0439453125 + 0.1171875 = 0.171875$$

The numbers in the sum are the first 4 values from the output of the function "dbinom(x,10,0.5)", which computes the probabilities of the values of the sample space.

In principle, the expectation of the Binomial random variable, like the expectation of any other (discrete) random variable is obtained from the application of the general formulae:

$$E(X) = \sum_x (x \times P(X = x)), \quad V(X) = \sum_x ((x - E(X))^2 \times P(x)).$$

However, in the specific case of the Binomial random variable, in which the probability P (X=x) obeys the specific mathematical formula of the Binomial distribution, the expectation and the variance reduce to the specific formulae:

$$E(X) = np, \quad V(X) = np(1 - p).$$

Hence, the expectation is the product of the number of trials nn with the probability of success in each trial pp. In the variance the number of trials is multiplied by the product of a probability of success (p) with the probability of a failure (1-p).

As illustration, let us compute for the given example the expectation and the variance according to the general formulae for the computation of the expectation and variance in random variables and compare the outcome to the specific formulae for the expectation and variance in the Binomial distribution:

```
X.val <- 0:10
P.val <- dbinom(X.val,10,0.5)
EX <- sum(X.val*P.val)
EX
```

```
## [1] 5
```

```
sum((X.val-EX)^2*P.val)
```

```
## [1] 2.5
```

This agrees with the specific formulae for Binomial variables, since 10×0.5=5 and 10×0.5×(1−0.5)=2.5.

Recall that the general formula for the computation of the expectation calls for the multiplication of each value in the sample space with the probability of that value, followed by the summation of all the products. The object "X.val" contains all the values of the random variable and the object "P.val" contains the probabilities of these values. Hence, the expression "X.val*P.val" produces the product of each value of the random variable times the probability of that value. Summation of these products with the function "sum" gives the expectation, which is saved in an object that is called "EX".

The general formula for the computation of the variance of a random variable involves the product of the squared deviation associated with each value with the probability of that value, followed by the summation of all products. The expression "(X.val-EX)^ 2" produces the sequence of squared deviations from the expectation for all the values of the random variable. Summation of the product of these squared deviations with the probabilities of the values (the outcome of "(X. val-EX)^2*P.val") gives the variance.

When the value of *pp* changes (without changing the number of trials *nn*) then the probabilities that are assigned to each of the values of the sample space of the Binomial random variable change, but the sample space itself does not. For example, consider rolling a die 10 times and counting the number of times that the face 3 was obtained. Having the face 3 turning up is a "Success". The probability *pp* of a success in this example is 1/6, since the given face is one out of 6 equally likely faces. The resulting random variable that counts the total number of success in 10 trials has a Binomial(10,1/6) distribution. The sample space is yet again equal to the set of integers {0,1,...,10}. However, the probabilities of values are different. These probabilities can again be computes with the aid of the function "dbinom":

```
dbinom(x,10,1/6)
```

```
##  [1] 1.615056e-01 3.230112e-01 2.907100e-01 1.550454e-01 5.426588e-02
##  [6] 1.302381e-02 2.170635e-03 2.480726e-04 1.860544e-05 8.269086e-07
## [11] 1.653817e-08
```

In this case smaller values of the random variable are assigned higher probabilities and larger values are assigned lower probabilities..

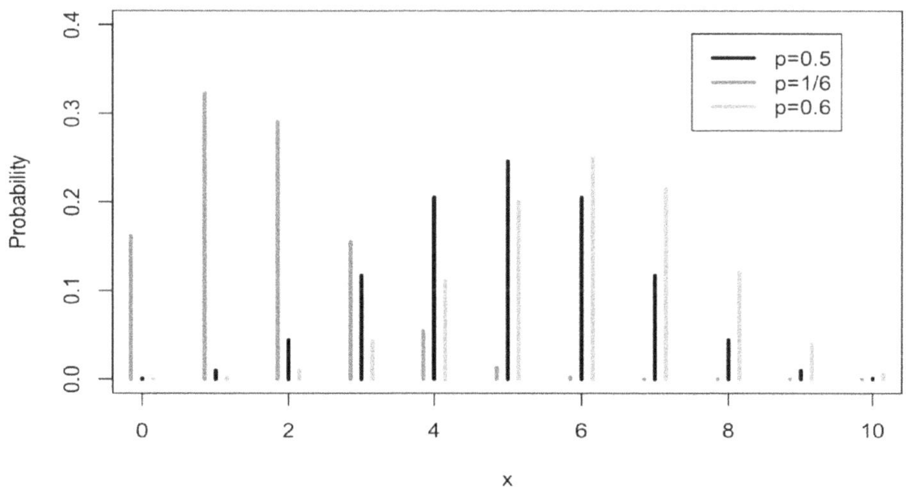

Figure 5.2: The Binomial Distribution for Various Probability of "Success"" p

In Figure 5.2 the probabilities for Binomial(10,1/6), the Binomial(10,1/2),and the Binomial(10,0.6) distributions are plotted side by side. In all these 3 distributions the sample space is the same, the integers between 0 and 10. However, the probabilities of the different values differ. (Note that all bars should be placed on top of the integers. For clarity of the presentation, the bars associated with the Binomial(10,1/6) are shifted slightly to the left and the bars associated with the Binomial(10,0.6) are shifted slightly to the right.)

The expectation of the Binomial(10,0.5) distribution is equal to 10×0.5=5. Compare this to the expectation of the Binomial(10,1/6) distribution, which is 10×(1/6)=1.666667 and to the expectation of the Binomial(10,0.6) distribution which equals 10×0.6=6.

The variance of the Binomial(10,0.5) distribution is 10×0.5×0.5=2.5. The variance when p=1/6 is 10×(1/6)×(5/6)=1.388889 and the variance when p=0.6 is 10×0.6×0.4=2.4.

Example 5.1 As an application of the Binomial distribution consider a pre-election poll. A candidate is running for office and is interested in knowing the percentage of support in the general population in its candidacy. Denote the probability of support by pp. In order to estimate the percentage a sample of size 300 is selected from the population. Let X be the count of supporters in the sample. A natural model for the distribution of X is the Binomial(300,p) distribution, since each subject in the sample may be a supporter ("Success") or may not be a supporter ("Failure"). The probability that a subject supports the candidate is pp and there are n=300 subjects in the sample.

Example 5.2 As another example consider the procedure for quality control that is described in Discussion Forum of Chapter 4. According to the procedure 20 items are tested and the number of faulty items is recorded. If pp is the probability that an item is identified as faulty then the distribution of the total number of faulty items may be modeled by the Binomial(20,p) distribution.

In both examples one may be interested in making statements on the probability pp based on the sample. Statistical inference relates the actual count obtained in the sample to the theoretical Binomial distribution in order to make such statements.

5.2.2 The Poisson Random Variable

The *Poisson* distribution is used as an approximation of the total number of occurrences of rare events. Consider, for example, the Binomial setting that involves nn trials with pp as the probability of success of each trial. Then, if p is small but nn is large then the number of successes X has, approximately, the Poisson distribution.

The sample space of the Poisson random variable is the unbounded collection of integers: {0,1,2,...}. Any integer value is assigned a positive probability. Hence, the Poisson random variable is a convenient model when the maximal number of occurrences of the events in a-priori unknown or is very large. For example, one may use the Poisson distribution to model the number of phone calls that enter a switchboard in a given interval of time or the number of malfunctioning components in a shipment of some product.

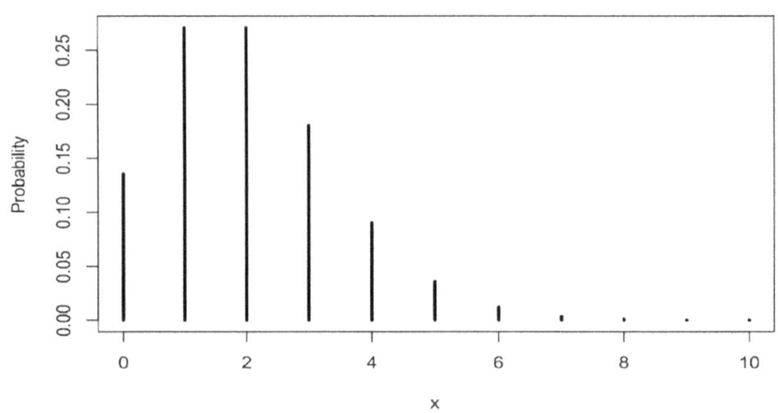

Figure 5.3: The Poisson(2) Distribution

The Binomial distribution was specified by the number of trials nn and probability of success in each trial pp. The Poisson distribution is specified by its expectation, which we denote by $\lambda\lambda$. The expression "X~Poisson(λ)" states that the random variable XX has a Poisson distribution[11] with expectation $E(X)=\lambda$. The function "dpois" computes the probability, according to the Poisson distribution, of values that are entered as the first argument to the function. The expectation of the distribution is entered in the second argument. The function "ppois" computes the cumulative probability. Consequently, we can compute the probabilities and the cumulative probabilities of the values between 0 and 10 for the Poisson(2) distribution via:

```
x <- 0:10
dpois(x,2)

## [1] 1.353353e-01 2.706706e-01 2.706706e-01 1.804470e-01 9.022352e-02
## [6] 3.608941e-02 1.202980e-02 3.437087e-03 8.592716e-04 1.909493e-04
## [11] 3.818985e-05

ppois(x,2)

## [1] 0.1353353 0.4060058 0.6766764 0.8571235 0.9473470 0.9834364 0.9954662
## [8] 0.9989033 0.9997626 0.9999535 0.9999917
```

The probability function of the Poisson distribution with λ=2, in the range between 0 and 10, is plotted in Figure 5.3. Observe that in this example probabilities of the values 8 and beyond are very small. As a matter of fact, the cumulative probability at x=7 (the 8th value in the output of "ppois(x,2)") is approximately 0.999, out of the total cumulative probability of 1.000, leaving a total probability of about 0.001 to be distributed among all the values larger than 7.

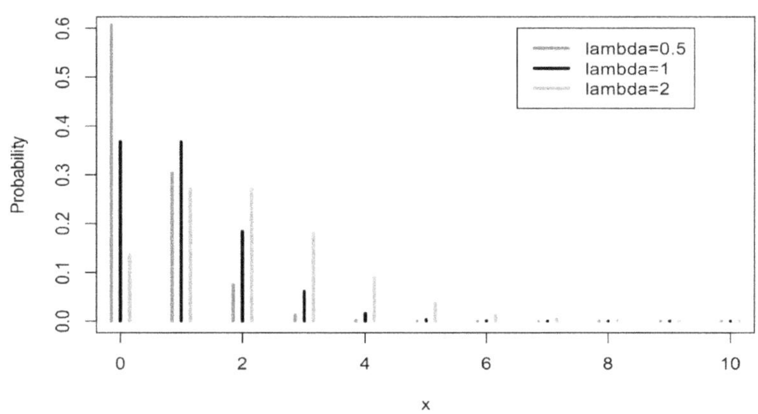

Figure 5.4: The Poisson Distribution for Various Values of λ

Let us compute the expectation of the given Poisson distribution:

```
X.val <- 0:10
P.val <- dpois(X.val,2)
sum(X.val*P.val)
```

```
## [1] 1.999907
```

Observe that the outcome is almost, but not quite, equal to 2.00, which is the actual value of the expectation. The reason for the inaccuracy is the fact that we have based the computation in R on the first 11 values of the distribution only, instead of the infinite sequence of values. A more accurate result may be obtained by the consideration of the first 101 values:

```
X.val <- 0:100
P.val <- dpois(X.val,2)
EX <- sum(X.val*P.val)
EX
```

```
## [1] 2
```

```
sum((X.val-EX)^2*P.val)
```

```
## [1] 2
```

In the last expression we have computed the variance of the Poisson distribution and obtained that it is equal to the expectation. This results can be validated mathematically. For the Poisson distribution it is always the case that the variance is equal to the expectation, namely to λ:

$$E(X) = V(X) = \lambda.$$

In Figure 5.4 you may find the probabilities of the Poisson distribution for λ=0.5, λ=1 and λ=2. Notice once more that the sample space is the same for all the Poisson distributions. What varies when we change the value of λ are the probabilities. Observe that as λ increases then probability of larger values increases as well.

Example 5.3 A radio active element decays by the release of subatomic particles and energy. The decay activity is measured in terms of the number of decays per second in a unit mass. A typical model for the distribution of the number of decays is the Poisson distribution. Observe that the number of decays in a second is a integer and, in principle, it may obtain any integer value larger or equal to zero. The event of a radio active decay of an atom is a relatively rare event. Therefore, the Poisson model is likely to fit this phenomena[3].

Example 5.4 Consider an overhead power line suspended between two utility poles. During rain, drops of water may hit the power line. The total number of drops that hit the line in a one minute period may be modeled by a Poisson random variable.

5.3 CONTINUOUS RANDOM VARIABLE

Various measurements, such as height, weight, angle, temperature, etc., can potentially have an infinite range of values. Continuous random variables are employed to represent uncertainty pertaining to future values of measurements. The primary distinction between discrete random variables, which we have already investigated, and the newly introduced continuous random variables is in the sample space, specifically the set of all potential outcomes. The former kind is employed when the potential results are distinct and can be categorized as integers. The latter category is employed when the potential results encompass the complete continuum of real numbers or when they constitute a range (which may be open-ended) of real numbers. The distinction between the two categories of sample spaces indicates variations in the manner in which the distribution of the random variables is being depicted. Discrete random variables can be represented by a table, formula, or bar plot, which displays the probability associated with each value in the sample space. For continuous random variables, probabilities are assigned to intervals of values rather than individual values. Therefore, densities are utilized to visually represent the distribution. Densities are analogous to histograms, where the areas beneath the graph represent probabilities. As we explore other instances of continuous random variables, we will offer a more comprehensive explanation of densities. When dealing with continuous random variables, integration is used instead of summation, and the density function is used instead of the probability function to calculate quantities such as the probability of an event, the expectation, and the variance.

Hence, if the expectation of a discrete random variable is given in the formula $\mathbf{E}(X) = \sum_x (x \times \mathbf{P}(x))$, which involves the summation over all values of the product between the value and the probability of the value, then for continuous random variable the definition becomes:

$$\mathbf{E}(X) = \int (x \times f(x))dx \ ,$$

where $f(x)$ is the density of X at the value xx. Therefore, in the expectation of a continuous random variable one multiplies the value by the density at the value. This product is then integrated over the sample space.

Likewise, the formula $\mathbf{V}(X) = \sum_x ((x - \mathbf{E}(X))^2 \times \mathbf{P}(x))$ for the variance is replaced by:

$$\mathbf{V}(X) = \int ((x - \mathbf{E}(X))^2 \times f(x))dx \ .$$

Nonetheless, the intuitive interpretation of the expectation as the central value of the distribution that identifies the location and the interpretation of the standard deviation (the square root of the variance) as the summary of the total spread of the distribution is still valid.

In this section we will describe two types of continuous random variables: Uniform and Exponential. In the next chapter another example - the Normal distribution - will be introduced.

5.3.1 The Uniform Random Variable

The Uniform distribution is used in order to model measurements that may have values in a given interval, with all values in this interval equally likely to occur.

For example, consider a random variable XX with the Uniform distribution over the interval [3,7], denoted by "$X \sim$Uniform(3,7)". The density function at given values may be computed with the aid of the function "dunif". For instance let us compute the density of the Uniform(3,7) distribution over the integers {0,1,...,10}:

```
dunif(0:10,3,7)
```

```
##  [1] 0.00 0.00 0.00 0.25 0.25 0.25 0.25 0.25 0.00 0.00 0.00
```

Notice that for the values 0, 1, and 2, and the values 8, 9 and 10 that are outside of the interval the density is equal to zero, indicating that such values cannot occur in the given distribution. The values of the density at integers inside the interval are positive and equal to each other. The density is not restricted to integer values. For example, at the point 4.73 we get that the density is positive and of the same height:

```
dunif(4.73,3,7)
```

```
## [1] 0.25
```

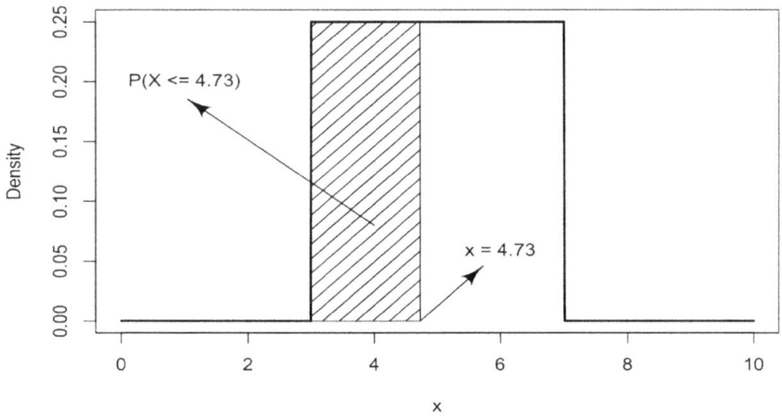

Figure 5.5: The Uniform(3,7) Distribution

A plot of the Uniform(3,7) density is given in Figure 5.5 in the form of a solid line. Observe that the density is positive over the interval [3,7] where its height is 1/4. Area under the curve in the density corresponds to probability. Indeed, the fact that the total probability is one is reflected in the total area under the curve being equal to 1. Over the interval [3,7] the density forms a rectangle. The base of the rectangle is the length of the interval 7-3=4. The height of the rectangle is thus equal to 1/4 in order to produce a total area of 4×(1/4)=1.

The function "punif" computes the cumulative probability of the uniform distribution. The probability $P(X \leq 4.73)$, for $X \sim \text{Uniform}(3,7)$, is given by:

```
punif(4.73,3,7)
```

```
## [1] 0.4325
```

This probability corresponds to the marked area to the left of the point x=4.73x=4.73 in Figure 5.5. This area of the marked rectangle is equal to the length of the base 4.73 - 3 = 1.73, times the height of the rectangle 1/(7-3) = 1/4. Indeed:

```
(4.73-3)/(7-3)
```

```
## [1] 0.4325
```

is the area of the marked rectangle and is equal to the probability.

Let us use R in order to plot the density and the cumulative probability functions of the Uniform distribution. We produce first a large number of points in the region we want to plot. The points are produced with aid of the function "seq". The output of this function is a sequence with equally spaced values. The starting value of the sequence is the first argument in the input of the function and the last value is the second argument in the input. The argument "length=1000" sets the length of the sequence, 1,000 values in this case:

```
x <- seq(0,10,length=1000)
den <- dunif(x,3,7)
plot(x,den)
```

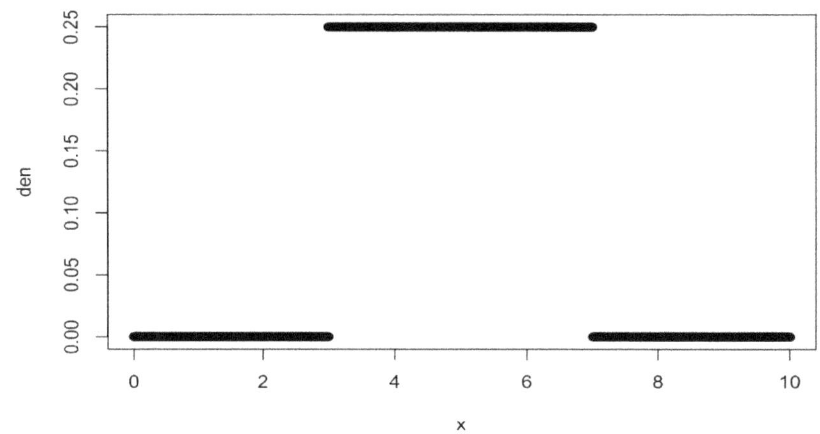

The object "den" is a sequence of length 1,000 that contains the density of the Uniform(3,7) evaluated over the values of "x". When we apply the function "plot" to the two sequences we get a scatter plot of the 1,000 points.

A scatter plot is a plot of points. Each point in the scatter plot is identify by its horizontal location on the plot (its "*x*" value) and by its vertical location on the plot (its *yy* value). The horizontal value of each point in the plot is determined by the first argument to the function "plot" and the vertical value is determined by the second argument. For example, the first value in the sequence "x" is 0. The value of the Uniform density at this point is 0. Hence, the first value of the sequence "den" is also 0. A point that corresponds to these values is produced in the plot. The horizontal value of the point is 0 and the vertical value is 0. In a similar way the other 999 points are plotted. The last point to be plotted has a horizontal value of 10 and a vertical value of 0.

The number of points that are plotted is large and they overlap each other in the graph and thus produce an impression of a continuum. In order to obtain nicer looking plots we may choose to connect the points to each other with segments and use smaller points. This may be achieved by the addition of the argument "type=l", with the letter l for line, to the plotting function:

```
plot(x,den,type="l")
```

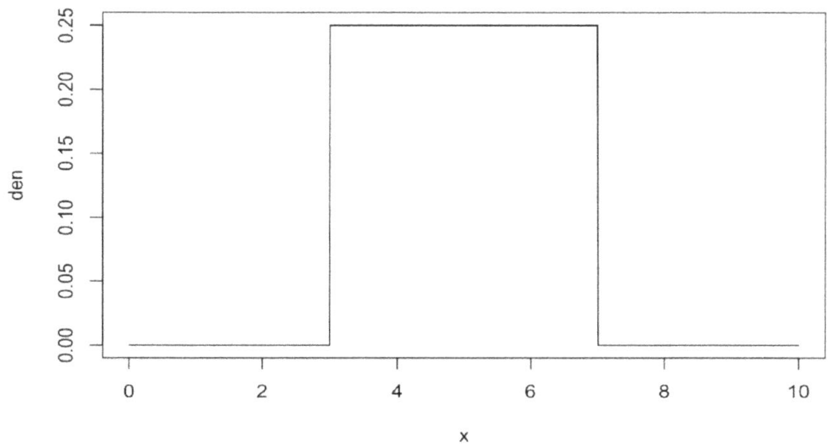

The cumulative probability of the Uniform(3,7) is produced by the code:

```
cdf <- punif(x,3,7)
plot(x,cdf,type="l")
```

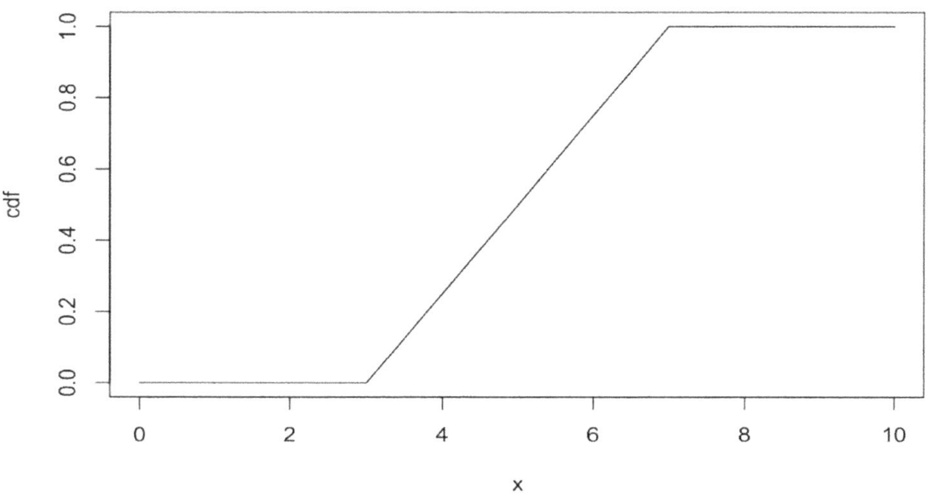

One can think of the density of the Uniform as an histogram. The expectation of a Uniform random variable is the middle point of it's histogram. Hence, if $X \sim \text{Uniform}(a,b)$ then:

$$E(X) = \frac{a+b}{2}\,.$$

For the $X \sim$Uniform(3,7) distribution the expectation is E (X)=(3+7)/2=5. Observe that 5 is the center of the Uniform density in Plot 5.5.

It can be shown that the variance of the Uniform(a,b) is equal to

$$V(X) = \frac{(b-a)^2}{12}\,,$$

with the standard deviation being the square root of this value. Specifically, for $X \sim$Uniform(3,7) we get that V $(X)=(7-3)^2/12=1.333333$. The standard deviation is equal to $\sqrt{1.333333} = 1.154701$.

Example 5.5 In Example 5.4 we considered rain drops that hit an overhead power line suspended between two utility poles. The **number** of drops that hit the line can be modeled using the Poisson distribution. The **position** between the two poles where a rain drop hits the line can be modeled by the Uniform distribution. The rain drop can hit any position between the two utility poles. Hitting one position along the line is as likely as hitting any other position.

Example 5.6 Meiosis is the process in which a diploid cell that contains two copies of the genetic material produces an haploid cell with only one copy (sperms or eggs, depending on the sex). The resulting molecule of genetic material is linear molecule (chromosome) that is composed of consecutive segments: a segment that originated from one of the two copies followed by a segment from the other copy and vice versa. The border points between segments are called points of crossover. The Haldane model for crossovers states that the position of a crossover between two given loci on the chromosome corresponds to the Uniform distribution and the total number of crossovers between these two loci corresponds to the Poisson distribution.

5.3.2 The Exponential Random Variable

The Exponential distribution is frequently used to model times between events. For example, times between incoming phone calls, the time until a component becomes malfunction, etc. We denote the Exponential distribution via "$X \sim$Exponential(λ)", where λ is a parameter that characterizes the distribution and is called the *rate* of the distribution. The overlap between the parameter used to characterize the Exponential distribution and the one used for the Poisson distribution is deliberate. The two distributions are tightly interconnected. As a matter of fact, it can be shown that if the distribution between occurrences of a phenomena has the Exponential distribution with rate λ then the total number of the occurrences of the phenomena within a unit interval of time has a Poisson(λ) distribution.

The sample space of an Exponential random variable contains all non-negative numbers. Consider, for example, $X \sim$Exponential(0.5). The density of the distribution in the range between 0 and 10 is presented in Figure 5.6. Observe that in the Exponential distribution smaller values are more likely to occur in comparison to larger values. This is indicated by the density being larger at the vicinity of 0. The density of the exponential distribution given in the plot is positive, but hardly so, for values larger than 10.

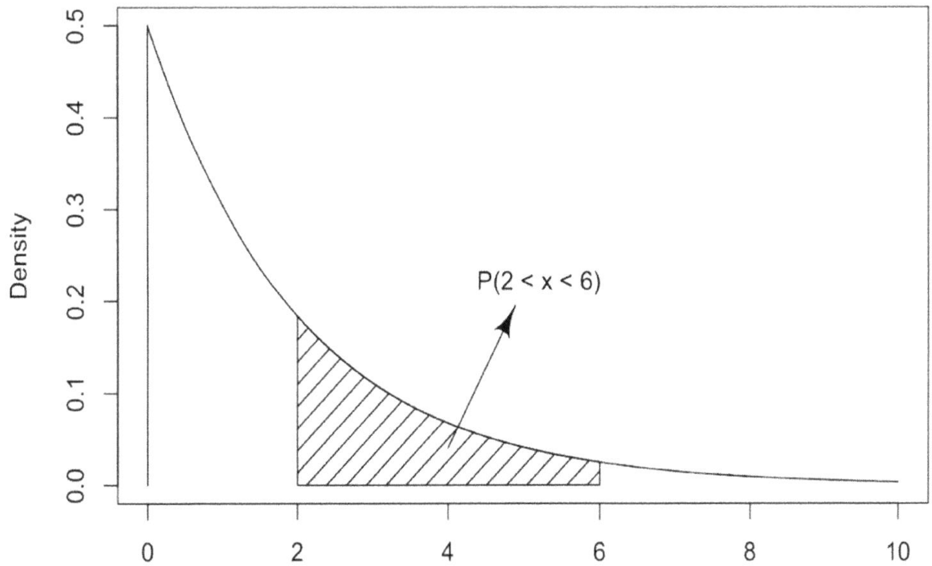

Figure 5.6: The Exponential(0.5) Distribution

The density of the Exponential distribution can be computed with the aid of the function "dexp". The cumulative probability can be computed with the function "pexp". For illustration, assume $X \sim$Exponential(0.5). Say one is interested in the computation of the probability P($2 < X \leq 6$) that the random variable obtains a value that belongs to the interval (2,6]. The required probability is indicated as the marked area in Figure 5.6. This area can be computed as the difference between the probability P($X \leq 6$), the area to the left of 6, and the probability P ($X \leq 2$), the area to the left of 2:

```
pexp(6,0.5) - pexp(2,0.5)
```

```
## [1] 0.3180924
```

The difference is the probability of belonging to the interval, namely the area marked in the plot.

The expectation of X, when $X \sim \text{Exponential}(\lambda)$, is given by the equation:

$$\mathrm{E}(X) = 1/\lambda ,$$

and the variance is given by:

$$\mathrm{V}(X) = 1/\lambda^2 .$$

The standard deviation is the square root of the variance, namely $1/\lambda$. Observe that the larger is the rate the smaller are the expectation and the standard deviation.

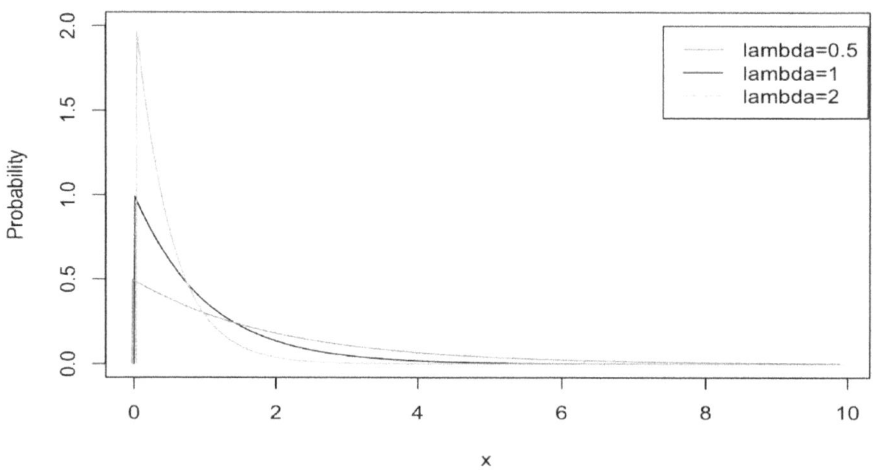

Figure 5.7: The Exponential Distribution for Various Values of λ

In Figure 5.7 the densities of the Exponential distribution are plotted for λ=0.5, λ=1, and λ=2. Notice that with the increase in the value of the parameter then the values of the random variable tends to become smaller. This inverse relation makes sense in connection to the Poisson distribution. Recall that the Poisson distribution corresponds to the total number of occurrences in a unit interval of time when the time between occurrences has an Exponential distribution. A larger expectation $\lambda\lambda$ of the Poisson corresponds to a larger number of occurrences that are likely to take place during the unit interval of time. The larger is the number of occurrences the smaller are the time intervals between occurrences.

Example 5.7 Consider Examples 5.4 and 5.5 that deal with rain dropping on a power line. The times between consecutive hits of the line may be modeled by the Exponential distribution. Hence, the time to the first hit has an Exponential distribution. The time between the first and the second hit is also Exponentially distributed, and so on.

Example 5.8 Return to Example 5.3 that deals with the radio activity of some element. The total count of decays per second is model by the Poisson distribution. The times between radio active decays is modeled according to the Exponential distribution. The rate λ of that Exponential distribution is equal to the expectation of the total count of decays in one second, i.e. the expectation of the Poisson distribution.

5.4 EXERCISES

Exercise 5.1 A particular measles vaccine produces a reaction (a fever higher that 102 Fahrenheit) in each vaccinee with probability of 0.09. A clinic vaccinates 500 people each day.

1. What is the expected number of people that will develop a reaction each day?
2. What is the standard deviation of the number of people that will develop a reaction each day?
3. In a given day, what is the probability that more than 40 people will develop a reaction?
4. In a given day, what is the probability that the number of people that will develop a reaction is between 50 and 45 (inclusive)?

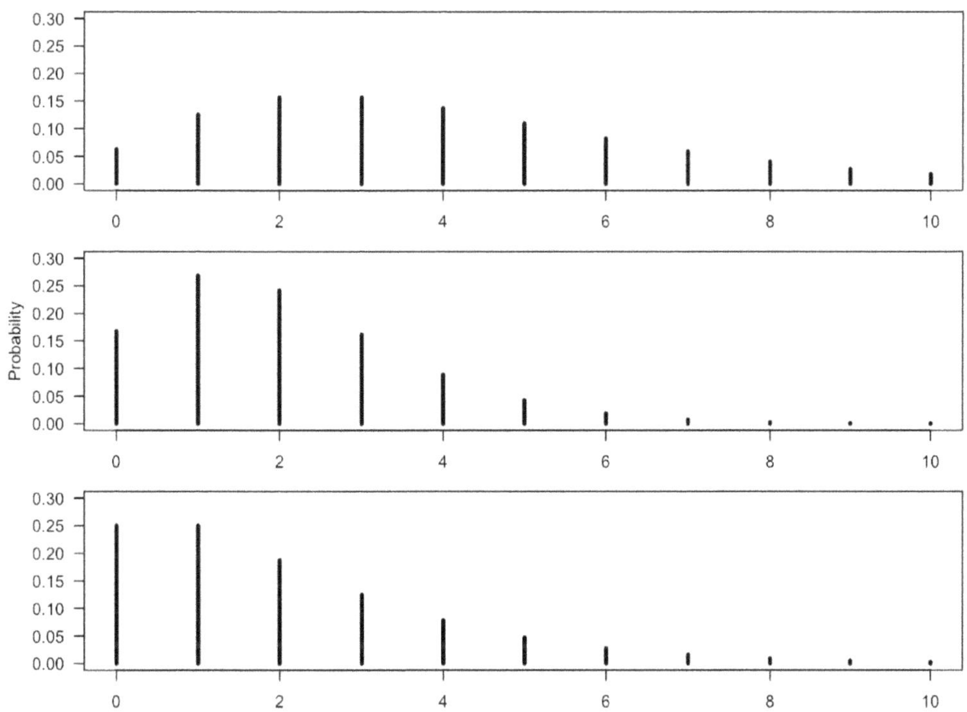

Figure 5.8: Bar Plots of the Negative-Binomial Distribution

Exercise 5.2 The Negative-Binomial distribution is yet another example of a discrete, integer valued, random variable. The sample space of the distribution are all non-negative integers {0,1,2,...}. The fact that a random variable X has this distribution is marked by "X~Negative-Binomial(r,p)X~Negative-Binomial(r,p)", where rr and p are parameters that specify the distribution.

Consider 3 random variables from the Negative-Binomial distribution:

- X_1~Negative-Binomial(2,0.5)
- X_2~Negative-Binomial(4,0.5)
- X_3~Negative-Binomial(8,0.8)

The bar plots of these random variables are presented in Figure 5.8, re-organizer in a random order.

1. Produce bar plots of the distributions of the random variables X_1, X_2, X_3 in the range of integers between 0 and 15 and thereby identify the pair of parameters that produced each one of the plots in Figure 5.8. Notice that the bar plots can be produced with the aid of the function "plot" and the function "dnbinom(x,r,p)", where "x" is a sequence of integers and "r" and "p" are the parameters of the distribution. Pay attention to the fact that you should use the argument "type = h" in the function "plot" in order to produce the horizontal bars.
2. Below is a list of pairs that includes an expectation and a variance. Each of the pairs is associated with one of the random variables X_1, X_2, and X_3:

- **E**(X) = 4, **V**(X) = 8.
- **E**(X) = 2, **V**(X) = 4.
- **E**(X) = 2, **V**(X) = 2.5.

Use Figure 5.8 in order to match the random variable with its associated pair. Do not use numerical computations or formulae for the expectation and the variance in the Negative-Binomial distribution in order to carry out the matching[15]. Use, instead, the structure of the bar-plots.

6 Chapter
THE NORMAL RANDOM VARIABLE

6.1 INTRODUCTION: AN OVERVIEW

This chapter presents the Normal distribution, which is a significant bell-shaped distribution. This text examines the calculations related to this distribution, such as the percentiles of the distribution and the determination of intervals with assigned probabilities. The Normal distribution can be used as an approximation for other distributions. We illustrate this characteristic by demonstrating that, under certain circumstances, the Binomial distribution can be approximated by the Normal distribution. The next chapter will illustrate the mathematical theory that establishes the Normal approximation, which will highlight this aspect of the Normal distribution.

6.2 THE NORMAL RANDOM VARIABLE

The Normal distribution is the preeminent distribution utilized in statistics. Often, it functions as a universal template for the dispersion of a measurement. Furthermore, even if the measurement is represented by alternative probability distributions such as Binomial, Poisson, Uniform, Exponential, etc., the Normal distribution arises as an estimate of the distribution of numerical properties of the data generated by these measurements.

6.2.1 The Normal Distribution

A Normal random variable has a continuous distribution over the sample space of all numbers, negative or positive. We denote the Normal distribution via "$X \sim \text{Normal}(\mu,\sigma^2)$", where $\mu=\text{E}(X)$ is the expectation of the random variable and $\sigma^2=\text{V}(X)$ is it's variance[1].

Consider, for example, $X \sim \text{Normal}(2,9)$. The density of the distribution is presented in Figure 6.1. Observe that the distribution is symmetric about the expectation 2. The random variable is more likely to obtain its value in the vicinity of the expectation. Values much larger or much smaller than the expectation are substantially less likely.

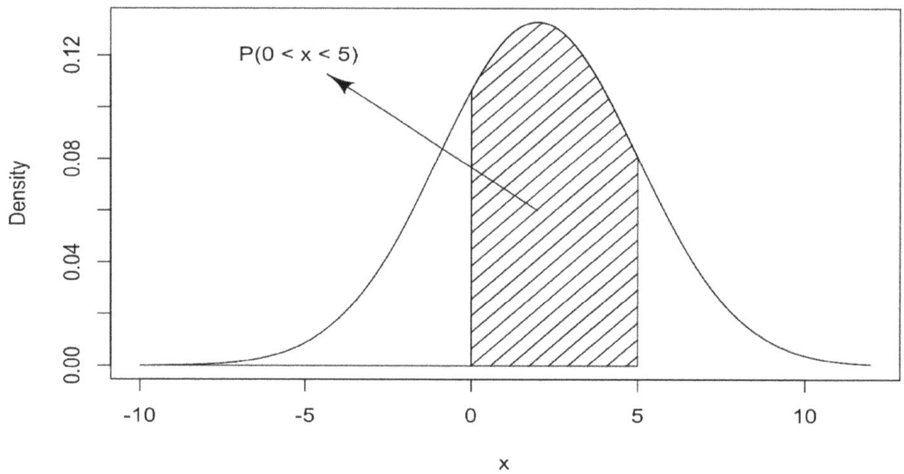

Figure 6.1: The Normal(2,9) Distribution

The density of the Normal distribution can be computed with the aid of the function “dnorm”. The cumulative probability can be computed with the function “pnorm”. For illustrating the use of the latter function, assume that $X \sim$Normal(2,9). Say one is interested in the computation of the probability P $(0<X\leq5)$ that the random variable obtains a value that belongs to the interval (0,5]. The required probability is indicated by the marked area in Figure 6.1. This area can be computed as the difference between the probability P $(X\leq5)$, the area to the left of 5, and the probability $P(X\leq0)$, the area to the left of 0:

```
pnorm(5,2,3) - pnorm(0,2,3)
```

```
## [1] 0.5888522
```

The difference is the indicated area that corresponds to the probability of being inside the interval, which turns out to be approximately equal to 0.589. Notice that the expectation μ of the Normal distribution is entered as the second argument to the function. The third argument to the function is the standard deviation, i.e. the square root of the variance. In this example, the standard deviation is $\sqrt{9} = 3$.

Figure 6.2 displays the densities of the Normal distribution for the combinations $\mu=0$, $\sigma^2=1$ (the *red* line); $\mu=2$, $\sigma^2=9$ (the *black* line); and $\mu=-3$, $\sigma^2=1/4$ (the *green* line). Observe that the smaller the variance the more concentrated is the distribution of the random variable about the expectation.

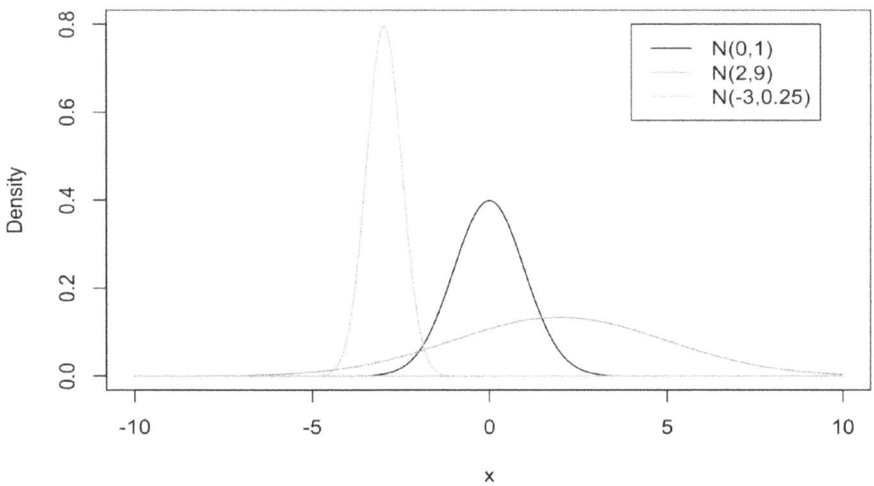

Figure 6.2: The Normal Distribution for Various Values of μ and σ^2

Example 6.1 IQ tests are a popular (and controversial) mean for measuring intelligence. They are produced as (weighted) average of a response to a long list of questions, designed to test different abilities. The score of the test across the entire population is set to be equal to 100 and the standard deviation is set to 15. The distribution of the score is Normal. Hence, if X is the IQ score of a random subject then $X \sim \text{Normal}(100,15^2)$.

Example 6.2 Any measurement that is produced as a result of the combination of many independent influencing factors is likely to poses the Normal distribution. For example, the hight of a person is influenced both by genetics and by the environment in which that person grew up. Both the genetic and the environmental influences are a combination of many factors. Thereby, it should not come as a surprise that the heights of people in a population tend to follow the Normal distribution.

6.2.2 The Standard Normal Distribution

The standard normal distribution is a normal distribution of standardized values, which are called zz-scores. A z-score is the original measurement measured in units of the standard deviation from the expectation. For example, if the expectation of a Normal distribution is 2 and the standard deviation is $3 = \sqrt{9}$, then the value of 0 is 2/3 standard deviations smaller than (or to the left of) the expectation. Hence, the z-score of the value 0 is -2/3. The calculation of the z-score emerges from the equation:

$$(0 =)\ x = \mu + z \cdot \sigma\ (= 2 + z \cdot 3)$$

The z-score is obtained by solving the equation

$$0 = 2 + z \cdot 3 \quad \Longrightarrow \quad z = (0 - 2)/3 = -2/3\ .$$

In a similar way, the z-score of the value x=5 is equal to 1, following the solution of the equation 5=2+z·3, which leads to z=(5–2)/3=1.

The standard Normal distribution is the distribution of a standardized Normal measurement. The expectation for the standard Normal distribution is 0 and the variance is 1. When $X \sim N(\mu,\sigma^2)$ has a Normal distribution with expectation μμ and variance σ^2 then the transformed random variable $Z=(X-\mu)/\sigma$ produces the standard Normal distribution $Z \sim N(0,1)$. The transformation corresponds to the reexpression of the original measurement in terms of a new "zero" and a new unit of measurement. The new "zero" is the expectation of the original measurement and the new unit is the standard deviation of the original measurement.

Computation of probabilities associated with a Normal random variable XX can be carried out with the aid of the standard Normal distribution. For example, consider the computation of the probability P(0<X≤5) for $X \sim N(2,9)$, that has expectation μ=2 and standard deviation σ=3σ=3. Consider X's standardized values: $Z=(X-2)/3$. The boundaries of the interval [0,5], namely 0 and 5, have standardized z-scores of (0–2)/3=–2/3 and (5–2)/3=1, respectively. Clearly, the original measurement X falls between the original boundaries (0<X≤5) if, and only if, the standardized measurement Z falls between the standardized boundaries (–2/3<Z≤1). Therefore, the probability that XX obtains a value in the range [0,5] is equal to the probability that Z obtains a value in the range [–2/3,1].

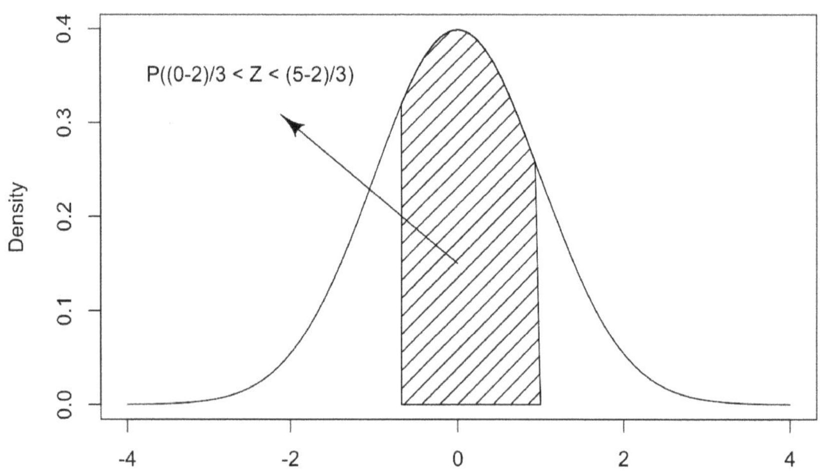

Figure 6.3: The Standard Normal Distribution

The function "pnorm" was used in the previous subsection in order to compute that probability that X obtains values between 0 and 5. The computation produced the probability 0.5888522. We can repeat the computation by the application of the same function to the standardized values:

```
pnorm((5-2)/3) - pnorm((0-2)/3
```

```
## [1] 0.5888522
```

The value that is being computed, the area under the graph for the standard Normal distribution, is presented in Figure 6.3. Recall that 3 arguments where specified in the previous application of the function "pnorm": the x value, the expectation, and the standard deviation. In the given application we did not specify the last two arguments, only the first one. (Notice that the output of the expression "(5-2)/3" is a single number and, likewise, the output of the expression "(0-2)/3" is also a single number.)

Most R function have many arguments that enables flexible application in a wide range of settings. For convenience, however, default values are set to most of these arguments. These default values are used unless an alternative value for the argument is set when the function is called. The default value of the second argument of the function "pnorm" that specifies the expectation is "mean=0", and the default value of the third argument that specifies the standard deviation is "sd=1". Therefore, if no other value is set for these arguments the function computes the cumulative distribution function of the standard Normal distribution.

6.2.3 Computing Percentiles

Consider the issue of determining the range that contains 95% of the probability for a Normal random variable. We start with the standard Normal distribution. Consult Figure 6.4. The figure displays the standard Normal distribution with the central region shaded. The area of the shaded region is 0.95.

We may find the zz-values of the boundaries of the region, denoted in the figure as z_0 and z_1 by the investigation of the cumulative distribution function. Indeed, in order to have 95% of the distribution in the central region one should leave out 2.5% of the distribution in each of the two tails. That is, 0.025 should be the area of the unshaded region to the right of z_1 and, likewise, 0.025 should be the area of the unshaded region to the left of z_0. In other words, the cumulative probability up to z0z_0 should be 0.025 and the cumulative distribution up to z_1 should be 0.975.

In general, given a random variable X and given a percent pp, the x value with the property that the cumulative distribution up to x is equal to the probability p is called the *p-percentile* of the distribution. Here we seek the 2.5%-percentile and the 97.5%-percentile of the standard Normal distribution.

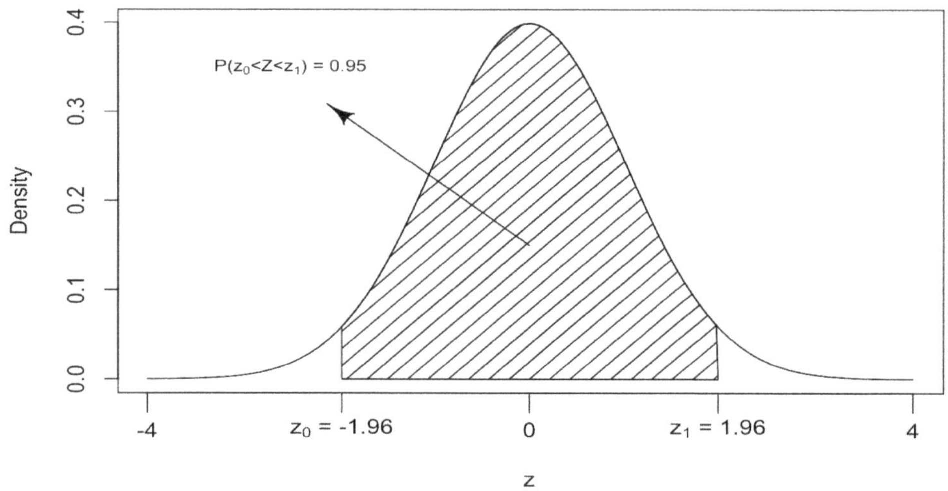

Figure 6.4: Central 95%% of the Standard Normal Distribution

The percentiles of the Normal distribution are computed by the function "qnorm". The first argument to the function is a probability (or a sequence of probabilities), the second and third arguments are the expectation and the standard deviations of the normal distribution. The default values to these arguments are set to 0 and 1, respectively. Hence if these arguments are not provided the function computes the percentiles of the standard Normal distribution. Let us apply the function in order to compute z_1□1 and z0z_0:

```
qnorm(0.975)
```

```
## [1] 1.959964
```

```
qnorm(0.025)
```

```
## [1] -1.959964
```

Observe that z_1 is practically equal to 1.96 and z_0=-1.96=-z_1. The fact that z0z_0 is the negative of z_1 results from the symmetry of the standard Normal distribution about 0. As a conclusion we get that for the standard Normal distribution 95% of the probability is concentrated in the range [-1.96,1.96].

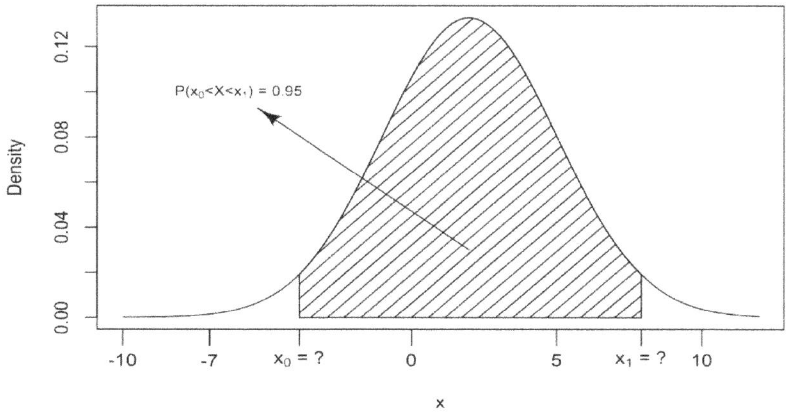

Figure 6.5: Central 95%% of the Normal(2,9) Distribution

The problem of determining the central range that contains 95% of the distribution can be addresses in the context of the original measurement X (See Figure 6.5). We seek in this case an interval centered at the expectation 2, which is the center of the distribution of XX, unlike 0 which was the center of the standardized values Z. One way of solving the problem is via the application of the function "qnorm" with the appropriate values for the expectation and the standard deviation:

```
qnorm(0.975,2,3)

## [1] 7.879892

qnorm(0.025,2,3)

## [1] -3.879892
```

Hence, we get that x_0=-3.88 has the property that the total probability to its left is 0.025 and x_1=7.88 has the property that the total probability to its right is 0.025. The total probability in the range [-3.88,7.88] is 0.95.

An alternative approach for obtaining the given interval exploits the interval that was obtained for the standardized values. An interval [-1.96,1.96] of standardized zz-values corresponds to an interval [2-1.96·3,2+1.96·3] of the original x-values:

```
2 + qnorm(0.975)*3
```

```
## [1] 7.879892
```

```
2 + qnorm(0.025)*3
```

```
## [1] -3.879892
```

Hence, we again produce the interval [-3.88,7.88], the interval that was obtained before as the central interval that contains 95% of the distribution of the Normal(2,9) random variable.

In general, if $X \sim N(\mu,\sigma)$ is a Normal random variable then the interval $[\mu-1.96\cdot\sigma,\mu+1.96\cdot\sigma]$ contains 95% of the distribution of the random variable. Frequently one uses the notation $\mu\pm1.96\cdot\sigma$ to describe such an interval.

6.2.4 Outliers and the Normal Distribution

Consider, next, the computation of the interquartile range in the Normal distribution. Recall that the interquartile range is the length of the central interval that contains 50% of the distribution. This interval starts at the first quartile (Q1), the value that splits the distribution so that 25% of the distribution is to the left of the value and 75% is to the right of it. The interval ends at the third quartile (Q3) where 75% of the distribution is to the left and 25% is to the right.

For the standard Normal the third and first quartiles can be computed with the aid of the function "qnorm":

```
qnorm(0.75)
```

```
## [1] 0.6744898
```

```
qnorm(0.25)
```

```
## [1] -0.6744898
```

Observe that for the standard Normal distribution one has that 75% of the distribution is to the left of the value 0.6744898, which is the third quartile of this distribution. Likewise, 25% of the standard Normal distribution are to the left of the value -0.6744898, which is the first quartile. the interquartile range is the length of the interval between the third and the first quartiles. In the case of the standard Normal distribution this length is equal to 0.6744898-(-0.6744898)=1.348980.

In Chapter 3 we considered box plots as a mean for the graphical display of numerical data. The box plot includes a vertical rectangle that initiates at the first quartile and ends at the third quartile, with the median marked within the box. The rectangle contains 50% of the data. Whiskers extends from the ends of this rectangle to the smallest and to the largest data values that are not outliers. Outliers are values that lie outside of the normal range of the data. Outliers are identified as values that are more then 1.5 times the interquartile range away from the ends of the central rectangle. Hence, a value is an outlier if it is larger than the third quartile plus 1.5 times the interquartile range or if it is less than the first quartile minus 1.5 times the interquartile range.

How likely is it to obtain an outlier value when the measurement has the standard Normal distribution? We obtained that the third quartile of the standard Normal distribution is equal to 0.6744898 and the first quartile is minus this value. The interquartile range is the difference between the third and first quartiles. The upper and lower thresholds for the defining outliers are:

```
qnorm(0.75) + 1.5*(qnorm(0.75)-qnorm(0.25))

## [1] 2.697959

qnorm(0.25) - 1.5*(qnorm(0.75)-qnorm(0.25))

## [1] -2.697959
```

Hence, a value larger than 2.697959 or smaller than -2.697959 would be identified as an outlier.

The probability of being less than the upper threshold 2.697959 in the standard Normal distribution is computed with the expression "pnorm(2.697959)". The probability of being above the threshold is 1 minus that probability, which is the outcome of the expression "1-pnorm(2.697959)".

By the symmetry of the standard Normal distribution we get that the probability of being below the lower threshold -2.697959 is equal to the probability of being above the upper threshold. Consequently, the probability of obtaining an outlier is equal to twice the probability of being above the upper threshold:

```
2*(1-pnorm(2.697959))

## [1] 0.006976603
```

We get that for the standard Normal distribution the probability of an outlier is approximately 0.7%.

6.3 APPROXIMATION OF THE BINOMIAL DISTRIBUTION

The Normal distribution often arises as an approximation of the distribution of data features. The mathematical theory that provides such approximation is known as the Central Limit Theorem and will be discussed in the next chapter. This section illustrates the Normal approximation within the framework of the Binomial distribution.

6.3.1 Approximate Binomial Probabilities and Percentiles

Consider, for example, the probability of obtaining between 1940 and 2060 heads when tossing 4,000 fair coins. Let XX be the total number of heads. The tossing of a coin is a trial with two possible outcomes: "Head" and "Tail." The probability of a "Head" is 0.5 and there are 4,000 trials. Let us call obtaining a "Head" in a trial a "Success". Observe that the random variable X counts the total number of successes. Hence, $X \sim$Binomial(4000,0.5).

The probability P(1940≤X≤2060) can be computed as the difference between the probability P(X≤2060) of being less or equal to 2060 and the probability P (X<1940) of being strictly less than 1940. However, 1939 is the largest integer that is still strictly less than the integer 1940. As a result we get that P(X<1940)= P (X≤1939). Consequently, P (1940≤X≤2060)=P (X≤2060)-P (X≤1939).

Applying the function "pbinom" for the computation of the Binomial cumulative probability, namely the probability of being less or equal to a given value, we get that the probability in the range between 1940 and 2060 is equal to

```
pbinom(2060,4000,0.5) - pbinom(1939,4000,0.5)
```

```
## [1] 0.9442883
```

This is a precise calculation. The Normal approximation yields an estimated evaluation, rather than a precise computation. The Normal approximation is a method that replaces calculations done for the Binomial distribution with calculations done for the Normal distribution. The calculation of the probability for a Binomial random variable is substituted with the calculation of the probability for a Normal random variable that possesses the identical mean and standard deviation as the Binomial random variable.

Notice that if $X \sim$Binomial(4000,0.5) then the expectation is E (X)=4,000×0.5=2,000 and the variance is V(X)=4,000×0.5×0.5=1,000, with the standard deviation being the square root of the variance. Repeating the same computation that we conducted for the Binomial random variable, but this time with the function "pnorm" that is used for the computation of the Normal cumulative probability, we get:

```
mu <- 4000*0.5
sig <- sqrt(4000*0.5*0.5)
pnorm(2060,mu,sig) - pnorm(1939,mu,sig)
```

```
## [1] 0.9442441
```

Observe that in this example the Normal approximation of the probability (0.9442441) agrees with the Binomial computation of the probability (0.9442883) up to 3 significant digits.

Normal computations may also be applied in order to find approximate percentiles of the Binomial distribution. For example, let us identify the central region that contains for a Binomial(4000,0.5)Binomial(4000,0.5) random variable (approximately) 95% of the distribution. Towards that end we can identify the boundaries of the region for the Normal distribution with the same expectation and standard deviation as that of the target Binomial distribution:

```
qnorm(0.975,mu,sig)

## [1] 2061.98

qnorm(0.025,mu,sig)

## [1] 1938.02
```

After rounding to the nearest integer we get the interval [1938,2062] as a proposed central region.

In order to validate the proposed region we may repeat the computation under the actual Binomial distribution:

```
qbinom(0.975,4000,0.5)

## [1] 2062

qbinom(0.025,4000,0.5)

## [1] 1938
```

Again, we get the interval [1938,2062] as the central region, in agreement with the one proposed by the Normal approximation. Notice that the function “qbinom” produces the percentiles of the Binomial distribution. It may not come as a surprise to learn that “qpois”, “qunif”, “qexp” compute the percentiles of the Poisson, Uniform and Exponential distributions, respectively.

The ability to approximate one distribution by the other, when computation tools for both distributions are handy, seems to be of questionable importance. Indeed, the significance of the Normal approximation is not so much in its ability to approximate the Binomial distribution as such. Rather, the important point is that the Normal distribution may serve as an approximation to a wide class of distributions, with the Binomial distribution being only one example. Computations that are based on the Normal approximation will be valid for all members in the class of distributions, including cases where we don't have the computational tools at our disposal or even in cases where we do not know what the exact distribution of the member is! As promised, a more detailed discussion of the Normal approximation in a wider context will be presented in the next chapter.

On the other hand, one need not assume that any distribution is well approximated by the Normal distribution. For example, the distribution of wealth in the population tends to be skewed, with more than 50% of the people possessing less than 50% of the wealth and small percentage of the people possessing the majority of the wealth. The Normal distribution is not a good model for such distribution. The Exponential distribution, or distributions similar to it, may be more appropriate.

6.3.2 Continuity Corrections

To completely comprehend this part, let us examine the Normal approximations of the Binomial distribution with further scrutiny.

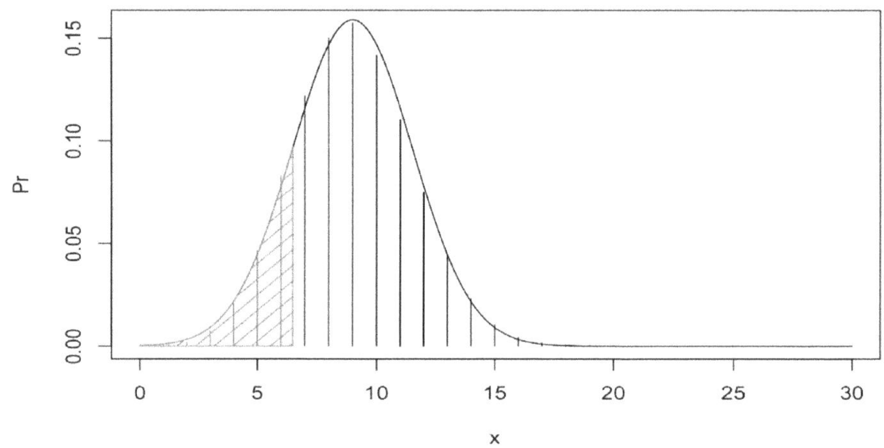

Figure 6.6: Normal Approximation of the Binomial Distribution

In principle, the Normal approximation is valid when nn, the number of independent trials in the Binomial distribution, is large. When nn is relatively small the approximation may not be so good. Indeed, take X~Binomial(30,0.3) and consider the probability $P(X \le 6)$. Compare the actual probability to the Normal approximation:

```
pbinom(6,30,0.3)
```

```
## [1] 0.159523
```

```
pnorm(6,30*0.3,sqrt(30*0.3*0.7))
```

```
## [1] 0.1159989
```

The Normal approximation, which is equal to 0.1159989, is not too close to the actual probability, which is equal to 0.1595230.

A naïve application of the Normal approximation for the Binomial(n,p) distribution may not be so good when the number of trials nn is small. Yet, a small modification of the approximation may produce much better results. In order to explain the modification consult Figure 6.6 where you will find the bar plot of the Binomial distribution with the density of the approximating Normal distribution superimposed on top of it. The target probability is the sum of heights of the bars that are painted in *red*. In the naïve application of the Normal approximation we used the area under the normal density which is to the left of the bar associated with the value x=6.

Alternatively, you may associate with each bar located at xx the area under the normal density over the interval [x-0.5,x+0.5]. The resulting correction to the approximation will use the Normal probability of the event {X≤6.5}, which is the area shaded in *red*. The application of this approximation, which is called *continuity correction* produces:

```
pnorm(6.5,30*0.3,sqrt(30*0.3*0.7))
```

```
## [1] 0.1596193
```

Observe that the corrected approximation is much closer to the target probability, which is 0.1595230, and is substantially better that the uncorrected approximation which was 0.1159989. Generally, it is recommended to apply the continuity correction to the Normal approximation of a discrete distribution.

Consider the Binomial(n,p) distribution. Another situation where the Normal approximation may fail is when pp, the probability of "Success" in the Binomial distribution, is too close to 0 (or too close to 1). Recall, that for large n the Poisson distribution emerged as an approximation of the Binomial distribution in such a setting. One may expect that when nn is large and pp is small then the Poisson distribution may produce a better approximation of a Binomial probability. When the Poisson distribution is used for the approximation we call it a *Poisson Approximation.*

Let us consider an example. Let us analyze 3 Binomial distributions. The expectation in all the distributions is equal to 2 but the number of trials, n, vary. In the first case n=20 (and hence p=0.1), in the second n=200 (and p=0.01), and in the third n=2,000 (and p=0.001. In all three cases we will be interested in the probability of obtaining a value less or equal to 3.

The Poisson approximation replaces computations conducted under the Binomial distribution with Poisson computations, with a Poisson distribution that has the same expectation as the Binomial. Since in all three cases the expectation is equal to 2 we get that the same Poisson approximation is used to the three probabilities:

```
ppois(3,2)

## [1] 0.8571235
```

The actual Binomial probability in the first case (n=20, p=0.1) and a Normal approximation thereof are:

```
pbinom(3,20,0.1)

## [1] 0.8670467

pnorm(3.5,2,sqrt(20*0.1*0.9))

## [1] 0.8682238
```

Observe that the Normal approximation (with a continuity correction) is better than the Poisson approximation in this case.

In the second case (n=200, p=0.01) the actual Binomial probability and the Normal approximation of the probability are:

```
pbinom(3,200,0.01)

## [1] 0.858034

pnorm(3.5,2,sqrt(200*0.01*0.99))

## [1] 0.856789
```

Observe that the Poisson approximation that produces 0.8571235 is slightly closer to the target than the Normal approximation. The greater accuracy of the Poisson approximation for the case where nn is large and pp is small is more pronounced in the final case (n=2000, p=0.001) where the target probability and the Normal approximation are:

```
pbinom(3,2000,0.001)

## [1] 0.8572138

pnorm(3.5,2,sqrt(2000*0.001*0.999))

## [1] 0.8556984
```

Compare the actual Binomial probability, which is equal to 0.8572138, to the Poisson approximation that produced 0.8571235. The Normal approximation, 0.8556984, is slightly off, but is still acceptable.

6.4 EXERCISES

Exercise 6.1 Consider the problem of establishing regulations concerning the maximum number of people who can occupy a lift. In particular, we would like to assess the probability of exceeding maximal weight when 8 people are allowed to use the lift simultaneously and compare that to the probability of allowing 9 people into the lift.

Assume that the total weight of 8 people chosen at random follows a normal distribution with a mean of 560kg and a standard deviation of 57kg. Assume that the total weight of 9 people chosen at random follows a normal distribution with a mean of 630kg and a standard deviation of 61kg.

1. What is the probability that the total weight of 8 people exceeds 650kg?
2. What is the probability that the total weight of 9 people exceeds 650kg?
3. What is the central region that contains 80% of distribution of the total weight of 8 people?
4. What is the central region that contains 80% of distribution of the total weight of 9 people?

Exercise 6.2 Assume $X \sim \text{Binomial}(27, 0.32)$. We are interested in the probability $P(X > 11)$.

1. Compute the (exact) value of this probability.
2. Compute a Normal approximation to this probability, without a continuity correction.
3. Compute a Normal approximation to this probability, with a continuity correction.
4. Compute a Poisson approximation to this probability.

7 Chapter THE SAMPLING DISTRIBUTION

7.1 INTRODUCTION: AN OVERVIEW

This section combines the notion of data derived from a sample with the concept of a random variable. The concept of sampling distribution serves as a bridge between these two ideas. The observed data is a consequence of the particular sample that was chosen. The sampling distribution, akin to random variables, encompasses all possible samples that could have been chosen. (Alternatively, expressed in an alternative grammatical form, referring to the sample that will be chosen before the actual selection takes place.) The data's distribution summaries, such as the sample mean and sample standard deviation, transform into random variables when examined within the sampling distribution framework. In this part, we examine the distribution of data summaries obtained from sampling. Specifically, it has been shown that, for large samples, the sampling distribution of the sample average may be estimated using the Normal distribution. The mathematical theorem that provides evidence for this approximation is known as the Central Limit Theorem.

7.2 THE SAMPLING DISTRIBUTION

The concept of a random variable was introduced in Chapter 5. During the introduction, we provided an illustration that entailed randomly choosing an individual from the community and measuring their height. Before the process of selection, the height of an individual is a variable that occurs by chance. It can achieve any of the heights found in the population, which represents the sample space in this case. The distribution of heights reflects the relative frequencies of each height in the population, determining the probabilities of the values. Upon the individual's selection and the subsequent measurement of their height, a certain value is obtained. The value being discussed is the one that has been observed, and it is no longer subject to randomness. Within this part, we expand upon the notion of a random variable and provide the definition of a random sample.

7.2.1 A Random Sample

The relationship between the random sample and the data is analogous to the relationship between a random variable and the observed value. The data represents the empirical measurements obtained from a subset of individuals selected from a larger group. The data's content is known. A random sample, analogous to a random variable, refers to the specific data that will be chosen during the process of sampling, before the actual selection takes place. The composition of the random sample is indeterminate, as the sample has not yet been collected. Similarly, as with the random variable, it is feasible to determine the probable outcomes of the sample and, depending on how the sample is selected, the probabilities of these distinct outcomes can be determined. The sample space of a random sample is the set of all potential evaluations of the sample, while the distribution of the random sample is determined by the probability associated with each evaluation. (Alternatively, if one chooses to use the past tense, the sample space of a random sample can be defined as the set of possible outcomes that could have occurred during the sample, with the distribution of the random sample representing the probability associated with these outcomes.)

A *statistic* is a function of the data. Example of statistics are the average of the data, the sample variance and standard deviation, the median of the data, etc. In each case a given formula is applied to the data. In each type of statistic a different formula is applied.

The same formula that is applied to the observed data may, in principle, be applied to random samples. Hence, for example, one may talk of the sample average, which is the average of the elements in the data. The average, considered in the context of the observed data, is a number and its value is known. However, if we think of the average in the context of a random sample then it becomes a random variable. Prior to the selection of the actual sample we do not know what values it will include. Hence, we cannot tell what the outcome of the average of the values will be. However, due to the identification of all possible evaluations that the sample can possess we may say in advance what is the collection of values the sample average can have. This is the sample space of the sample average. Moreover, from the sampling distribution of the random sample one may identify the probability of each value of the sample average, thus obtaining the *sampling distribution* of the sample average.

The same line of argumentation applies to any statistic. Computed in the context of the observed data, the statistic is a known number that may, for example, be used to characterize the variation in the data. When thinking of a statistic in the context of a random sample it becomes a random variable. The distribution of the statistic is called the sampling distribution of the statistic. Consequently, we may talk of the sampling distribution of the median, the sample distribution of the sample variance, etc.

Random variables are also applied as models for uncertainty in future measurements in more abstract settings that need not involve a specific population. Specifically, we introduced the Binomial and Poisson random variables for settings that involve counting and the Uniform, Exponential, and Normal random variables for settings where the measurement is continuous.

The concept of a sampling distribution can be expanded to situations where multiple measures are collected, with each measurement being independent of the others. Consequently, one acquires a series of measures. The term "sample" is used to refer to this sequence. The sequence's distribution is sometimes referred to as the sampling distribution. A series consisting entirely of Binomial measurements is referred to as a Binomial sample. If all the measurements exhibit an exponential distribution, we classify it as an exponential sample, and so on. Once again, it is possible to apply a formula, such as the average, to the elements of the random sequence, resulting in the creation of a random variable. The phrase "sampling distribution" refers to the distribution of the random variable generated by the formula, which is influenced by the characteristics of the sample. In the following subsection, we will analyze an instance of a specimen extracted from a population. Next, we will examine instances that pertain to a series of measurements derived from a hypothetical model.

7.2.2 Sampling From a Population

Consider taking a sample from a population. Let us use again for the illustration the file "pop1.csv" like we did in Chapter 4. The data frame produced from the file contains the sex and hight of the 100,000 members of some imaginary population. Recall that in Chapter 4 we applied the function "sample" to randomly sample the height of a single subject from the population. Let us apply the same function again, but this time in order to sample the heights of 100 subjects:

```
pop.1 <- read.csv("_data/pop1.csv")
X.samp <- sample(pop.1$height,100)
X.samp
```

```
##   [1] 183 175 161 160 164 167 164 169 182 153 157 158 160 163 163 175 157
##  [18] 143 156 175 161 201 173 165 177 157 203 179 180 161 189 170 185 174
##  [35] 156 170 186 159 170 171 178 178 162 164 184 166 178 181 173 157 167
##  [52] 161 177 173 180 162 180 187 167 183 158 191 165 180 149 157 175 167
##  [69] 186 178 151 157 154 177 172 172 173 176 165 167 187 159 160 167 175
##  [86] 179 181 190 189 184 182 170 168 180 163 184 164 181 175 176
```

In the first line of code we produce a data frame that contains the information on the entire population. In the second line we select a sample of size 100 from the population, and in the third line we present the content of the sample.

The first argument to the function "sample" that selects the sample is the sequence of length 100,000 with the list of heights of all the members of the population. The second argument indicates the sample size, 100 in this case. The outcome of the random selection is stored in the object "X.samp", which is a sequence that contains 100 heights.

Typically, a researcher does not get to examine the entire population. Instead, measurements on a sample from the population are made. In relation to the imaginary setting we simulate in the example, the typical situation is that the research does not have the complete list of potential measurement evaluations, i.e. the complete list of 100,000 heights in "pop.1$height", but only a sample of measurements, namely the list of 100 numbers that are stored in "X.samp" and are presented above. The role of statistics is to make inference on the parameters of the unobserved population based on the information that is obtained from the sample.

For example, we may be interested in estimating the mean value of the heights in the population. A reasonable proposal is to use the sample average to serve as an estimate:

```
mean(X.samp)
```

```
## [1] 171.14
```

In our artificial example we can actually compute the true population mean:

```
mean(pop.1$height)
```

```
## [1] 170.035
```

Hence, we may see that although the match between the estimated value and the actual value is not perfect still they are close enough.

The actual estimate that we have obtained resulted from the specific sample that was collected. Had we collected a different subset of 100 individuals we would have obtained different numerical value for the estimate. Consequently, one may wonder: Was it pure luck that we got such good estimates? How likely is it to get estimates that are close to the target parameter?

Notice that in realistic settings we do not know the actual value of the target population parameters. Nonetheless, we would still want to have at least a probabilistic assessment of the distance between our estimates and the parameters they try to estimate. The sampling distribution is the vehicle that may enable us to address these questions.

In order to illustrate the concept of the sampling distribution let us select another sample and compute its average:

```
X.samp <- sample(pop.1$height,100)
X.bar <- mean(X.samp)
X.bar

## [1] 169.3
```

and do it once more:

```
X.samp <- sample(pop.1$height,100)
X.bar <- mean(X.samp)
X.bar

## [1] 171.26
```

In each case we got a different value for the sample average. In the first of the last two iterations the result was more than 1 centimeter away from the population average, which is equal to 170.035, and in the second it was within the range of 1 centimeter. Can we say, prior to taking the sample, what is the probability of falling within 1 centimeter of the population mean?

Chapter 4 discussed the random variable that emerges by randomly sampling a single number from the population presented by the sequence "pop.1$height". The distribution of the random variable resulted from the assignment of the probability 1/100,000 to each one of the 100,000 possible outcomes. The same principle applies when we randomly sample 100 individuals. Each possible outcome is a collection of 100 numbers and each collection is assigned equal probability. The resulting distribution is called *the sampling distribution.*

The distribution of the average of the sample emerges from this distribution: With each sample one may associate the average of that sample. The probability assigned to that average outcome is the probability of the sample. Hence, one may assess the probability of falling within 1 centimeter of the population mean using the sampling distribution. Each sample produces an average that either falls within the given range or not. The probability of the sample average falling within the given range is the proportion of samples for which this event happens among the entire collection of samples.

However, we face a technical difficulty when we attempt to assess the sampling distribution of the average and the probability of falling within 1 centimeter of the population mean. Examination of the distribution of a sample of a single individual is easy enough. The total number of outcomes, which is 100,000 in the given example, can be handled with no effort by the computer. However, when we consider samples of size 100 we get that the total number of ways to select 100 number out of 100,000 numbers is in the order of 10342 (1 followed by 342 zeros) and cannot be handled by any computer. Thus, the probability cannot be computed.

As a compromise we will approximate the distribution by selecting a large number of samples, say 100,000, to represent the entire collection, and use the resulting distribution as an approximation of the sampling distribution. Indeed, the larger the number of samples that we create the more accurate the approximation of the distribution is. Still, taking 100,000 repeats should produce approximations which are good enough for our purposes.

Consider the sampling distribution of the sample average. We simulated above a few examples of the average. Now we would like to simulate 100,000 such examples. We do this by creating first a sequence of the length of the number of evaluations we seek (100,000) and then write a small program that produces each time a new random sample of size 100 and assigns the value of the average of that sample to the appropriate position in the sequence. Do first and explain later:

```
X.bar <- rep(0,10^5)
for(i in 1:10^5) {
  X.samp <- sample(pop.1$height,100)
  X.bar[i] <- mean(X.samp)
}
```

In the first line we produce a sequence of length 100,000 that contains zeros. The function "rep" creates a sequence that contains repeats of its first argument a number of times that is specified by its second argument. In this example, the numerical value 0 is repeated 100,000 times to produce a sequence of zeros of the length we seek.

The main part of the program is a "for" loop. The argument of the function "for" takes the special form: "*index.name* in *index.values*", where *index.name* is the name of the running index and *index.values* is the collection of values over which the running index is evaluated. In each iteration of the loop the running index is assigned a value from the collection and the expression that follows the brackets of the "for" function is evaluated with the given value of the running index.

In the given example the collection of values is produced by the expression "1:n". Recall that the expression "1:n" produces the collection of integers between 1 and n. Here, n = 100,000. Hence, in the given application the collection of values is a sequence that contains the integers between 1 and 100,000. The running index is called "i". the expression is evaluated 100,000 times, each time with a different integer value for the running index "i".

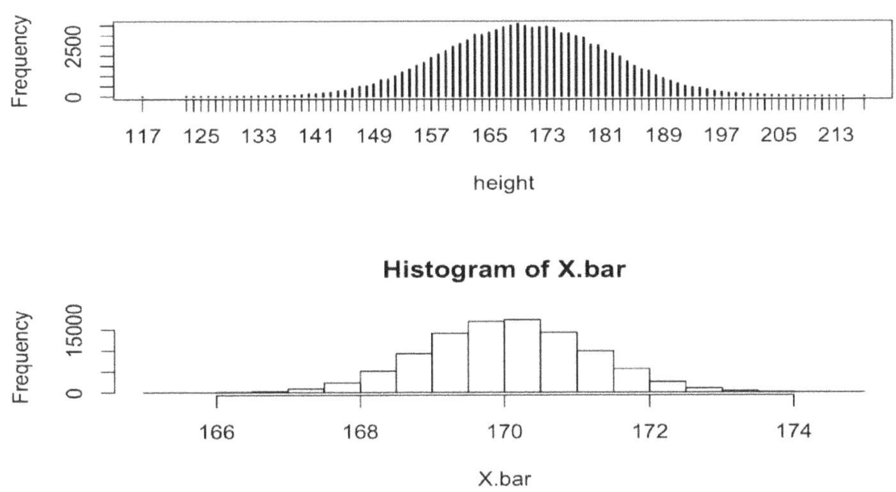

Figure 7.1: Distribution of Height and the Sampling Distribution of Averages

The R system treats a collection of expressions enclosed within curly brackets as one entity. Therefore, in each iteration of the "for" loop, the lines that are within the curly brackets are evaluated. In the first line a random sample of size 100 is produced and in the second line the average of the sample is computed and stored in the *ii*-th position of the sequence "X.bar". Observe that the specific position in the sequence is referred to by using square brackets.

The program changes the original components of the sequence, from 0 to the average of a random sample, one by one. When the loop ends all values are changed and the sequence "X.bar" contains 100,000 evaluations of the sample average. The last line, which is outside the curly brackets and is evaluated after the "for" loop ends, produces an histogram of the averages that were simulated. The histogram is presented in the lower panel of Figure 7.1.

Compare the distribution of the sample average to the distribution of the heights in the population that was presented first in Figure 4.1 and is currently presented in the upper panel of Figure 7.1. Observe that both distributions are centered at about 170 centimeters. Notice, however, that the range of values of the sample average lies essentially between 166 and 174 centimeters, whereas the range of the distribution of heights themselves is between 127 and 217 centimeter. Broadly speaking, the sample average and the original measurement are centered around the same location but the sample average is less spread.

Specifically, let us compare the expectation and standard deviation of the sample average to the expectation and standard deviation of the original measurement:

```
mean(pop.1$height)

## [1] 170.035

sd(pop.1$height)

## [1] 11.23205

mean(X.bar)

## [1] 170.0311

sd(X.bar)

## [1] 1.118308
```

Observe that the expectation of the population and the expectation of the sample average, are practically the same, the standard deviation of the sample average is about 10 times smaller than the standard deviation of the population. This result is not accidental and actually reflects a general phenomena that will be seen below in other examples.

We may use the simulated sampling distribution in order to compute an approximation of the probability of the sample average falling within 1 centimeter of the population mean. Let us first compute the relevant probability and then explain the details of the computation:

```
mean(abs(X.bar - mean(pop.1$height)) <= 1)

## [1] 0.62981
```

Hence we get that the probability of the given event is about 62.6%.

The object "X.bar" is a sequence of length 100,000 that contains the simulated sample averages. This sequence represents the distribution of the sample average. The expression "abs(X.bar - mean(pop.1$height)) <= 1" produces a sequence of logical "TRUE" or "FALSE" values, depending on the value of the sample average being less or more than one unit away from the population mean. The application of the function "mean" to the output of the last expression results in the computation of the relative frequency of TRUEs, which corresponds to the probability of the event of interest.

Example 7.1 A poll for the determination of the support in the population for a candidate was describe in Example 5.1. The proportion in the population of supporters was denoted by pp. A sample of size n=300n=300 was considered in order to estimate the size of pp. We identified that the distribution of X, the number of supporters in the sample, is Binomial(300,p). This distribution is the sampling distribution of X. One may use the proportion in the sample of supporters, the number of supporters in the sample divided by 300, as an estimate to the parameter pp. The sampling distribution of this quantity, $X/300$, may be considered in order to assess the discrepancy between the estimate and the actual value of the parameter.

7.2.3 Theoretical Models

Sampling distribution can also be considered in the context of theoretical distribution models. For example, take a measurement $X\sim$Binomial(10,0.5) from the Binomial distribution. Assume 64 independent measurements are produced with this distribution: $X_1, X_2, \ldots, X_{64}$. The sample average in this case corresponds to the distribution of the random variable produced by averaging these 64 random variables:

$$\bar{X} = \frac{X_1 + X_2 + \cdots + X_{64}}{64} = \frac{1}{64}\sum_{i=1}^{64} X_i \ .$$

Again, one may wonder what is the distribution of the sample average $\bar{X}$ in this case?

We can approximate the distribution of the sample average by simulation. The function "rbinom" produces a random sample from the Binomial distribution. The first argument to the function is the sample size, which we take in this example to be equal to 64. The second and third arguments are the parameters of the Binomial distribution, 10 and 0.5 in this case. We can use this function in the simulation:

```
X.bar <- rep(0,10^5)
for(i in 1:10^5) {
  X.samp <- rbinom(64,10,0.5)
  X.bar[i] <- mean(X.samp)
}
```

Observe that in this code we created a sequence of length 100,000 with evaluations of the sample average of 64 Binomial random variables. We start with a sequence of zeros and in each iteration of the "for" loop a zero is replaced by the average of a random sample of 64 Binomial random variables.

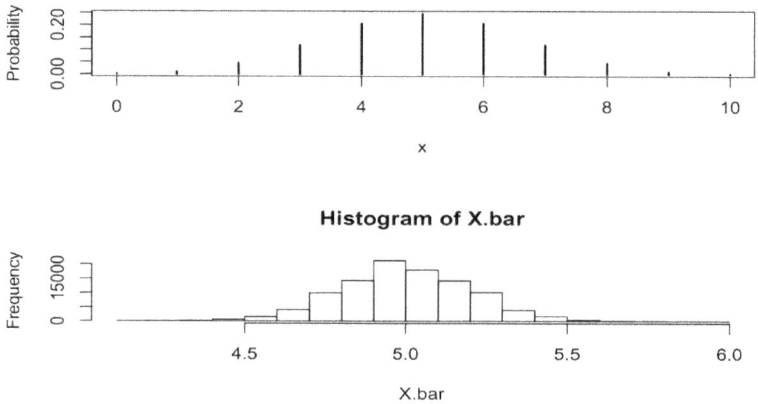

Figure 7.2: Distributions of an Average and a Single Binomial(10,0.5)

Examine the sampling distribution of the Binomial average:

```
mean(X.bar)
```

```
## [1] 5.00008
```

```
sd(X.bar)
```

```
## [1] 0.1973577
```

The histogram of the sample average is presented in the lower panel of Figure 7.2. Compare it to the distribution of a single Binomial random variable that appears in the upper panel. Notice, once more, that the center of the two distributions coincide but the spread of the sample average is smaller. The sample space of a single Binomial random variable is composed of integers. The sample space of the average of 64 Binomial random variables, on the other hand, contains many more values and is closer to the sample space of a random variable with a continuous distribution.

Recall that the expectation of a Binomial(10,0.5) random variable is E(X)=10·0.5=5 and the variance is V(X)=10·0.5·0.5=2.5 (thus, the standard deviation is $\sqrt{2.5} = 1.581139$). Observe that the expectation of the sample average that we got from the simulation is essentially equal to 5 and the standard deviation is 0.1982219.

One may prove mathematically that the expectation of the sample mean is equal to the theoretical expectation of its components:

$$\mathbf{E}(\bar{X}) = \mathbf{E}(X) \ .$$

The results of the simulation for the expectation of the sample average are consistent with the mathematical statement. The mathematical theory of probability may also be used in order to prove that the variance of the sample average is equal to the variance of each of the components, divided by the sample size:

$$\mathbf{V}(\bar{X}) = \mathbf{V}(X)/n ,$$

here nn is the number of observations in the sample. Specifically, in the Binomial example we get that $\mathbf{V}(\bar{X}) = 2.5/64$, since the variance of a Binomial component is 2.5 and there are 64 observations. Consequently, the standard deviation is $\sqrt{2.5/64} = 0.1976424$, in agreement, more or less, with the results of the simulation (that produced 0.1982219 as the standard deviation).

Consider the problem of identifying the central interval that contains 95% of the distribution. In the Normal distribution we were able to use the function "qnorm" in order to compute the percentiles of the theoretical distribution. A function that can be used for the same purpose for simulated distribution is the function "quantile". The first argument to this function is the sequence of simulated values of the statistic, "X.bar" in the current case. The second argument is a number between 0 and 1, or a sequence of such numbers:

```
quantile(X.bar,c(0.025,0.975))
```

```
##     2.5%    97.5%
## 4.609375 5.390625
```

We used the sequence "c(0.025,0.975)" as the input to the second argument. As a result we obtained the output 4.609375, which is the 2.5%-percentile of the sampling distribution of the average, and 5.390625, which is the 97.5%-percentile of the sampling distribution of the average.

Of interest is to compare these percentiles to the parallel percentiles of the Normal distribution with the same expectation and the same standard deviation as the average of the Binomials:

```
qnorm(c(0.025,0.975),mean(X.bar),sd(X.bar))
```

```
## [1] 4.613266 5.386894
```

Observe the similarity between the percentiles of the distribution of the average and the percentiles of the Normal distribution. This similarity is a reflection of the Normal approximation of the sampling distribution of the average, which is formulated in the next section under the title: *The Central Limit Theorem.*

Example 7.2 The distribution of the number of events of radio active decay in a second was modeled in Example 5.3 according to the Poisson distribution. A quantity of interest is $\lambda\lambda$, the expectation of that Poisson distribution. This quantity may be estimated by measuring the total number of decays over a period of time and dividing the outcome by the number of seconds in that period of time. Let nn be this number of second. The procedure just described corresponds to taking the sample average of Poisson(λ) observations for a sample of size nn. The expectation of the sample average is λ and the variance is λ/n, leading to a standard deviation of size $\sqrt{\lambda/n}$. The Central Limit Theorem states that the sampling distribution of this average corresponds, approximately, to the Normal distribution with this expectation and standard deviation.

7.3 LAW OF LARGE NUMBERS AND CENTRAL LIMIT THEOREM

The Law of Large Numbers and the Central Limit Theorem are mathematical theorems that describe the sampling distribution of the average for large samples.

7.3.1 The Law of Large Numbers

The Law of Large Numbers states that, as the sample size becomes larger, the sampling distribution of the sample average becomes more and more concentrated about the expectation.

Let us demonstrate the Law of Large Numbers in the context of the Uniform distribution. Let the distribution of the measurement X be Uniform(3,7). Consider three different sample sizes n: n=10, n=100, and n=1000. Let us carry out a simulation similar to the simulations of the previous section. However, this time we run the simulation for the three sample sizes in parallel:

```
unif.10 <- rep(0,10^5)
unif.100 <- rep(0,10^5)
unif.1000 <- rep(0,10^5)
for(i in 1:10^5) {
  X.samp.10 <- runif(10,3,7)
  unif.10[i] <- mean(X.samp.10)
  X.samp.100 <- runif(100,3,7)
  unif.100[i] <- mean(X.samp.100)
  X.samp.1000 <- runif(1000,3,7)
  unif.1000[i] <- mean(X.samp.1000)
}
```

Observe that we have produced 3 sequences of length 100,000 each: “unif.10”, “unif.100”, and “unif.1000”. The first sequence is an approximation of the sampling distribution of an average of 10 independent Uniform measurements, the second approximates the sampling distribution of an average of 100 measurements and the third the distribution of an average of 1000 measurements. The distribution of single measurement in each of the examples is Uniform(3,7).

Consider the expectation of sample average for the three sample sizes:

```
mean(unif.10)
```

```
## [1] 4.999856
```

```
mean(unif.100)
```

```
## [1] 4.999809
```

```
mean(unif.1000)
```

```
## [1] 4.999975
```

For all sample size the expectation of the sample average is equal to 5, which is the expectation of the Uniform(3,7) distribution.

Recall that the variance of the Uniform(a,b) distribution is $(b-a)^2/12$. Hence, the variance of the given Uniform distribution is $V(X)=(7-3)^2/12=16/12\approx 1.3333$. The variances of the sample averages are:

```
var(unif.10)
```

```
## [1] 0.1337174
```

```
var(unif.100)
```

```
## [1] 0.01334807
```

```
var(unif.1000)
```

```
## [1] 0.001335726
```

Notice that the variances decrease with the increase of the sample sizes. The decrease is according to the formula $\mathrm{V}(\bar{X}) = \mathrm{V}(X)/n$.

Variance is a statistical term that quantifies the extent to which data points in a distribution deviate from the mean. A distribution with a smaller variance is more tightly concentrated around its expectation. Therefore, in accordance with the Law of Large Numbers, as the sample size increases, the sampling distribution of the sample average becomes more tightly clustered around the expected value.

7.3.2 The Central Limit Theorem (CLT)

The Law of Large Numbers states that the distribution of the sample average tends to be more concentrated as the sample size increases. The Central Limit Theorem (CLT in short) provides an approximation of this distribution.

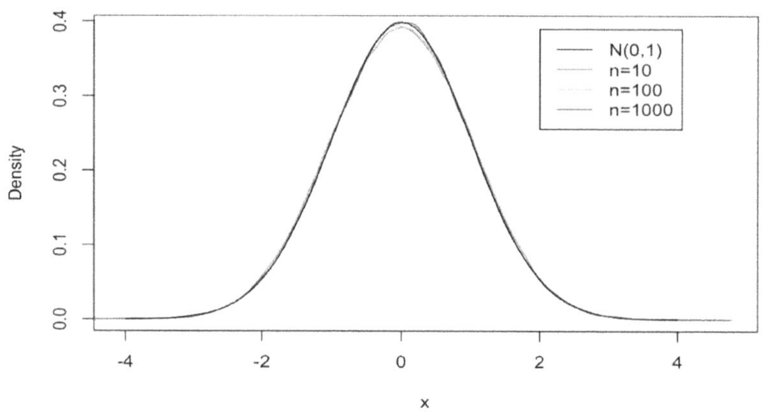

Figure 7.3: The CLT for the Uniform(3,7) Distribution

The deviation between the sample average and the expectation of the measurement tend to decreases with the increase in sample size. In order to obtain a refined assessment of this deviation one needs to magnify it. The appropriate way to obtain the magnification is to consider the standardized sample average, in which the deviation of the sample average from its expectation is divided by the standard deviation of the sample average:

$$Z = \frac{\bar{X} - \mathbf{E}(\bar{X})}{\sqrt{\mathbf{V}(\bar{X})}} .$$

Recall that the expectation of the sample average is equal to the expectation of a single random variable $\left(\mathbf{E}(\bar{X}) = \mathbf{E}(X)\right)$ and that the variance of the sample average is equal to the variance of a single observation, divided by the sample size $\left(\mathbf{V}(\bar{X}) = \mathbf{V}(X)/n\right)$. Consequently, one may rewrite the standardized sample average in the form:

$$Z = \frac{\bar{X} - \mathbf{E}(X)}{\sqrt{\mathbf{V}(X)/n}} = \frac{\sqrt{n}(\bar{X} - \mathbf{E}(X))}{\sqrt{\mathbf{V}(X)}} .$$

The second equality follows from placing in the numerator the square root of n which *divides* the term in the denominator. Observe that with the increase of the sample size the decreasing difference between the average and the expectation is magnified by the square root of n.

The Central Limit Theorem states that, with the increase in sample size, the sample average converges (after standardization) to the standard Normal distribution.

Let us examine the Central Normal Theorem in the context of the example of the Uniform measurement. In Figure 7.3 you may find the (approximated) density of the standardized average for the three sample sizes based on the simulation that we carried out previously (as *red*, *green*, and *blue* lines). Along side with these densities you may also find the theoretical density of the standard Normal distribution (as a *black* line). Observe that the four curves are almost one on top of the other, proposing that the approximation of the distribution of the average by the Normal distribution is good even for a sample size as small as n=10.

However, before jumping to the conclusion that the Central Limit Theorem applies to any sample size, let us consider another example. In this example we repeat the same simulation that we did with the Uniform distribution, but this time we take Exponential(0.5) measurements instead:

```
exp.10 <- rep(0,10^5)
exp.100 <- rep(0,10^5)
exp.1000 <- rep(0,10^5)
for(i in 1:10^5) {
  X.samp.10 <- rexp(10,0.5)
  exp.10[i] <- mean(X.samp.10)
  X.samp.100 <- rexp(100,0.5)
  exp.100[i] <- mean(X.samp.100)
  X.samp.1000 <- rexp(1000,0.5)
  exp.1000[i] <- mean(X.samp.1000)
}
```

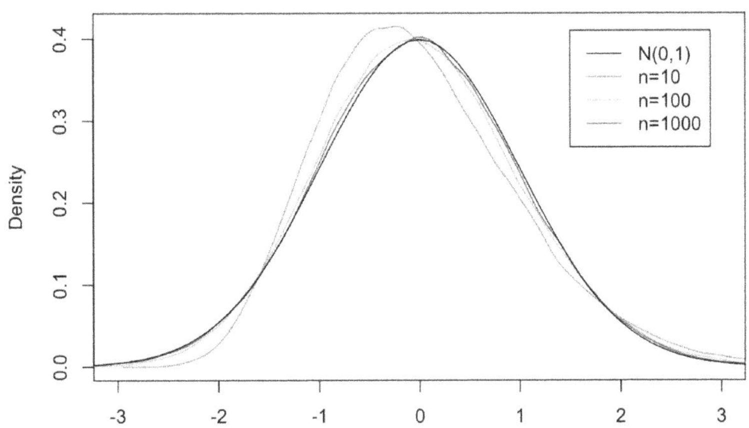

Figure 7.4: The CLT for the Exponential(0.5) Distribution

The expectation of an Exponential(0.5) random variable is $\mathbf{E}(X) = 1/\lambda = 1/0.5 = 2$ and the variance is $\mathbf{V}(X) = 1/\lambda^2 = 1/(0.5)^2 = 4$. Observe below that the expectations of the sample averages are equal to the expectation of the measurement and the variances of the sample averages follow the relation $\mathbf{V}(\bar{X}) = \mathbf{V}(X)/n$:

```
mean(exp.10)

## [1] 1.999671

mean(exp.100)

## [1] 2.000088

mean(exp.1000)

## [1] 1.999788
```

So the expectations of the sample average are all equal to 2. For the variance we get:

```
var(exp.10)

## [1] 0.399315
var(exp.100)

## [1] 0.0402442

var(exp.1000)

## [1] 0.004011308
```

Which is in agreement with the decrease proposed by the theory,

However, when one examines the densities of the sample averages in Figure @reF(fig:SampDist9) one may see a clear distinction between the sampling distribution of the average for a sample of size 10 and the normal distribution (compare the *red* curve to the *black* curve. The match between the *green* curve that corresponds to a sample of size n=100 and the *black* line is better, but not perfect. When the sample size is as large as n=1000 (the *blue* curve) then the agreement with the normal curve is very good.

7.3.3 Applying the Central Limit Theorem

The Central Limit Theorem states that the sampling distribution of the sample average can be approximated by the Normal distribution, independent of the distribution of the original measurement. However, this approximation holds true only when the sample size is sufficiently big. This assertion is crucial because it enables us to perform probabilistic calculations using the Normal distribution, specifically in the context of the sample average. This is possible even if we are unaware of the true distribution of the measurement. The computation requires knowledge of the measurement's expectation, variance (or standard deviation), and the sample size.

The theorem can be applied whenever probability computations associated with the sampling distribution of the average are required. The computation of the approximation is carried out by using the Normal distribution with the same expectation and the same standard deviation as the sample average.

An example of such computation was conducted in Subsection 7.2.3 where the central interval that contains 95% of the sampling distribution of a Binomial average was required. The 2.5%- and the 97.5%-percentiles of the Normal distribution with the same expectation and variance as the sample average produced boundaries for the interval. These boundaries were in good agreement with the boundaries produced by the simulation. More examples will be provided in the Solved Exercises of this chapter and the next one.

Despite its utility, it is important to approach the Central Limit Theorem with caution. The approximation is generally reliable for big samples, but may be unreliable for samples that are not sufficiently large. Using the Central Limit Theorem without caution when the sample size is tiny can lead to inaccurate findings.

7.4 EXERCISES

Exercise 7.1 The file "pop2.csv" contains information associated to the blood pressure of an imaginary population of size 100,000. The file can be found on the internet (http://pluto.huji.ac.il/~msby/StatThink/Datasets/pop2.csv). The variables in this file are:

id: A numerical variable. A 7 digits number that serves as a unique identifier of the subject.

sex: A factor variable. The sex of each subject. The values are either "MALE" or "FEMALE".

age: A numerical variable. The age of each subject.

bmi: A numerical variable. The body mass index of each subject.

systolic: A numerical variable. The systolic blood pressure of each subject.

diastolic: A numerical variable. The diastolic blood pressure of each subject.

group: A factor variable. The blood pressure category of each subject. The values are "NORMAL" both the systolic blood pressure is within its normal range (between 90 and 139) and the diastolic blood pressure is within its normal range (between 60 and 89). The value is "HIGH" if either measurements of blood pressure are above their normal upper limits and it is "LOW" if either measurements are below their normal lower limits.

Our goal in this question is to investigate the sampling distribution of the sample average of the variable "bmi". We assume a sample of size n=150.

1. Compute the population average of the variable "bmi".
2. Compute the population standard deviation of the variable "bmi".
3. Compute the expectation of the sampling distribution for the sample average of the variable.
4. Compute the standard deviation of the sampling distribution for the sample average of the variable.
5. Identify, using simulations, the central region that contains 80% of the sampling distribution of the sample average.
6. Identify, using the Central Limit Theorem, an approximation of the central region that contains 80% of the sampling distribution of the sample average.

Exercise 7.2 A subatomic particle hits a linear detector at random locations. The length of the detector is 10 nm and the hits are uniformly distributed. The location of 25 random hits, measured from a specified endpoint of the interval, are marked and the average of the location computed.

1. What is the expectation of the average location?
2. What is the standard deviation of the average location?
3. Use the Central Limit Theorem in order to approximate the probability the average location is in the left-most third of the linear detector.
4. The central region that contains 99% of the distribution of the average is of the form 5±c. Use the Central Limit Theorem in order to approximate the value of c.

8 Chapter INTEGRATION: CONCEPTS AND METHODS

8.1 INTRODUCTION: AN OVERVIEW

This section offers a concise summary of the principles and techniques that were introduced in the initial portion of the book. We strive to establish a connection between them and place them in the appropriate context. A set of problems is given. The resolutions to these issues necessitate the amalgamation of several technologies that were introduced in preceding chapters.

8.2 INTEGRATION: AN OVERVIEW

The initial section of the book aims to acquaint readers with the basic principles of statistics and impart the fundamental notions of probability. These concepts are crucial for comprehending the statistical methods employed in data analysis. The second half of the book presents and discusses these procedures. Data is commonly acquired by sampling a population and conducting measurements on the selected sample. There are various methods for selecting a sample, but it is crucial that these approaches do not compromise the fundamental requirement of a sample: to accurately represent the population it is derived from. This book focuses exclusively on the method of simple random sampling. Nevertheless, it is important for the reader to acknowledge that alternative sample designs are available and may be more suited for particular applications. The primary focus of the field of statistics is to draw conclusions about population parameters based on acquired data. These deductions are made using statistics, which are mathematical functions based on the data. Data is commonly kept in the form of a data frame, where the columns represent the measured variables and the rows represent the observations related to the chosen sample. The primary categories of variables include numeric variables, which can be either discrete or continuous, as well as factors. We acquired the knowledge of generating data frames and importing data into R for subsequent analysis. Statistics is focused on addressing and analyzing variability. Diversity can manifest in various ways and due to various causes. It can be summarized, analyzed, and managed using a variety of techniques. Oftentimes, a tool that has a strong similarity to another instrument can be utilized in several contexts and for different types of variations. To maintain a clear understanding, it is crucial to comprehend the origin and characteristics of the variability being analyzed in each situation. A significant division in terms of the origin of variability exists between descriptive statistics and probability. Descriptive statistics analyzes the dispersion of data. The frame of reference refers to the actual data being considered. Various visual representations, such as bar plots, histograms, and box plots, along with tables displaying frequency, relative frequency, and cumulative relative frequency, as well as numerical summaries like mean, median, and standard deviation, can all be utilized to comprehend the distribution of a given data set. In the context of probability, the frame of reference is not limited to the current data, but rather encompasses all possible data sets that could have been selected (known as the sample space of the sampling distribution). One can employ analogous plots, tables, and numerical summaries to examine the distribution of functions of the sample (statistics), however the interpretation of the analysis varies. The relevance of the probabilistic analysis to the sampled data is indirectly related. The provided sample is a single instance inside the sample space, representing one of many potential instances. In the realm of probability, the observed realization does not hold any unique significance when compared to all other possible realizations. The absence of a direct correlation between probabilistic variability and the observed data does not diminish the significance of this relationship. Conversely, this indirect relationship serves as the foundation for drawing statistical inferences. Statistical inference is utilizing the properties of the data to make predictions about the complete population based on a sample. The dependability of the extrapolation is assessed by utilizing a probabilistic description of the distribution of the sample. For instance, one can attempt to calculate the values of population parameters, such as the population mean and the population standard deviation, by considering the corresponding properties of the data. The variability of the sampling distribution is utilized to measure the precision of this estimation. (Refer to Example 5 below.)

Statistics, like to other empirical sciences, employs theoretical modeling to evaluate and interpret observational data. In statistics, the modeling component typically involves using a probabilistic model to represent the measurements as random variables. Throughout the initial section of this book, we have come across numerous models of this nature. The basic sampling model assumes that every subset of a certain size from the population has an equal likelihood of being chosen as the sample. Alternative, more organized models, presumed a particular pattern in the distribution of the measurements. The distributions we examined included the Binomial, Poisson, Uniform, Exponential, and Normal distributions. Additional models can be identified in the existing body of research and can be utilized as needed. Several alternative models include R functions that enable the computation of the distribution and generation of simulations. A statistic is a mathematical function that is applied to a sample of data in order to draw conclusions or make predictions about a larger population. When a statistical measure, such as the mean, is calculated based on a randomly selected sample, the result might be considered a random variable from a probabilistic perspective. The probability distribution of this random variable is influenced by the distribution of the measurements used to create the sample, but it is not exactly the same as that distribution. Therefore, the distribution of the mean of a sample taken from the Uniform distribution does not conform to the Uniform distribution. Typically, the connection between the distribution of a measurement and the distribution of a statistic calculated from a sample drawn from that distribution can be intricate. Fortunately, the relationship for the sample average is very straightforward, particularly for sufficiently large samples. The Central Limit Theorem offers an estimate of the distribution of the sample mean, which generally becomes more accurate as the sample size increases. The mean of the sample average is equivalent to the mean of a single measurement, whereas the standard deviation is equivalent to the standard deviation of a single measurement divided by the sample size. The Central Limit Theorem states that the distribution of the sample average can be approximated by a Normal distribution, with the same mean and standard deviation as the sample average. This approximation is applicable to virtually any distribution of the measurement. In the case of the sample average, the conclusion is that the distribution of the statistic is influenced by the expectation and variance of the measurements, but not by any other aspects of the distribution. The theorem's conclusion applies to quantities that are directly proportional to the sample average. Consequently, by multiplying the sample average by the sample size n, we may derive the total of the sample. This theorem can then be applied to estimate the distribution of sums. Indeed, the theorem can be extended to a far broader range of cases. For instance, it can be demonstrated that the theorem applies to a differentiable function of the mean value, thus expanding the range of situations where the theory is relevant and enhancing its significance. In the following section, we will address several real-world situations and provide solutions. To solve these problems, you must have a thorough understanding of the concepts and tools that were introduced in the earlier part of the book. Therefore, it is highly advisable that you carefully reread and thoroughly examine all the preceding chapters of the book prior to proceeding to the following section.

8.3 INTEGRATED APPLICATIONS

The Central Limit Theorem states that while calculating the sample average, we can use the Normal distribution to estimate probabilities and achieve accurate approximations, as long as the sample size is sufficiently large. The only information required for the calculations are the expected value and variance of the underlying measurement. Alternatively, the specific distribution of that parameter is inconsequential. We will illustrate the practicality of the Central Limit Theorem through two cases.

8.3.1 Example 1

A study involving stress is done on a college campus among the students. The stress scores follow a (continuous) Uniform distribution with the lowest stress score equal to 1 and the highest equal to 5. Using a sample of 75 students, find:

1. The probability that the average stress score for the 75 students is less than 2.
2. The 90th percentile for the average stress score for the 75 students.
3. The probability that the total of the 75 stress scores is less than 200.
4. The 90th percentile for the total stress score for the 75 students.

Solution:

Denote by X the stress score of a random student. We are given that $X \sim$Uniform(1,5). We use the formulas $E(X)=(a+b)/2$ and $V(X)=(b-a)^2/12$ in order to obtain the expectation and variance of a single observation and then we use the relations $E(\bar{X}) = E(X)$ and $V(\bar{X}) = V(X)/n$ to translated these results to the expectation and variance of the sample average:

```
a <- 1
b <- 5
n <- 75
mu.bar <- (a+b)/2
sig.bar <- sqrt((b-a)^2/(12*n))
mu.bar

## [1] 3

sig.bar

## [1] 0.1333333
```

After obtaining the expectation and the variance of the sample average we can forget about the Uniform distribution and proceed only with the R functions that are related to the Normal distribution. By the Central Limit Theorem we get that the distribution of the sample average is approximately Normal(μ,σ^2), with μ = mu.bar and σ = sig.bar.

In the Question 1.1 we are asked to find the value of the cumulative distribution function of the sample average at x=2:

```
pnorm(2,mu.bar,sig.bar)
```

```
## [1] 3.190892e-14
```

The goal of Question 1.2 is to identify the 90%-percentile of the sample average:

```
qnorm(0.9,mu.bar,sig.bar)
```

```
## [1] 3.170874
```

The sample average is equal to the total sum divided by the number of observations, n=75 in this example. The total sum is less than 200 if, and only if the average is less than $200/n$. Therefore, for Question 1.3:

```
pnorm(200/n,mu.bar,sig.bar)
```

```
## [1] 0.006209665
```

Finally, if 90% of the distribution of the average is less that 3.170874 then 90% of the distribution of the total sum is less than 3.170874n3.170874n. In Question 1.4 we get:

```
n*qnorm(0.9,mu.bar,sig.bar)
```

```
## [1] 237.8155
```

8.3.2 Example 2

Consider again the same stress study that was described in Example 1 and answer the same questions. However, this time assume that the stress score may obtain only the values 1, 2, 3, 4 or 5, with the same likelihood for obtaining each of the values.

Solution:

Denote again by X the stress score of a random student. The modified distribution states that the sample space of X are the integers {1,2,3,4,5}, with equal probability for each value. Since the probabilities must sum to 1 we get that P (X=x)=1/5, for all x in the sample space. In principle we may repeat the steps of the solution of previous example, substituting the expectation and standard deviation of the continuous measurement by the discrete counterpart:

```
x <- 1:5
p <- rep(1/5,5)
n <- 75
mu.X <- sum(x*p)
sig.X <- sum((x-mu.X)^2*p)
mu.bar <- mu.X
sig.bar <- sqrt(sig.X/n)
mu.bar

## [1] 3

sig.bar

## [1] 0.1632993
```

Notice that the expectation of the sample average is the same as before but the standard deviation is somewhat larger due to the larger variance in the distribution of a single response.

We may apply the Central Limit Theorem again in order to conclude that distribution of the average is approximately Normal(μ,σ^2), with μ = mu.bar as before and for the new σ = sig.bar.

For Question 2.1 we compote that the cumulative distribution function of the sample average at x=2 is approximately equal:

```
pnorm(2,mu.bar,sig.bar)

## [1] 4.570649e-10
```

and the 90%-percentile is:

```
qnorm(0.9,mu.bar,sig.bar)

## [1] 3.209276
```

which produces the answer to Question 2.2.

Similarly to the solution of Question 1.3 we may conclude that the total sum is less than 200 if, and only if the average is less than $200/n$. Therefore, for Question 2.3:

```
pnorm(200/n,mu.bar,sig.bar)

## [1] 0.02061342
```

Observe that in the current version of the question we have the score is integer-valued. Clearly, the sum of scores is also integer valued. Hence we may choose to apply the continuity correction for the Normal approximation whereby we approximate the probability that the sum is less than 200 (i.e. is less than or equal to 199) by the probability that a Normal random variable is less than or equal to 199.5. Translating this event back to the scale of the average we get the approximation:

```
pnorm(199.5/n,mu.bar,sig.bar)
```

```
## [1] 0.01866821
```

Finally, if 90% of the distribution of the average is less that 3.170874 then 90% of the distribution of the total sum is less than 3.170874n. Therefore:

```
n*qnorm(0.9,mu.bar,sig.bar)
```

```
## [1] 240.6957
```

or, after rounding to the nearest integer we get for Question 2.4 the answer 241.

8.3.3 Example 3

Suppose that a market research analyst for a cellular phone company conducts a study of their customers who exceed the time allowance included on their basic cellular phone contract. The analyst finds that for those customers who exceed the time included in their basic contract, the excess time used follows an exponential distribution with a mean of 22 minutes. Consider a random sample of 80 customers and find

1. The probability that the average excess time used by the 80 customers in the sample is longer than 20 minutes.
2. The 95th percentile for the average excess time for samples of 80 customers who exceed their basic contract time allowances.

Solution:

Let X be the excess time for customers who exceed the time included in their basic contract. We are told that $X \sim \text{Exponential}(\lambda)$. For the Exponential distribution $\text{E}(X)=1/\lambda$. Hence, given that $\text{E}(X)=22$ we can conclude that $\lambda=1/22$. For the Exponential we also have that $\text{V}(X)=1/\lambda^2$. Therefore:

```
lam <- 1/22
n <- 80
mu.bar <- 1/lam
sig.bar <- sqrt(1/(lam^2*n))
mu.bar
```

```
## [1] 22
```

```
sig.bar
```

```
## [1] 2.459675
```

Like before, we can forget at this stage about the Exponential distribution and refer henceforth to the Normal Distribution. In Question 2.1 we are asked to compute the probability above x=20. The total probability is 1. Hence, the required probability is the difference between 1 and the probability of being less or equal to x=20:

```
1-pnorm(20,mu.bar,sig.bar)
```

```
## [1] 0.7919241
```

The goal in Question 2.2 is to find the 95%-percentile of the sample average:

```
qnorm(0.95,mu.bar,sig.bar)
```

```
## [1] 26.0458
```

8.3.4 Example 4

A beverage company produces cans that are supposed to contain 16 ounces of beverage. Under normal production conditions the expected amount of beverage in each can is 16.0 ounces, with a standard deviation of 0.10 ounces.

As a quality control measure, each hour the QA department samples 50 cans from the production during the previous hour and measures the content in each of the cans. If the average content of the 50 cans is below a control threshold then production is stopped and the can filling machine is re-calibrated.

1. Compute the probability that the amount of beverage in a random can is below 15.95.
2. Compute the probability that the amount of beverage in a sample average of 50 cans is below 15.95.
3. Find a threshold with the property that the probability of stopping the machine in a given hour is 5% when, in fact, the production conditions are

normal.

4. Consider the data in the file "QC.csv". It contains measurement results of 8 hours. Assume that we apply the threshold that was obtained in Question 4.3. At the end of which of the hours the filling machine needed re-calibration?
5. Based on the data in the file "QC.csv", which of the hours contains measurements which are suspected outliers in comparison to the other measurements conducted during that hour?

Solution

The only information we have on the distribution of each measurement is its expectation (16.0 ounces under normal conditions) and its standard deviation (0.10, under the same condition). We do not know, from the information provided in the question, the actual distribution of a measurement. (The fact that the production conditions are normal does not imply that the distribution of the measurement in the Normal distribution!) Hence, the correct answer to Question 4.1 is that there is not enough information to calculate the probability.

When we deal with the sample average, on the other hand, we may apply the Central Limit Theorem in order to obtain at least an approximation of the probability. Observe that the expectation of the sample average is 16.0 ounces and the standard deviation is $0.1/\sqrt{50}$. The distribution of the average is approximately the Normal distribution:

```
pnorm(15.95,16,0.1/sqrt(50))
```

```
## [1] 0.000203476
```

Hence, we get that the probability of the average being less than 15.95 ounces is (approximately) 0.0002, which is a solution to Question 4.2.

In order to solve Question 4.3 we may apply the function "qnorm" in order to compute the 5%-percentile of the distribution of the average:

```
qnorm(0.05,16,0.1/sqrt(50))
```

```
## [1] 15.97674
```

Consider the data in the file "QC.csv". Let us read the data into a data frame by the by the name "QC" and apply the function "summary" to obtain an overview of the content of the file:

```
QC <- read.csv("_data/QC.csv")
summary(QC)
```

```
##        h1              h2              h3              h4
##  Min.   :15.86   Min.   :15.82   Min.   :15.68   Min.   :15.75
##  1st Qu.:15.94   1st Qu.:15.93   1st Qu.:15.84   1st Qu.:15.91
##  Median :16.02   Median :16.01   Median :15.91   Median :15.99
##  Mean   :16.02   Mean   :16.01   Mean   :15.91   Mean   :15.99
##  3rd Qu.:16.09   3rd Qu.:16.08   3rd Qu.:15.98   3rd Qu.:16.06
##  Max.   :16.22   Max.   :16.22   Max.   :16.11   Max.   :16.31
##        h5              h6              h7              h8
##  Min.   :15.75   Min.   :15.73   Min.   :15.73   Min.   :15.78
##  1st Qu.:15.93   1st Qu.:15.93   1st Qu.:15.94   1st Qu.:15.92
##  Median :15.99   Median :15.98   Median :15.99   Median :15.97
##  Mean   :15.99   Mean   :15.98   Mean   :15.99   Mean   :15.97
##  3rd Qu.:16.05   3rd Qu.:16.06   3rd Qu.:16.05   3rd Qu.:16.04
##  Max.   :16.17   Max.   :16.23   Max.   :16.18   Max.   :16.25
```

Observe that the file contains 8 quantitative variables that are given the names h1, ..., h8. Each of these variables contains the 50 measurements conducted in the given hour.

Observe that the mean is computed as part of the summary. The threshold that we apply to monitor the filling machine is 15.97674. Clearly, the average of the measurements at the third hour "h3" is below the threshold. Not enough significance digits of the average of the 8th hour are presented to be able to say whether the average is below or above the threshold. A more accurate presentation of the computed mean is obtained by the application of the function "mean" directly to the data:

```
mean(QC$h8)
```

```
## [1] 15.9736
```

Now we can see that the average is below the threshold. Hence, the machine required re-calibration after the 3rd and the 8th hours, which is the answer to Question 4.4.

In Chapter 3 it was proposed to use box plots in order to identify points that are suspected to be outliers. We can use the expression "boxplot(QC$h1)" in order to obtain the box plot of the data of the first hour and go through the names of the variable one by one in order to screen all variable. Alternatively, we may apply the function "boxplot" directly to the data frame "QC" and get a plot with box plots of all the variables in the data frame plotted side by side:

```
boxplot(QC)
```

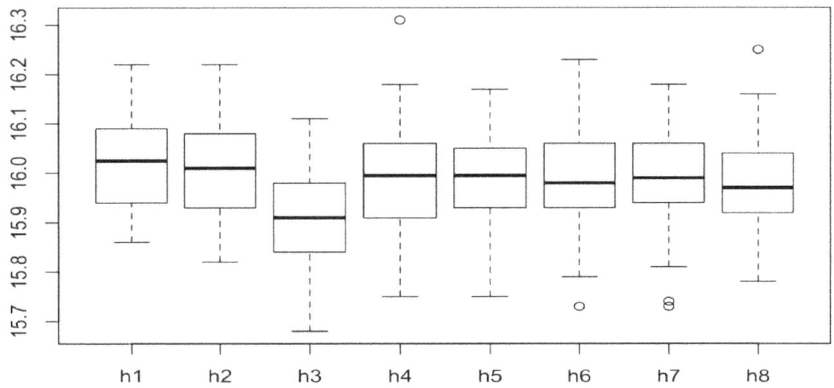

Examining the plots we may see that evidence for the existence of outliers can be spotted on the 4th, 6th, 7th, and 8th hours, providing an answer to Question 4.5

9 Chapter | STATISTICAL INFERENCE

9.1 INTODUCTION: AN OVERVIEW

In the following section of this chapter, the fundamental concepts and techniques of statistical inference will be presented. The second section of this book focuses on these tools. Chapters 9–15 utilize data on automotive specifications to illustrate the practical usage of statistical inference tools. In this chapter's third section, we introduce the data frame that encompasses this dataset. The fourth section examines probability concepts that were previously addressed in the first half of the book and are applicable to the second portion.

9.2 KEY TERMS

The initial section of the book focuses on descriptive statistics and probability. Descriptive statistics involves examining the attributes of data through the use of visual aids and numerical summaries. The frame of reference refers to the data that is noticed. In the context of probability, the frame of reference is expanded to encompass all possible data sets that may have conceivably occurred, with the observed data being just one of many possibilities. The latter portion of the book focuses on inferential statistics. The objective of statistical inference is to obtain understanding about the population parameters based on the observed data. The process of acquiring such understanding entails utilizing formal computations on the data. The analysis of the results of these formal calculations is conducted within the framework of probability, where one examines the application of these formal computations to all possible data sets. The rationale for employing the particular method of computing on the observed data arises from the analysis of the probabilistic characteristics of the formal computations. Generally, the formal calculations will entail statistical analysis, which are mathematical functions that operate on the data. The evaluation of the likelihood characteristics of the calculations will arise from the sample distribution of these statistics. An instance of a predicament that necessitates statistical inference is the process of estimating a population parameter based on the available data. Point estimate aims to derive the most accurate approximation of the value of a given parameter. An estimator is a statistical measure that generates an approximation or prediction. One might favor an estimator with a sample distribution that is more tightly clustered around the true value of the population parameter, compared to another estimator with a less concentrated sampling distribution. Therefore, the reason for choosing a particular statistic as an estimator is determined by the probabilistic properties of that statistic inside the sampling distribution. For instance, an automobile manufacturer may have a keen interest in the fuel efficiency of a novel car model. To do this, the manufacturer may administer a standardized test cycle to a subset of 10 newly manufactured automobiles of the specified model and quantify their fuel usage. The parameter of interest is the mean fuel consumption across all cars of the specified kind. The mean consumption of the 10 autos serves as a point estimate for the parameter of interest. Another method for estimating a parameter is to create a range that is very probable to contain the population parameter. A confidence interval is a computed interval based on the data. The confidence level refers to the possibility that the confidence interval will contain the parameter value. Confidence intervals are created in order to achieve a predetermined level of confidence. Another issue encountered in statistical inference is hypothesis testing. The scientific paradigm entails the formulation of novel theories and hypotheses that aim to offer a more accurate depiction of the principles governing the natural world. Based on these hypotheses, one can suggest predictions that can be tested empirically. If the empirical evidence aligns with the predictions of the new hypothesis but contradicts those of the previous theory, the old theory is discarded in favor of the new one. Alternatively, the established theory remains unchanged in its status. Statistical hypothesis testing is a rigorous approach to determine which of two hypotheses should be accepted, employing this particular framework. Both the old and the new hypotheses anticipate distinct distributions for the empirical measurements. To determine which distribution aligns better with the data, a statistic is calculated. The term used to refer to this numerical value is "test statistic". A predetermined threshold is established, and based on the position of the test statistic relative to this threshold, a determination is made as to whether or not to reject the previous hypothesis in favor of the new one. This decision rule is not infallible, as the test statistic may coincidentally fall on the incorrect side of the threshold. However, by analyzing the sampling distribution of the test statistic, one can determine the likelihood of making a mistake. The significance level of a test refers to the probability of incorrectly rejecting the currently accepted theory, also known as the old theory. Indeed, the threshold is chosen to provide a sufficiently low significance level. Resuming the discussion on the car maker. Let's assume that the car in question is produced at two distinct factories. It is advisable to investigate the idea that the car's fuel consumption is same for both plants. If 5 automobiles were produced in one factory and the remaining 5 in another plant, the test could be conducted by comparing the absolute difference between the average fuel consumption of the first 5 cars and the average fuel consumption of the other 5 cars. The approach of hypothesis testing is also utilized in several practical contexts where it is necessary to make informed decisions. Prior to receiving marketing approval from the relevant authorities, a new medical therapy for a specific ailment must undergo a rigorous process of objective evaluation through clinical trials. During these studies, the new treatment is given to certain individuals, while others receive the current standard treatment. Statistical tests are utilized to compare the two groups of patients. The new medicine is made available to the market only if it demonstrates significant statistical benefits and is found to have no undesirable side effects. In the following chapters, we will delve into the computation of point estimate, the building of confidence intervals, and the implementation of hypothesis testing with greater elaboration. The talk will commence by considering a solitary measurement, but will thereafter encompass scenarios that entail the comparison multiple measurements. An instance of such examination is the analysis of clinical trials, wherein the response of patients subjected to the novel process is juxtaposed with the response of patients who underwent the standard treatment. This comparison entails the application of the identical measurement to two distinct sub-samples. In order to make this comparison, statistical inference procedures such as hypothesis testing, point estimation, and confidence interval creation can be utilized. Additional comparisons may pertain to two measurements obtained for the full sample. Regression is a crucial tool for investigating the relationships between two measures or variables. Regression models elucidate the alteration in the distribution of one variable based on the other variable. Regression models can be examined using point estimates, confidence intervals, and hypothesis testing. The variable under research, whose distribution is the focus, is referred to as the response. The explanatory variable is another factor that can potentially influence the distribution.

9.3 THE CARS DATA SET

Statistical inference is applied to data in order to address specific research question. We will demonstrate different inferential procedures using a specific data set with the aim of making the discussion of the different procedures more concrete. The same data set will be used for all procedures that are presented in Chapters 10–15[22]. This data set contains information on various models of cars and is stored in the CVS file "cars.csv"[23]. The file can be found on the internet at http://pluto.huji.ac.il/~msby/StatThink/Datasets/cars.csv. You are advised to download this file to your computer and store it in the working directory of R.

Let us read the content of the CSV file into an R data frame and produce a brief summary:

```
cars <- read.csv("_data/cars.csv")
summary(cars)
```

```
##          make       fuel.type   num.of.doors       body.style drive.wheels
##  toyota     : 32   diesel: 20   four:114     convertible: 6   4wd:  9
##  nissan     : 18   gas   :185   two : 89     hardtop    : 8   fwd:120
##  mazda      : 17                NA's:  2     hatchback  :70   rwd: 76
##  honda      : 13                             sedan      :96
##  mitsubishi: 13                              wagon      :25
##  subaru     : 12
##  (Other)    :100
##  engine.location   wheel.base         length           width
##  front:202       Min.   : 86.60   Min.   :141.1   Min.   :60.30
##  rear :  3       1st Qu.: 94.50   1st Qu.:166.3   1st Qu.:64.10
##                  Median : 97.00   Median :173.2   Median :65.50
##                  Mean   : 98.76   Mean   :174.0   Mean   :65.91
##                  3rd Qu.:102.40   3rd Qu.:183.1   3rd Qu.:66.9
##                  Max.   :120.90   Max.   :208.1   Max.   :72.3
##
##      height        curb.weight     engine.size      horsepower
##  Min.   :47.80   Min.   :1488   Min.   : 61.0   Min.   : 48.0
##  1st Qu.:52.00   1st Qu.:2145   1st Qu.: 97.0   1st Qu.: 70.0
##  Median :54.10   Median :2414   Median :120.0   Median : 95.0
##  Mean   :53.72   Mean   :2556   Mean   :126.9   Mean   :104.3
##  3rd Qu.:55.50   3rd Qu.:2935   3rd Qu.:141.0   3rd Qu.:116.0
##  Max.   :59.80   Max.   :4066   Max.   :326.0   Max.   :288.0
##                                                 NA's   :2
##     peak.rpm       city.mpg      highway.mpg        price
##  Min.   :4150   Min.   :13.00   Min.   :16.00   Min.   : 5118
##  1st Qu.:4800   1st Qu.:19.00   1st Qu.:25.00   1st Qu.: 7775
##  Median :5200   Median :24.00   Median :30.00   Median :10295
##  Mean   :5125   Mean   :25.22   Mean   :30.75   Mean   :13207
##  3rd Qu.:5500   3rd Qu.:30.00   3rd Qu.:34.00   3rd Qu.:16500
##  Max.   :6600   Max.   :49.00   Max.   :54.00   Max.   :45400
##  NA's   :2                                      NA's   :4
```

Observe that the first 6 variables are factors, i.e. they contain qualitative data that is associated with categorization or the description of an attribute. The last 11 variable are numeric and contain quantitative data.

Factors are summarized in R by listing the attributes and the frequency of each attribute value. If the number of attributes is large then only the most frequent attributes are listed. Numerical variables are summarized in R with the aid of the smallest and largest values, the three quartiles (Q1, the median, and Q3) and the average (mean).

The third factor variable, “num.of.doors”, as well as several of the numerical variables have

a special category titled “NA’s”. This category describes the number of missing values among the observations. For a given variable, the observations for which a value for the variable is not recorded, are marked as missing. R uses the symbol “NA” to identify a missing value.

Missing observations are a concern in the analysis of statistical data. If the relative frequency of missing values is substantial and the reason for not obtaining the data for specific observations is related to the phenomena under investigation than naïve statistical inference may produce biased conclusions. In the “cars” data frame missing values are less of a concern since their relative frequency is low.

One should be on the lookout for missing values when applying R to data since the different functions may have different ways for dealing with missing values. One should make sure that the appropriate way is applied for the specific analysis.

Consider the variables of the data frame “cars”:

make: The name of the car producer (a factor).

fuel.type: The type of fuel used by the car, either diesel or gas (a factor).

num.of.doors: The number of passenger doors, either two or four (a factor).

body.style: The type of the car (a factor).

drive.wheels: The wheels powered by the engine (a factor).

engine.location: The location in the car of the engine (a factor).

wheel.base: The distance between the centers of the front and rear wheels in inches (numeric).

length: The length of the body of the car in inches (numeric).

width: The width of the body of the car in inches (numeric).

height: The height of the car in inches (numeric).

curb.weight: The total weight in pounds of a vehicle with standard equipment and a full tank of fuel, but with no passengers or cargo (numeric).

engine.size: The volume swept by all the pistons inside the cylinders in cubic inches (numeric).

horsepower: The power of the engine in horsepowers (numeric).

peak.rpm: The top speed of the engine in rounds-per-minute (numeric).

city.mpg: The fuel consumption of the car in city driving conditions, measured as miles per gallon of fuel (numeric).

highway.mpg: The fuel consumption of the car in highway driving conditions, measured as miles per gallon of fuel (numeric).

price: The retail price of the car in US Dollars (numeric).

9.4 THE SAMPLING DISTRIBUTION

9.4.1 Statistics

Statistical inferences, be it point estimation, confidence intervals, or testing hypothesis, are based on statistics computed from the data. Examples of statistics are the sample average and the sample standard deviation. These are important examples, but clearly not the only ones. Given numerical data, one may compute the smallest value, the largest value, the quartiles, and the median. All are examples of statistics. Statistics may also be associated with factors. The frequency of a given attribute among the observations is a statistic. (An example of such statistic is the frequency of diesel cars in the data frame.) As part of the discussion in the subsequent chapters we will consider these and other types of statistics.

Any statistic, when computed in the context of the data frame being analyzed, obtains a single numerical value. However, once a sampling distribution is being considered then one may view the same statistic as a random variable. A statistic is a function or a formula which is applied to the data frame. Consequently, when a random collection of data frames is the frame of reference then the application of the formula to each of the data frames produces a random collection of values, which is the sampling distribution of the statistic.

We distinguish in the text between the case where the statistic is computed in the context of the given data frame and the case where the computation is conducted in the context of the random sample. This distinguishing is emphasized by the use of small letters for the former and capital letters for the later. Consider, for example, the sample average. In the context of the observed data we denote the data values for a specific variable by $x_1,x_2,\ldots,x_{□}$. The sample average computed for these values is denoted by

$$\bar{x} = \frac{x_1 + x_2 + \cdots + x_n}{n} .$$

On the other hand, if the discussion of the sample average is conducted in the context of a random sample then the sample is a sequence $X_1,X_2,\ldots,X_{□}$ of random variables. The sample average is denoted in this context as

$$\bar{X} = \frac{X_1 + X_2 + \cdots + X_n}{n} .$$

The same formula that was applied to the data values is applied now to the random components of the random sample. In the first context $\bar{X}$ is an observed non-random quantity. In the second context $\bar{X}$ is a random variable, an abstract mathematical concept.

A second example is the sample variance. When we compute the sample variance for the observed data we use the formula:

$$s^2 = \frac{\text{Sum of the squares of the deviations}}{\text{Number of values in the sample} - 1} = \frac{\sum_{i=1}^{n}(x_i - \bar{x})^2}{n-1}.$$

However, when we discuss the sampling distribution of the sample variance we apply the same formula to the random sample:

$$S^2 = \frac{\text{Sum of the squares of the deviations}}{\text{Number of values in the sample} - 1} = \frac{\sum_{i=1}^{n}(X_i - \bar{X})^2}{n-1}.$$

Again, S^2 is a random variable whereas s^2 is a non-random quantity: The evaluation of the random variable at the specific sample that is being observed.

9.4.2 The Sampling Distribution

The sampling distribution may emerge as random selection of samples from a particular population. In such a case, the sampling distribution of the sample, and hence of the statistic, is linked to the distribution of values of the variable in the population.

Alternatively, one may assign theoretical distribution to the measurement associated with the variable. In this other case the sampling distribution of the statistic is linked to the theoretical model.

Consider, for example, the variable "price" that describes the prices of the 205 car types (with 4 prices missing) in the data frame "cars". In order to define a sampling distribution one may imagine a larger population of car types, perhaps all the car types that were sold during the 80's in the United States, or some other frame of reference, with the car types that are included in the data frame considered as a random sample from that larger population. The observed sample corresponds to car types that where sold in 1985. Had one chosen to consider car types from a different year then one may expect to obtain other evaluations of the price variable. The reference population, in this case, is the distribution of the prices of the car types that were sold during the 80's and the sampling distribution is associated with a random selection of a particular year within this period and the consideration of prices of car types sold in that year. The data for 1985 is what we have at hand. But in the sampling distribution we take into account the possibility that we could have obtained data for 1987, for example, rather than the data we did get.

An alternative approach for addressing sampling distribution is to consider a theoretical model. Referring again to the variable "price" one may propose an Exponential model for the distribution of the prices of cars. This model implies that car types in the lower spectrum of the price range are more frequent than cars with a higher price tag. With this model in mind, one may propose the sampling distribution to be composed of 205 unrelated copies from the Exponential distribution (or 201 if we do not want to include the missing values). The rate λ of the associated Exponential distribution is treated as an unknown parameter. One of the roles of statistical inference is to estimate the value of this parameter with the aid of the data at hand.

Sampling distribution is relevant also for factor variables. Consider the variable "fuel.type" as an example. In the given data frame the frequency of diesel cars is 20. However, had one considered another year during the 80's one may have obtained a different frequency, resulting in a sampling distribution. This type of sampling distribution refers to all cars types that were sold in the United States during the 80's as the frame of reference.

Alternatively, one may propose a theoretical model for the sampling distribution. Imagine there is a probability p that a car runs on diesel (and probability $1-p$ that it runs on gas). Hence, when one selects 205 car types at random then one obtains that the distribution of the frequency of car types that run on diesel has the Binomial(205,p) distribution. This is the sampling distribution of the frequency statistic. Again, the value of pp is unknown and one of our tasks is to estimate it from the data we observe.

In the context of statistical inference the use of theoretical models for the sampling distribution is the standard approach. There are situation, such as the application surveys to a specific target population, where the consideration of the entire population as the frame of reference is more natural. But, in most other applications the consideration of theoretical models is the method of choice. In this part of the book, where we consider statistical inference, we will always use the theoretical approach for modeling the sampling distribution.

9.4.3 Theoretical Distributions of Observations

In the first part of the book we introduced several theoretical models that may describe the distribution of an observation. Let us take the opportunity and review the list of models:

Binomial: The Binomial distribution is used in settings that involve counting the number of occurrences of a particular outcome. The parameters that determine the distribution are nn, the number of observations, and p, the probability of obtaining the particular outcome in each observation. The expression "Binomial(n,p)" is used to mark the Binomial distribution. The sample space for this distribution is formed by the integer values $\{0,1,2,...,n\}$. The expectation of the distribution is npnp and the variance is $np(1-p)$. The functions "dbinom", "pbinom", and "qbinom" may be used in order to compute the probability, the cumulative probability, and the percentiles, respectively, for the Binomial distribution. The function "rbinom" can be used in order to simulate a random sample from this distribution.

Poisson: The Poisson distribution is also used in settings that involve counting. This distribution approximates the Binomial distribution when the number of examinations nn is large but the probability pp of the particular outcome is small. The parameter that determines the distribution is the expectation λ. The expression "Poisson(λ)" is used to mark the Poisson distribution. The sample space for this distribution is the entire collection of natural numbers $\{0,1,2,...\}$. The expectation of the distribution is λ and the variance is also λ. The functions "dpois", "ppois", and "qpois" may be used in order to compute the probability, the cumulative probability, and the percentiles, respectively, for the Poisson distribution. The function "rpois" can be used in order to simulate a random sample from this distribution.

Uniform: The Uniform distribution is used in order to model measurements that may have values in a given interval, with all values in this interval equally likely to occur. The parameters that determine the distribution are a and b, the two end points of the interval. The expression "Uniform(a,b)" is used to identify the Uniform distribution. The sample space for this distribution is the interval $[a,b]$. The expectation of the distribution is $(a+b)/2$ and the variance is $(b-a)^2/12$. The functions "dunif", "punif", and "qunif" may be used in order to compute the density, the cumulative probability, and the percentiles for the Uniform distribution. The function "runif" can be used in order to simulate a random sample from this distribution.

Exponential: The Exponential distribution is frequently used to model times between events. It can also be used in other cases where the outcome of the measurement is a positive number and where a smaller value is more likely than a larger value. The parameter that determines the distribution is the rate λ. The expression "Exponential(λ)" is used to identify the Exponential distribution. The sample space for this distribution is the collection of positive numbers. The expectation of the distribution is $1/\lambda$ and the variance is $1/\lambda^2$. The functions "dexp", "pexp", and "qexp" may be used in order to compute the density, the cumulative probability, and the percentiles, respectively, for the Exponential distribution. The function "rexp" can be used in order to simulate a random sample from this distribution.

Normal: The Normal distribution frequently serves as a generic model for the distribution of a measurement. Typically, it also emerges as an approximation of the sampling distribution of statistics. The parameters that determine the distribution are the expectation μ and the variance σ^2. The expression "Normal(μ,σ^2)" is used to mark the Normal distribution. The sample space for this distribution is the collection of all numbers, negative or positive. The expectation of the distribution is μμ and the variance is σ^2. The functions "dnorm", "pnorm", and "qnorm" may be used in order to compute the density, the cumulative probability, and the percentiles for the Normal distribution. The function "rnorm" can be used in order to simulate a random sample from this distribution.

9.4.4 Sampling Distribution of Statistics

Theoretical models describe the distribution of a measurement as a function of a parameter, or a small number of parameters. For example, in the Binomial case the distribution is determined by the number of trials nn and by the probability of success in each trial p. In the Poisson case the distribution is a function of the expectation λ. For the Uniform distribution we may use the end-points of the interval, a and b, as the parameters. In the Exponential case, the rate λ is a natural parameter for specifying the distribution and in Normal case the expectation μμ and the variance σ^2 my be used for that role.

The general formulation of statistical inference problems involves the identification of a theoretical model for the distribution of the measurements. This theoretical model is a function of a parameter whose value is unknown. The goal is to produce statements that refer to this unknown parameter. These statements are based on a sample of observations from the given distribution.

For example, one may try to guess the value of the parameter (point estimation), one may propose an interval which contains the value of the parameter with some subscribed probability (confidence interval) or one may test the hypothesis that the parameter obtains a specific value (hypothesis testing).

The vehicles for conducting the statistical inferences are statistics that are computed as a function of the measurements. In the case of point estimation these statistics are called *estimators*. In the case where the construction of an interval that contains the value of the parameter is the goal then the statistics are called *confidence interval*. In the case of testing hypothesis these statistics are called *test statistics*.

In all cases of inference, The relevant statistic possesses a distribution that it inherits from the sampling distribution of the observations. This distribution is the sampling distribution of the statistic. The properties of the statistic as a tool for inference are assessed in terms of its sampling distribution. The sampling distribution of a statistic is a function of the sample size and of the parameters that determine the distribution of the measurements, but otherwise may be of complex structure.

In order to assess the performance of the statistics as agents of inference one should be able to determine their sampling distribution. We will apply two approaches for this determination. One approach is to use a Normal approximation. This approach relies on the Central Limit Theorem. The other approach is to simulate the distribution. This other approach relies on the functions available in R for the simulation of a random sample from a given distribution.

9.4.5 The Normal Approximation

In general, the sampling distribution of a statistic is not the same as the sampling distribution of the measurements from which it is computed. For example, if the measurements are from the Uniform distributed then the distribution of a function of the measurements will, in most cases, not possess the Uniform distribution. Nonetheless, in many cases one may still identify, at least approximately, what the sampling distribution of the statistic is.

The most important scenario where the limit distribution of the statistic has a known shape is when the statistic is the sample average or a function of the sample average. In such a case the Central Limit Theorem may be applied in order to show that, at least for a sample size not too small, the distribution of the statistic is approximately Normal.

In the case where the Normal approximation may be applied then a probabilistic statement associated with the sampling distribution of the statistic can be substituted by the same statement formulated for the Normal distribution. For example, the probability that the statistic falls inside a given interval may be approximated by the probability that a Normal random variable with the same expectation and the same variance (or standard deviation) as the statistic falls inside the given interval.

For the special case of the sample average one may use the fact that the expectation of the average of a sample of measurements is equal to the expectation of a single measurement and the fact that the variance of the average is the variance of a single measurement, divided by the sample size. Consequently, the probability that the sample average falls within a given interval may be approximate by the probability of the same interval according to the Normal distribution. The expectation that is used for the Normal distribution is the expectation of the measurement. The standard deviation is the standard deviation of the measurement, divided by the square root of the number of observations.

The Normal approximation of the distribution of a statistic is valid for cases other than the sample average or functions thereof. For example, it can be shown (under some conditions) that the Normal approximation applies to the sample median, even though the sample median is not a function of the sample average.

On the other hand, one need not always assume that the distribution of a statistic is necessarily Normal. In many cases it is not, even for a large sample size. For example, the minimal value of a sample that is generated from the Exponential distribution can be shown to follow the Exponential distribution with an appropriate rate[25], regardless of the sample size.

9.4.6 Simulations

In most problems of statistical inference that will be discussed in this book we will be using the Normal approximation for the sampling distribution of the statistic. However, every now and then we may want to check the validity of this approximation in order to reassure ourselves of its appropriateness. Computerized simulations can be carried out for that checking. The simulations are equivalent to those used in the first part of the book.

A model for the distribution of the observations is assumed each time a simulation is carried out. The simulation itself involves the generation of random samples from that model for the given sample size and for a given value of the parameter. The statistic is evaluated and stored for each generated sample. Thereby, via the generation of many samples, an approximation of the sampling distribution of the statistic is produced. A probabilistic statement inferred from the Normal approximation can be compared to the results of the simulation. Substantial disagreement between the Normal approximation and the outcome of the simulations is an evidence that the Normal approximation may not be valid in the specific setting.

As an illustration, assume the statistic is the average price of a car. It is assumed that the price of a car follows an Exponential distribution with some unknown rate parameter λλ. We consider the sampling distribution of the average of 201 Exponential random variables. (Recall that in our sample there are 4 missing values among the 205 observations.) The expectation of the average is $1/\lambda$, which is the expectation of a single Exponential random variable. The variance of a single observation is $1/\lambda^2$. Consequently, the standard deviation of the average is

$$\sqrt{(1/\lambda^2)/201} = (1/\lambda)/\sqrt{201} = (1/\lambda)/14.17745 = 0.0705/\lambda.$$

In the first part of the book we found out that for Normal(μ,σ^2), the Normal distribution with expectation μμ and variance σ^2, the central region that contains 95% of the distribution takes the form $\mu \pm 1.96\sigma$ (namely, the interval $[\mu - 1.96\sigma, \mu + 1.96\sigma]$). Thereby, according to the Normal approximation for the sampling distribution of the average price we state that the region $1/\lambda \pm 1.96 \cdot 0.0705/\lambda$ should contain 95% of the distribution.

We may use simulations in order to validate this approximation for selected values of the rate parameter λ. Hence, for example, we may choose $\lambda=1/12{,}000$ (which corresponds to an expected price of $12,000 for a car) and validate the approximation for that parameter value.

The simulation itself is carried out by the generation of a sample of size n=201n=201 from the Exponential(1/1200) distribution using the function "rexp" for generating Exponential samples. The function for computing the average (mean) is applied to each sample and the result stored. We repeat this process a large number of times (100,000 is the typical number we use) in order to produce an approximation of the sampling distribution of the sample average. Finally, we check the relative frequency of cases where the simulated average is within the given range. This relative frequency is an approximation of the required probability and may be compared to the target value of 0.95.

Let us run the proposed simulation for the sample size of n=201 and for a rate parameter equal to λ=1/12000. Observe that the expectation of the sample average is equal to 12,000 and the standard deviation is 0.0705×12000. Hence:

```
X.bar <- rep(0,10^5)
for(i in 1:10^5) {
  X <- rexp(201,1/12000)
  X.bar[i] <- mean(X)
}
mean(abs(X.bar-12000) <= 1.96*0.0705*12000)


## [1] 0.95002
```

Observe that the simulation produces 0.9496 as the probability of the interval. This result is close enough to the target probability of 0.95, proposing that the Normal approximation is adequate in this example.

The simulation demonstrates the appropriateness of the Normal approximation for the specific value of the parameter that was used. In order to gain more confidence in the approximation we may want to consider other values as well. However, simulations in this book are used only for demonstration. Hence, in most cases where we conduct a simulation experiment, we conduct it only for a single evaluation of the parameters. We leave it to the curiosity of the reader to expand the simulations and try other evaluations of the parameters.

Simulations may also be used in order to compute probabilities in cases where the Normal approximation does not hold. As an illustration, consider the mid-range statistic. This statistic is computed as the average between the largest and the smallest values in the sample. This statistic is discussed in the next chapter.

Consider the case where we obtain 100 observations. Let the distribution of each observation be Uniform. Suppose we are interested as before in the central range that contains 95% of the distribution of the mid-range statistic. The Normal approximation does not apply in this case. Yet, if we specify the parameters of the Uniform distribution then we may use simulations in order to compute the range.

As a specific example let the distribution of an observation be Uniform(3,7). In the simulation we generate a sample of size n=100 from this distribution[28] and compute the mid-range for the sample.

For the computation of the statistic we need to obtain the minimal and the maximal values of the sample. The minimal value of a sequence is compute with the function "min". The input to this function is a sequence and the output is the minimal value of the sequence. Similarly, the maximal value is computed with the function "max". Again, the input to the function is a sequence and the output is the maximal value in the sequence. The statistic itself is obtained by adding the two extreme values to each other and dividing the sum by two.

We produce, just as before, a large number of samples and compute the value of the statistic to each sample. The distribution of the simulated values of the statistic serves as an approximation of the sampling distribution of the statistic. The central range that contains 95% of the sampling distribution may be approximated with the aid of this simulated distribution.

Specifically, we approximate the central range by the identification of the 0.025-percentile and the 0.975-percentile of the simulated distribution. Between these two values are 95% of the simulated values of the statistic. The percentiles of a sequence of simulated values of the statistic can be identified with the aid of the function "quantile" that was presented in the first part of the book. The first argument to the function is a sequence of values and the second argument is a number pp between 0 and 1. The output of the function is the pp-percentile of the sequence[30]. The pp-percentile of the simulated sequence serves as an approximation of the pp-percentile of the sampling distribution of the statistic.

The second argument to the function "quantile" may be a sequence of values between 0 and 1. If so, the percentile for each value in the second argument is computed.

Let us carry out the simulation that produces an approximation of the central region that contains 95% of the sampling distribution of the mid-range statistic for the Uniform distribution:

```
mid.range <- rep(0,10^5)
for(i in 1:10^5) {
  X <- runif(100,3,7)
```

```
  mid.range[i] <- (max(X)+min(X))/2
}
quantile(mid.range,c(0.025,0.975))

##     2.5%    97.5%
## 4.941024 5.058786
```

Observe that (approximately) 95% of the sampling distribution of the statistic are in the range [4.941680,5.059004].

Simulations can be used in order to compute the expectation, the standard deviation or any other numerical summary of the sampling distribution of a statistic. All one needs to do is compute the required summary for the simulated sequence of statistic values and hence obtain an approximation of the required summary. For example, we my use the sequence "mid.range" in order to obtain the expectation and the standard deviation of the mid-range statistic of a sample of 100 observations from the Uniform(3,7) distribution:

```
mean(mid.range)

## [1] 5.000067

sd(mid.range)

## [1] 0.02778315
```

The expectation of the statistic is obtained by the application of the function "mean" to the sequence. Observe that it is practically equal to 5. The standard deviation is obtained by the application of the function "sd". Its value is approximately equal to 0.028.

9.5 EXERCISES

Magnetic fields have been shown to have an effect on living tissue and were proposed as a method for treating pain. In the case study presented here, Carlos Vallbona and his colleagues sought to answer the question "Can the chronic pain experienced by postpolio patients be relieved by magnetic fields applied directly over an identified pain trigger point?"

A total of 50 patients experiencing post-polio pain syndrome were recruited. Some of the patients were treated with an active magnetic device and the others were treated with an inactive placebo device. All patients rated their pain before (score1) and after application of the device (score2). The variable "change" is the difference between "score1" and "score2. The treatment condition is indicated by the variable "active." The value "1" indicates subjects receiving treatment with the active magnet and the value "2" indicates subjects treated with the inactive placebo.

This case study is taken from the Rice Virtual Lab in Statistics. More details on this case study can be found in the case study Magnets and Pain Relief that is presented in that site.

Exercise 9.1 The data for the 50 patients is stored in file "magnets.csv". The file can be found on the internet at http://pluto.huji.ac.il/~msby/StatThink/Datasets/magnets.csv. Download this file to your computer and store it in the working directory of R. Read the content of the file into an R data frame. Produce a summary of the content of the data frame and answer the following questions:

What is the sample average of the change in score between the patient's rating before the application of the device and the rating after the application?

Is the variable "active" a factor or a numeric variable?

Compute the average value of the variable "change" for the patients that received and active magnet and average value for those that received an inactive placebo. (Hint: Notice that the first 29 patients received an active magnet and the last 21 patients received an inactive placebo. The sub-sequence of the first 29 values of the given variables can be obtained via the expression "change[1:29]" and the last 21 vales are obtained via the expression "change[30:50]".)

Compute the sample standard deviation of the variable "change" for the patients that received and active magnet and the sample standard deviation for those that received an inactive placebo.

Produce a boxplot of the variable "change" for the patients that received and active magnet and for patients that received an inactive placebo. What is the number of outliers in each subsequence?

Exercise 9.2 In Chapter 13 we will present a statistical test for testing if there is a difference between the patients that received the active magnets and the patients that received the inactive placebo in terms of the *expected* value of the variable that measures the change. The test statist for this problem is taken to be

$$\frac{\bar{X}_1 - \bar{X}_2}{\sqrt{S_1^2/29 + S_2^2/21}},$$

where $\bar{X}_1$ and $\bar{X}_2$ are the sample averages for the 29 patients that receive active magnets and for the 21 patients that receive inactive placebo, respectively. The quantities S_1^2 and S_2^2 are the sample variances for each of the two samples. Our goal is to investigate the sampling distribution of this statistic in a case where both expectations are equal to each other and to compare this distribution to the observed value of the statistic.

Assume that the expectation of the measurement is equal to 3.5, regardless of what the type of treatment that the patient received. We take the standard deviation of the measurement for patients the receives an active magnet to be equal to 3 and for those that received the inactive placebo we take it to be equal to 1.5. Assume that the distribution of the measurements is Normal and there are 29 patients in the first group and 21 in the second. Find the interval that contains 95% of the sampling distribution of the statistic.

Does the observed value of the statistic, computed for the data frame "magnets", falls inside or outside of the interval that is computed in 1?

10 Chapter POINT ESTIMATION STATISTIC

10.1 INTRODUCTION: AN OVERVIEW

This chapter focuses on the process of determining the value of a parameter using available data. An estimator is a mathematical function that is utilized to approximate or calculate an unknown parameter or quantity based on available data. The text discusses the criteria for selecting estimators, aiming to find an estimator that consistently produces values that are as close as feasible to the true value of the parameter. Various instances of estimate issues are presented and discussed.

10.2 ESTIMATING PARAMETERS

Statistics is the scientific discipline that involves analyzing data. The main objective in statistics is to derive significant and reliable conclusions about a certain phenomenon based on observable data. Usually, the data arises as a subset of observations. An observation is the result of a measurement (or several measurements) done for a subject that is part of the sample. These observations can be utilized to explore the phenomena of interest. The results are derived from the examination of the observations. An essential component of statistical inference involves establishing a connection between the observations and a probabilistic model. The fundamental premise is that the observed data originates from a particular distribution. Typically, it is assumed that the distribution is associated with a theoretical model, such as the Normal, Exponential, Poisson, or any other model that accurately represents the characteristics of the measurement taken. In statistical inference, it is common to have a series of data as a standard setting. It is assumed that all the observations originated from a shared distribution. The parameters one aims to estimate are summaries or characteristics of that distribution. For instance, an individual can have a curiosity regarding the price distribution of automobiles. It can be reasonably assumed that the prices follow an Exponential(λ) distribution. By examining a set of observed prices, it is possible to determine the rate λ that characterizes the distribution. The objective of statistical point estimation is to generate the most accurate estimation of a parameter's value using the given data. An estimator is the statistical measure used to estimate the value of a parameter. An estimate is a mathematical formula that is applied to the data in order to generate a numerical value. This number represents the approximation of the parameter's value. A crucial attribute of a distribution, which is consistently of significance, is the expectation of the measurement, namely the central location of the distribution. The sample average is a reliable estimate of the expectation. Alternatively, one can suggest alternative estimators that are logical, such as the sample mid-range discussed in the preceding chapter. The primary focus of this chapter is to identify the criteria that can assist us in selecting the most suitable estimator for estimating a specific parameter. In the following part, we will address the concerns related to estimating the expected value of a measurement. This section focuses on the estimation of the variance and standard deviation, which are statistical measures that describe the extent to which data points are spread out in a distribution. The final section pertains to the theoretical models of distribution that were presented in the initial portion of the book. The text explores methods for estimating the parameters that define these distributions.

10.3 ESTIMATION OF THE EXPECTATION

A natural candidate for the estimation of the expectation of a random variable on the basis of a sample of observations is the sample average. Consider, as an example, the estimation of the expected price of a car using the information in the data file "cars.csv". Let us read the data into a data frame named "cars" and compute the average of the variable "price":

```
cars <- read.csv("_data/cars.csv")
mean(cars$price)
```

```
## [1] NA
```

The application of the function "mean" for the computation of the sample average produced a missing value. The reason is that the variable "price" contains 4 missing values. As default, when applied to a sequence that contains missing values, the function "mean" produce as output a missing value.

The behavior of the function "mean" at the presence of missing values is determined by the argument "na.rm". If we want to compute the average of the non-missing values in the sequence we should specify the argument "na.rm" as "TRUE". This can be achieved by the inclusion of the expression "na.rm=TRUE" in the arguments of the function:

```
mean(cars$price,na.rm=TRUE)

## [1] 13207.13
```

The resulting average price is, approximately, $13,000.

10.3.1 The Accuracy of the Sample Average

How close is the estimated value of the expectation – the average price – to the expected price?

There is no way of answering this question on the basis of the data we observed. Indeed, we think of the price of a random car as a random variable. The expectation we seek to estimate is the expectation of that random variable. However, the actual value of that expectation is unknown. Hence, not knowing what is the target value, how can we determine the distance between the computed average 13207.13 and that unknown value?

As a remedy for not being able to answer the question we would like to address we, instead, change the question. In the new formulation of the question we ignore the data at hand altogether. The new formulation considers the sample average as a statistic and the question is formulated in terms of the sampling distribution of that statistic. The question, in its new formulation is: How close is the sample average of the price, taken as a random variable, to the expected price?

Notice that in the new formulation of the question the observed average price $\bar{x} = 13207.13$ has no special role. The question is formulated in terms of the sampling distribution of the sample average $(\bar{X})$. The observed average value is only one among many in the sampling distribution of the average.

The advantage of the new formulation of the question is that it can be addressed. We do have means for investigating the closeness of the estimator to the parameter and thereby producing meaningful answers. Specifically, consider the current case where the estimator is the sample average $\bar{X}$. This estimator attempts to estimate the expectation E(X) of the measurement, which is the parameter. Assessing the closeness of the estimator to the parameter corresponds to the comparison between the distribution of the random variable, i.e. the estimator, and the value of the parameter.

For this comparison we may note that the expectation E(X) is also the expectation of the sample average $\bar{X}$. Consequently, in this problem the assessment of the closeness of the estimator to the parameter is equivalent to the investigation of the spread of the distribution of the sample average about its expectation.

Consider an example of such investigation. Imagine that the expected price of a car is equal to $13,000. A question one may ask is how likely it is that the estimator's guess at the value is within $1,000 of the actual value? In other words, what is the probability that sample average falls in the range [12,000,14,000]?

Let us investigate this question using simulations. Recall our assumption that the distribution of the price is Exponential. An expectation of 13,000 corresponds to a rate parameter of λ=1/13,000. We simulate the sampling distribution of the estimator by the generation of a sample of 201 Exponential random variables with this rate. The sample average is computed for each sample and stored. The sampling distribution of the sample average is approximated via the production of a large number of sample averages:

```
lam <- 1/13000
X.bar <- rep(0,10^5)
for(i in 1:10^5) {
  X <- rexp(201,lam)
  X.bar[i] <- mean(X)
}
mean(abs(X.bar - 1/lam) <= 1000)

## [1] 0.72251
```

In the last line of the code we compute the probability of being within $1,000 of the expected price. Recall that the expected price in the Exponential case is the reciprocal of the rate λ. In this simulation we obtained 0.7247 as an approximation of the probability.

In the case of the sample average we may also apply the Normal approximation in order to assess the probability under consideration. In particular, if λ=1/13,000 then the expectation of an Exponential observation is $E(X)=1/\lambda=13{,}000$ and the variance is $V(X)=1/\lambda^2=(13{,}000)^2$. The expectation of the sample average is equal to the expectation of the measurement, 13,000 in this example. The variance of the sample average is equal to the variance of the observation, divided by the sample size. In the current setting it is equal to $(13{,}000)^2/201$. The standard deviation is equal to the square root of the variance.

The Normal approximation uses the Normal distribution in order to compute probabilities associated with the sample average. The Normal distribution that is used has the same expectation and standard deviation as the sample average:

```
mu <- 13000
sig <- 13000/sqrt(201)
pnorm(14000,mu,sig) - pnorm(12000,mu,sig)
```

```
## [1] 0.7245391
```

The probability of falling within the interval [12000,14000] is computed as the difference between the cumulative Normal probability at 14,000 and the cumulative Normal probability at 12,000.

These cumulative probabilities are computed with the function "pnorm". Recall that this function computes the cumulative probability for the Normal distribution. If the first argument is 14,000 then the function produces the probability that a Normal random variable is less than or equal to 14,000. Likewise, if the first argument is 12,000 then the computed probability is the probability of being less than or equal to 12,000. The expectation of the Normal distribution enters in the second argument of the function and the standard deviation enters in the third argument.

The Normal approximation of falling in the interval [12000,14000], computed as the difference between the two cumulative probabilities, produces 0.7245391 as the probability. Notice that the probability 0.7247 computed in the simulations is in agreement with the Normal approximation.

If we wish to assess the accuracy of the estimator at other values of the parameter, say E (X)=12,000 (which corresponds to λ=1/12,000) or E(X)=14,033, (which corresponds to λ=1/14,033) all we need to do is change the expression "lam <- 1/13000" to the new value and rerun the simulation.

Alternatively, we may use a Normal approximation with modified interval, expectation, and standard deviation. For example, consider the case where the expected price is equal to $12,000. In order to asses the probability that the sample average falls within $1,000 of the parameter we should compute the probability of the interval [11,000,13,000] and change the entries to the first argument of the function "pnorm" accordingly. The new expectation is 12,000 and the new standard deviation is $12,000/\sqrt{201}$:

```
mu <- 12000
sig <- 12000/sqrt(201)
pnorm(13000,mu,sig) - pnorm(11000,mu,sig)
```

```
## [1] 0.7625775
```

This time we get that the probability is, approximately, 0.763.

The fact that the computed value of the average 13,207.13 belongs to the interval [12,000,14,000] that was considered in the first analysis but does not belong to the interval [11,000,13,000] that was considered in the second analysis is irrelevant to the conclusions drawn from the analysis. In both cases the theoretical properties of the sample average as an estimator were considered and not its value at specific data.

In the simulation and in the Normal approximation we applied one method for assessing the closeness of the sample average to the expectation it estimates. This method involved the computation of the probability of being within $1,000 of the expected price. The higher this probability, the more accurate is the estimator.

An alternative method for assessing the accuracy of an estimator of the expectation may involve the use of an overall summary of the spread of the distribution. A standard method for quantifying the spread of a distribution about the expectation is the variance (or its square root, the standard deviation). Given an estimator of the expectation of a measurement, the sample average for example, we may evaluate the accuracy of the estimator by considering its variance. The smaller the variance the more accurate is the estimator.

Consider again the case where the sample average is used in order to estimate the expectation of a measurement. In such a situation the variance of the estimator, i.e. the variance of the sample average, is obtained as the ratio between the variance of the measurement $V(X)$, divided by the sample size n:

$$\mathbf{V}(\bar{X}) = \mathbf{V}(X)/n \ .$$

Notice that for larger sample sizes the estimator is more accurate. The lager the sample size nn the smaller is the variance of the estimator, in which case the values of the estimator tend to be more concentrated about the expectation. Hence, one may make the estimator more accurate by increasing the sample size.

Another method for improving the accuracy of the average of measurements in estimating the expectation is the application of a more accurate measurement device. If the variance $V(X)$ of the measurement device decreases so does the variance of the sample average of such measurements.

When examining the precision of estimators in the subsequent analysis, we will typically rely on comprehensive summaries of the extent to which their distribution deviates from the desired value of the parameter.

10.3.2 Comparing Estimators

The formulation of the accuracy of estimate that we employ substitutes the inquiry: "To what extent does the provided value of the estimator align with the undisclosed value of the parameter?" The inquiry is asking about the proximity of the unknown and random values of the estimator to a certain value of the parameter. The second formulation of the question is purely theoretical and has no connection to real-world measurement values. Within this academic framework, we might contemplate many prospective values of the parameter. Once the parameter value has been chosen, it can be considered as a known quantity inside the academic discourse. It is evident that this does not indicate that we possess knowledge of the real value of the parameter. The sample average is a valid estimate of the expected value of the measurement. Alternatively, one can suggest alternative estimators. When the distribution of a measurement is symmetrical around the expected value, the median of the distribution is equal to the expected value. The sample median, which is a reliable estimate of the measurement median, can also be used as an alternative estimator of the expectation in this scenario. When dealing with a symmetric distribution, which of the two options, the sample average or the sample median, is more preferable as an estimate for the expectation? The unequivocal response to this inquiry is to favor the superior option, the one that exhibits greater precision. As part of the completed tasks, you are required to compare the sample average and the sample median as estimators of the expectation. In this analysis, we are comparing the sample average to another alternative estimator known as the mid-range estimator. The mid-range estimate is calculated by taking the average of the smallest and greatest observations in the sample. When comparing estimators, we do not assess them based on the observed data. Instead, we evaluate them as stochastic variables. The comparison focuses on the characteristics of the estimators within a certain theoretical framework. This theoretical framework is based on the actual circumstances that we are aware of. However, it is important to note that the frame of reference remains the theoretical model rather than the evidence that has been collected. Therefore, based on the given circumstances, we can infer that in the comparison, the observations arise from a certain distribution. We can define specific values for the parameters of this distribution and determine the suitable sample size. Once the scene has been set, we may proceed to compare the accuracy of one estimator with that of the other. Evaluating the performance of different estimators by testing them at various parameter values inside the provided theoretical model or in other theoretical models can offer valuable insights and improve our understanding of their respective strengths and limitations.

Let us compare the sample average to the sample mid-range as estimators of the expectation in a situation that we design. Consider a Normal measurement X with expectation $\mathrm{E}(X)=3$ and variance that is equal to 2. Assume that the sample size is n=100n=100. Both estimators, due to the symmetry of the Normal distribution, are centered at the expectation. Hence, we may evaluate the accuracy of the two estimators using their variances. These variances are the measure of the spread of the distributions of each estimator about the target parameter value.

We produce the sampling distribution and compute the variances using a simulation. Recall that the distribution of the mid-range statistic was simulated in the previous chapter. In the computation of the mid-range statistic we used the function "max" that computes the maximum value of its input and the function "min" that computes the minimum value:

```
mu <- 3
sig <- sqrt(2)
X.bar <- rep(0,10^5)
mid.range <- rep(0,10^5)
for(i in 1:10^5) {
  X <- rnorm(100,mu,sig)
  X.bar[i] <- mean(X)
  mid.range[i] <- (max(X)+min(X))/2
}
var(X.bar)

## [1] 0.01996425

var(mid.range)

## [1] 0.1865454
```

We get that the variance of the sample average is approximately equal to 0.02. The variance of the mid-range statistic is approximately equal to 0.185, more than 9 times as large. We see that the accuracy of the sample average is better in this case than the accuracy of the mid-range estimator. Evaluating the two estimators at other values of the parameter will produce the same relation. Hence, in the current example it seems as if the sample average is the better of the two.

Is the sample average necessarily the best estimator for the expectation? The next example will demonstrate that this need not always be the case.

Consider again a situation of observing a sample of size n=100n=100. However, this time the measurement X is Uniform and not Normal. Say X~Uniform(0.5,5.5) has the Uniform distribution over the interval [0.5,5.5]. The expectation of the measurement is equal to 3 like before, since E(X)=(0.5+5.5)/2=3. The variance on an observation is V (X)=$(5.5-0.5)^2/12$=2.083333, not much different from the variance that was used in the Normal case. The Uniform distribution, like the Normal distribution, is a symmetric distribution about the center of the distribution. Hence, using the mid-range statistic as an estimator of the expectation makes sense.

We re-run the simulations, using the function "runif" for the simulation of a sample from the Uniform distribution and the parameters of the Uniform distribution instead of the function "rnorm" that was used before:

```
a <- 0.5
b <- 5.5
X.bar <- rep(0,10^5)
mid.range <- rep(0,10^5)
for(i in 1:10^5) {
  X <- runif(100,a,b)
  X.bar[i] <- mean(X)
  mid.range[i] <- (max(X)+min(X))/2
}
var(X.bar)

## [1] 0.02084876

var(mid.range)

## [1] 0.001221015
```

Again, we get that the variance of the sample average is approximately equal to 0.02, which is close to the theoretical value. The variance of mid-range statistic is approximately equal to 0.0012.

Observe that in the current comparison between the sample average and the mid-range estimator we get that the latter is a clear winner. Examination of other values of a and b for the Uniform distribution will produce the same relation between the two competitors. Hence, we may conclude that for the case of the Uniform distribution the sample average is an inferior estimator.

The last example may serve as yet another reminder that life is never simple. A method that is good in one situation may not be as good in a different situation.

Still, the estimator of choice of the expectation is the sample average. Indeed, in some cases we may find that other methods may produce more accurate estimates. However, in most settings the sample average beats its competitors. The sample average also possesses other useful benefits. Its sampling distribution is always centered at the expectation it is trying to estimate. Its variance has a simple form, i.e. it is equal to the variance of the measurement divided by the sample size. Moreover, its sampling distribution can be approximated by the Normal distribution. Henceforth, due to these properties, we will use the sample average whenever estimation of the expectation is required.

10.4 ESTIMATION OF THE VARIANCE AND STANDARD DEVIATION

The spread of the measurement about its expected value may be measured by the variance or by the standard deviation, which is the square root of the variance. The standard estimator for the variance of the measurement is the sample variance and the square root of the sample variance is the default estimator of the standard deviation.

The computation of the sample variance from the data is discussed in Chapter 3. Recall that the sample variance is computed via the formula:

$$s^2 = \frac{\text{Sum of the squares of the deviations}}{\text{Number of values in the sample} - 1} = \frac{\sum_{i=1}^{n}(x_i - \bar{x})^2}{n-1},$$

where $\bar{X}$ is the sample average and nn is the sample size. The term $x_i - \bar{x}$ is the deviation from the sample average of the ith observation and $\sum_{i=1}^{n}(x_i - \bar{x})^2$ is the sum of the squares of deviations. It is pointed out in Chapter 3 that the reason for dividing the sum of squares by (n-1), rather than nn, stems from considerations of statistical inference. A promise was made that these reasonings will be discussed in due course. Now we want to deliver on this promise.

Let us compare between two competing estimators for the variance, both considered as random variables. One is the estimator S^2, which is equal to the formula for the sample variance applied to a random sample:

$$S^2 = \frac{\text{Sum of the squares of the deviations}}{\text{Number of values in the sample} - 1} = \frac{\sum_{i=1}^{n}(X_i - \bar{X})^2}{n-1}.$$

The computation of this statistic can be carried out with the function "var".

The second estimator is the one obtained when the sum of squares is divided by the sample size (instead of the sample size minus 1):

$$\frac{\text{Sum of the squares of the deviations}}{\text{Number of values in the sample}} = \frac{\sum_{i=1}^{n}(X_i - \bar{X})^2}{n}.$$

Observe that the second estimator can be represented in the form:

$$\frac{\sum_{i=1}^{n}(X_i - \bar{X})^2}{n} = \frac{n-1}{n} \cdot \frac{\sum_{i=1}^{n}(X_i - \bar{X})^2}{n-1} = [(n-1)/n]S^2 .$$

In order to make the comparison concrete, let us consider it in the context of a Normal measurement with expectation μ=5μ=5 and variance σ2=3σ^2=3. Let us assume that the sample is of size 20 (n=20).

Under these conditions we carry out a simulation. Each iteration of the simulation involves the generation of a sample of size n=20 from the given Normal distribution. The sample variance S^2 is computed from the sample with the application of the function "var". The resulting estimate of the variance is stored in an object that is called "X.var":

```
mu <- 5
std <- sqrt(3)
X.var <- rep(0,10^5)
for(i in 1:10^5) {
  X <- rnorm(20,mu,std)
  X.var[i] <- var(X)
}
```

The content of the object "X.var", at the end of the simulation, approximates the sampling distribution of the estimator S^2.

Our goal is to compare between the performance of the estimator of the variance S2S^2 and that of the alternative estimator. In this alternative estimator the sum of squared deviations is divided by the sample size (n=20) and not by the sample size minus 1 (n–1=19). Consequently, the alternative estimator is obtained by multiplying S^2 by the ratio 19/2019/20. The sampling distribution of the values of S^2 is approximated by the content of the object "X.var". It follows that the sampling distribution of the alternative estimator is approximated by the object "(19/20)*X.var", in which each value of S^2 is multiplied by the appropriate ratio. The comparison between the sampling distribution of S^2 and the sampling distribution of the alternative estimator is obtained by comparing between "X.var" and "(19/20)*X.var".

Let us start by the investigation of the expectation of the estimators. Recall that when we analyzed the sample average as an estimator of the expectation of a measurement we obtained that the expectation of the sampling distribution of the estimator is equal to the value of the parameter it is trying to estimate. One may wonder: What is the situation for the estimators of the variance? Is it or is it not the case that the expectation of their sampling distribution equals the value of the variance? In other words, is the distribution of either estimators of the variance centered at the value of the parameter they are trying to estimate?

Compute the expectations of the two estimators:

```
mean(X.var)

## [1] 3.00401

mean((19/20)*X.var)

## [1] 2.853809
```

Note that 3 is the value of the variance of the measurement that was used in the simulation. Observe that the expectation of S^2 is essentially equal to 3, whereas the expectation of the alternative estimator is less than 3. Hence, at least in the example that we consider, the center of the distribution of S^2 is located on the target value. On the other hand, the center of the sampling distribution of the alternative estimator is located off that target value.

As a matter of fact it can be shown mathematically that the expectation of the estimator S^2 is always equal to the variance of the measurement. This holds true regardless of what is the actual value of the variance. On the other hand the expectation of the alternative estimator is always off the target value.

An estimator is called *unbiased* if its expectation is equal to the value of the parameter that it tries to estimate. We get that S^2 is an unbiased estimator of the variance. Similarly, the sample average is an unbiased estimator of the expectation. Unlike these two estimators, the alternative estimator of the variance is a *biased* estimator.

The default is to use S^2 as the estimator of the variance of the measurement and to use its square root as the estimator of the standard deviation of the measurement. A justification, which is frequently quoted to justify this selection, is the fact that S2S^2 is an unbiased estimator of the variance.

In the previous section, when comparing two competing estimators of the expectation, or main concern was the quantification of the spread of the sampling distribution of either estimator about the target value of the parameter. We used that spread as a measure of the distance between the estimator and the value it tries to estimate. In the setting of the previous section both estimators were unbiased. Consequently, the variance of the estimators, which measures the spread of the distribution about its expectation, could be used in order to quantify the distance between the estimator and the parameter. (Since, for unbiased estimators, the parameter is equal to the expectation of the sampling distribution.)

In the current section one of the estimators (S^2) is unbiased, but the other (the alternative estimator) is not. In order to compare their accuracy in estimation we need to figure out a way to quantify the distance between a biased estimator and the value it tries to estimate.

Towards that end let us recall the definition of the variance. Given a random variable X with an expectation $\mathrm{E}(X)$, we consider the square of the deviations ($(X$-\ $\mathrm{E}(X))^2$, which measure the (squared) distance between each value of the random variable and the expectation. The variance is defined as the expectation of the squared distance: $\mathrm{V}(X)$= E [$(X$-\E $(X))^2$]. One may think of the variance as an overall measure of the distance between the random variable and the expectation.

Assume now that the goal is to assess the distance between an estimator and the parameter it tries to estimate. In order to keep the discussion on an abstract level let us use the Greek letter $\hat{\theta}$ (read: theta) to denote this parameter. The estimator is denoted by θ^ (read: theta hat). It is a statistic, a formula applied to the data. Hence, with respect to the sampling distribution, $\hat{\theta}$ is a random variable. The issue is to measure the distance between the random variable ^θθ^ and the parameter θ.

Motivated by the method that led to the definition of the variance we consider the deviations between the estimator and the parameter. The square deviations $(\hat{\theta} - \theta)^2$ may be considered in the current context as a measure of the (squared) distance between the estimator and the parameter. When we take the expectation of these square deviations we get an overall measure of the distance between the estimator and the parameter. This overall distance is called the *mean square error* of the estimator and is denoted by MSE:

$$\text{MSE} = \mathbf{E}\left[(\hat{\theta} - \theta)^2\right] .$$

The mean square error of an estimator is tightly linked to the bias and the variance of the estimator. The bias of an estimator $\hat{\theta}$ is the difference between the expectation of the estimator and the parameter it seeks to estimate:

$$\text{Bias} = \mathbf{E}(\hat{\theta}) - \theta .$$

In an unbiased estimator the expectation of the estimator and the estimated parameter coincide, i.e. the bias is equal to zero. For a biased estimator the bias is either negative, as is the case for the alternative estimator of the variance, or else it is positive.

The variance of the estimator, Variance=V $(\hat{\theta})$, is a measure of the spread of the sampling distribution of the estimator about its expectation.

The link between the mean square error, the bias, and the variance is described by the formula:

$$\text{MSE} = \text{Variance} + (\text{Bias})^2 .$$

Hence, the mean square error of an estimator is the sum of its variance, the (squared) distance between the estimator and its expectation, and the square of the bias, the square of the distance between the expectation and the parameter. The mean square error is influenced both by the spread of the distribution about the expected value (the variance) and by the distance between the expected value and the parameter (the bias). The larger either of them become the larger is the mean square error, namely the distance between the estimator and the parameter.

Let us compare between the mean square error of the estimator S^2 and the mean square error of the alternative estimator [19/20]S^2. Recall that we have computed their expectations and found out that the expectation of S2S^2 is essentially equal to 3, the target value of the variance. The expectation of the alternative estimator turned out to be equal to 2.845630, which is less than the target value. It turns out that the bias of S2S^2 is zero (or essentially zero in the simulations) and the bias of the alternative estimator is 2.845630−3=−0.15437≈−0.15.

In order to compute the mean square errors of both estimators, let us compute their variances:

```
var(X.var)

## [1] 0.949878

var((19/20)*X.var)

## [1] 0.8572649
```

Observe that the variance of S^2 is essentially equal to 0.936 and the variance of the alternative estimator is essentially equal to 0.845.

The estimator S^2 is unbiased. Consequently, the mean square error of S2S^2 is equal to its variance. The bias of the alternative is -0.15. As a result we get that the mean square error of this estimator, which is the sum of the variance and the square of the bias, is essentially equal to

$$0.845 + (-0.15)^2 = 0.845 + 0.0225 = 0.8675 \ .$$

Observe that the mean square error of the estimator S^2, which is equal to 0.936, is larger than the mean square error of the alternative estimator.

Notice that even though the alternative estimator is biased it still has a smaller mean square error than the default estimator S^2. Indeed, it can be prove mathematically that when the measurement has a Normal distribution then the mean square error of the alternative estimator is always smaller than the mean square error of the sample variance S^2.

Still, although the alternative estimator is slightly more accurate than S^2 in the estimation of the variance, the tradition is to use the latter. Obeying this tradition we will henceforth use S^2 whenever estimation of the variance is required. Likewise, we will use S, the square root of the sample variance, to estimate the standard deviation.

In order to understand how is it that the biased estimator produced a smaller mean square error than the unbiased estimator let us consider the two components of the mean square error. The alternative estimator is biased but, on the other hand, it has a smaller variance. Both the bias and the variance contribute to the mean square error of an estimator. The price for reducing the bias in estimation is usually an increase in the variance and vice versa. The consequence of producing an unbiased estimator such as S^2 is an inflated variance. A better estimator is an estimator that balances between the error that results from the bias and the error that results from the variance. Such is the alternative estimator.

We will use S^2 in order to estimate the variance of a measurement. A context in which an estimate of the variance of a measurement is relevant is in the assessment of the variance of the sample mean. Recall that the variance of the sample mean is equal to $V(X)/n$, where V(X) is the variance of the measurement and nn is the size of the sample. In the case where the variance of the measurement is not known one may estimate it from the sample using S^2. It follows that the estimator of the variance of the sample average is S^2/n. Similarly, $S/\sqrt{n}$ can be used as an estimator of the standard deviation of the sample average.

10.5 ESTIMATION OF OTHER PARAMETERS

In the preceding two sections, we examined the estimation of the mean and the variance of a measurement. The suggested estimators, the sample mean for the expected value and the sample variance for the variability, are not dependent on any particular model for the distribution of the measurement. These methods can be used on data regardless of whether a theoretical model for the distribution of the measurement is adopted. If a theoretical model is assumed for the measurement, one would want to estimate the specific parameters associated with this model. The initial section of the book presented the Binomial, Poisson, Uniform, Exponential, and Normal models as means to describe the distribution of measurements. In this section, we focus on estimating the parameters that define each of these theoretical distributions using a sample drawn from the same distribution. Occasionally, the estimators align with the estimators discussed in the preceding sections. Alternatively, there are instances where the estimators vary.

Start with the Binomial distribution. We will be interested in the special case $X \sim \text{Binomial}(1,p)$. This case involves the outcome of a single trial. The trial has two possible outcomes, one of them is designated as "success" and the other as "failure". The parameter pp is the probability of the success. The Binomial(1,p) distribution is also called *the Bernoulli distribution*. Our concern is the estimation of the parameter pp based on a sample of observations from this Bernoulli distribution.

This estimation problem emerges in many settings that involve the assessment of the probability of an event based on a sample of nn observations. In each observation the event either occurs or not. A natural estimator of the probability of the event is its relative frequency in the sample. Let us show that this estimator can be represented as an average of a Bernoulli sample and the sample average is used for the estimation of a Bernoulli expectation.

Consider an event, one may code a measurement X, associated with an observation, by 1 if the event occurs and by 0 if it does not. Given a sample of size nn, one thereby produces nn observations with values 0 or 1. An observation has the value 1 if the event occurs for that observation or, else, the value is 0.

Notice that E $(X)=1\cdot p=p$. Consequently, the probability of the event is equal to the expectation of the Bernoulli measurement[43]. It turns out that the parameter one seeks to estimate is the expectation of a Bernoulli measurement. The estimation is based on a sample of size n of Bernoulli observations.

In Section 10.3 it was proposed to use the sample average as an estimate of the expectation. The sample average is the sum of the observations, divided by the number of observation. In the specific case of a sample of Bernoulli observations, the sum of observation is the sum of zeros and one. The zeros do not contribute to the sum. Hence, the sum is equal to the number of times that 1 occurs, namely the frequency of the occurrences of the event. When we divide by the sample size we get the relative frequency of the occurrences. The conclusion is that the sample average of the Bernoulli observations and the relative frequency of occurrences of the event in the sample are the same. Consequently, the sample relative frequency of the event is also a sample average that estimates the expectation of the Bernoulli measurement.

We seek to estimate pp, the probability of the event. The estimator is the relative frequency of the event in the sample. We denote this estimator by ^PP^. This estimator is a sample average of Bernoulli observations that is used in order to estimate the expectation of the Bernoulli distribution. From the discussion in Section 10.3 one may conclude that this estimator is an unbiased estimator of pp (namely, $\mathrm{E}(\hat{P}) = p$) and that its variance is equal to:

$$\mathbf{V}(\hat{P}) = \mathbf{V}(X)/n = p(1-p)/n \ ,$$

where the variance of the measurement is obtained from the formula for the variance of a Binomial(1,p) distribution.

The second example of an integer valued random variable that was considered in the first part of the book is the Poisson(λ) distribution. Recall that λλ is the expectation of a Poisson measurement. Hence, one may use the sample average of Poisson observations in order to estimate this parameter.

The first example of a continuous distribution that was discussed in the first part of the book is the Uniform(a,b) distribution. This distribution is parameterized by a and b, the end-points of the interval over which the distribution is defined. A natural estimator of a is the smallest value observed and a natural estimator of b is the largest value. One may use the function "min" for the computation of the former estimate from the sample and use the function "max" for the computation of the later. Both estimators are slightly biased but have a relatively small mean square error.

Next considered the $X \sim$Exponential(λ) random variable. This distribution was applied in this chapter to model the distribution of the prices of cars. The distribution is characterized by the rate parameter λ. In order to estimate the rate one may notice the relation between it and the expectation of the measurement:

The rate is equal to the reciprocal of the expectation. The expectation can be estimated by the sample average. Hence a natural proposal is to use the reciprocal of the sample average as an estimator of the rate:

$$\hat{\lambda} = 1/\bar{X} \ .$$

The final example that we mention is the Normal (μ,σ^2) case. The parameter μμ is the expectation of the measurement and may be estimated by the sample average $\bar{X}$. The parameter σ^2 is the variance of a measurement, and can be estimated using the sample variance S^2.

10.6 EXERCISES

Exercise 10.1 In Subsection 10.3.2 we compare the average against the mid-range as estimators of the expectation of the measurement. The goal of this exercise is to repeat the analysis, but this time compare the average to the median as estimators of the expectation in symmetric distributions.

Simulate the sampling distribution of average and the median of a sample of size n=100 from the Normal(3,2) distribution. Compute the expectation and the variance of the sample average and of the sample median. Which of the two estimators has a smaller mean square error?

Simulate the sampling distribution of average and the median of a sample of size n=100 from the Uniform(0.5,5.5) distribution. Compute the expectation and the variance of the sample average and of the sample median. Which of the two estimators has a smaller mean square error?

Exercise 10.2 The goal in this exercise is to assess estimation of a proportion in a population on the basis of the proportion in the sample.

The file "pop2.csv" was introduced in Exercise 7.1 of Chapter 7. This file contains information associated to the blood pressure of an imaginary population of size 100,000. The file can be found on the internet (http://pluto.huji.ac.il/~msby/StatThink/Datasets/pop2.csv). One of the variables in the file is a factor by the name "group" that identifies levels of blood pressure. The levels of this variable are "HIGH", "LOW", and "NORMAL".

The file "ex2.csv" contains a sample of size n=150n=150 taken from the given population. This file can also be found on the internet (http://pluto.huji.ac.il/~msby/StatThink/Datasets/ex2.csv). It contains the same variables as in the file "pop2.csv". The file "ex2.csv" corresponds in this exercise to the observed sample and the file "pop2.csv" corresponds to the unobserved population.

Download both files to your computer and answer the following questions:

1. Compute the proportion in the sample of those with a high level of blood pressure[45].
2. Compute the proportion in the population of those with a high level of blood pressure.
3. Simulate the sampling distribution of the sample proportion and compute its expectation.
4. Compute the variance of the sample proportion.
5. It is proposed in Section 10.5 that the variance of the sample proportion is $\mathrm{V}(\hat{P}) = p(1 - p)/n$, where p is the probability of the event (having a high blood pressure in our case) and nn is the sample size (n=150 in our case). Examine this proposal in the current setting.

11 Chapter | CONFIDENCE INTERVALS

11.1 INTRODUCTION: AN OVERVIEW

A confidence interval is a statistical estimate of an unknown parameter, represented by a range of values. The range encompasses the parameter value that corresponds to a predetermined probability, known as the confidence level. This chapter focuses on constructing confidence intervals for the mean and variance of a measurement, as well as for the likelihood of an event. Occasionally, the construction will utilize the Normal approximation as recommended by the Central Limit Theorem. This approximation is accurate when the sample size is sufficiently high. The process of determining confidence intervals for a small sample is examined within the framework of Normal measurements.

11.2 INTERVALS FOR MEAN AND PROPORTION

A confidence interval, similar to a point estimator, is a technique used to estimate the unknown value of a parameter. However, rather than generating a solitary value, the confidence interval is a range of values. The range of values is determined from the data. The confidence interval is expected to encompass the population parameter that is not known. The confidence level of the confidence intervals represents the probability of the event of inclusion. This section outlines a technique for calculating confidence intervals for the mean value of a measurement, as well as a related technique for calculating a confidence interval for the probability of an event. These methods depend on the utilization of the Central Limit Theorem to calculate the sample average in one scenario, and the sample proportion in the other scenario.

In the first subsection we compute a confidence interval for the expectation of the variable "price" and a confidence interval for the proportion of diesel cars. The confidence intervals are computed based on the data in the file "cars.csv". In the subsequent subsections we discuss the theory behind the computation of the confidence intervals and explain the meaning of the confidence level. Subsection 11.2.2 does so with respect to the confidence interval for the expectation and Subsection 11.2.3 with respect to the confidence interval for the proportion.

11.2.1 Examples of Confidence Intervals

A point estimator of the expectation of a measurement is the sample average of the variable that is associated with the measurement. A confidence interval is an interval of numbers that is likely to contain the parameter value. A natural interval to consider is an interval centered at the sample average ¯xx¯. The interval is set to have a width that assures the inclusion of the parameter value in the prescribed probability, namely the confidence level.

Consider the confidence interval for the expectation. The structure of the confidence interval of confidence level 95% is $[\bar{x} - 1.96 \cdot s/\sqrt{n}, \bar{x} + 1.96 \cdot s/\sqrt{n}]$, where ss is the estimated standard deviation of the measurement (namely, the sample standard deviation) and nn is the sample size. This interval may be expressed in the form:

$$\bar{x} \pm 1.96 \cdot s/\sqrt{n}\ .$$

As an illustration, let us construct a 0.95-confidence interval for the expected price of a car. :

```
cars <- read.csv("_data/cars.csv")
x.bar <- mean(cars$price,na.rm=TRUE)
s <- sd(cars$price,na.rm=TRUE)
n <- 201
```

In the first line of code the data in the file "cars.csv" is stored in a data frame called "cars". In the second line the average ¯xx¯ is computed for the variable "price" in the data frame "cars". This average is stored under the name "x.bar". Recall that the variable "price" contains 4 missing values. Hence, in order to compute the average of the non-missing values we should set a "TRUE" value to the argument "na.rm". The sample standard deviation "s" is computed in the third line by the application of the function "sd". We set once more the argument "na. rm=TRUE" in order to deal with the missing values. Finally, in the last line we store the sample size "n", the number of non-missing values.

Let us compute the lower and the upper limits of the confidence interval for the expectation of the price:

```
x.bar - 1.96*s/sqrt(n)
```

```
## [1] 12108.47
```

```
x.bar + 1.96*s/sqrt(n)
```

```
## [1] 14305.79
```

The lower limit of the confidence interval turns out to be $12,108.47 and the upper limit is $14,305.79. The confidence interval is the range of values between these two numbers.

Consider, next, a confidence interval for the probability of an event. The estimate of the probability p is $\hat{p}$, the relative proportion of occurrences of the event in the sample. Again, we construct an interval about this estimate. In this case, a confidence interval of confidence level 95% is of the form $[\hat{p} - 1.96 \cdot \sqrt{\hat{p}(1-\hat{p})/n}, \hat{p} + 1.96 \cdot \sqrt{\hat{p}(1-\hat{p})/n}]$, where nn is the sample size. Observe that ^pp^ replaces ¯xx¯ as the estimate of the parameter and that $\hat{p}(1-\hat{p})/n$ replace s^2/n as the estimate of the variance of the estimator. The confidence interval for the probability may be expressed in the form:

$$\hat{p} \pm 1.96 \cdot \sqrt{\hat{p}(1-\hat{p})/n} .$$

As an example, let us construct a confidence interval for the proportion of car types that use diesel fuel. The variable "fuel.type" is a factor that records the type of fuel the car uses, either diesel or gas:

```
table(cars$fuel.type)
```

```
##
## diesel    gas
##     20    185
```

Only 20 of the 205 types of cars are run on diesel in this data set. The point estimation of the probability of such car types and the confidence interval for this probability are:

```
n <- 205
p.hat <- 20/n
p.hat

## [1] 0.09756098

p.hat - 1.96*sqrt(p.hat*(1-p.hat)/n)

## [1] 0.05694226

p.hat + 1.96*sqrt(p.hat*(1-p.hat)/n)

## [1] 0.1381797
```

The point estimation of the probability is $\hat{p} = 20/205 \approx 0.098$ and the confidence interval, after rounding up, is [0.057,0.138].

11.2.2 Confidence Intervals for the Mean

In the preceding subsection, we calculated a confidence interval for the anticipated price of a car and a confidence interval for the likelihood that a car operates on diesel fuel. This subsection provides an explanation of the theoretical basis for constructing confidence intervals for the expectation. The theory offers valuable understanding regarding the proper interpretation of confidence intervals. In the following subsection, we will examine the theoretical basis for constructing confidence intervals for the probability of an event.

Assume one is interested in a confidence interval for the expectation of a measurement X. For a sample of size nn, one may compute the sample average $\bar{X}$, which is the point estimator for the expectation. The expected value of the sample average is the expectation E(X), for which we are trying to produce the confidence interval. Moreover, the variance of the sample average is V(X)/n, where V(X) is the variance of a single measurement and nn is the sample size.

The construction of a confidence interval for the expectation relies on the Central Limit Theorem and on estimation of the variance of the measurement. The Central Limit Theorem states that the distribution of the (standardized) sample average $Z = (\bar{X} - \mathbf{E}(X)/\sqrt{\mathbf{V}(X)/n}$ is approximately standard Normal for a large enough sample size. The variance of the measurement can be estimated using the sample variance S^2.

Supposed that we are interested in a confidence interval with a confidence level of 95%. The value 1.96 is the 0.975-percentile of the standard Normal. Therefore, about 95% of the distribution of the standardized sample average is concentrated in the range [-1.96,1,96]:

$$\mathrm{P}\left(\left|\frac{\bar{X} - \mathrm{E}(X)}{\sqrt{\mathrm{V}(X)/n}}\right| \leq 1.96\right) \approx 0.95$$

The event, the probability of which is being described in the last display, states that the absolute value of deviation of the sample average from the expectation, divided by the standard deviation of the sample average, is no more than 1.96. In other words, the distance between the sample average and the expectation is at most 1.96 units of standard deviation. One may rewrite this event in a form that puts the expectation within an interval that is centered at the sample average:

$$\left\{|\bar{X} - \mathrm{E}(X)| \leq 1.96 \cdot \sqrt{\mathrm{V}(X)/n}\right\} \quad \Longleftrightarrow$$
$$\left\{\bar{X} - 1.96 \cdot \sqrt{\mathrm{V}(X)/n} \leq \mathrm{E}(X) \leq \bar{X} + 1.96 \cdot \sqrt{\mathrm{V}(X)/n}\right\}.$$

Clearly, the probability of the later event is (approximately) 0.95 since we are considering the same event, each time represented in a different form. The second representation states that the expectation E(X) belongs to an interval about the sampleaverage: $\bar{X} \pm 1.96\sqrt{\mathrm{V}(X)/n}$. Thisintervalis,almost,theconfidenceintervalweseek.

The difficulty is that we do not know the value of the variance \Var(X)\Var(X), hence we cannot compute the interval in the proposed form from the data. In order to overcome this difficulty we recall that the unknown variance may nonetheless be estimated from the data:

$$S^2 \approx \mathrm{V}(X) \quad \Longrightarrow \quad \sqrt{\mathrm{V}(X)/n} \approx S/\sqrt{n}\,,$$

where S is the sample standard deviation.

When the sample size is sufficiently large, so that SS is very close to the value of the standard deviation of an observation, we obtain that the interval $\bar{X} \pm 1.96\sqrt{\mathrm{V}(X)/n}$ and the interval $\bar{X} \pm 1.96 \cdot S/\sqrt{n}$ almost coincide. Therefore:

$$\mathrm{P}\left(\bar{X} - 1.96 \cdot \frac{S}{\sqrt{n}} \leq \mathrm{E}(X) \leq \bar{X} + 1.96 \cdot \frac{S}{\sqrt{n}}\right) \approx 0.95\,.$$

Hence, $\bar{X} \pm 1.96 \cdot S/\sqrt{n}$ is an (approximate) confidence interval of the (approximate) confidence level 0.95.

Let us demonstrate the issue of confidence level by running a simulation. We are interested in a confidence interval for the expected price of a car. In the simulation we assume that the distribution of the price is Exponential(1/13000). (Consequently, E (X)=13,000). We take the sample size to be equal to n=201 and compute the actual probability of the confidence interval containing the value of the expectation:

```
lam <- 1/13000
n <- 201
X.bar <- rep(0,10^5)
S <- rep(0,10^5)
for(i in 1:10^5) {
  X <- rexp(n,lam)
  X.bar[i] <- mean(X)
  S[i] <- sd(X)
}
LCL <- X.bar - 1.96*S/sqrt(n)
UCL <- X.bar + 1.96*S/sqrt(n)
mean((13000 >= LCL) & (13000 <= UCL))
```

```
## [1] 0.94441
```

Below we will go over the code and explain the simulation. But, before doing so, notice that the actual probability that the confidence interval contains the expectation is about 0.945, which is slightly below the nominal confidence level of 0.95. Still quoting the nominal value as the confidence level of the confidence interval is not too far from reality.

Let us look now at the code that produced the simulation. In each iteration of the simulation a sample is generated. The sample average and standard deviations are computed and stored in the appropriate locations of the sequences "X.bar" and "S". At the end of all the iterations the content of these two sequences represents the sampling distribution of the sample average $\bar{X}$ and the sample standard deviation S, respectively.

The lower and the upper end-points of the confidence interval are computed in the next two lines of code. The lower level of the confidence interval is stored in the object "LCL" and the upper level is stored in "UCL". Consequently, we obtain the sampling distribution of the confidence interval. This distribution is approximated by 100,000 random confidence intervals that are generated by the sampling distribution. Some of these random intervals contain the value of the expectation, namely 13,000, and some do not. The proportion of intervals that contain the expectation is the (simulated) confidence level. The last expression produces this confidence level, which turns out to be equal to about 0.945.

The last expression involves a new element, the term "&", which calls for more explanations. Indeed, let us refer to the last expression in the code. This expression involves the application of the function "mean". The input to this function contains two sequences with logical values ("TRUE" or "FALSE"), separated by the character

"&". The character "&" corresponds to the logical "AND" operator. This operator produces a "TRUE" if a "TRUE" appears at both sides. Otherwise, it produces a "FALSE". (Compare this operator to the operator "OR", that is expressed in R with the character "|", that produces a "TRUE" if at least one "TRUE" appears at either sides.)

In order to clarify the behavior of the terms "&" and "|" consider the following example:

```
a <- c(TRUE, TRUE, FALSE, FALSE)
b <- c(FALSE, TRUE, TRUE, FALSE)
a & b

## [1] FALSE  TRUE FALSE FALSE

a | b

## [1]  TRUE  TRUE  TRUE FALSE
```

The term "&" produces a "TRUE" only if parallel components in the sequences "a" and "b" both obtain the value "TRUE". On the other hand, the term "|" produces a "TRUE" if at least one of the parallel components are "TRUE". Observe, also, that the output of the expression that puts either of the two terms between two sequences with logical values is a sequence of the same length (with logical components as well).

The expression "(13000 >= LCL)" produces a logical sequence of length 100,000 with "TRUE" appearing whenever the expectation is larger than the lower level of the confidence interval. Similarly, the expression "(13000 <= UCL)" produces "TRUE" values whenever the expectation is less than the upper level of the confidence interval. The expectation belongs to the confidence interval if the value in both expressions is "TRUE". Thus, the application of the term "&" to these two sequences identifies the confidence intervals that contain the expectation. The application of the function "mean" to a logical vector produces the relative frequency of TRUE's in the vector. In our case this corresponds to the relative frequency of confidence intervals that contain the expectation, namely the confidence level.

We calculated before the confidence interval [12108.47,14305.79] for the expected price of a car. This confidence interval was obtained via the application of the formula for the construction of confidence intervals with a 95% confidence level to the variable "price" in the data frame "cars". Casually speaking, people frequently refer to such an interval as an interval that contains the expectation with probability of 95%.

However, one should be careful when interpreting the confidence level as a probabilistic statement. The probability computations that led to the method for constructing confidence intervals were carried out in the context of the sampling distribution. Therefore, probability should be interpreted in the context of all data sets that could have emerged and not in the context of the given data set. No probability is assigned to the statement "The expectation belongs to the interval [12108.47,14305.79]". The probability is assigned to the statement "The expectation belongs to the interval $\bar{X} \pm 1.96 \cdot S/\sqrt{n}$", where ¯XX¯ and SS are interpreted as random variables. Therefore the statement that the interval [12108.47,14305.79] contains the expectation with probability of 95% is meaningless. The assertion that is significant is that the provided interval was created using a method that, when applied to random samples, creates intervals that have the assigned probability of containing the expectation.

11.2.3 Confidence Intervals for a Proportion

The next issue is the construction of a confidence interval for the probability of an event. Recall that a probability pp of some event can be estimated by the observed relative frequency of the event in the sample, denoted $\hat{P}$. The estimation is associated with the Bernoulli random variable X, that obtains the value 1 when the event occurs and the value 0 when it does not. In the estimation problem p is the expectation of X and $\hat{P}$. is the sample average of this measurement. With this formulation we may relate the problem of the construction of a confidence interval for p to the problem of constructing a confidence interval for the expectation of a measurement. The latter problem was dealt with in the previous subsection.

Specifically, the discussion regarding the steps in the construction – staring with an application of the Central Limit Theorem in order to produce an interval that depends on the sample average and its variance and proceeding by the replacement of the unknown variance by its estimate – still apply and may be taken as is. However, in the specific case we have a particular expression for the variance of the estimate $\hat{P}$:

$$\mathbf{V}(\hat{P}) = p(1-p)/n \approx \hat{P}(1-\hat{P})/n \ .$$

The tradition is to estimate this variance by using the estimator ^PP^ for the unknown pp instead of using the sample variance. The resulting confidence interval of significance level 0.95 takes the form:

$$\bar{P} \pm 1.96 \cdot \sqrt{\hat{P}(1-\hat{P})/n} \ .$$

Let us run a simulation in order to assess the confidence level of the confidence interval for the probability. Assume that n=205 and p=0.12. The simulation we run is very similar to the simulation of Subsection 11.2.2. In the first stage we produce the sampling distribution of $\hat{P}$. (stored in the sequence "P.hat") and in the second stage we compute the relative frequency in the simulation of the intervals that contain the actual value of pp that was used in the simulation:

```
p <- 0.12
n <- 205
P.hat <- rep(0,10^5)
for(i in 1:10^5) {
  X <- rbinom(n,1,p)
  P.hat[i] <- mean(X)
}
LCL <- P.hat - 1.96*sqrt(P.hat*(1-P.hat)/n)
UCL <- P.hat + 1.96*sqrt(P.hat*(1-P.hat)/n)
mean((p >= LCL) & (p <= UCL))
```

```
## [1] 0.95182
```

In this simulation we obtained that the actual confidence level is approximately 0.951, which is slightly above the nominal confidence level of 0.95.

The formula $\bar{X} \pm 1.96 \cdot S/\sqrt{n}$ that is used for a confidence interval for the expectation and the formula $\hat{P} \pm 1.96 \cdot \{\hat{P}(1-\hat{P})/n\}^{1/2}$ for the probability both refer to a confidence intervals with confidence level of 95%. If one is interested in a different confidence level then the width of the confidence interval should be adjusted: a wider interval for higher confidence and a narrower interval for smaller confidence level.

Specifically, if we examine the derivation of the formulae for confidence intervals we may notice that the confidence level is used to select the number 1.96, which is the 0.975-percentile of the standard Normal distribution (1.96 =qnorm(0.975)). The selected number satisfies that the interval [-1.96,1.96] contains 95% of the standard Normal distribution by leaving out 2.5% on both tails. For a different confidence level the number 1.96 should be replace by a different number.

For example, if one is interested in a 90% confidence level then one should use 1.645, which is the 0.95-percentile of the standard Normal distribution (qnorm(0.95)), leaving out 5% in both tails. The resulting confidence interval for an expectation is $\bar{X} \pm 1.645 \cdot S/\sqrt{n}$ and the confidence interval for a probability is $\hat{P} \pm 1.645 \cdot \{\hat{P}(1-\hat{P})/n\}^{1/2}$.

11.3 INTERVALS FOR NORMAL MEASUREMENTS

In the preceding section, it was assumed that the sample size is sufficiently large when constructing confidence intervals. This assumption was employed in both the application of the Central Limit Theorem and the substitution of the unknown variance with its estimated value. The above logic may no longer be true when dealing with a tiny sample size. The Normal distribution may not adequately approximate the sampling distribution of the sample average, and the sample variance may significantly deviate from the true value of the measurement variance. Typically, when drawing conclusions from tiny samples, it is necessary to employ more intricate modeling techniques to accurately represent the distribution of the values. For the purpose of this section, we shall assume that the measurements follow a Normal distribution. This assumption may not be applicable in all cases. For instance, the Normal distribution is not an accurate model for the price of a car, whereas the Exponential distribution provides a more suitable model. Therefore, it is not advisable to blindly apply the methodologies presented in this section to variables like price when the sample size is small, as this may result in questionable findings. If the distribution of the measurements follows a Normal distribution, the approach described in this section will generate reliable confidence intervals for the expected value of the measurement, even when the sample size is small. In addition, we will expand the methodology to allow for the creation of confidence intervals for the measurement's variance. Prior to delving into the specifics of the techniques, allow us to provide an illustration of inference that pertains to a limited sample. Let's examine the matter of gasoline use. The "cars" data frame has two variables that provide information on fuel use. The first file, "city.mpg", provides information on the car's fuel efficiency in urban driving conditions, measured in miles per gallon. The second file, "highway.mpg", provides information on the car's fuel efficiency in highway driving situations, also measured in miles per gallon. Driving in urban environments typically involves frequent stops and changes in speed, resulting in decreased fuel efficiency. Therefore, it is anticipated that the mileage per gallon will be lower when driving in urban settings as compared to driving in highway conditions. We compute the disparity variable for each car type, which quantifies the difference between the highway fuel efficiency and the urban fuel efficiency in terms of miles per gallon. The cars are categorized into two groups: those powered by diesel and those powered by gasoline. Our objective is to calculate the expected value and variation of a specific variable for each type of fuel. Specifically, we are focused in constructing confidence intervals for the mean and variance.

Box plots of the difference in fuel consumption between highway and urban conditions are presented in Figure 11.1. The box plot on the left hand side corresponds to cars that run on diesel and the box plot on the right hand side corresponds to cars that run on gas. Recall that 20 of the 205 car types use diesel and the other 185 car types use gas. One may suspect that the fuel consumption characteristics vary between the two types of fuel. Indeed, the measurement tends to have sightly higher values for vehicles that use gas.

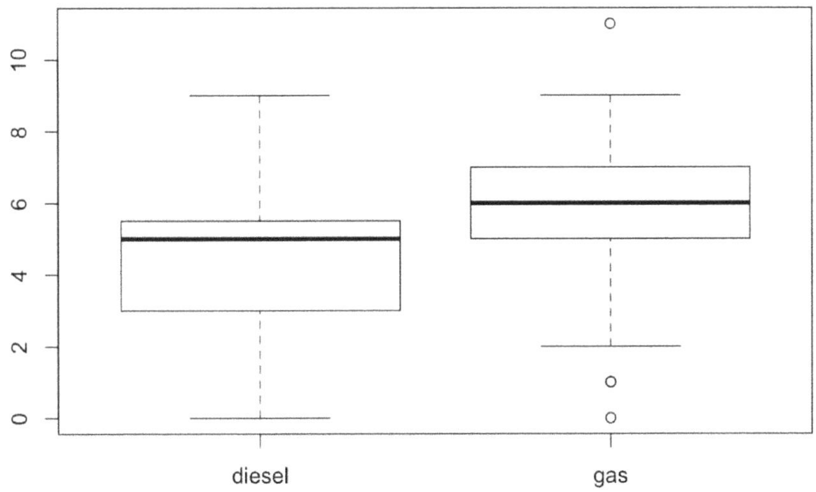

Figure 11.1: Box Plots of Differences in MPG

We conduct inference for each fuel type separately. However, since the sample size for cars that run on diesel is only 20, one may have concerns regarding the application of methods that assume a large sample size to a sample size this small.

11.3.1 Confidence Intervals for a Normal Mean

Consider the construction of a confidence interval for the expectation of a Normal measurement. In the previous section, when dealing with the construction of a confidence interval for the expectation, we exploited the Central Limit Theorem in order to identify that the distribution of the standardized sample average $(\bar{X} - \mathbf{E}(X))/\sqrt{\mathbf{V}(X)/n}$ is, approximately, standard Normal. Afterwards, we substituted the standard deviation of the measurement by the sample standard deviation S, which was an accurate estimator of the former due to the magnitude sample size.

In the case where the measurements themselves are Normally distributed one can identify the exact distribution of the standardized sample average, with the sample variance substituting the variance of the measurement: $(\bar{X} - \mathbf{E}(X))/(S/\sqrt{n})$. This specific distribution is called the Student's t-distribution, or simply the t-distribution.

The t-distribution is bell shaped and symmetric. Overall, it looks like the standard Normal distribution but it has wider tails. The t-distribution is characterized by a parameter called the number of *degrees of freedom*. In the current setting, where we deal with the standardized sample average (with the sample variance substituting the variance of the measurement) the number of degrees of freedom equals the number of observations associated with the estimation of the variance, minus 1. Hence, if the sample size is nn and if the measurement is Normally distributed then the standardized sample average (with SS substituting the standard deviation of the measurement) has a t-distribution on $(n-1)$ degrees of freedom. We use $t(n-1)$ to denote this t-distribution.

The R system contains functions for the computation of the density, the cumulative probability function and the percentiles of the t-distribution, as well as for the simulation of a random sample from this distribution. Specifically, the function "qt" computes the percentiles of the t-distribution. The first argument to the function is a probability and the second argument is the number of degrees of freedom. The output of the function is the percentile associated with the probability of the first argument. Namely, it is a value such that the probability that the t-distribution is below the value is equal to the probability in the first argument.

For example, let "n" be the sample size. The output of the expression "qt(0.975,n-1)" is the 0.975-percentile of the t-distribution on (n-1)$(n-1)$ degrees of freedom. By definition, 97.5% of the t-distribution are below this value and 2.5% are above it. The symmetry of the t distribution implies that 2.5% of the distribution is below the negative of this value. The middle part of the distribution is bracketed by these two values $[-\texttt{qt(0.975,n-1)}, \texttt{qt(0.975,n-1)}]$, and it contains 95% of the distribution.

Summarizing the above claims in a single formula produces the statement:

$$\frac{\bar{X} - \mathbf{E}(X)}{S/\sqrt{n}} \sim t_{(n-1)} \quad \Longrightarrow \quad \mathbf{P}\left(\left|\frac{\bar{X} - \mathbf{E}(X)}{S/\sqrt{n}}\right| \leq \texttt{qt(0.975,n-1)}\right) = 0.95 \, .$$

Notice that the equation associated with the probability is not an approximation but an exact relation. Rewriting the event that is described in the probability in the form of a confidence interval, produces

$$\bar{X} \pm \texttt{qt(0.975,n-1)} \cdot S/\sqrt{n}$$

as a confidence interval for the expectation of the Normal measurement with a confidence level of 95%.

The structure of the confidence interval for the expectation of a Normal measurement is essentially identical to the structure proposed in the previous section. The only difference is that the number 1.96, the percentile of the standard Normal distribution, is substituted by the percentile of the t-distribution.

Consider the construction of a confidence interval for the expected difference in fuel consumption between highway and urban driving conditions. In order to save writing we created two new variables; a factor called "fuel" that contains the data on the fuel type of each car, and a numerical vector called "dif.mpg" that contains the difference between highway and city fuel consumption for each car type:

```
fuel <- cars$fuel.type
dif.mpg <- cars$highway.mpg - cars$city.mpg
```

We are interested in confidence intervals based on the data stored in the variable "dif.mpg". One confidence interval will be associated with the level "diesel" of the factor "fuel" and the other will be associated with the level "gas" of the same factor.

In order to compute these confidence intervals we need to compute, for each level of the factor "fuel", the sample average and the sample standard deviation of the data points of the variable "dif.mpg" that are associated with that level.

The function "tapply" is a helpful tool for this operation. This function utilizes three parameters. The initial parameter is the series of data on which we intend to perform a calculation. The second parameter is a multiplier. The third parameter represents the name of a function utilized for the computation. The "tapply" function applies the function specified in the third parameter to each subset of values in the first argument. The sub-collections are defined based on the levels of the second parameter.

Sounds complex but it is straightforward enough to apply:

```
tapply(dif.mpg,fuel,mean)

##   diesel      gas
## 4.450000 5.648649

tapply(dif.mpg,fuel,sd)

##   diesel      gas
## 2.781045 1.433607
```

Sample averages are computed in the first application of the function "tapply". Observe that an average was computed for cars that run on diesel and an average was computed for cars that run on gas. In both cases the average corresponds to the difference in fuel consumption. Similarly, the standard deviations were computed in the second application of the function. We obtain that the point estimates of the expectation for diesel and gas cars are 4.45 and 5.648649, respectively and the point estimates for the standard deviation of the variable are 2.781045 and 1.433607.

Let us compute the confidence interval for each type of fuel:

```
x.bar <- tapply(dif.mpg,fuel,mean)
s <- tapply(dif.mpg,fuel,sd)
n <- c(20,185)
x.bar - qt(0.975,n-1)*s/sqrt(n)
```

```
##   diesel      gas
## 3.148431 5.440699
```

```
x.bar + qt(0.975,n-1)*s/sqrt(n)
```

```
##   diesel      gas
## 5.751569 5.856598
```

The objects "x.bar" and "s" contain the sample averages and sample standard deviations, respectively. Both are sequences of length two, with the first component referring to "diesel" and the second component referring to "gas". The object "n" contains the two sample sizes, 20 for "diesel" and 185 for "gas". In the expression next to last the lower boundary for each of the confidence intervals is computed and in the last expression the upper boundary is computed. The confidence interval for the expected difference in diesel cars is [3.148431,5.751569]. and the confidence interval for cars using gas is [5.440699,5.856598].

The 0.975-percentiles of the t-distributions are computed with the expressions "qt(0.025,n-1)":

```
qt(0.975,n-1)
```

```
## [1] 2.093024 1.972941
```

The second argument of the function "qt" is a sequence with two components, the number 19 and the number 184. Accordingly, The first position in the output of the function is the percentile associated with 19 degrees of freedom and the second position is the percentile associated to 184 degrees of freedom.

Compare the resulting percentiles to the 0.975-percentile of the standard Normal distribution, which is essentially equal to 1.96. When the sample size is small, 20 for example, the percentile of the t-distribution is noticeably larger than the percentile of the standard Normal. However, for a larger sample size the percentiles, more or less, coincide. It follows that for a large sample the method proposed in Subsection 11.2.2 and the method discussed in this subsection produce essentially the same confidence intervals.

11.3.2 Confidence Intervals for a Normal Variance

The subsequent objective is to calculate confidence intervals for the variance of a measurement that follows a Normal distribution. The primary concept behind constructing a confidence interval is to determine the probability distribution of a random variable that is linked to the parameter of interest. The identified zone corresponds to the middle portion of the probability distribution, encompassing 95% of the random variable's distribution (or, more broadly, the portion of the distribution with a probability equal to the confidence level). The confidence interval arises from the rephrasing of the occurrence linked to that particular place. The revised formulation places the parameter inside a defined range, bounded by a lower limit and an upper limit. The lower and upper bounds are calculated based on the data and serve as the boundaries of the confidence interval.

We start with the sample variance, $S^2 = \sum_{i=1}^{n}(X_i - \bar{X})^2/(n-1)$, which serves as a point estimator of the parameter of interest. When the measurements are Normally distributed then the random variable $(n-1)S^2/\sigma^2$ possesses a special distribution called the chi-square distribution. (Chi is the Greek letter χ, which is read "Kai".) This distribution is associated with the sum of squares of Normal variables. It is parameterized, just like the t-distribution, by a parameter called the number of degrees of freedom. This number is equal to $(n-1)$ in the situation we discuss. The chi-square distribution on $(n-1)$ degrees of freedom is denoted with the symbol $\chi^2(n-1)$.

The R system contains functions for the computation of the density, the cumulative probability function and the percentiles of the chi-square distribution, as well as for the simulation of a random sample from this distribution. Specifically, the percentiles of the chi-square distribution are computed with the aid of the function "qchisq". The first argument to the function is a probability and the second argument is the number of degrees of freedom. The output of the function is the percentile associated with the probability of the first argument. Namely, it is a value such that the probability that the chi-square distribution is below the value is equal to the probability in the first argument.

Forexample,let"n"bethesamplesize.Theoutputoftheexpression"qt(0.975,n-1)" is the 0.975-percentile of the chi-square distribution. By definition, 97.5% of the chi-square distribution are below this value and 2.5% are above it. Similarly, the expression "qchisq(0.025,n-1)" is the 0.025-percentile of the chi-square distribution, with 2.5% of the distribution below this value. Notice that between these two percentiles, namely within the interval `[qchisq(0.025,n-1), qchisq(0.975,n-1)]`, are 95% of the chi-square distribution.

We may summarize that for Normal measurements:

$$(n-1)S^2/\sigma^2 \sim \chi^2_{(n-1)} \quad \Longrightarrow$$
$$\mathrm{P}\big(\texttt{qchisq(0.025,n-1)} \le (n-1)S^2/\sigma^2 \le \texttt{qchisq(0.975,n-1)}\big) = 0.95\,.$$

The chi-square distribution is not symmetric. Therefore, in order to identify the region that contains 95% of the distribution region we have to compute both the 0.025- and the 0.975-percentiles of the distribution.

The event associated with the 95% region is rewritten in a form that puts the parameter σ^2 in the center:

$$\big\{(n-1)S^2/\texttt{qchisq(0.975,n-1)} \le \sigma^2 \le (n-1)S^2/\texttt{qchisq(0.025,n-1)}\big\}\,.$$

The left most and the right most expressions in this event mark the end points of the confidence interval. The structure of the confidence interval is:

$$\big[\{(n-1)/\texttt{qchisq(0.975,n-1)}\}\times S^2,\ \{(n-1)/\texttt{qchisq(0.025,n-1)}\}\times S^2\big]\,.$$

Consequently, the confidence interval is obtained by the multiplication of the estimator of the variance by a ratio between the number of degrees of freedom (n-1) and an appropriate percentile of the chi-square distribution. The percentile on the left hand side is associated with the larger probability (making the ratio smaller) and the percentile on the right hand side is associated with the smaller probability (making the ratio larger).

Consider, specifically, the confidence intervals for the variance of the measurement "diff.mpg" for cars that run on diesel and for cars that run on gas. Here, the size of the samples is 20 and 185, respectively:

```
(n-1)/qchisq(0.975,n-1)
```

```
## [1] 0.5783456 0.8234295
```

```
(n-1)/qchisq(0.025,n-1)
```

```
## [1] 2.133270 1.240478
```

The ratios that are used in the left hand side of the intervals are 0.5783456 and 0.8234295, respectively. Both ratios are less than one. On the other hand, the ratios associated with the other end of the intervals, 2.133270 and 1.240478, are both larger than one.

Let us compute the point estimates of the variance and the associated confidence intervals. Recall that the object "s" contains the sample standard deviations of the difference in fuel consumption for diesel and for gas cars. The object “n” contains the two sample sizes:

```
s^2
```

```
##    diesel       gas
## 7.734211 2.055229
```

```
(n-1)*s^2/qchisq(0.975,n-1)
```

```
##    diesel       gas
## 4.473047 1.692336
```

```
(n-1)*s^2/qchisq(0.025,n-1)
```

```
##     diesel        gas
## 16.499155  2.549466
```

The variance of the difference in fuel consumption for diesel cars is estimated to be 7.734211 with a 95%-confidence interval of [4.473047,16.499155] and for cars that use gas the estimated variance is 2.055229, with a confidence interval of [1.692336,2.549466].

As a final example in this section let us simulate the confidence level for a confidence interval for the expectation and for a confidence interval for the variance of a Normal measurement. In this simulation we assume that the expectation is equal to μ=3μ=3 and the variance is equal to σ^2=32=9. The sample size is taken to be n=20. We start by producing the sampling distribution of the sample average $\bar{X}$ and of the sample standard deviation S:

```
mu <- 4
sig <- 3
n <- 20
X.bar <- rep(0,10^5)
S <- rep(0,10^5)
for(i in 1:10^5) {
  X <- rnorm(n,mu,sig)
  X.bar[i] <- mean(X)
  S[i] <- sd(X)
}
```

Consider first the confidence interval for the expectation:

```
mu.LCL <- X.bar - qt(0.975,n-1)*S/sqrt(n)
mu.UCL <- X.bar + qt(0.975,n-1)*S/sqrt(n)
mean((mu >= mu.LCL) & (mu <= mu.UCL))
```

```
## [1] 0.94934
```

The nominal significance level of the confidence interval is 95%, which is practically identical to the confidence level that was computed in the simulation.

The confidence interval for the variance is obtained in a similar way. The only difference is that we apply now different formulae for the computation of the upper and lower confidence limits:

```
var.LCL <- (n-1)*S^2/qchisq(0.975,n-1)
var.UCL <- (n-1)*S^2/qchisq(0.025,n-1)
mean((sig^2 >= var.LCL) & (sig^2 <= var.UCL))
```

```
## [1] 0.94896
```

Again, we obtain that the nominal confidence level of 95% coincides with the confidence level computed in the simulation.

11.4 CHOOSING THE SAMPLE SIZE

Statistics plays a significant role in research by offering valuable guidance for the design of experiments and surveys. A meticulously designed experiment has the potential to yield sufficiently precise responses to the research inquiries while maximizing the utilization of resources. Conversely, inadequately organized experiments may not yield desired outcomes or may squander precious resources.

Regrettably, the topic of experiment design is not included in this book. However, we would want to provide a concise analysis of a specific component in design: The process of determining the appropriate sample size. During the planning phase of an experiment or survey, it is crucial to determine the appropriate number of observations to collect. Undoubtedly, a larger sample size is generally more desirable from a statistical perspective. Nevertheless, a larger sample size usually results in higher costs. Hence, it is preferable to gather the minimum amount of observations that are still adequate to arrive at a meaningful conclusion.

As an example, consider an opinion poll aimed at the estimation of the proportion in the population of those that support a specific candidate that considers running for an office. How large the sample must be in order to assure, with high probability, that the percentage in the sample of supporters is within 0.5% of the percentage in the population? Within 0.25%?

A natural way to address this problem is via a confidence interval for the proportion. If the range of the confidence interval is no more than 0.05 (or 0.025 in the other case) then with a probability equal to the confidence level it is assured that the population relative frequency is within the given distance from the sample proportion.

Consider a confidence level of 95%. Recall that the structure of the confidence interval for the proportion is $\hat{P} \pm 1.96 \cdot \{\hat{P}(1-\hat{P})/n\}^{1/2}$. The range of the confidence interval is $1.96 \cdot \{\hat{P}(1-\hat{P})/n\}^{1/2}$. How large should nn be in order to guarantee that the range is no more than 0.05?

The answer to this question depends on the magnitude of $\hat{P}(1-\hat{P})$, which is a random quantity. Luckily, one may observe that the maximal value[49] of the quadratic function $f(p)=p(1-p)$ is 1/4. It follows that

$$1.96 \cdot \{\hat{P}(1-\hat{P})/n\}^{1/2} \le 1.96 \cdot \{0.25/n\}^{1/2} = 0.98/\sqrt{n} \, .$$

Finally,

$$0.98/\sqrt{n} \le 0.05 \quad \Longrightarrow \quad \sqrt{n} \ge 0.98/0.05 = 19.6 \quad \Longrightarrow \quad n \ge (19.6)^2 = 384.16 \, .$$

The conclusion is that nn should be larger than 384 in order to assure the given range. For example, n=385 should be sufficient.

If the request is for an interval of range 0.025 then the last line of reasoning should be modified accordingly:

$$0.98/\sqrt{n} \le 0.025 \quad \Longrightarrow \quad \sqrt{n} \ge \frac{0.98}{0.025} = 39.2 \quad \Longrightarrow \quad n \ge (39.2)^2 = 1536.64 \, .$$

Consequently, n=1537n=1537 will do. Increasing the accuracy by 50% requires a sample size that is 4 times larger.

More examples that involve selection of the sample size will be considered as part of the homework.

11.5 EXERCISES

Exercise 11.1 This exercise deals with an experiment that was conducted among students. The aim of the experiment was to assess the effect of rumors and prior reputation of the instructor on the evaluation of the instructor by her students. The experiment was conducted by Towler and Dipboye. This case study is taken from the Rice Virtual Lab in Statistics. More details on this case study can be found in the case study "Instructor Reputation and Teacher Ratings" that is presented in that site.

The experiment involved 49 students that were randomly assigned to one of two conditions. Before viewing the lecture, students were give one of two "summaries" of the instructor's prior teaching evaluations. The first type of summary, i.e. the first condition, described the lecturer as a charismatic instructor. The second type of summary (second condition) described the lecturer as a punitive instructor. We code the first condition as “C” and the second condition as “P”. All subjects watched the same twenty-minute lecture given by the exact same lecturer. Following the lecture, subjects rated the lecturer.

The outcomes are stored in the file “teacher.csv”. The file can be found on the internet at http://pluto.huji.ac.il/~msby/StatThink/Datasets/teacher.csv. Download this file to your computer and store it in the working directory of R. Read the content of the file into an R data frame. Produce a summary of the content of the data frame and answer the following questions:

1. Identify, for each variable in the file “teacher.csv”, the name and the type of the variable (factor or numeric).
2. Estimate the expectation and the standard deviation among all students of the rating of the teacher.
3. Estimate the expectation and the standard deviation of the rating only for students who were given a summary that describes the teacher as charismatic.
4. Construct a confidence interval of 99% confidence level for the expectation of the rating among students who were given a summary that describes the teacher as charismatic. (Assume the ratings have a Normal distribution.)
5. Construct a confidence interval of 90% confidence level for the variance of the rating among students who were given a summary that describes the teacher as charismatic. (Assume the ratings have a Normal distribution.)

Exercise 11.2 Twenty observations are used in order to construct a confidence interval for the expectation. In one case, the construction is based on the Normal approximation of the sample average and in the other case it is constructed under the assumption that the observations are Normally distributed. Assume that in reality the measurement is distributed Exponential(1/4).

1. Compute, via simulation, the actual confidence level for the first case of a confidence interval with a nominal confidence level of 95%.
2. Compute, via simulation, the actual confidence level for the second case of a confidence interval with a nominal confidence level of 95%.
3. Which of the two approaches would you prefer?

Exercise 11.3 Insurance companies are interested in knowing the population percent of drivers who always buckle up before riding in a car.

1. When designing a study to determine this proportion, what is the minimal sample size that is required for a 99% confident that the population proportion is accurately estimated, up to an error of 0.03?
2. Suppose that the insurance companies did conduct the study by surveying 400 drivers. They found that 320 of the drives claim to always buckle up. Produce an 80% confidence interval for the population proportion of drivers who claim to always buckle up.

12 Chapter — TESTING HYPOTHESIS

12.1 INTRODUCTION: AN OVERVIEW

Hypothesis testing plays a vital role in decision making when there is a requirement to choose between two conflicting choices. Statistical hypothesis testing offers explicit criteria for making such a choice. This chapter focuses on the development of statistical hypothesis testing and explains the corresponding decision criteria. More precisely, we examine hypothesis testing in relation to the anticipated value of a measurement and the likelihood of an occurrence. In the next chapters, we address the process of hypothesis testing within the framework of several parameters.

12.2 THE THEORY OF HYPOTHESIS TESTING

Statistical inference is employed to identify and describe significant occurrences that may be obscured in a setting affected by random noise. Hypothesis testing is a crucial initial stage in the process of drawing conclusions. During this stage, one endeavors to determine whether a phenomenon exists or not. The fundamental strategy is to ascertain whether the observed data can be plausibly accounted for by a model of randomness that does not incorporate the phenomena. This section provides an overview of the framework and properties of statistical hypothesis testing. We begin by using a statistical test in a casual manner and then move on to providing formal definitions. In the following part, we will provide a more comprehensive analysis of hypothesis testing for both the expected value of a measurement and the likelihood of an event. Additional illustrations are examined in following chapters.

12.2.1 An Example of Hypothesis Testing

The variable "price" in the file "cars.csv" contains data on the prices of different types of cars that were sold in the United States during 1985. The average price of a car back then — the average of the variable "price" — was $13,207. One may be interested in the question: Do Americans pay today for cars a different price than what they used to pay in the 80's? Has the price of cars changed significantly since 1985?

The average price of a car in the United States in 2009 was $27,958. Clearly, this figure is higher than $13,207. However, in order to produce a fair answer to the question we have to take into account that, due to inflation, the prices of all products went up during these years. A more meaningful comparison will involve the current prices of cars in terms of 1985 Dollars. Indeed, if we take into account inflation then we get that, on the average, the cost of today's cars corresponds to an average price of $13,662 in 1985 values. This price is still higher than the prices in the 1985 but not as much. The question we are asking is: "Is the difference between $13,207 and $13,662 significant or is it not so?".

In order to give a statistical answer to this question we carry out a statistical test. The specific test is conducted with the aid of the function "t.test". Later we will discuss in more details some of the arguments that may be used in this function. Currently, we simply apply it to the data stored in the variable "price" to test that the expected price is different than the $13,662, the average price of a car in 2009, adjusted for inflation:

```
cars <- read.csv("_data/cars.csv")
t.test(cars$price,mu=13662)


##
##  One Sample t-test
##
## data:  cars$price
## t = -0.81148, df = 200, p-value = 0.4181
## alternative hypothesis: true mean is not equal to 13662
## 95 percent confidence interval:
##  12101.80 14312.46
## sample estimates:
## mean of x
##  13207.13
```

The data in the file "cars.csv" is read into a data frame that is given the name "cars". Afterwards, the data on prices of car types in 1985 is entered as the first argument to the function "t.test". The other argument is the expected value that we want to test, the current average price of cars, given in terms of 1985 Dollar value. The output of the function is reported under the title: "One Sample t-test".

Let us read the report from the bottom up. The bottom part of the report describes the confidence interval and the point estimate of the expected price of a car in 1985, based on the given data. Indeed, the last line reports the sample average of the price, which is equal to 13,207.13. This number, the average of the 201 non-missing values of the variable "price", serves as the estimate of the expected price of a car in 1985. The 95% confidence interval of the expectation, the interval 12101.80, 14312.46, is presented on the 4th line from the bottom. This is the confidence interval for the expectation that was computed in Subsection 11.2.2.

The information relevant to conducting the statistical test itself is given in the upper part of the report. Specifically, it is reported that the data in "cars$price" is used in order to carry out the test. Based on this data a test statistic is computed and obtains the value of "t = -0.8115". This statistic is associated with the t-distribution with "df = 200" degrees of freedom. The last quantity that is being reported is denoted the *p-value* and it obtains the value "p-value = 0.4181". The test may be carried out with the aid of the value of the t statistic or, more directly, using the p-value. Currently we will use the p-value.

The test itself examines the hypothesis that the expected price of a car in 1985 was equal to $13,662, the average price of a car in 2009, given in 1985 values. This hypothesis is called the null hypothesis. The alternative hypothesis is that the expected price of a car in 1985 was not equal to that figure. The specification of the alternative hypothesis is reported on the third line of the output of the function "t.test".

One may decide between the two hypothesis on the basis of the size of the p-value . The rule of thumb is to reject the null hypothesis, and thus accept the alternative hypothesis, if the p-value is less than 0.05. In the current example the p-value is equal 0.4181 and is larger than 0.05. Consequently, we may conclude that the expected price of a car in 1985 was not significantly different than the current price of a car.

In the rest of this section we give a more rigorous explanation of the theory and practice of statistical hypothesis testing.

12.2.2 The Structure of a Statistical Test of Hypotheses

The initial step in statistical inference in general, and in statistical hypothesis testing in particular, is the formulation of the statistical model and the identification of the parameter/s that should be investigated. In the current situation the statistical model may correspond to the assumption that the data in the variable "price" are an instance of a *random* sample (of size n=201). The parameter that we want to investigate is the expectation of the measurement that produced the sample. The variance of the measurement is also relevant for the investigation.

After the statistical model has been set, one may split the process of testing a statistical hypothesis into three steps: (i) formulation of the hypotheses, (ii) specification of the test, and (iii) reaching the final conclusion. The first two steps are carried out on the basis of the probabilistic characteristics of the statistical model and in the context of the sampling distribution. In principal, the first two steps may be conducted in the planning stage prior to the collection of the observations. Only the third step involves the actual data. In the example that was considered in the previous subsection the third step was applied to the data in the variable "price" using the function "t.test".

(i) Formulating the hypotheses: A statistical model involves a parameter that is the target of the investigation. In principle, this parameter may obtain any value within a range of possible values. The formulation of the hypothesis corresponds to splitting the range of values into two sub-collections: a sub-collection that emerges in response to the presence of the phenomena and a sub-collection that emerges in response to the situation when the phenomena is absent. The sub-collection of parameter values where the phenomena is absent is called the *null hypothesis* and is marked as "H0H_0". The other sub-collection, the one reflecting the presence of the phenomena, is denoted the *alternative hypothesis* and is marked "H_1".

For example, consider the price of cars. Assume that the phenomena one wishes to investigate is the change in the relative price of a car in the 80's as compared to prices today. The parameter of interest is the expected price of cars back then, which we denote by $E(X)$. The formulation of the statement that the expected price of cars has changed is "$E(X)\neq 13{,}662$". This statement corresponds to the *presence* of a phenomena, to a change, and is customarily defined as the alternative hypothesis. On the other hand, the situation "$E(X)=13{,}662$" corresponds to not having any change in the price of cars. Hence, this situation corresponds to the *absence* of the phenomena and is denoted the null hypothesis. In summary, in order to investigate the change in the relative price of cars we my consider the null hypothesis "$H_0:E(X)=13{,}662$" and test it against the alternative hypothesis "$H_1: E(X)\neq 13{,}662$".

A variation in the formulation of the phenomena can change the definition of the null and alternative hypotheses. For example, if the intention is to investigate the *rise* in the price of cars then the phenomena will correspond to the expected price in 1985 being less than $13,662. Accordingly, the alternative hypothesis should be defined as $H_1: E(X)<13{,}662$, with the null hypothesis defined as $H_0:E(X)\geq 13{,}662$. Observe that in this case an expected price larger than $13,662 relates to the phenomena of rising (relative) prices *not* taking place.

On the other hand, if one would wants to investigate a *decrease* in the price then one should define the alternative hypothesis to be $H_1:E(X)>13{,}662$, with the null hypothesis being $H_0: E(X)\leq 13{,}662$.

The type of alternative that was considered in the example, $H_1:(X)\neq 13{,}622$ is called a *two-sided* alternative. The other two types of alternative hypotheses that were considered thereafter, $H_1:E(X)<13{,}662$ and $H_1:E(X)>13{,}662$, are both called *one-*

sided alternatives.

In summary, the formulation of the hypothesis is a reflection of the phenomena one wishes to examine. The setting associated with the presence of the phenomena is denoted the alternative hypothesis and the complimentary setting, the setting where the phenomena is absent, is denoted the null hypothesis.

(ii) Specifying the test: The second step in hypothesis testing involves the selection of the decision rule, i.e. the statistical test, to be used in order to decide between the two hypotheses. The decision rule is composed of a statistic and a subset of values of the statistic that correspond to the rejection of the null hypothesis. The statistic is called the *test statistic* and the subset of values is called the *rejection region*. The decision is to reject the null hypothesis (and consequently choose the alternative hypothesis) if the test statistic falls in the rejection region. Otherwise, if the test statistic does not fall in the rejection region then the null hypothesis is selected.

Return to the example in which we test between H_0:E (X)=13,662 and H_1: E(X)≠13,662. One may compute the statistic:

$$T = \frac{\bar{X} - 13,662}{S/\sqrt{n}} \,,$$

where $\bar{X}$ is the sample average (of the variable "price"), S is the sample standard deviation, and n is the sample size (n=201 in the current example).

The sample average $\bar{X}$ is an estimator of a expected price of the car. In principle, the statistic T measures the discrepancy between the estimated value of the expectation ($\bar{X}$) and the expected value under the null hypothesis (E(X)=13,662). This discrepancy is measured in units of the (estimated) standard deviation of the sample average.

If the null hypothesis H_0:E(X)=13,662 is true then the sampling distribution of the sample average $\bar{X}$ should be concentrated about the value 13,662. Values of the sample average much larger or much smaller than this value may serve as evidence against the null hypothesis.

In reflection, if the null hypothesis holds true then the values of the sampling distribution of the statistic T should tend to be in the vicinity of 0. Values with a relative small absolute value are consistent with the null hypothesis. On the other hand, extremely positive or extremely negative values of the statistic indicate that the null hypothesis is probably false.

It is natural to set a value c and to reject the null hypothesis whenever the absolute value of the statistic T is larger than c. The resulting rejection region is of the form $\{|T|>c\}$. The rule of thumb, again, is to take threshold c to be equal the

0.975-percentile of the t-distribution on n-1 degrees of freedom, where n is the sample size. In the current example, the sample size is n=201 and the percentile of the t-distribution is qt(0.975,200) = 1.971896. Consequently, the subset $\{|T|>1.971896\}$ is the rejection region of the test.

A change in the hypotheses that are being tested may lead to a change in the test statistic and/or the rejection region. For example, for testing H_0:E $(X)\geq 13{,}662$ versus H_1:E $(X)<13{,}662$ one may still use the same test statistic T as before. However, only very negative values of the statistic are inconsistent with the null hypothesis. It turns out that the rejection region in this case is of the form $\{T<-1.652508\}$, where qt(0.05,200) = -1.652508 is the 0.05-percentile of the t-distribution on 200 degrees of freedom. On the other hand, the rejection region for testing between H_0: E $(X)\leq 13{,}662$ and H_1: E $(X)>13{,}662$ is $\{T>1.652508\}$. In this case, qt(0.95,200) = 1.652508 is the 0.95-percentile of the t-distribution on 200 degrees of freedom.

Selecting the test statistic and deciding what rejection region to use specifies the statistical test and completes the second step.

(iii) Reaching a conclusion: After the stage is set, all that is left is to apply the test to the observed data. This is done by computing the observed value of the test statistic and checking whether or not the observed value belongs to the rejection region. If it does belong to the rejection region then the decision is to reject the null hypothesis. Otherwise, if the statistic does not belong to the rejection region, then the decision is to accept the null hypothesis.

Return to the example of testing the price of car types. The observed value of the T statistic is part of the output of the application of the function "t.test" to the data. The value is "t = -0.8115". As an exercise, let us recompute directly from the data the value of the T statistic:

```
x.bar <- mean(cars$price,na.rm=TRUE)
x.bar

## [1] 13207.13

s <- sd(cars$price,na.rm=TRUE)
```

The observed value of the sample average is $\bar{x} = 13207.13$ and the observed value of the sample standard deviation is s=7947.066. The sample size (due to having 4 missing values) is n=201. The formula for the computation of the test statistic in this example is $t = [\bar{x} - 13,662]/[s/\sqrt{n}]$. Plugging in this formula the sample size and the computed values of the sample average and standard deviation produces:

```
(x.bar - 13662)/(s/sqrt(201))
```

```
## [1] -0.8114824
```

This value, after rounding up, is equal to the value "t = -0.8115" that is reported in the output of the function "t.test".

The critical threshold for the absolute value of the T statistic on 201−1=200 degrees of freedom is qt(0.975,200) = 1.971896. Since the absolute observed value ($|t|$=0.8114824) is less then the threshold we get that the value of the statistic does not belong to the rejection region (which is composed of absolute values larger than the threshold). Consequently, we accept the null hypothesis. This null hypothesis declares that the expected price of a car was equal to the current expected price (after adjusting for the change in Consumer Price Index).

12.2.3 Error Types and Error Probabilities

The TT statistic was proposed for testing a change in the price of a car. This statistic measures the discrepancy between the sample average price of a car and the expected value of the sample average, where the expectation is computed under the null hypothesis. The structure of the rejection region of the test is $\{|T|>c\}$, where cc is an appropriate threshold. In the current example the value of the threshold cc was set to be equal to qt(0.975,200) = 1.971896. In general, the specification of the threshold cc depends on the error probabilities that are associated with the test. In this section we describe these error probabilities.

The process of making decisions may involve errors. In the case of hypothesis testing one may specify two types of error. On the one hand, the case may be that the null hypothesis is correct (in the example, E(X)=13,662). However, the data is such that the null hypothesis is rejected (here, $|T|$>1.971896). This error is called a *Type I* error.

A different type of error occurs when the alternative hypothesis holds (E(X)≠13,662) but the null hypothesis is not rejected ($|T|$≤1.971896). This other type of error is called *Type II* error. A summary of the types of errors can be found in Table 12.1:

Table 12.1: Error

	H_0:E(X)=13,662	H_1:E(X)≠13,662
Accept H_0: $|T|$≤1.971896		Type II Error
Reject H_0: $|T|$>1.971896	Type I Error	

In statistical testing of hypothesis the two types of error are not treated symmetrically. Rather, making a Type I error is considered more severe than making a Type II error. Consequently, the test's decision rule is designed so as to assure an acceptable probability of making a Type I error. Reducing the probability of a Type II error is desirable, but is of secondary importance.

Indeed, in the example that deals with the price of car types the threshold was set as high as qt(0.975,200) = 1.971896 in order to reject the null hypothesis. It is not sufficient that the sample average is not equal to 13,662 (corresponding to a threshold of 0), but it has to be significantly different from the expectation under the null hypothesis, the distance between the sample average and the null expectation should be relatively large, in order to exclude H_0 as an option.

The significance level of the evidence for rejecting the null hypothesis is based on the probability of the Type I error. The probabilities associated with the different types of error are presented in Table 12.2:

Table 12.2: Error Probabilities

	H_0:E(X)=13,662	H_1: E(X)≠13,662
P(|T|≤c)		Prob. of Type II Error
P(|T|>c)	Significance Level	Statistical Power

Observe that the probability of a Type I error is called the significance level. The significance level is set at some pre-specified level such as 5% or 1%, with 5% being the most widely used level. In particular, setting the threshold in the example to be equal to qt(0.975,200) = 1.971896 produces a test with a 5% significance level.

This lack of symmetry between the two hypothesis proposes another interpretation of the difference between the hypothesis. According to this interpretation the null hypothesis is the one in which the cost of making an error is greater. Thus, when one separates the collection of parameter values into two subsets then the subset that is associated with a more severe error is designated as the null hypothesis and the other subset becomes the alternative.

For example, a new drug must pass a sequence of clinical trials before it is approved for distribution. In these trials one may want to test whether the new drug produces beneficial effect in comparison to the current treatment. Naturally, the null hypothesis in this case would be that the new drug is no better than the current treatment and the alternative hypothesis would be that it is better. Only if the clinical trials demonstrates a significant beneficiary effect of the new drug would it be released for marketing.

In scientific research, in general, the currently accepted theory, the conservative explanation, is designated as the null hypothesis. A claim for novelty in the form of an alternative explanation requires strong evidence in order for it to be accepted and be favored over the traditional explanation. Hence, the novel explanation is designated as the alternative hypothesis. It replaces the current theory only if the empirical data clearly supports its. The test statistic is a summary of the empirical data. The rejection region corresponds to values that are unlikely to be observed according to the current theory. Obtaining a value in the rejection region is an indication that the current theory is probably not adequate and should be replaced by an explanation that is more consistent with the empirical evidence.

The second type of error probability in Table tab: *tab:Testing_2* is the probability of a Type II error. Instead of dealing directly with this probability the tradition is to consider the complementary probability that corresponds to the probability of *not* making a Type II error. This complementary probability is called the *statistical power*:

Statistical Power=1-Probability of Type II Error

The statistical power is the probability of rejecting the null hypothesis when the state of nature is the alternative hypothesis. (In comparison, the significance level is the probability of rejecting the null hypothesis when the state of nature is the null hypothesis.) When comparing two decision rules for testing hypothesis, both having the same significance level, the one that possesses a higher statistical power should be favored.

12.2.4 p-Values

The p-value is another test statistic. It is associated with a specific test statistic and a structure of the rejection region. The p-value is equal to the significance level of the test in which the observed value of the statistic serves as the threshold. In the current example, where the T is the underlying test statistic and the structure of the rejection region is of the form $\{|T|>c\}$ then the p-value is equal to the probability of rejecting the null hypothesis in the case where the threshold cc is equal to the observed absolute value of the T statistic. In other words:

$$p\text{-value} = \mathbf{P}(|T| > |t|) = \mathbf{P}(|T| > |-0.8114824|) = \mathbf{P}(|T| > 0.8114824)\,,$$

where t=-0.8114824 is the observed value of the T statistic and the computation of the probability is conducted under the null hypothesis.

Specifically, under the null hypothesis H_0: E(X)=13,662 we get that the distribution of the statistic $T = [\bar{X} - 13,662]/[S/\sqrt{n}]$ is the t-distribution on n-1=200 degrees of freedom. The probability of the event $\{|T|>0.8114824\}$ corresponds to the sum of the probabilities of both tails of the distribution. By the symmetry of the t-distribution this equals twice the probability of the upper tail:

$$P(|T| > 0.8114824) = 2 \cdot P(T > 0.8114824) = 2 \cdot [1 - P(|T| \leq 0.8114824)] .$$

When we compute this probability in R we get:

```
2*(1-pt(0.8114824,200))

## [1] 0.4180534
```

This probability is equal, after rounding up, to the probability "p-value = 0.4181" that is reported in the output of the function "t.test".

The *p*-value is a function of the data. In the particular data set the computed value of the *T* statistic was -0.8114824. For a different data set the evaluation of the statistic would have produced a different value. As a result, the threshold that would have been used in the computation would have been different, thereby changing the numerical value of the *p*-value. Being a function of the data, we conclude that the *p*-value is a statistic.

The *p*-value is used as a test statistic by comparing its value to the pre-defined significance level. If the significance level is 1% then the null hypothesis is rejected for *p*-values less that 0.01. Likewise, if the significance level is set at the 5% level then the null hypothesis is rejected for *p*-values less than 0.05.

The statistical test that is based directly on the *T* statistic and the statistical test that is based on the *p*-value are equivalent to each other. The one rejects the null hypothesis if, and only if, the other does so. The advantage of using the *p*-value as the test statistic is that no further probabilistic computations are required. The *p*-value is compared directly to the significance level we seek. For the test that examines the *T* statistic we still need to identify the threshold associated with the given significance level.

In the next 2 sections we extend the discussion of the *t*-test and give further examples to the use of the function "t.test". We also deal with tests on probabilities of events and introduce the function "prop.test" for conducting such tests.

12.3 TESTING HYPOTHESIS ON EXPECTATION

Let us consider the variable "dif.mpg" that contains the difference in fuel consumption between highway and city conditions. This variable was considered in Chapter 11. Examine the distribution of this variable:

```
dif.mpg <- cars$highway.mpg - cars$city.mpg
summary(dif.mpg)

##    Min. 1st Qu.  Median    Mean 3rd Qu.    Max.
##   0.000   5.000   6.000   5.532   7.000  11.000

plot(table(dif.mpg))
```

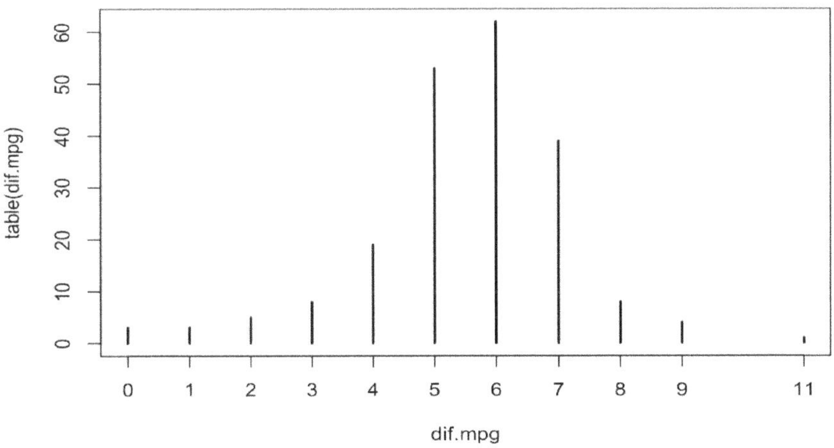

In the first expression we created the variable "dif.mpg" that contains the difference in miles-per-gallon. The difference is computed for each car type between highway driving conditions and urban driving condition. The summary of this variable is produced in the second expression. Observe that the values of the variable range between 0 and 11, with 50% of the distribution concentrated between 5 and 7. The median is 6 and the mean is 5.532. The last expression produces the bar plot of the distribution. It turns out that the variable "dif.mpg" obtains integer values.

In this section we test hypotheses regarding the expected difference in fuel consumption between highway and city conditions.

Energy is required in order to move cars. For heavier cars more energy is required. Consequently, one may conjecture that milage per gallon for heavier cars is less than the milage per gallon for lighter cars.

The relation between the weight of the car and the difference between the milage-per-gallon in highway and city driving conditions is less clear. On the one hand, urban traffic involves frequent changes in speed in comparison to highway conditions. One may presume that this change in speed is a cause for reduced efficiency in fuel consumption. If this is the case then one may predict that heavier cars, which require more energy for acceleration, will be associated with a bigger difference between highway and city driving conditions in comparison to lighter cars.

One the other hand, heavier cars do less miles per gallon overall. The difference between two smaller numbers (the milage per gallon in highway and in city conditions for heavier cars) may tend to be smaller than the difference between two larger numbers (the milage per gallon in highway and in city conditions for lighter cars). If this is the case then one may predict that heavier cars will be associated with a smaller difference between highway and city driving conditions in comparison to lighter cars.

The average difference between highway and city conditions is approximately 5.53 for all cars. Divide the cars into to two groups of equal size: One group is composed of the heavier cars and the other group is composed of the lighter cars. We will examine the relation between the weight of the car and difference in miles per gallon between the two driving conditions by testing hypotheses separately for each weight group. For each such group we start by testing the two-sided hypothesis H_1:E(X)≠5.53, where X is the difference between highway and city miles-per-gallon in cars that belong to the given weight group. After carrying the test for the two-sided alternative we will discuss results of the application of tests for one-sided alternatives.

We start by the definition of the weight groups. The variable "curb.weight" measures the weight of the cars in the data frame "cars". Let us examine the summary of the content of this variable:

```
summary(cars$curb.weight)
```

```
##    Min. 1st Qu.  Median    Mean 3rd Qu.    Max.
##    1488    2145    2414    2556    2935    4066
```

Half of the cars in the data frame weigh less than 2,414 lb and half the cars weigh more. The average weight of a car is 2,556 lb. Let us take 2,414 as a threshold and denote cars below this weight as "light" and cars above this threshold as "heavy":

```
heavy <- cars$curb.weight > 2414
table(heavy)
```

```
## heavy
## FALSE  TRUE
##   103   102
```

The variable "heavy" indicates for each car type whether its weight is above or below the threshold weight of 2,414 lb. The variable is composed of a sequence with as many components as the number of observations in the data frame "cars" (n=205). Each component is a logical value: "TRUE" if the car is heavier than the threshold and "FALSE" if it is not. When we apply the function "table" to this sequence we get that 102 of the cars are heavier than the threshold and 103 are not so.

We would like to apply the t-test first to the subset of all cars with weight above 2,414 lb (cars that are associated with the value "TRUE" in the variable "heavy"), and then to all cars with weights not exceeding the threshold (cars associated with value "FALSE"). In the past we showed that one may address components of a sequence using its position in the sequence[57]. Here we demonstrate an alternative approach for addressing specific locations by using a sequence with logical components.

In order to illustrate this second approach consider the two sequences:

```
w <- c(5,3,4,6,2,9)
d <- c(13,22,0,12,6,20)
```

Say we want to select the components of the sequence "d" in all the locations where the components of the sequence "w" obtain values larger than 5. Consider the code:

```
w > 5

## [1] FALSE FALSE FALSE  TRUE FALSE  TRUE

d[w > 5]

## [1] 12 20
```

The expression "w > 5" is a sequence of logical components, with the value "TRUE" at the positions where "w" is above the threshold and the value "FALSE" at the positions where "w" is below the threshold. We may use the sequence with logical components as an index to the sequence of the same length "d". The relevant expression is "d[w > 5]". The output of this expression is the sub-sequence of elements from "d" that are associated with the "TRUE" values of the logical sequence. Indeed, "TRUE" values are present at the 4th and the 6th positions of the logical sequence. Consequently, the output of the expression "d[w > 5]" contains the 4th and the 6th components of the sequence "d".

The operator "!", when applied to a logical value, reverses the value. A "TRUE" becomes "FALSE" and a "FALSE" becomes "TRUE". Consider the code:

```
!(w > 5)

## [1]  TRUE  TRUE  TRUE FALSE  TRUE FALSE

d[!(w > 5)]
```

Observe that the sequence "!(w > 5)" obtains a value of "TRUE" at the positions where "w" is less or equal to 5. Consequently, the output of the expression "d[!(w > 5)]" are all the values of "d" that are associated with components of "w" that are less or equal to 5.

The variable "dif.mpg" contains data on the difference in miles-per-gallon between highway and city driving conditions for all the car types. The sequence "heavy" identifies the car types with curb weight above the threshold of 2,414 lb. The components of this sequence are logical with the value "TRUE" at positions associated with the heavier car types and the "FALSE" at positions associated with the lighter car types. Observe that the output of the expression "dif.mpg[heavy]" is the subsequence of differences in miles-per-gallon for the cars with curb weight above the given threshold. We apply the function "t.test" to this expression in order to conduct the *t*-test on the expectation of the variable "dif.mpg" for the heavier cars:

```
t.test(dif.mpg[heavy],mu=5.53)
```

```
##
##  One Sample t-test
##
## data:  dif.mpg[heavy]
## t = -1.5385, df = 101, p-value = 0.127
## alternative hypothesis: true mean is not equal to 5.53
## 95 percent confidence interval:
##  4.900198 5.609606
## sample estimates:
## mean of x
##  5.254902
```

The target population are the heavier car types. Notice that we test the null hypothesis that expected difference among he heavier cars is equal to 5.53 against the alternative hypothesis that the expected difference among heavier cars is not equal to 5.53. The null hypothesis is not rejected at the 5% significance level since the *p*-value , which is equal to 0.1735, is larger than 0.05. Consequently, based on the data at hand, we cannot conclude that the expected difference in miles-per-gallon for heavier cars is significantly different than the average difference for all cars.

Observe also that the estimate of the expectation, the sample mean, is equal to 5.254902, with a confidence interval of the form [4.900198,5.609606].

Next, let us apply the same test to the lighter cars. The expression "dif. pmg[!heavy]" produces the subsequence of differences in miles-per-gallon for the cars with curb weight below the given threshold. The application of the function "t.test" to this subsequence gives:

```
t.test(dif.mpg[!heavy],mu=5.53)

##
##  One Sample t-test
##
## data:  dif.mpg[!heavy]
## t = 1.9692, df = 102, p-value = 0.05164
## alternative hypothesis: true mean is not equal to 5.53
## 95 percent confidence interval:
##  5.528002 6.083649
## sample estimates:
## mean of x
##  5.805825
```

Again, the null hypothesis is not rejected at the 5% significance level since a p-value of 0.05164 is still larger than 0.05. However, unlike the case for heavier cars where the p-value was undeniably larger than the threshold. In this example it is much closer to the threshold of 0.05. Consequently, we may almost conclude that the expected difference in miles-per-gallon for lighter cars is significantly different than the average difference for all car.

Why did we not reject the null hypothesis for the heavier cars but almost did so for the lighter cars? Both tests are based on the T statistic, which measures the ratio between the deviation of the sample average from its expectation under the null, divided by the estimate of the standard deviation of the sample average. The value of this statistic is "t = -1.5385" for heavier cars and it is "t = 1.9692" for lighter cars, an absolute value of about 25% higher.

The deviation of the sample average for the heavier cars and the expectation under the null is 5.254902-5.53=-0.275098. On the other hand, the deviation of the sample average for the lighter cars and the expectation under the null is 5.805825-5.53=0.275825. The two deviations are practically equal to each other in the absolute value.

The estimator of the standard deviation of the sample average is $S/\sqrt{n}$, where SS is the sample standard deviation and nn is the sample size. The sample sizes, 103 for lighter cars and 102 for heavier cars, are almost equal. Therefore, the reason for the difference in the values of the T statistics for both weight groups must be differences in the sample standard deviations. Indeed, when we compute the sample standard deviation for lighter and heavier cars we get that the standard deviation for lighter cars (1.421531) is much smaller than the standard deviation for heavier cars (1.805856):

```
tapply(dif.mpg,heavy,sd)
```

```
##    FALSE     TRUE
## 1.421531 1.805856
```

The important lesson to learn from this exercise is that simple minded notion of significance and statistical significance are not the same. A simple minded assessment of the discrepancy from the null hypothesis will put the evidence from the data on lighter cars and the evidence from the data on heavier cars on the same level. In both cases the estimated value of the expectation is the same distance away from the null value.

However, statistical assessment conducts the analysis in the context of the sampling distribution. The deviation of the sample average from the expectation is compared to the standard deviation of the sample average. Consequently, in statistical testing of hypothesis a smaller deviation of the sample average from the expectation under the null may be more significant than a larger one if the sampling variability of the former is much smaller than the sampling variability of the later.

Let us proceed with the demonstration of the application of the *t*-test by the testing of one-sided alternatives in the context of the lighter cars. One may test the one-sided alternative H_1: E(X)>5.53 that the expected value of the difference in miles-per-gallon among cars with curb weight no more than 2,414 lb is *greater* than 5.53 by the application of the function "t.test" to the data on lighter cars. This data is the output of the expression "dif.mpg[!heavy]". As before, we specify the null value of the expectation by the introduction of the expression "mu=5.53". The fact that we are interested in the testing of the specific alternative is specified by the introduction of a new argument of the form: "alternative=greater". The default value of the argument "alternative" is "two.sided", which produces a test of a two-sided alternative. By changing the value of the argument to "greater" we produce a test for the appropriate one-sided alternative:

```
t.test(dif.mpg[!heavy],mu=5.53,alternative="greater")
```

```
##
##  One Sample t-test
##
## data:  dif.mpg[!heavy]
```

```
## t = 1.9692, df = 102, p-value = 0.02582
## alternative hypothesis: true mean is greater than 5.53
## 95 percent confidence interval:
##  5.573323       Inf
## sample estimates:
## mean of x
##  5.805825
```

The value of the test statistic (t = 1.9692) is the same as for the test of the two-sided alternative and so is the number of degrees of freedom associated with the statistic (df = 102). However, the p-value is smaller (p-value = 0.02582), compared to the p-value in the test for the two-sided alternative (p-value = 0.05164). The p-value for the one-sided test is the probability under the sampling distribution that the test statistic obtains vales larger than the observed value of 1.9692. The p-value for the two-sided test is twice that figure since it involves also the probability of being less than the negative of the observes value.

The estimated value of the expectation, the sample average, is unchanged. However, instead of producing a confidence interval for the expectation the report produces a *one-sided* confidence interval of the form $[5.573323,\infty)$. Such an interval corresponds to the *smallest* value that the expectation may reasonably obtain on the basis of the observed data.

Finally, consider the test of the other one-sided alternative H_1: E(X)<5.53:

```
t.test(dif.mpg[!heavy],mu=5.53,alternative="less")
```

```
##
##  One Sample t-test
##
## data:  dif.mpg[!heavy]
## t = 1.9692, df = 102, p-value = 0.9742
## alternative hypothesis: true mean is less than 5.53
## 95 percent confidence interval:
##      -Inf 6.038328
## sample estimates:
## mean of x
##  5.805825
```

The alternative here is determined by the expression "alternative=less". The p-value is equal to 0.9742, which is the probability that the test statistic obtains values less than the observed value of 1.9692. Clearly, the null hypothesis is not rejected in this test.

12.4 TESTING HYPOTHESIS ON PROPORTION

Consider the problem of testing hypothesis on the probability of an event. Recall that a probability p of some event can be estimated by the observed relative frequency of the event in the sample, denoted $\hat{P}$. The estimation is associated with the Bernoulli random variable X, that obtains the value 1 when the event occurs and the value 0 when it does not. The statistical model states that p is the expectation of X. The estimator $\hat{P}$ is the sample average of this measurement.

With this formulation we may relate the problem of testing hypotheses formulated in terms of p to the problem of tests associated to the expectation of a measurement. For the latter problem we applied the t-test. A similar, though not identical, test is used for the problem of testing hypothesis on proportions.

Assume that one in interested in testing the null hypothesis that the probability of the event is equal to some specific value, say one half, versus the alternative hypothesis that the probability is not equal to this value. These hypotheses are formulated as $H_0{:}p=0.5$ and $H_1{:}p\neq0.5$.

The sample proportion of the event ^PP^ is the basis for the construction of the test statistic. Recall that the variance of the estimator $\hat{P}$ is given by V $(\hat{P})$ =p(1-p)/n. Under the null hypothesis we get that the variance is equal to V$(\hat{P})$ =0.5(1−0.5)/n. A natural test statistic is the standardized sample proportion:

$$Z = \frac{\hat{P} - 0.5}{\sqrt{0.5(1 - 0.5)/n}},$$

that measures the ratio between the deviation of the estimator from its null expected value and the standard deviation of the estimator. The standard deviation of the sample proportion is used in the ratio.

If the null hypothesis that p=0.5 holds true then one gets that the value 0 is the center of the sampling distribution of the test statistic Z. Values of the statistic that are much larger or much smaller than 0 indicate that the null hypothesis is unlikely. Consequently, one may consider a rejection region of the form $\{|Z|>c\}$, for some threshold value c. The threshold cc is set at a high enough level to assure the required significance level, namely the probability under the null hypothesis of obtaining a value in the rejection region. Equivalently, the rejection region can be written in the form $\{Z^2>c^2\}$.

As a result of the Central Limit Theorem one may conclude that the distribution of the test statistic is approximately Normal. Hence, Normal computations may be used in order to produce an approximate threshold or in order to compute an approximation for the p-value. Specifically, if Z has the standard Normal distribution then Z^2 has a chi-square distribution on one degree of freedom.

In order to illustrate the application of hypothesis testing for proportion consider the following problem: In the previous section we obtained the curb weight of 2,414 lb as the sample median. The weights of half the cars in the sample were above that level and the weights of half the cars were below this level. If this level was actually the population median then the probability that the weight of a random car is not exceeding this level would be equal to 0.5.

Let us test the hypothesis that the median weight of cars that run on diesel is also 2,414 lb. Recall that 20 out of the 205 car types in the sample have diesel engines. Let us use the weights of these cars in order to test the hypothesis.

The variable "fuel.type" is a factor with two levels "diesel" and "gas" that identify the fuel type of each car. The variable "heavy" identifies for each car whether its weight is above the level of 2414 or not. Let us produce a 2×2 table that summarizes the frequency of each combination of weight group and the fuel type:

```
fuel <- cars$fuel.type
table(fuel,heavy)
```

```
##           heavy
## fuel      FALSE TRUE
##   diesel      6   14
##   gas        97   88
```

Originally the function "table" was applied to a single factor and produced a sequence with the frequencies of each level of the factor. In the current application the input to the function are two factors. The output is a table of frequencies. Each entry to the table corresponds to the frequency of a combination of levels, one from the first input factor and the other from the second input factor. In this example we obtain that 6 cars use diesel and their curb weight was below the threshold. There are 14 cars that use diesel and their curb weight is above the threshold. Likewise, there are 97 light cars that use gas and 88 heavy cars with gas engines.

The function "prop.test" produces statistical tests for proportions. The relevant information for the current application of the function is the fact that frequency of light diesel cars is 6 among a total number of 20 diesel cars. The first entry to the function is the frequency of the occurrence of the event, 6 in this case, and the second entry is the relevant sample size, the total number of diesel cars which is 20 in the current example:

```
prop.test(6,20)

##
##  1-sample proportions test with continuity correction
##
## data:  6 out of 20, null probability 0.5
## X-squared = 2.45, df = 1, p-value = 0.1175
## alternative hypothesis: true p is not equal to 0.5
## 95 percent confidence interval:
##  0.1283909 0.5433071
## sample estimates:
##   p
## 0.3
```

The function produces a report that is printed on the screen. The title identifies the test as a one-sample test of proportions. In later chapters we will apply the same function to more complex data structures and the title will change accordingly. The title also identifies the fact that a continuity correction is used in the computation of the test statistic.

The line under the title indicates the frequency of the event in the sample and the sample size. (In the current example, 6 diesel cars with weights below the threshold among a total of 20 diesel cars.) The probability of the event, under the null hypothesis, is described. The default value of this probability is "p = 0.5", which is the proper value in the current example. This default value can be modified by replacing the value 0.5 by the appropriate probability.

The next line presents the information relevant for the test itself. The test statistic, which is essentially the square of the ZZ statistic described above[60], obtains the value 2.45. The sampling distribution of this statistic under the null hypothesis is, approximately, the chi-square distribution on 1 degree of freedom. The p-value, which is the probability that chi-square distribution on 1 degree of freedom obtains a value above 2.45, is equal to 0.1175. Consequently, the null hypothesis is not rejected at the 5% significance level.

The bottom part of the report provides the confidence interval and the point estimate for the probability of the event. The confidence interval for the given data is [0.1283909,0.5433071] and the point estimate is $\hat{p} = 6/20 = 0.3$.

It is interesting to note that although the deviation between the estimated proportion ^p=0.3p^=0.3 and the null value of the probability p=0.5p=0.5 is relatively large still the null hypothesis was not rejected. The reason for that is the smallness of the sample, n=20n=20, that was used in order to test the hypothesis. Indeed, as an exercise let us examine the application of the same test to a setting where n=200n=200 and the number of occurrences of the event is 60:

```
prop.test(60,200)

##
##  1-sample proportions test with continuity correction
##
## data:  60 out of 200, null probability 0.5
## X-squared = 31.205, df = 1, p-value = 2.322e-08
## alternative hypothesis: true p is not equal to 0.5
## 95 percent confidence interval:
##  0.2384423 0.3693892
## sample estimates:
##   p
## 0.3
```

The estimated value of the probability is the same as before since $\hat{p} = 60/200$ =0.3. However, the *p*-value is 2.322×10-8, which is way below the significance threshold of 0.05. In this scenario the null hypothesis is rejected with flying colors.

This last example is yet another demonstration of the basic characteristic of statistical hypothesis testing. The consideration is based not on the discrepancy of the estimator of the parameter from the value of the parameter under the null. Instead, it is based on the *relative* discrepancy in comparison to the sampling variability of the estimator. When the sample size is larger the variability is smaller. Hence, the chances of rejecting the null hypothesis for the same discrepancy increases.

12.5 EXERCISES

Exercise 12.1 Consider a medical condition that does not have a standard treatment. The recommended design of a clinical trial for a new treatment to such condition involves using a placebo treatment as a control. A placebo treatment is a treatment that externally looks identical to the actual treatment but, in reality, it does not have the active ingredients. The reason for using placebo for control is the "placebo effect". Patients tent to react to the fact that they are being treated regardless of the actual beneficial effect of the treatment.

As an example, consider the trial for testing magnets as a treatment for pain that was described in Question $ex{:}Inference$.1. The patients that where randomly assigned to the control (the last 21 observations in the file "magnets.csv") were treated with devises that looked like magnets but actually were not. The goal in this exercise is to test for the presence of a placebo effect in the case study "Magnets and Pain Relief" of Question $ex{:}Inference$.1using the data in the file "magnets.csv".

1. Let X be the measurement of change, the difference between the score of pain before the treatment and the score after the treatment, for patients

that were treated with the inactive placebo. Express, in terms of the expected value of X, the null hypothesis and the alternative hypothesis for a statistical test to determine the presence of a placebo effect. The null hypothesis should reflect the situation that the placebo effect is absent.

2. Identify the observations that can be used in order to test the hypotheses.
3. Carry out the test and report your conclusion. (Use a significance level of 5%.)

Exercise 12.2 It is assumed, when constructing the t-test, that the measurements are Normally distributed. In this exercise we examine the robustness of the test to divergence from the assumption. You are required to compute the significance level of a two-sided t-test of H_0:E(X)=4 versus H_1: E(X)≠4. Assume there are n=20n=20 observations and use a t-test with a nominal 5% significance level.

1. Consider the case where $X \sim$Exponential(1/4).
2. Consider the case where $X \sim$Uniform(0,8).

Exercise 12.3 Assume that you are interested in testing H_0:E (X)=20 versus H_1: E (X)≠20 with a significance level of 5% using the t-test. Let the sample average, of a sample of size n=55, be equal to $\bar{x} = 22.7$ and the sample standard deviation be equal to s=5.4.

1. Do you reject the null hypothesis?
2. Use the same information. Only now you are interested in a significance level of 1%. Do you reject the null hypothesis?
3. Use the information the presentation of the exercise. But now you are interested in testing H_0:E(X)=24 versus H_1:E(X)≠24 (with a significance level of 5%). Do you reject the null hypothesis?

13 Chapter COMPARING TWO SAMPLES

13.1 INTRODUCTION: AN OVERVIEW

The following three chapters focus on the statistical inference pertaining to the relationship between two variables. The relation represents the impact of one variable on the distribution of the other. The variable under investigation, which is being examined for its distribution, is referred to as the response. The variable that can influence the distribution of the response is referred to as the explanatory variable. This section focuses on the scenario where the explanatory variable is a categorical variable with just two distinct levels. This factor divides the sample into two distinct sub-samples. Statistical inference involves comparing the distributions of the response variable in two sub-samples. Statistical inference encompasses point estimation, confidence intervals, and hypothesis testing. R functions can be utilized to do statistical inference.

13.2 COMPARING TWO DISTRIBUTIONS

So far in the book, we have been discussing methods to examine the properties of a single measurement's distribution. However, in most applications, the focus lies on making inferences about the correlations between several measurements. Specifically, it is important to comprehend how the result of one measurement influences the result of another measurement. An example of a prevalent mathematical relationship between two variables occurs when one variable is a dependent function of the other. When such a correlation exists, the value of the first variable is dictated by the value of the second. Nevertheless, inside the statistical framework, the interconnections between variables exhibit greater intricacy. Generally, a statistical relationship between variables does not imply that one variable is a direct effect of the other. Conversely, the value of one variable influences the distribution of values of another variable. The first variable may exhibit one distribution for a specific value of the second variable, but the distribution of the first variable may vary for a different value of the second variable. In statistical parlance, the second variable in this context is referred to as an explanatory variable, whereas the first variable, whose distribution is influenced by the second variable, is known as the response. To demonstrate the connection between the response and the explanatory variable, consider the following example. In a clinical trial, which is a prerequisite for the commercialization of a novel medical intervention, a cohort of patients is randomly allocated into a treatment group and a control group. The new treatment is provided to the treatment sub-group in an anonymous manner. Simultaneously, the patients in the control sub-group get the existing established treatment. The novel treatment undergoes a trial and is authorized for commercialization by the Health Authorities only if the response to the medical intervention is superior for the treatment sub-group compared to the control sub-group. The treatment-control experimental design, which involves measuring a response under two different experimental conditions, is commonly employed in various scientific and industrial contexts. In the context of a clinical trial, there are two variables that can be identified. A single variable quantifies the outcome of the medical intervention for every patient involved in the experiment. This variable is the dependent variable, the distribution of which one aims to examine. The second variable denotes the specific subgroup, either treatment or control, to which each patient is assigned. This variable serves as the independent variable. In a clinical trial, the explanatory variable is a factor that has two levels, namely "treatment" and "control". This variable divides the sample into two sub-samples. Statistical inference involves comparing the distribution of the response variable in the treatment sub-sample with the distribution of the response in the control sub-group. The analysis of experimental settings, such as a treatment-control trial, is a unique scenario that entails studying the impact of an explanatory variable on the response variable. In this particular instance, the explanatory variable is a categorical variable with two unique levels. Each level of the factor corresponds to a sub-sample, which can be either a treatment or a control group. The study aims to compare the distribution of the response in one subset with the distribution in the other subset. If the response is a numerical measurement, the analysis can involve comparing the expected value of the response in one subgroup to the expected value in the other subgroup. Alternatively, the analysis may entail the comparison of variances. In an alternative scenario, if the answer serves as an indicator of an event's happening, the analysis can compare two probabilities: the probability of the event occurring in the treatment group vs the probability of the identical event occurring in the control group. This chapter focuses on statistical inference, specifically the comparison of the distribution of a numerical response variable between two sub-groups defined by a factor. The inference involves the examination of hypotheses, specifically the null hypothesis that the distribution of the response is identical in both subgroups, as opposed to the alternative hypothesis that the distribution is different. Another component of the inference process involves determining point estimates and constructing confidence intervals for relevant parameters. In the following chapter, we will examine the scenario when the explanatory variable is numeric. In the upcoming chapter, we will explain the inference process utilized when the response variable indicates the existence of an event.

13.3 COMPARING THE SAMPLE MEANS

This section focuses on the topic of statistical inference when comparing the mean of the response variable in two different sub-samples. Inference is employed to examine questions regarding the equivalence of two expectations and, if they are not equivalent, to evaluate the disparity between them. To address the initial question, statistical hypothesis testing can be employed. To evaluate the situation, point estimates and/or confidence intervals can be utilized. The first subsection is an illustrative example of a hypothesis test to determine if the expectations are equivalent. The report generated by the R function that performs the test provides a confidence range for the difference between expectations. The second paragraph discusses the establishment of the confidence interval, while the third subsection explores the theoretical foundation of the statistical test.

13.3.1 An Example of a Comparison of Means

In order to illustrate the statistical inference that compars two expectations let us return to an example that was considered in Chapter 12. The response of interest is the difference in miles-per-gallon between driving in highway conditions and driving in city conditions. This response is produced as the difference between the variable "cars$highway.mpg" and the variable "cars$city.mpg". It is stored in the object "dif.mpg", which is a numerical sequence:

```
cars <- read.csv("_data/cars.csv")
dif.mpg <- cars$highway.mpg - cars$city.mpg
```

The object "heavy" was defined in the previous chapter as a sequence with logical components. A component had the value "TRUE" if the curb weight of the car type associated with this component was above the median level of 2,414 lb. The component obtained the value "FALSE" if the curb weight did not exceed that level. The logical sequence "heavy" was used in order to select the subsequences associated with each weight sub-group. Statistical inference was applied separately to each subsequence.

In the current analysis we want to examine directly the relation between the response variable "dif.mpg" and an explanatory factor variable "heavy". In order to do so we redefine the variable "heavy" to be a factor:

```
heavy <- factor(cars$curb.weight > 2414)
```

The variable "curb.weight" is numeric and the expression "cars$curb.weight > 2414" produces a sequence with logical "TRUE" or "FALSE" components. This sequence is not a factor. In order to produce a factor we apply the function "factor" to the sequence. The function "factor" transforms its input into a factor. Specifically, the application of this function to a sequence with logical components produces a factor with two levels that are given the names "TRUE" and "FALSE".

We want to examine the relation between the response variable "dif.mpg" and the explanatory factor "heavy". Towards that end we produce a plot of the relation with the function "plot" and test for the equality of the expectations of the response with the function "t.test". First the plot:

```
plot(dif.mpg~heavy)
```

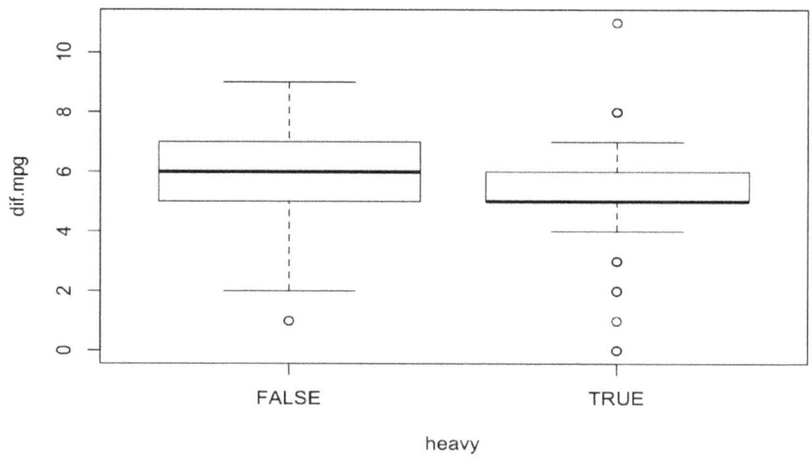

Observe that the figure contains two box plots, one associated with the level "FALSE" of the explanatory factor and the other with the level "TRUE" of that factor. The box plots describe the distribution of the response variable for each level of the explanatory factor. Overall, the distribution of the response for heavier cars (cars associated with the level "TRUE") tends to obtain smaller values than the distribution of the response for lighter cars (cars associated with the level "FALSE").

The input to the function "plot" is a *formula* expression of the form: "*response~explanatory.variable*". A formula identifies the role of variables. The variable to the left of the tilde character (~) in a formula is the response and the variable to the right is the explanatory variable. In the current case the variable "dif.mpg" is the response and the variable "heavy" is the explanatory variable.

Let us use a formal test in order to negate the hypothesis that the expectation of the response for the two weight groups is the same. The test is provided by the application of the function "t.test" to the formula "dif.mpg\;\tilde{}\;heavy":

```
t.test(dif.mpg~heavy)

##
##  Welch Two Sample t-test
##
## data:  dif.mpg by heavy
## t = 2.4255, df = 191.56, p-value = 0.01621
## alternative hypothesis: true difference in means is not equal to 0
## 95 percent confidence interval:
##  0.1029150 0.9989315
## sample estimates:

## mean in group FALSE  mean in group TRUE
##            5.805825            5.254902
```

The function "t.test", when applied to a formula that describes the relation between a numeric response and a explanatory factor with two level, produces a special form of a *t*-test that is called the *Welch Two Sample t-test*. The statistical model associated with this test assumes the present of two independent sub-samples, each associated with a level of the explanatory variable. The relevant parameters for this model are the two expectations and the two variances associated with the sub-samples.

The hypotheses tested in the context of the Welch test are formulated in terms of the difference between the expectation of the first sub-sample and the expectation of the second sub-sample. In the default application of the test the null hypothesis is that the difference is equal to 0 (or, equivalently, that the expectations are equal to each other). The alternative is that the difference is not equal to 0 (hence, the expectations differ).

The test is conducted with the aid of a test statistic. The computed value of the test statistic in this example is "t = 2.4255". Under the null hypothesis the distribution of the test statistic is (approximately) equal to the *t*-distribution on "df = 191.561" degrees of freedom. The resulting *p*-value is "p-value = 0.01621". Since the computed *p*-value is less than 0.05 we reject the null hypothesis with a significance level of 5% and declare that the expectations are not equal to each other.

The bottom part of the report presents points estimates and a confidence interval. The point estimates of the two expectations are the sub-samples averages. The estimated value of the expected difference in miles-per-gallon for lighter cars is 5.805825, which is the average of the measurements associated with the level "FALSE". The estimated value of the expected difference for heavier cars is 5.254902, the average of measurements associated with the level "TRUE".

The point estimate for the difference between the two expectations is the difference between the two sample averages: 5.805825–5.254902=0.550923. A confidence interval for the *difference* between the expectations is reported under the title “95 percent confidence interval:”. The computed value of the confidence interval is [0.1029150,0.9989315].

In the following section, we will explain the underlying principles of constructing the confidence interval and conducting the statistical test.

13.3.2 Confidence Interval for the Difference

Examine the statistical model utilized in constructing the confidence interval. The primary concern is that the model addresses two distinct populations instead of a single population. In our earlier theoretical discussions, we made the assumption that there is only one population and that a measurement was performed for all the individuals in this population. When the measurement was considered as a random variable it was denoted by a capital Latin letter such as X. Of concern were characteristics of the distribution of X such as E(X), the expectation of X, and V(X), the variance.

For the present inquiry, two populations are being considered. There are two populations: one is linked to the first level of the factor, and the other is linked to the second level. The measurement is conducted on individuals from both sub-populations. Nevertheless, the measurement entails two stochastic variables, one linked to the initial sub-population and the other linked to the subsequent sub-population. Furthermore, the distribution of the measurement for one population may vary from the distribution for the other population. We denote the random variable associated with the first sub-population by X_a and the one associated with the other sub-population by X_b.

Consider the example in which the measurement is the difference in miles-per-gallon between highway and city driving conditions. In this example X_a is the measurement for cars with curb weight up to 2,414 lb and X_b is the same measurement for cars with curb weight above that threshold.

The random variables XaX_a and XbX_b may have different distributions. Consequently, the characteristics of their distributions may also vary. Denote by E (X_a) and E(X_b) the expectations of the first and second random variable, respectively. Likewise, V (X_a) and V (X_b) are the variances of the two random variables. These expectations and variances are subjects of the statistical inference.

The sample itself may also be divided into two sub-samples according to the sub-population each observation originated from. In the example, one sub-sample is associated with the lighter car types and the other sub-sample with the heavier ones. These sub-samples can be used in order to make inference with respect to the parameters of X_a and X_b, respectively. For example, the average of the observations from first sub-sample, $\bar{X}_a$, can serve as the estimator of the of the expectation E(X_a) and the second sub-sample's average $\bar{X}_b$ may be used in order to estimate E(Xb).

Our goal in this section is to construct a confidence interval for the difference in expectations E(X_a) -E(X_b). A natural estimator for this difference in expectations is the difference in averages $\bar{X}_a - \bar{X}_b$. The average difference will also serve as the basis for the construction of a confidence interval.

Recall that the construction of the confidence interval for a signal expectation was based on the sample average $\bar{X}$. We exploited the fact that the distribution of $Z = (\bar{X} - \mathbf{E}(X)/\sqrt{\mathbf{V}(X)/n}$. the standardized sample average, is approximately standard Normal. From this Normal approximation we obtained an approximate 0.95 probability for the event

$$\left\{ - 1.96 \cdot \sqrt{\mathbf{V}(X)/n} \leq \bar{X} - \mathbf{E}(X) \leq 1.96 \cdot \sqrt{\mathbf{V}(X)/n} \right\},$$

where 1.96={qnorm(0.975) is the 0.975-percentile of the standard Normal distribution. Substituting the estimator S for the unknown variance of the measurement and rewriting the event in a format that puts the expectation E(X) in the center, between two boundaries, produced the confidence interval:

$$\bar{X} \pm 1.96 \cdot S/\sqrt{n} \,.$$

Similar considerations can be used in the construction of a confidence interval for the difference between expectations on the basis of the difference between sub-sample averages. The deviation $\{\bar{X}_a - \bar{X}_b\} - \{\mathbf{E}(X_a) - \mathbf{E}(X_b)\}$,between the difference of the averages and the difference of the expectations that they estimate can be standardized. By the Central Limit Theorem one may obtain that the distribution of the standardized deviation is approximately standard Normal.

Standardization is obtained by dividing by the standard deviation of the estimator. In the current setting the estimator is the difference between the averages. The variance of the difference is given by

$$\mathbf{V}(\bar{X}_a - \bar{X}_b) = \mathbf{V}(\bar{X}_a) + \mathbf{V}(\bar{X}_b) = \frac{\mathbf{V}(X_a)}{n_a} + \frac{\mathbf{V}(X_b)}{n_b} \,,$$

where n_a is the size of the sub-sample that produces the sample average $\bar{X}_a$ and nbn_b is the size of the sub-sample that produces the sample average $\bar{X}_b$. Observe that both $\bar{X}_a$ and $\bar{X}_b$ contribute to the variability of the difference. The total variability is the sum of the two contributions. Finally, we use the fact that the variance of the sample average is equal to he variance of a single measurement divided by the sample size. This fact is used for both averages in order to obtain a representation of the variance of the estimator in terms of the variances of the measurement in the two sub-population and the sizes of the two sub-samples.

The standardized deviation takes the form:

$$Z = \frac{\bar{X}_a - \bar{X}_b - \{\mathbf{E}(X_a) - \mathbf{E}(X_b)\}}{\sqrt{\mathbf{V}(X_a)/n_a + \mathbf{V}(X_b)/n_b}} .$$

When both sample sizes nan$_a$ and nbn$_b$ are large then the distribution of ZZ is approximately standard Normal. As a corollary from the Normal approximation one gets that $P(-1.96 \le Z \le 1.96) \approx 0.95$.

The values of variances $V(X_a)$ and $V(X_b)$ that appear in the definition of Z are unknown. However, these values can be estimated using the sub-samples variances S^2_a and S^2_b. When the size of both sub-samples is large then these estimators will produce good approximations of the unknown variances:

$$\mathbf{V}(X_a) \approx S_a^2,\ \mathbf{V}(X_b) \approx S_b^2 \quad \Longrightarrow \quad \frac{\mathbf{V}(X_a)}{n_a} + \frac{\mathbf{V}(X_b)}{n_b} \approx \frac{S_a^2}{n_a} + \frac{S_b^2}{n_b} .$$

The event $\{-1.96 \le Z \le 1.96\}$ may be approximated by the event:

$$\left\{ -1.96 \cdot \sqrt{\frac{S_a^2}{n_a} + \frac{S_b^2}{n_b}} \le \bar{X}_a - \bar{X}_b - \{\mathbf{E}(X_a) - \mathbf{E}(X_b)\} \le 1.96 \cdot \sqrt{\frac{S_a^2}{n_a} + \frac{S_b^2}{n_b}} \right\} .$$

The approximation results from the use of the sub-sample variances as a substitute for the unknown variances of the measurement in the two sub-populations. When the two sample sizes n_a and n_b are large then the probability of the given event will also be approximately equal to 0.95.

Finally, reexpressing the least event in a format that puts the parameter $E(X_a) - E(X_b)$ in the center will produce the confidence interval with boundaries of the form:

$$\bar{X}_a - \bar{X}_b \pm 1.96 \cdot \sqrt{S_a^2/n_a + S_b^2/n_b}$$

To demonstrate the calculations required to create a confidence interval for the disparity between two expectations, let us revisit the example of the variation in miles-per-gallon between lighter and heavier cars. Calculate the sample sizes, sample means, and sample variances for two samples:

```
table(heavy)
```

```
## heavy
## FALSE  TRUE
##   103   102
```

```
tapply(dif.mpg,heavy,mean)
```

```
##    FALSE     TRUE
## 5.805825 5.254902
```

```
tapply(dif.mpg,heavy,var)
```

```
##    FALSE     TRUE
## 2.020750 3.261114
```

Observe that there 103 lighter cars and 102 heavier ones. These counts were obtained by the application of the function "table" to the factor "heavy". The lighter cars are associated with the level "FALSE" and heavier cars are associated with the level "TRUE".

The average difference in miles-per-gallon for lighter cars is 5.805825 and the variance is 2.020750. The average difference in miles-per-gallon for heavier cars is 5.254902 and the variance is 3.261114. These quantities were obtained by the application of the functions "mean" or "var" to the values of the variable "dif. mpg" that are associated with each level of the factor "heavy". The application was carried out using the function "tapply".

The computed values of the means are equal to the vales reported in the output of the application of the function "t.test" to the formula "dif.mpg\;\tilde{}\;heavy". The difference between the averages is $\bar{x}_a - \bar{x}_b$ =5.805825-5.254902=0.550923. This value is the center of the confidence interval. The estimate of the standard deviation of the difference in averages is:

$$\sqrt{s_a^2/n_a + s_b^2/n_b} = \sqrt{2.020750/103 + 3.261114/102} = 0.227135 .$$

Therefore, the confidence interval for the difference in expectations is

$$\bar{x}_a - \bar{x}_b \pm 1.96 \cdot \sqrt{\frac{s_a^2}{n_a} + \frac{s_b^2}{n_b}} = 0.550923 \pm 1.96 \cdot 0.227135 = [0.1057384, 0.9961076] ,$$

which is (essentially) the confidence interval that is presented in the report[64].

13.3.3 The t-Test for Two Means

The statistical model that involves two sub-populations may be considered also in the context of hypothesis testing. Hypotheses can be formulated regarding the relations between the parameters of the model. These hypotheses can be tested using the data. For example, in the current application of the *t*-test, the null hypothesis is H_0: E (X_a)= E(X_b) and the alternative hypothesis is H_1:E(X_a)≠E(X_b). In this subsection we explain the theory behind this test.

Recall that the construction of a statistical test included the definition of a test statistic and the determination of a rejection region. The null hypothesis is rejected if, and only if, the test statistic obtains a value in the rejection region. The determination of the rejection region is based on the sampling distribution of the test statistic under the null hypothesis. The significance level of the test is the probability of rejecting the null hypothesis (i.e., the probability that the test statistic obtains a value in the rejection region) when the null hypothesis is correct (the distribution of the test statistic is the distribution under the null hypothesis). The significance level of the test is set at a given value, say 5%, thereby restricting the size of the rejection region.

In the previous chapter we consider the case where there is one population. For review, consider testing the hypothesis that the expectation of the measurement is equal to zero (H_0:E(X)=0) against the alternative hypothesis that it is not (H_1:E(X)≠0). A sample of size n is obtained from this population. Based on the sample one may compute a test statistic:

$$T = \frac{\bar{X} - 0}{S/\sqrt{n}} = \frac{\bar{X}}{S/\sqrt{n}} ,$$

where $\bar{X}$ is the sample average and S is the sample standard deviation. The rejection region of this test is {|T|>{qt(0.975,n-1)}}, for "qt(0.975,n-1)" the 0.975-percentile of the *t*-distribution on n−1n−1 degrees of freedom.

Alternatively, one may compute the *p*-value and reject the null hypothesis if the *p*-value is less than 0.05. The *p*-value in this case is equal to P(|T|>|t|), where t is the computed value of the test statistic. The distribution of T is the *t*-distribution of n−1 degrees of freedom.

A similar approach can be used in the situation where two sub-population are involved and one wants to test the null hypothesis that the expectations are equal versus the alternative hypothesis that they are not. The null hypothesis can be written in the form H_0: E (X_a)- E (X_b)=0 with the alternative hypothesis given as H_1:E(X_a)-\Expec$(X_b)$≠0.

It is natural to base the test static on the difference between sub-samples averages $\bar{X}_a - \bar{X}_b$. The T statistic is the ratio between the deviation of the estimator from the null value of the parameter, divided by the (estimated) standard deviation of the estimator. In the current setting the estimator is difference in sub-samples averages $\bar{X}_a - \bar{X}_b$, the null value of the parameter, the difference between the expectations, is 0, and the (estimated) standard deviation of the estimator is $\sqrt{S_a^2/n_a + S_b^2/n_b}$. It turns out that the test statistic in the current setting is:

$$T = \frac{\bar{X}_a - \bar{X}_b - 0}{\sqrt{S_a^2/n_a + S_b^2/n_b}} = \frac{\bar{X}_a - \bar{X}_b}{\sqrt{S_a^2/n_a + S_b^2/n_b}} .$$

Consider as a measurement the difference in miles-per-gallon. Define the sub-population a to the lighter cars and the sub-population b to be the heavier cars. Recall that the sub-sample sizes are n_a=103 and n_b=102. Also, the sub-sample averages are $\bar{x}_a = 5.805825$ and $\bar{x}_b = 5.254902$, and the sub-sample variances are $s_a^2 = 2.020750$ and $s_b^2 = 5.254902$.

In order to calculate the observed value of the test statistic we use once more the fact that the difference between the averages is $\bar{x}_a - \bar{x}_b = 5.805825 - 5.254902 = 0.550923$ and the estimated value of the standard deviation of the sub-samples average difference is:

$$\sqrt{s_a^2/n_a + s_b^2/n_b} = \sqrt{2.020750/103 + 3.261114/102} = 0.227135 .$$

It follows that the observed value of the T statistic is

$$t = \frac{\bar{x}_a - \bar{x}_b}{\sqrt{s_a^2/n_a + s_b^2/n_b}} = \frac{0.550923}{0.227135} = 2.425531 ,$$

which, after rounding up, is equal to the value presented in the report that was produced by the function "t.test".

The p-value is computed as the probability of obtaining values of the test statistic more extreme than the value that was obtained in our data. The computation is carried out under the assumptions of the null hypothesis. The limit distribution of the T statistic, when both sub-sample sizes n_a and n_b are large, is standard Normal. In the case when the measurements are Normally distributed then a refined approximation of the distribution of the statistic is the t-distribution. Both the standard Normal and the t-distribution are symmetric about the origin.

The probability of obtaining a value in either tails for a symmetric distribution is equal to twice the probability of obtaining a value in the upper tail:

$$\mathrm{P}(|T| > 2.4255) = 2 \times \mathrm{P}(T > 2.4255) = 2 \times [1 - \mathrm{P}(T \leq 2.4255)] .$$

The function "t.test" computes the p-value using the t-distribution. For the current data, the number of degrees of freedom that are used in this approximation is df = 191.561. When we apply the function "pt" for the computation of the cumulative probability of the t-distribution we get:

```
2*(1-pt(2.4255,191.561))

## [1] 0.01621458
```

which (after rounding) is equal to the reported p-value of 0.01621. This p-value is less than 0.05, hence the null hypothesis is rejected in favor of the alternative hypothesis that assumes an effect of the weight on the expectation.

13.4 COMPARING SAMPLE VARIANCES

In the previous section we discussed inference associated with the comparison of the expectations of a numerical measurement between two sub-population. Inference included the construction of a confidence interval for the difference between expectations and the testing of the hypothesis that the expectations are equal to each other.

In this section we consider a comparisons between variances of the measurement in the two sub-populations. For this inference we consider the ratio between estimators of the variances and introduce a new distribution, the F-distribution, that is associated with this ratio.

Assume, again, the presence of two sub-populations, denoted a and b. A numerical measurement is taken over a sample. The sample can be divided into two sub-samples according to the sub-population of origin. In the previous section we were interested in inference regarding the relation between the expectations of the measurement in the two sub-populations. Here we are concerned with the comparison of the variances.

Specifically, let X_a be the measurement at the first sub-population and let X_b be the measurement at the second sub-population. We want to compare V (X_a), the variance in the first sub-population, to $\mathrm{V}(X_b)$, the variance in the second sub-population. As the basis for the comparison we may use S^2_a and S^2_b, the sub-samples variances, which are computed from the observations in the first and the second sub-sample, respectively.

Consider the confidence interval for the ratio of the variances. In Chapter 11 we discussed the construction of the confidence interval for the variance in a single sample. The derivation was based on the sample variance S2S^2 that serves as an estimator of the population variance V(X). In particular, the distribution of the random variable $(n-1)S^2/\text{V}(X)$ was identified as the chi-square distribution on n-1 degrees of freedom. A confidence interval for the variance was obtained as a result of the identification of a central region in the chi-square distribution that contains a pre-subscribed probability.

In order to construct a confidence interval for the ratio of the variances we consider the random variable that is obtained as a ratio of the estimators of the variances:

$$\frac{S_a^2/\mathbf{V}(X_a)}{S_b^2/\mathbf{V}(X_b)} \sim F_{(n_a-1,n_b-1)} \; .$$

The distribution of this random variable is denoted the F-distribution. This distribution is characterized by the number of degrees of freedom associated with the estimator of the variance at the numerator and by the number of degrees of freedom associated with the estimator of the variance at the denominator. The number of degrees of freedom associated with the estimation of each variance is the number of observation used for the computation of the estimator, minus 1. In the current setting the numbers of degrees of freedom are n_a-1 and n_b-1, respectively.

The percentiles of the F-distribution can be computed in R using the function "qf". For example, the 0.025-percentile of the distribution for the ratio between sample variances of the response for two sub-samples is computed by the expression "qf(0.025,dfa,dfb)", where dfa=n_a-1 and dfb=n_b-1. Likewise, the 0.975-percentile is computed by the expression "qf(0.975,dfa,dfb)". Between these two numbers lie 95% of the given F-distribution. Consequently, the probability that the random variable $\{S_a^2/\mathbf{V}(X_a)\}/\{S_b^2/\mathbf{V}(X_b)\}$ obtains its values between these two percentiles is equal to 0.95:

$$\frac{S_a^2/\mathbf{V}(X_a)}{S_b^2/\mathbf{V}(X_b)} \sim F_{(n_a-1,n_b-1)} \quad \Longrightarrow$$

$$\mathbf{P}\left(\texttt{qf(0.025,dfa,dfb)} \le \frac{S_a^2/\mathbf{V}(X_a)}{S_b^2/\mathbf{V}(X_b)} \le \texttt{qf(0.975,dfa,dfb)}\right) = 0.95 \; .$$

A confidence interval for the ratio between V(X_a) and V(X_b) is obtained by reformulation of the last event. In the reformulation, the ratio of the variances is placed in the center:

$$\left\{\frac{S_a^2/S_b^2}{\texttt{qf(0.975,dfa,fdb)}} \le \frac{\mathbf{V}(X_a)}{\mathbf{V}(X_b)} \le \frac{S_a^2/S_b^2}{\texttt{qf(0.025,dfa,dfb)}}\right\} .$$

This confidence interval has a significance level of 95%.

Next, consider testing hypotheses regarding the relation between the variances. Of particular interest is testing the equality of the variances. One may formulate the null hypothesis as H_0:V(X_a)/V(X_b)=1 and test it against the alternative hypothesis H_1: Var(X_a) /Var(X_b)≠1.

The statistic $F = S_a^2/S_b^2$ can used in order to test the given null hypothesis. Values of this statistic that are either much larger or much smaller than 1 are evidence against the null hypothesis and in favor of the alternative hypothesis. The sampling distribution, under that null hypothesis, of this statistic is the $F(n_a-1,n_b-1)$ distribution. Consequently, the null hypothesis is rejected either if F<qf(0.025,dfa,dfb) or if F>qf(0.975,dfa,dfb, where dfa=n_a-1 and dfb=n_b-1. The significance level of this test is 5%.

Given an observed value of the statistic, the *p*-value is computed as the significance level of the test which uses the observed value as the threshold. If the observed value *ff* is less than 1 then the *p*-value is twice the probability of the lower tail: 2·P(*F*<*f*). On the other hand, if *f* is larger than 1 one takes twice the upper tail as the *p*-value : 2·P (*F*>*f*)=2·[1-\P (*F*≤*f*)]. The null hypothesis is rejected with a significance level of 5% if the *p*-value is less than 0.05.

In order to illustrate the inference that compares variances let us return to the variable "dif.mpg" and compare the variances associated with the two levels of the factor "heavy". The analysis will include testing the hypothesis that the two variances are equal and an estimate and a confidence interval for their ratio.

The function "var.test" may be used in order to carry out the required tasks. The input to the function is a formula such "dif.mpg\;\tilde{}\;heavy", with a numeric variable on the left and a factor with two levels on the right. The default application of the function to the formula produces the desired test and confidence interval:

```
var.test(dif.mpg~heavy)
```

```
##
##  F test to compare two variances
##
## data:  dif.mpg by heavy
## F = 0.61965, num df = 102, denom df = 101, p-value = 0.01663
## alternative hypothesis: true ratio of variances is not equal to 1
## 95 percent confidence interval:
##  0.4189200 0.9162126
## sample estimates:
## ratio of variances
##          0.6196502
```

Consider the report produced by the function. The observed value of the test statistic is "F = 0.6197", and it is associated with the FF-distribution on "num df = 102" and "denom df = 101" degrees of freedom. The test statistic can be used in order to test the null hypothesis H_0:V(X_a)/V(X_b)=1, that states that the two variance are equal, against the alternative hypothesis that they are not. The p-value for this test is "p-value = 0.01663", which is less than 0.05.

Consequently, the null hypothesis is rejected and the conclusion is that the two variances are significantly different from each other. The estimated ratio of variances, given at the bottom of the report, is 0.6196502. The confidence interval for the ratio is reported also and is equal to [0.4189200,0.9162126].

In order to relate the report to the theoretical discussion above let us recall that the sub-samples variances are s^2_a=2.020750 and s^2_b=3.261114. The sub-samples sizes are n_a=103 and n_b=102, respectively. The observed value of the statistic is the ratio s^2a/s^2b=2.020750/3.261114=0.6196502, which is the value that appears in the report. Notice that this is the estimate of the ration between the variances that is given at the bottom of the report.

The p-value of the two-sided test is equal to twice the probability of the tail that is associated with the observed value of the test statistic as a threshold. The number of degrees of freedom is dfa=n_a-1=102 and dfb=n_b-1=101. The observed value of the ratio test statistic is f=0.6196502. This value is less than one. Consequently, the probability P (F<0.6196502) enters into the computation of the p-value , which equals twice this probability:

```
2*pf(0.6196502,102,101)
```

```
## [1] 0.01662612
```

Compare this value to the p-value that appears in the report and see that, after rounding up, the two are the same.

For the confidence interval of the ratio compute the percentiles of the F distribution:

```
qf(0.025,102,101)
```

```
## [1] 0.676317
```

```
qf(0.975,102,101)
```

```
## [1] 1.479161
```

The confidence interval is equal to:

$$\left[\frac{s_a^2/s_b^2}{\texttt{qf(0.975,102,101)}}, \frac{s_a^2/s_b^2}{\texttt{qf(0.025,102,101)}}\right] = \left[\frac{0.6196502}{1.479161}, \frac{0.6196502}{0.676317}\right]$$
$$= [0.4189200, 0.9162127] \,,$$

which coincides with the reported interval.

13.5 EXERCISES

Exercise 13.1 In this exercise we would like to analyze the results of the trial that involves magnets as a treatment for pain. The trial is described in Question *ex:Inference*.1. The results of the trial are provided in the file "magnets.csv".

Patients in this trail where randomly assigned to a treatment or to a control. The responses relevant for this analysis are either the variable "change", which measures the difference in the score of pain reported by the patients before and after the treatment, or the variable "score1", which measures the score of pain before a device is applied. The explanatory variable is the factor "active". This factor has two levels, level "1" to indicate the application of an active magnet and level "2" to indicate the application of an inactive placebo.

1. In the following questions you are required to carry out tests of hypotheses. All tests should conducted at the 5% significance level:
2. Is there a significance difference between the treatment and the control groups in the expectation of the reported score of pain before the application of the device?
3. Is there a significance difference between the treatment and the control groups in the variance of the reported score of pain before the application of the device?
4. Is there a significance difference between the treatment and the control groups in the expectation of the change in score that resulted from the application of the device?

Is there a significance difference between the treatment and the control groups in the variance of the change in score that resulted from the application of the device?

Exercise 13.2 It is assumed, when constructing the F-test for equality of variances, that the measurements are Normally distributed. In this exercise we what to examine the robustness of the test to divergence from the assumption. You are required to compute the significance level of a two-sided F-test of H_0: V (X_a)= V (X_b) versus H_1: V (X_a)≠V(X_b). Assume there are n_a=29 observations in one group and nb=21n_b=21 observations in the other group. Use an F-test with a nominal 5% significance level.

1. Consider the case where X~Normal(4,4^2).

2. Consider the case where $X \sim \text{Exponential}(1/4)$.

Exercise 13.3 The sample average in one sub-sample is $\bar{x}_a = 124.3$ and the sample standard deviation is sa=13.4. The sample average in the second sub-sample is $\bar{x}_b = 80.5$ and the sample standard deviation is sb=16.7. The size of the first sub-sample is n_a=15 and this is also the size of the second sub-sample. We are interested in the estimation of the ratio of variances $V(X_a)/V(X_b)$.

1. Compute the estimate of parameter of interest.
2. Construct a confidence interval, with a confidence level of 95%, to the value of the parameter of interest.
3. It is discovered that the size of each of the sub-samples is actually equal to 150, and no to 15 (but the values of the other quantities are unchanged). What is the corrected estimate? What is the corrected confidence interval?

14 Chapter | LINEAR REGRESSION

14.1 INTRODUCTION: AN OVERVIEW

In the previous chapter, we analyzed a scenario in which the response variable is numerical and the explanatory variable is a factor with just two levels. This chapter focuses on situations where both the answer and explanatory variables are numerical. Regression is the method used to describe the relationships between two variables. In this context, we utilize linear regression to address a linear correlation between two numerical variables. This regression model uses linear regression to find the best-fitting line for the given data. The statement encapsulates the impact of the explanatory variable on the distribution of the response. Regression analysis provides a framework for doing statistical inference. One can apply the regression model to the data. This refers to the process of estimating the values of the parameters in the model. Additionally, it is possible to generate confidence intervals for the parameters and do hypothesis testing. Another factor that is taken into account is the evaluation of the proportion of variation in the answer that is accounted for by the regression model.

14.2 POINTS AND LINES

This section focuses on the visual depiction of the relationship between the answer and explanatory variables on a single graph. The data corresponding to both variables is graphed as points on a two-dimensional plane. Linear equations can be graphically represented as straight lines on a two-dimensional coordinate plane. This section provides the necessary context for the subsequent discussion on the linear regression model. The forthcoming section presents the current iteration of the linear regression model.

14.2.1 The Scatter Plot

Consider two number variables. A scatter plot is an effective tool for visually illustrating data that encompasses two variables. A scatter plot is a visual display in which individual data points are represented as discrete points. An examination of the scatter plot can unveil connections between the two variables.

Consider an example. A marine biologist measured the length (in millimeters) and the weight (in grams) of 10 fish that where collected in one of her expeditions. The results are summarized in a data frame that is presented in Table

$$tab{:}Regression\_1.$$

Notice that the data frame contains 10 observations. The variable x corresponds to the length of the fish and the variable y corresponds to the weight.

$$tab{:}Regression\_1$$

Table 14.1: Data

Observation	x	y
1	4.5	9.5
2	3.7	8.2
3	1.8	4.9
4	1.3	6.7
5	3.2	12.9
6	3.8	14.1
7	2.5	5.6
8	4.5	8.0
9	4.1	12.6
10	1.1	7.2

Let us display this data in a scatter plot. Towards that end, let us read the length data into an object by the name "x" and the weight data into an object by the name "y". Finally, let us apply the function "plot" to the formula that relates the response "y" to the explanatory variable "x":

```
x <- c(4.5,3.7,1.8,1.3,3.2,3.8,2.5,4.5,4.1,1.1)
y <- c(9.5,8.2,4.9,6.7,12.9,14.1,5.6,8.0,12.6,7.2)
plot(y~x)
```

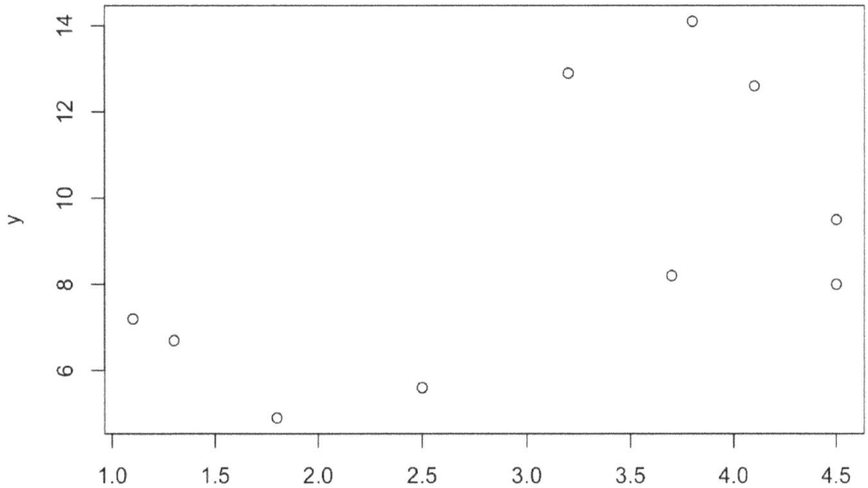

Figure 14.1: A Scatter Plot

The scatter plot that is produced by the last expression is presented in Figure 14.1.

A scatter plot is a graph that displays jointly the data of two numerical variables. The variables ("x" and "y" in this case) are represented by the x*x*-axis and the y*y*-axis, respectively. The x*x*-axis is associated with the explanatory variable and the y*y*-axis is associated with the response.

Each observation is represented by a point. The x*x*-value of the point corresponds to the value of the explanatory variable for the observation and the y*y*-value corresponds to the value of the response. For example, the first observation is represented by the point (x=4.5,y=9.5). The two rightmost points have an x*x* value of 4.5. The higher of the two has a y value of 9.5 and is therefore point associated with the first observation. The lower of the two has a y value of 8.0, and is thus associated with the 8th observation. Altogether there are 10 points in the plot, corresponding to the 10 observations in the data frame.

Let us consider another example of a scatter plot. The file "cars.csv" contains data regarding characteristics of cars. Among the variables in this data frame are the variables "horsepower" and the variable "engine.size". Both variables are numeric.

The variable "engine.size" describes the volume, in cubic inches, that is swept by all the pistons inside the cylinders. The variable "horsepower" measures the power of the engine in units of horsepower. Let us examine the relation between these two variables with a scatter plot:

```
cars <- read.csv("_data/cars.csv")
plot(horsepower ~ engine.size, data=cars)
```

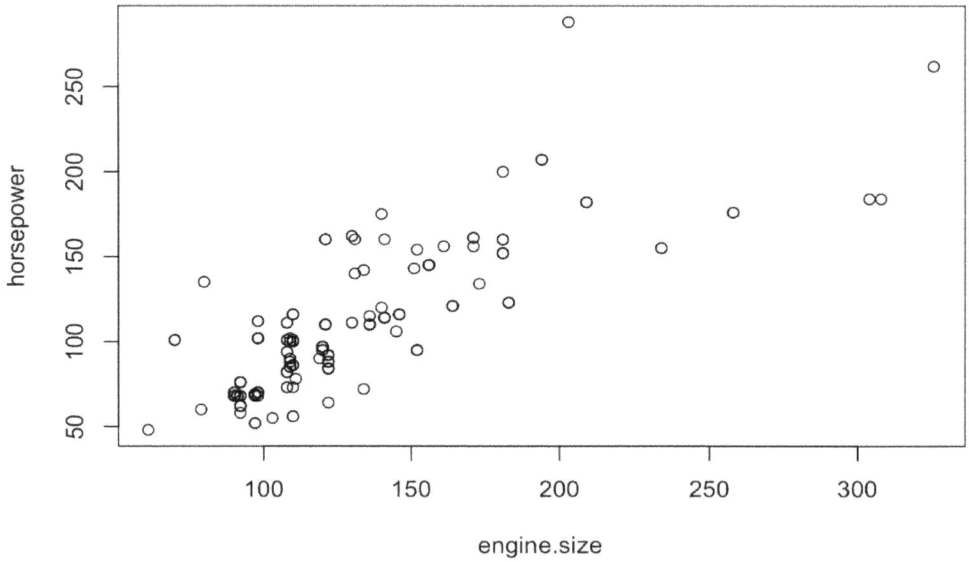

Figure 14.2: The Scatter Plot of Power versus Engine Size

In the first line of code we read the data from the file into an R data frame that is given the name "cars". In the second line we produce the scatter plot with "horsepower" as the response and "engine.size" as the explanatory variable. Both variables are taken from the data frame "cars". The plot that is produced by the last expression is presented in Figure $fig{:}Regression\_2$.

Consider the expression "plot(horsepower~engine.size, data=cars)". Both the response variable and the explanatory variables that are given in this expression do not exist in the computer's memory as independent objects, but only as variables within the object "cars". In some cases, however, one may refer to these variables directly within the function, provided that the argument "data=*data.frame.name*" is added to the function. This argument informs the function in which data frame the variables can be found, where *data.frame.name* is the name of the data frame. In the current example, the variables are located in the data frame "cars".

Examine the scatter plot in Figure 14.2. It is evident that the horsepower values generally rise as the engine size values grow. In general, the rise shows a linear pattern, with a straight line, although the data points are not precisely aligned on a single line. The purpose of linear regression, which will be explained in the following sections, is to analyze and evaluate the linear pattern.

14.2.2 Linear Equation

Linear regression is a statistical technique employed to examine and describe the linear correlation between a dependent variable and an independent variable. Linear trends can be characterized by the use of linear equations. This subsection examines the relationship between a linear equation and a linear trend, which is graphically represented by a straight line.A linear equation is an equation of the form:

$$y=a+b \cdot x,$$

where y and x are variables and a and b are the coefficients of the equation. The coefficient a is called the *intercept* and the coefficient b is called the *slope.*

A linear equation can be used in order to plot a line on a graph. With each value on the x-axis one may associate a value on the y-axis: the value that satisfies the linear equation. The collection of all such pairs of points, all possible x values and their associated y values, produces a straight line in the two-dimensional plane.

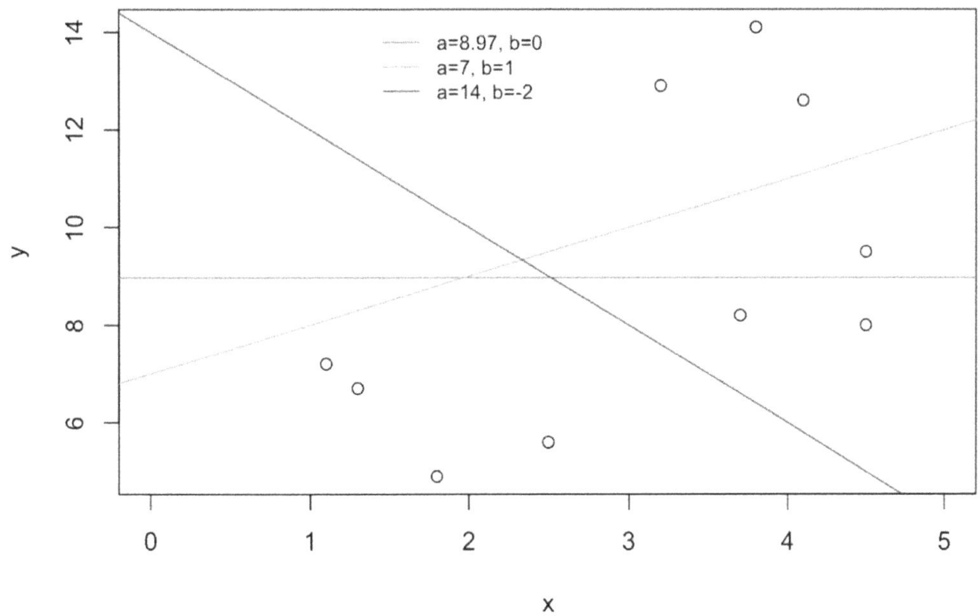

Figure 14.3: Lines

As an illustration consider the three lines in Figure 14.3. The *green* line is produced via the equation $y=7+x$, the intercept of the line is 7 and the slope is 1. The *blue* is a result of the equation $y=14-2x$. For this line the intercept is 14 and the slope is -2. Finally, the *red* line is produced by the equation $y=8.97$. The intercept of the line is 8.97 and the slope is equal to 0.

The intercept describes the value of yy when the line crosses the yy-axis. Equivalently, it is the result of the application of the linear equation for the value $x=0$. Observe in Figure 14.3 that the *green* line crosses the yy-axis at the level $y=7$. Likewise, the *blue* line crosses the y-axis at the level $y=14$. The *red* line stays constantly at the level $y=8.97$, and this is also the level at which it crosses the y-axis.

The slope is the change in the value of y for each unit change in the value of xx. Consider the *green* line. When x=0 the value of y is y=7. When xx changes to x=1 then the value of yy changes to y=8. A change of one unit in xx corresponds to an *increase* in one unit in yy. Indeed, the slope for this line is b=1. As for the *blue* line, when x changes from 0 to 1 the value of yy changes from y=14 to y=12; a *decrease* of two units. This decrease is associated with the slope b=-2. Lastly, for the constant *red* line there is no change in the value of y when x changes its value from x=0x=0 to x=1x=1. Therefore, the slope is b=0. A positive slope is associated with an increasing line, a negative slope is associated with a decreasing line and a zero slope is associated with a constant line.

Lines can be considered in the context of scatter plots. Figure 14.3 contains the scatter plot of the data on the relation between the length of fish and their weight. A regression line is the line that best describes the linear trend of the relation between the explanatory variable and the response. Neither of the lines in the figure is the regression line, although the *green* line is a better description of the trend than the *blue* line. The regression line is the best description of the linear trend.

The *red* line is a fixed line that is constructed at a level equal to the average value of the variable yy. This line partly reflects the information in the data. The regression line, which we fit in the next section, reflects more of the information by including a description of the trend in the data.

Lastly, let us see how one can add lines to a plot in R. Functions to produce plots in R can be divided into two categories: high level and low level plotting functions. High level functions produce an entire plot, including the axes and the labels of the plot. The plotting functions that we encountered in the past such as "plot", "hist", "boxplot" and the like are all high level plotting functions. Low level functions, on the other hand, add features to an existing plot.

An example of a low level plotting function is the function "abline". This function adds a straight line to an existing plot. The first argument to the function is the intercept of the line and the second argument is the slope of the line. Other arguments may be used in order to specify the characteristics of the line. For example, the argument "col=*color.name*" may be used in order to change the color of the line from its default black color. A plot that is very similar to plot in Figure 14.3 may be produced with the following code:

```
plot(y~x)
abline(7,1,col="green")
abline(14,-2,col="blue")
abline(mean(y),0,col="red")
```

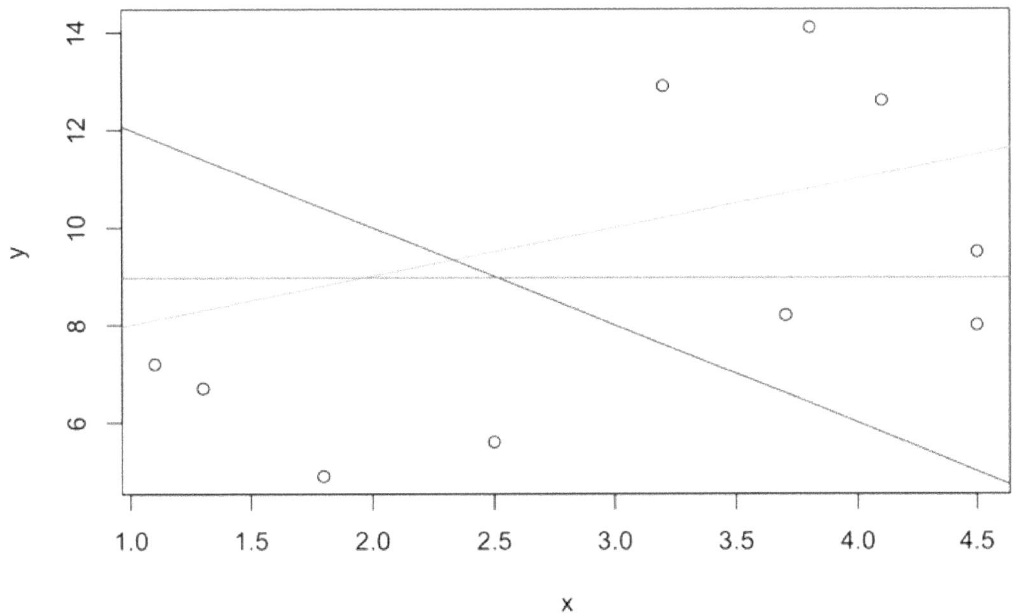

Initially, the scatter plot is created and the lines are added to the plot one after the other. Observe that color of the first line that is added is green, it has an intercept of 7 and a slope of 1. The second line is blue, with a intercept of 14 and a negative slope of -2. The last line is red, and its constant value is the average of the variable *y*.

In the next section we discuss the computation of the regression line, the line that describes the linear trend in the data. This line will be added to scatter plots with the aid of the function "abline".

14.3 LINEAR REGRESSION

Data that describes the joint distribution of two numeric variables can be represented with a scatter plot. The y*y*-axis in this plot corresponds to the response and the x*x*-axis corresponds to the explanatory variable. The regression line describes the linear trend of the response as a function of the explanatory variable. This line is characterized by a linear equation with an intercept and a slope that are computed from the data.

In the first subsection we present the computation of the regression linear equation from the data. The second subsection discusses regression as a statistical model. Statistical inference can be carried out on the basis of this model. In the context of the statistical model, one may consider the intercept and the slope of the regression model that is fitted to the data as point estimates of the model's parameter. Based on these estimates, one may test hypotheses regarding the regression model and construct confidence intervals for parameters.

14.3.1 Fitting the Regression Line

The R function that fits the regression line to data is called “lm”, an acronym for *Linear Model*. The input to the function is a formula, with the response variable to the left of the tilde character and the explanatory variable to the right of it. The output of the function is the fitted linear regression model.

Let us apply the linear regression function to the data on the weight and the length of fish. The output of the function is saved by us in a object called “fit”. Subsequently, the content of the object “fit” is displayed:

```
fit <- lm(y~x)
fit

##
## Call:
## lm(formula = y ~ x)
##
## Coefficients:
## (Intercept)            x
##       4.616        1.427
```

When displayed, the output of the function “lm” shows the formula that was used by the function and provides the coefficients of the regression linear equation. Observe that the intercept of the line is equal to 4.616. The slope of the line, the coefficient that multiplies “x” in linear equation, is equal to 1.427.

One may add the regression line to the scatter plot with the aid of the function “abline”:

```
plot(y~x)
abline(fit)
```

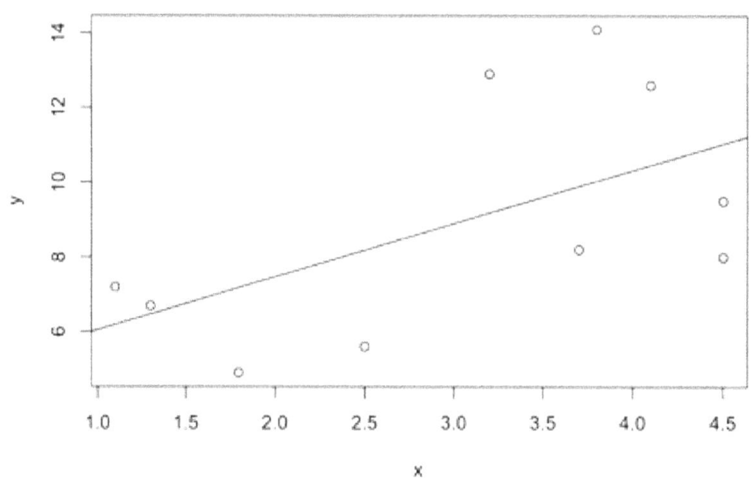

Figure 14.4: A Fitted Regression Line

The first expression produces the scatter plot of the data on fish. The second expression adds the regression line to the scatter plot. When the input to the graphical function "abline" is the output of the function "lm" that fits the regression line, then the result is the addition of the regression line to the existing plot. The line that is added is the line characterized by the coefficients that are computed by the function "lm". The coefficients in the current setting are 4.616 for the intercept and 1.427 for the slope.

The scatter plot and the added regression line are displayed in Figure 14.4. Observe that line passes through the points, balancing between the points that are above the line and the points that are below. The line captures the linear trend in the data.

Examine the line in Figure 14.4. When x=1 then the yy value of the line is slightly above 6. When the value of x is equal to 2, a change of one unit, then value of y is below 8, and is approximately equal to 7.5. This observation is consistent with the fact that the slop of the line is 1.427. The value of x is decreased by 1 when changing from x=1 to x=0. Consequently, the value of yy when x=0x=0 should decrease by 1.427 in comparison to its value when x=1. The value at x=1 is approximately 6. Therefore, the value at x=0 should be approximately 4.6. Indeed, we do get that the intercept is equal to 4.616.

The coefficients of the regression line are computed from the data and are hence statistics. Specifically, the slope of the regression line is computed as the ratio between the *covariance* of the response and the explanatory variable, divided by the variance of the explanatory variable. The intercept of the regression line is computed using the sample averages of both variables and the computed slope.

Start with the slope. The main ingredient in the formula for the slope, the numerator in the ratio, is the covariance between the two variables. The covariance measures the joint variability of two variables. Recall that the formula for the sample variance of the variable xx is equal to::

$$s^2 = \frac{\text{Sum of the squares of the deviations}}{\text{Number of values in the sample} - 1} = \frac{\sum_{i=1}^{n}(x_i - \bar{x})^2}{n-1}\,.$$

The formula of the sample covariance between x and y replaces the square of the deviations by the product of deviations. The product is between an y deviation and the parallel x deviation:

$$\text{covariance} = \frac{\text{Sum of products of the deviations}}{\text{Number of values in the sample} - 1} = \frac{\sum_{i=1}^{n}(y_i - \bar{y})(x_i - \bar{x})}{n-1}\,.$$

The function "cov" computes the sample covariance between two numeric variables. The two variables enter as arguments to the function and the sample covariance is the output. Let us demonstrate the computation by first applying the given function to the data on fish and then repeating the computations without the aid of the function:

```
cov(y,x)

## [1] 2.386111

sum((y-mean(y))*(x-mean(x)))/9

## [1] 2.386111
```

In both cases we obtained the same result. Notice that the sum of products of deviations in the second expression was divided by 9, which is the number of observations, minus 1.

The slope of the regression line is the ratio between the covariance and the variance of the explanatory variable.

The regression line passes through the point $(\bar{x}, \bar{y})$, a point that is determined by the means of the both the explanatory variable and the response. It follows that the intercept should obey the equation:

$$\bar{y} = a + b \cdot \bar{x} \quad \Longrightarrow \quad a = \bar{y} - b \cdot \bar{x} \,,$$

The left-hand-side equation corresponds to the statement that the value of the regression line at the average $\bar{x}$ is equal to the average of the response $\bar{y}$. The right-hand-side equation is the solution to the left-hand-side equation.

One may compute the coefficients of the regression model manually by computing first the slope as a ratio between the covariance and the variance of explanatory variable. The intercept can then be obtained by the equation that uses the computed slope and the averages of both variables:

```
b <- cov(x,y)/var(x)
a <- mean(y) - b*mean(x)
a

## [1] 4.616477

b

## [1] 1.427385
```

Applying the manual method we obtain, after rounding up, the same coefficients that were produced by the application of the function “lm” to the data.

As an exercise, let us fit the regression model to the data on the relation between the response "horsepower" and the explanatory variable "engine.size". Apply the function "lm" to the data and present the results:

```
fit.power <- lm(horsepower ~ engine.size, data=cars)
fit.power

##
## Call:
## lm(formula = horsepower ~ engine.size, data = cars)
##
## Coefficients:
## (Intercept)  engine.size
##      6.6414       0.7695
```

The fitted regression model is stored in an object called "fit.power". The intercept in the current setting is equal to 6.6414 and the slope is equal to 0.7695.

Observe that one may refer to variables that belong to a data frame, provided that the name of the data frame is entered as the value of the argument "data" in the function "lm". Here we refer to variables that belong to the data frame "cars".

Next we plot the scatter plot of the data and add the regression line:

```
plot(horsepower ~ engine.size, data=cars)
abline(fit.power)
```

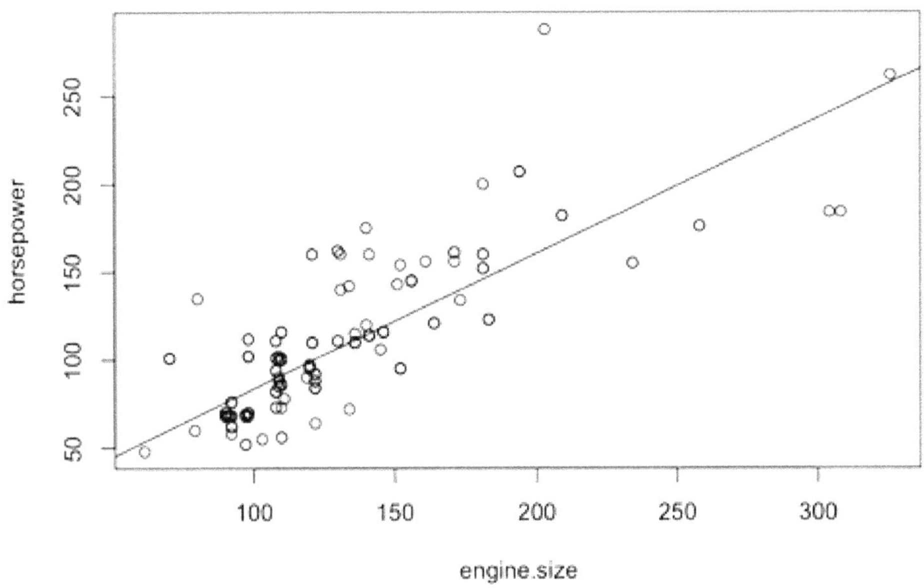

Figure 14.5: A Regression Model of Power versus Engine Size

The output of the plotting functions is presented in Figure 14.5. Again, the regression line describes the general linear trend in the data. Overall, with the increase in engine size one observes increase in the power of the engine.

14.3.2 Inference

So far, we have been examining the regression model within the framework of descriptive statistics. The objective of fitting the regression line to the data was to describe the linear pattern found in the data. Our upcoming objective is to address regression within the framework of inferential statistics. The objective is to generate assertions about the attributes of a whole population using the information gathered from the sample.

A statistical model is the basis for statistical inference in a certain context, as it generates the sampling distribution in that context. The sampling distribution serves as the basis for the study. Within this framework, the observed sample represents a solitary occurrence of the sampling distribution, serving as one instance out of an infinite number of possible instances that will never occur. Regression analysis involves the identification of a response variable and an explanatory variable. We present a comprehensive explanation of the statistical model used in this particular context.The relation between the response and the explanatory variable is such that the value of the later affects the distribution of the former. Still, the value of the response is not uniquely defined by the value of the explanatory variable. This principle also hold for the regression model of the relation between the response Y and the explanatory variable X. According to the model of linear regression the value of the *expectation* of the response for observation i, $\mathrm{E}(Y_i)$, is a linear function of the value of the explanatory variable for the same observation. Hence, there exist and intercept a and a slope b, common for all observations, such that if $X_i=x_i$ then

$$\mathrm{E}(Y_i) = a + b \cdot x_i \ .$$

The regression line can thus be interpreted as the average trend of the response in the population. This average trend is a linear function of the explanatory variable.

The intercept a and the slope b of the statistical model are parameters of the sampling distribution. One may test hypotheses and construct confidence intervals for these parameters based on the observed data and in relation to the sampling distribution.

Consider testing hypothesis. A natural null hypothesis to consider is the hypothesis that the slope is equal to zero. This hypothesis corresponds to statement that the expected value of the response is constant for all values of the explanatory variable. In other words, the hypothesis is that the explanatory variable does not affect the distribution of the response. One may formulate this null hypothesis as H_0:b=0 and test it against the alternative H_1:b≠0 that states that the explanatory variable does affect the distribution of the response.

A test of the given hypotheses can be carried out by the application of the function "summary" to the output of the function "lm". Recall that the function "lm" was used in order to fit the linear regression to the data. In particular, this function was applied to the data on the relation between the size of the engine and the power that the engine produces. The function fitted a regression line that describes the linear trend of the data. The output of the function was saved in an object by the name "fit.power". We apply the function "summary" to this object:

```
summary(fit.power)
```

```
##
## Call:
## lm(formula = horsepower ~ engine.size, data = cars)
##
## Residuals:
##      Min       1Q  Median       3Q      Max
## -59.643 -12.282  -5.515  10.251 125.153
##
## Coefficients:
##             Estimate Std. Error t value Pr(>|t|)
## (Intercept)  6.64138    5.23318   1.269    0.206
## engine.size  0.76949    0.03919  19.637   <2e-16 ***
## ---
## Signif. codes:  0 '***' 0.001 '**' 0.01 '*' 0.05 '.' 0.1 ' ' 1
##
## Residual standard error: 23.31 on 201 degrees of freedom
##   (2 observations deleted due to missingness)
## Multiple R-squared:  0.6574, Adjusted R-squared:  0.6556
## F-statistic: 385.6 on 1 and 201 DF,  p-value: < 2.2e-16
```

The output produced by the application of the function "summary" is long and detailed. We will discuss this output in the next section. Here we concentrate on the table that goes under the title "Coefficients:". The said table is made of 2 rows and 4 columns. It contains information for testing, for each of the coefficients, the null hypothesis that the value of the given coefficient is equal to zero. In particular, the second row may be used is order to test this hypothesis for the slope of the regression line, the coefficient that multiplies the explanatory variable.

Consider the second row. The first value on this row is 0.76949, which is equal (after rounding up) to the slope of the line that was fitted to the data in the previous subsection. However, in the context of statistical inference this value is the *estimate* of the slope of the population regression coefficient, the realization of the estimator of the slope.

The second value is 0.03919. This is an estimate of the standard deviation of the estimator of the slope. The third value is the test statistic. This statistic is the ratio between the deviation of the sample estimate of the parameter (0.76949) from the value of the parameter under the null hypothesis (0), divided by the estimated standard deviation (0.03919): (0.76949−0)/0.03919=0.76949/0.03919=19.63486, which is essentially the value given in the report.

The last value is the computed p-value for the test. It can be shown that the sampling distribution of the given test statistic, under the null distribution which assumes no slope, is asymptotically the standard Normal distribution. If the distribution of the response itself is Normal then the distribution of the statistic is the t-distribution on n−2 degrees of freedom. In the current situation this corresponds to 201 degrees of freedom[74]. The computed p-value is extremely small, practically eliminating the possibility that the slope is equal to zero.

The first row presents information regarding the intercept. The estimated intercept is 6.64138 with an estimated standard deviation of 5.23318. The value of the test statistic is 1.269 and the p-value for testing the null hypothesis that the intercept is equal to zero against the two sided alternative is 0.206. In this case the null hypothesis is not rejected since the p-value is larger than 0.05.

The report includes a deduction for the intercept. Nevertheless, it is recommended to approach this conclusion with caution in the present situation. Indeed, the intercept represents the predicted value of the response variable when the explanatory variable is set to zero. In this context, the explanatory variable refers to the size of the engine, while the response variable pertains to the power output of this engine. The power output of an engine with a size of zero is a value that lacks any tangible significance. Typically, if the intercept is not within the range of observations (meaning that the value 0 is not within the range of the observed explanatory variable), one should approach the inference on the intercept with caution. This type of reasoning necessitates extrapolation and is highly susceptible to the mis-specification of the regression model.Apart from testing hypotheses one may also construct confidence intervals for the parameters. A crude confidence interval may be obtained by taking 1.96 standard deviations on each side of the estimate of the parameter. Hence, a confidence interval for the slope is approximately equal to 0.76949±1.96×0.03919=[0.6926776,0.8463024]. In a similar way one may obtain a confidence interval for the slope: 6.64138±1.96×5.233 18=[-3.615653,16.89841].

Alternatively, one may compute confidence intervals for the parameters of the linear regression model using the function "confint". The input to this function is the fitted model and the output is a confidence interval for each of the parameters:

```
confint(fit.power)
```

```
##                  2.5 %     97.5 %
## (Intercept) -3.6775989 16.9603564
## engine.size  0.6922181  0.8467537
```

Observe the similarity between the confidence intervals that are computed by the function and the crude confidence intervals that were produced by us. The small discrepancies that do exist between the intervals result from the fact that the function "confint" uses the *t*-distribution whereas we used the Normal approximation.

14.4 R-SQUARED AND THE VARIANCE OF RESIDUALS

In this section we discuss the residuals between the values of the response and their estimated expected value according to the regression model. These residuals are the regression model equivalence of the deviations between the observations and the sample average. We use these residuals in order compute the variability that is not accounted for by the regression model. Indeed, the ratio between the total variability of the residuals and the total variability of the deviations from the average serves as a measure of the variability that is not explained by the explanatory variable. R-squared, which is equal to 1 minus this ratio, is interpreted as the fraction of the variability of the response that is explained by the regression model.

We start with the definition of residuals. Let us return to the artificial example that compared length of fish to their weight. The data for this example was given in Table

$$tab:Regression\_1$$

and was saved in the objects "x" and "y". The regression model was fitted to this data by the application of the function "lm" to the formula "y~x" and the fitted model was saved in an object called "fit". Let us apply the function "summary" to the fitted model:

```
summary(fit)

##
## Call:
## lm(formula = y ~ x)
##
## Residuals:
##     Min      1Q  Median      3Q     Max
## -3.0397 -2.1388 -0.6559  1.8518  4.0595
##
## Coefficients:
##             Estimate Std. Error t value Pr(>|t|)
## (Intercept)   4.6165     2.3653   1.952   0.0868 .
## x             1.4274     0.7195   1.984   0.0826 .
## ---
## Signif. codes:  0 '***' 0.001 '**' 0.01 '*' 0.05 '.' 0.1 ' ' 1
##
## Residual standard error: 2.791 on 8 degrees of freedom
## Multiple R-squared:  0.3297, Adjusted R-squared:  0.246
## F-statistic: 3.936 on 1 and 8 DF,  p-value: 0.08255
```

The given report contains a table with estimates of the regression coefficients and information for conducting hypothesis testing. The report contains other information that is associated mainly with the notion of the residuals from regression line. Our current goal is to understand what is that other information.

The residual from regression for each observation is the difference between the value of the response for the observation and the estimated expectation of the response under the regression model. An observation is a pair (x_i,y_i), with y_i being the value of the response. The expectation of the response according to the regression model is $a+b\cdot x_i$, where a and b are the coefficients of the model. The estimated expectation is obtained by using, in the formula for the expectation, the coefficients that are estimated from the data. The residual is the difference between y_i and $a+b\cdot x_i$.

Consider an example. The first observation on the fish is (4.5,9.5), where x_1=4.5 and y_1=9.5. The estimated intercept is 4.6165 and the estimated slope is 1.4274. The estimated expectation of the response for the first variable is equal to

$$4.6165 + 1.4274 \cdot x_1 = 4.6165 + 1.4274 \cdot 4.5 = 11.0398 .$$

The residual is the difference between the observes response and this value:

$$y_1 - (4.6165 + 1.4274 \cdot x_1) = 9.5 - 11.0398 = -1.5398 .$$

The residuals for the other observations are computed in the same manner. The values of the intercept and the slope are kept the same but the values of the explanatory variable and the response are changed.

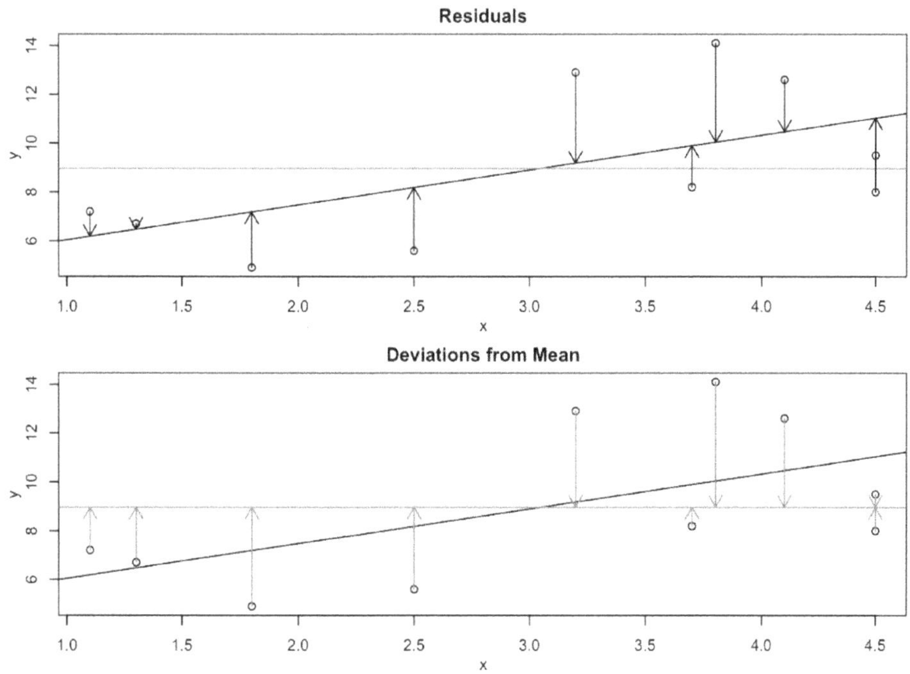

Figure 14.6: Residuals and Deviations from the Mean

Consult the upper plot in Figure 14.6. This is a scatter plot of the data, together with the regression line in *black* and the line of the average in *red*. A vertical arrow extends from each data point to the regression line. The point where each arrow hits the regression line is associated with the estimated value of the expectation for that point. The residual is the difference between the value of the response at the origin of the arrow and the value of the response at the tip of its head. Notice that there are as many residuals as there are observations.

The function "residuals" computes the residuals. The input to the function is the fitted regression model and the output is the sequence of residuals. When we apply the function to the object "fit", which contains the fitted regression model for the fish data, we get the residuals:

```
residuals(fit)
```

```
##          1          2          3          4          5          6
## -1.5397075 -1.6977999 -2.2857694  0.2279229  3.7158923  4.0594616
##          7          8          9         10
## -2.5849385 -3.0397075  2.1312463  1.0133998
```

Indeed, 10 residuals are produced, one for each observation. In particular, the residual for the first observation is -1.5397075, which is essentially the value that we obtained.

Return to the report produced by the application of the function "summary" to the fitted regression model. The first component in the report is the formula that identifies the response and the explanatory variable. The second component, the component that comes under the title "Residuals:", gives a summary of the distribution of the residuals. This summary includes the smallest and the largest values in the sequence of residuals, as well as the first and third quartiles and the median. The average is not reported since the average of the residuals from the regression line is always equal to 0.

The table that contains information on the coefficients was discussed in the previous section. Let us consider the last 3 lines of the report.

The first of the three lines contains the estimated value of the standard deviation of the response from the regression model. If the expectations of the measurements of the response are located on the regression line then the variability of the response corresponds to the variability about this line. The resulting variance is estimated by the sum of squares of the residuals from the regression line, divided by the number of observations minus 2. A division by the number of observation minus 2 produces an unbiased estimator of the variance of the response about the regression model. Taking the square root of the estimated variance produces an estimate of the standard deviation:

```
sqrt(sum(residuals(fit)^2)/8)
```

```
## [1] 2.790787
```

The last computation is a manual computation of the estimated standard deviation. It involves squaring the residuals and summing the squares. This sum is divided by the number of observations minus 2 (10-2=8). Taking the square root produces estimate. The value that we get for the estimated standard deviation is 2.790787, which coincides with the value that appears in the first of the last 3 lines of the report.

The second of these lines reports the R-squared of the linear fit. In order to explain the meaning of R-squared let us consider Figure 14.6 once again. The two plots in the figure present the scatter plot of the data together with the regression line and the line of the average. Vertical *black* arrows that represent the residuals from the regression are added to the upper plot. The lower plot contains vertical *red* arrows that extend from the data points to the line of the average. These arrows represent the deviations of the response from the average.

Consider two forms of variation. One form is the variation of the response from its average value. This variation is summarized by the sample variance, the sum of the squared lengths of the *red* arrows divided by the number of observations minus 1. The other form of variation is the variation of the response from the fitted regression line. This variation is summarized by the sample variation of the residuals, the sum of squared lengths of the *black* arrows divided by the number of observations minus 1. The ratio between these two quantities gives the relative variability of the response that remains after fitting the regression line to the data.

The line of the average is a straight line. The deviations of the observations from this straight line can be thought of as residuals from that line. The variability of these residuals, the sum of squares of the deviations from the average divided by the number of observations minus 1, is equal to the sample variance.

The regression line is the unique straight line that minimizes the variability of its residuals. Consequently, the variability of the residuals from the regression, the sum of squares of the residuals from the regression divided by the number of observations minus 1, is the smallest residual variability produced by any straight line. It follows that the sample variance of the regression residuals is less than the sample variance of the response. Therefore, the ratio between the variance of the residuals and the variance of the response is less than 1.

R-squared is the difference between 1 and the ratio of the variances. Its value is between 0 and 1 and it represents the fraction of the variability of the response that is *explained* by the regression line. The closer the points are to the regression line the larger the value of R-squared becomes. On the other hand, the less there is a linear trend in the data the closer to 0 is the value of R-squared. In the extreme case of R-squared equal to 1 all the data point are positioned exactly on a single straight line. In the other extreme, a value of 0 for R-squared implies no linear trend in the data.

Let us compte manually the difference between 1 and the ratio between the variance of the residuals and the variance of the response:

```
1-var(residuals(fit))/var(y)
```

```
## [1] 0.3297413
```

Observe that the computed value of R-squared is the same as the value "Multiple R-squared: 0.3297" that is given in the report.

The report provides another value of R-squared, titled *Adjusted R-squared*. The difference between the adjusted and unadjusted quantities is that in the former the sample variance of the residuals from the regression is replaced by an unbiased estimate of the variability of the response about the regression line. The sum of squares in the unbiased estimator is divided by the number of observations minus 2. Indeed, when we re-compute the ratio using the unbiased estimate, the sum of squared residuals divided by 10-2=8, we get:

```
1-(sum(residuals(fit)^2)/8)/var(y)
```

```
## [1] 0.245959
```

The value of this adjusted quantity is equal to the value "Adjusted R-squared: 0.246" in the report.

Which value of R-squared to use is a matter of personal taste. In any case, for a larger number of observations the difference between the two values becomes negligible.

The last line in the report produces an overall goodness of fit test for the regression model. In the current application of linear regression this test reduces to a test of the slope being equal to zero, the same test that is reported in the second row of the table of coefficients. The F statistic is simply the square of the t value that is given in the second row of the table. The sampling distribution of this statistic under the null hypothesis is the F-distribution on 1 and n-2 degrees of freedom, which is the sampling distribution of the square of the test statistic for the slope. The computed p-value, "p-value: 0.08255" is the identical (after rounding up) to the p-value given in the second line of the table.

Return to the R-squared coefficient. This coefficient is a convenient measure of the goodness of fit of the regression model to the data. Let us demonstrate this point with the aid of the "cars" data. In Subsection 14.3.2 we fitted a regression model to the power of the engine as a response and the size of the engine as an explanatory variable. The fitted model was saved in the object called "fit.power". A report of this fit, the output of the expression "summary(fit.power)" was also presented. The null hypothesis of zero slope was clearly rejected. The value of R-squared for this fit was 0.6574. Consequently, about 2/3 of the variability in the power of the engine is explained by the size of the engine.

Consider trying to fit a different regression model for the power of the engine as a response. The variable "length" describes the length of the car (in inches). How well would the length explain the power of the car? We may examine this question using linear regression:

```
summary(lm(horsepower ~ length, data=cars))
```

```
##
## Call:
## lm(formula = horsepower ~ length, data = cars)
##
## Residuals:
##     Min      1Q  Median      3Q     Max
## -53.57 -20.35   -6.69  14.45 180.72
##
## Coefficients:
##              Estimate Std. Error t value Pr(>|t|)
## (Intercept) -205.3971    32.8185  -6.259   2.3e-09 ***
## length         1.7796     0.1881   9.459   < 2e-16 ***
## ---
## Signif. codes:  0 '***' 0.001 '**' 0.01 '*' 0.05 '.' 0.1 ' ' 1
##
## Residual standard error: 33.12 on 201 degrees of freedom
##   (2 observations deleted due to missingness)
## Multiple R-squared:  0.308,  Adjusted R-squared:  0.3046
## F-statistic: 89.47 on 1 and 201 DF,  p-value: < 2.2e-16
```

We used one expression to fit the regression model to the data and to summarize the outcome of the fit.

A scatter plot of the two variables together with the regression line may be produced using the code:

```
plot(horsepower ~ length, data=cars)
abline(lm(horsepower ~ length, data=cars))
```

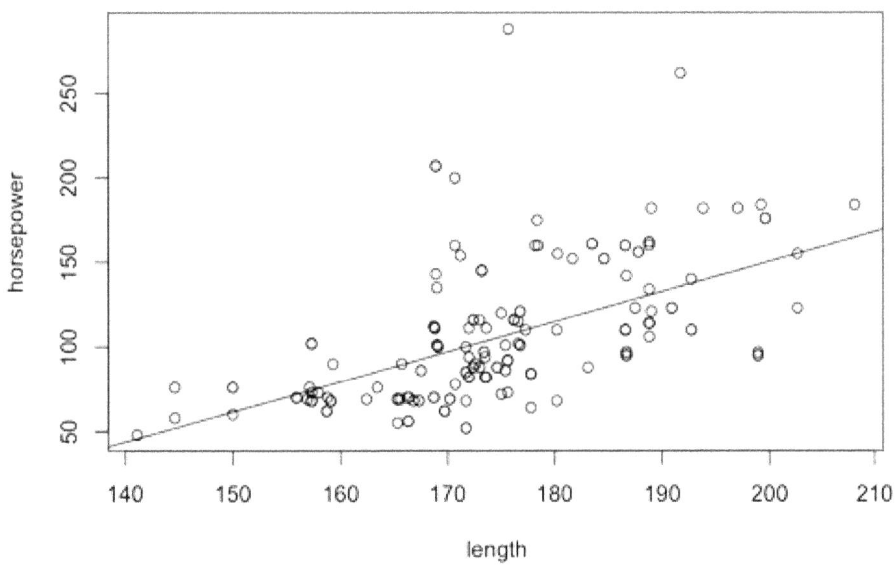

Upon analyzing the image, it is evident that there is a clear linear correlation between the car's length and its power. Generally, vehicles with greater length often possess a higher level of horsepower. Performing a hypothesis test to see if the slope is equal to zero yields a significantly low p-value, resulting in the rejection of the null hypothesis.

Both the car's length and the engine's size have a statistically significant relationship with the response. Nevertheless, which of the two explanatory factors yields a superior fit?An answer to this question may be provided by the examination of values of R-squared, the ratio of the variance of the response explained by each of the explanatory variable. The R-squared for the size of the engine as an explanatory variable is 0.6574, which is approximately equal to 2/3. The value of R-squared for the length of the car as an explanatory variable is 0.308, less than 1/3. It follows that the size of the engine explains twice as much of the variability of the power of the engine than the size of car and is a better explanatory variable.

14.5 EXERCISES

Exercise 14.1 Figure 14.7 presents 10 points and three lines. One of the lines is colored *red* and one of the points is marked as a *red triangle*. The points in the plot refer to the data frame in Table

$$tab:Regression\_2$$

and the three lines refer to the linear equations:

1. $y=4$
2. $y=5-2x$
3. $y=x$

You are asked to match the marked line to the appropriate linear equation and match the marked point to the appropriate observation:

1. Which of the three equations, 1, 2 or 3, describes the line marked in *red*?
2. The poind marked with a *red triangle* represents which of the observations. (Identify the observation number.)

$$tab:Regression\_2$$

Table 14.2: Points

Observation	x	y
1	2.3	-3.0
2	-1.9	9.8
3	1.6	4.3
4	-1.6	8.2

Observation	x	y
5	0.8	5.9
6	-1.0	4.3
7	-0.2	2.0
8	2.4	-4.7
9	1.8	1.8
10	1.4	-1.1

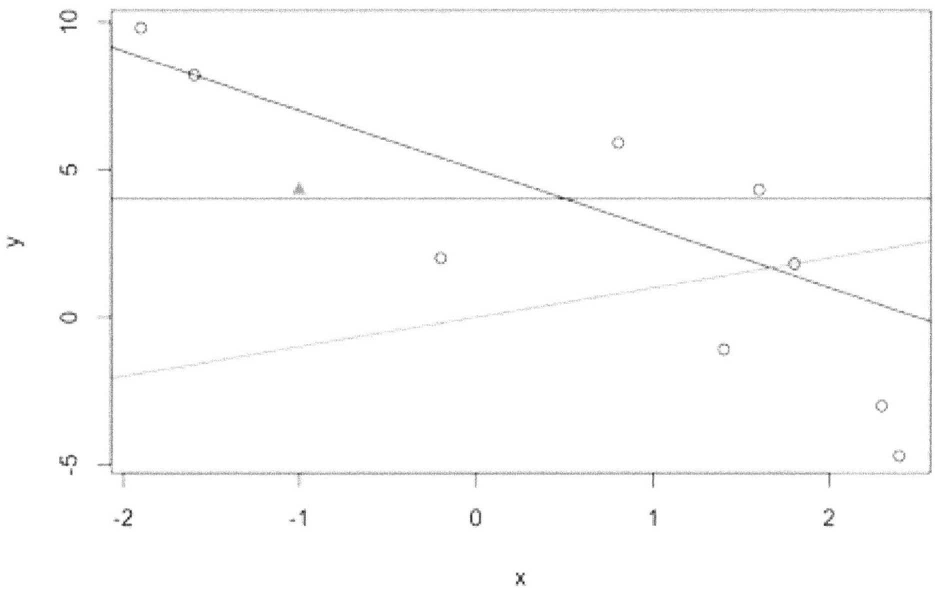

Figure 14.7: Lines and Points

Exercise 14.2 Assume a regression model that describes the relation between the expectation of the response and the value of the explanatory variable in the form:

$$E(Y_i) = 2.13 \cdot x_i - 3.60 \, .$$

1. What is the value of the intercept and what is the value of the slope in the linear equation that describes the model?
2. Assume the x_1=5.5, x_2=12.13, x_3=4.2, and x_4=6.7. What is the expected value of the response of the 3rd observation?

Exercise 14.3 The file "aids.csv" contains data on the number of diagnosed cases of Aids and the number of deaths associated with Aids among adults and adolescents in the United States between 1981 and 2002. The file can be found on the internet at http://pluto.huji.ac.il/~msby/StatThink/Datasets/aids.csv.

The file contains 3 variables: The variable "year" that tells the relevant year, the variable "diagnosed" that reports the number of Aids cases that were diagnosed in each year, and the variable "deaths" that reports the number of Aids related deaths in each year. The following questions refer to the data in the file:

1. Consider the variable "deaths" as response and the variable "diagnosed" as an explanatory variable. What is the slope of the regression line? Produce a point estimate and a confidence interval. Is it statistically significant (namely, significantly different than 0)?
2. Plot the scatter plot that is produced by these two variables and add the regression line to the plot. Does the regression line provided a good description of the trend in the data?
3. Consider the variable "diagnosed" as the response and the variable "year" as the explanatory variable. What is the slope of the regression line? Produce a point estimate and a confidence interval. Is the slope in this case statistically significant?
4. Plot the scatter plot that is produced by the later pair of variables and add the regression line to the plot. Does the regression line provided a good description of the trend in the data?

Exercise 14.4 Below are the percents of the U.S. labor force (excluding self-employed and unemployed) that are members of a labor union. We use this data in order to practice the computation of the regression coefficients.

tab:Regression_4

Table 14.3: Percent of Union Members

Year	Percent
1945	35.5
1950	31.5
1960	31.4
1970	27.3
1980	21.9
1986	17.5
1993	15.8

1. Produce the scatter plot of the data and add the regression line. Is the regression model reasonable for this data?
2. Compute the sample averages and the sample standard deviations of both variables. Compute the covariance between the two variables.
3. Using the summaries you have just computed, recompute the coefficients of the regression model.

Exercise 14.5 Assume a regression model was fit to some data that describes the relation between the explanatory variable x and the response y. Assume that the coefficients of the fitted model are a=2.5 and b=−1.13, for the intercept and the slope, respectively. The first 4 observations in the data are (x_1,y_1)=(5.5,3.22), (x_2,y_2)=(12.13,−6.02), (x_3,y_3)=(4.2,−8.3), and (x_4,y_4)=(6.7,0.17).

1. What is the estimated expectation of the response for the 4th observation?
2. What is the residual from the regression line for the 4th observation?

Exercise 14.6 In Chapter 13 we analyzed an example that involved the difference between fuel consumption in highway and city driving conditions as the response. The explanatory variable was a factor that was produced by splitting the cars into two weight groups. In this exercise we would like to revisit this example. Here we use the weight of the car directly as an explanatory variable. We also consider the size of the engine as an alternative explanatory variable and compare between the two regression models.

1. Fit the regression model that uses the variable "curb.weight" as an explanatory variable. Is the slope significantly different than 0? What fraction of the standard deviation of the response is explained by a regression model involving this variable?
2. Fit the regression model that uses the variable "engine.size" as an explanatory variable. Is the slope significantly different than 0? What fraction of the standard deviation of the response is explained by a regression model involving this variable?
3. Which of the two models fits the data better?

15 Chapter | A BERNOULLI RESPONSE

15.1 INTRODUCTION: AN OVERVIEW

Chapters 13 and 14 introduced the concept of statistical inference, which includes analyzing the relationship between a response variable and an explanatory variable that may have an impact on the distribution of the response. Numerical responses were observed in both chapters. The two chapters exhibited dissimilarities in the data type of the explanatory variable. Chapter 13 introduced an explanatory variable that is a factor with two levels, which divides the sample into two distinct sub-samples. Chapter 14 had a numeric explanatory variable that, when combined with the response variable, resulted in a linear trend. The objective of this chapter is to examine the scenario in which the response is a Bernoulli variable. A variable may arise as an indicator of the presence of an event related to the response or as a component with two levels. The explanatory variable can either be a categorical variable with two levels or a numerical variable. When the explanatory variable is a binary factor, we can utilize the "prop.test" function. This function was utilized in Chapter 12 to analyze the probability of an event occurring in a single sample. Here we utilize it to do comparisons between two sub-samples. This is analogous to the manner in which the "t.test" function was employed to analyze a numerical answer in both a single sample and in the comparison of sub-samples. To analyze a situation where the explanatory variable is numeric, we can utilize the "glm" function, which stands for Generalized Linear Model. This function allows us to accurately fit a regression model to the given data.

15.2 COMPARING SAMPLE PROPORTIONS

This chapter focuses on analyzing a Bernoulli response. A response can be categorized into two levels: "TRUE" or "FALSE", and it can serve as a signal of an event. Alternatively, it might be linked to a binary component and represent the indication of one of the two levels. The response was examined in Chapters 11 and 12, where confidence intervals and tests for the probability of an event were presented within the framework of a single sample. This chapter focuses on examining the connections between a specific type of reaction and a variable that provides an explanation for it. Let's consider the scenario when the explanatory variable is a factor with two distinct levels. These levels correspond to two distinct sub-populations or situations. The objective of the analysis is to compare the likelihood of the event between the two sub-populations or settings. The discussion in this section is analogous to the discussion in Section 13.3. The part focused on comparing the anticipated numerical response between two sub-populations.

We denoted these sub-populations *a* and *b* with expectations E (X_a) and E (X_b), respectively. The inference used the average $\bar{X}_a$, which was based on a sub-sample of size nan$_a$, and the average $\bar{X}_b$, which was based on the other sub-sample of size nbn$_b$. The sub-samples variances S^2_a and S^2_b participated in the inference as well. The application of a test for the equality of the expectations and a confidence interval where produced by the application of the function "t.test" to the data.

The inference problem, which is considered in this chapter, involves an event. This event is being examined in two different settings that correspond to two different sub-population *a* and *b*. Denote the probabilities of the event in each of the sub-populations by *pa* and *pb*. Our concern is the statistical inference associated with the comparison of these two probabilities to each other.

Natural estimators of the probabilities are $\hat{P}_a$ and $\hat{P}_b$, the sub-samples proportions of occurrence of the event. These estimators are used in order to carry out the inference. Specifically, we consider here the construction of a confidence interval for the difference *pa-pb* and a test of the hypothesis that the probabilities are equal.

The methods for producing the confidence intervals for the difference and for testing the null hypothesis that the difference is equal to zero are similar is principle to the methods that were described in Section for making parallel inferences regarding the relations between expectations. However, the derivations of the tools that are used in the current situation are not identical to the derivations of the tools that were used there. The main differences between the two cases is the replacement of the sub-sample averages by the sub-sample proportions, a difference in the way the standard deviation of the statistics are estimated, and the application of a continuity correction. We do not discuss in this chapter the theoretical details associated with the derivations. Instead, we demonstrate the application of the inference in an example.

The variable "num.of.doors" in the data frame "cars" describes the number of doors a car has. This variable is a factor with two levels, "two" and "four". We treat this variable as a response and investigate its relation to explanatory variables. In this section the explanatory variable is a factor with two levels and in the next section it is a numeric variable. Specifically, in this section we use the factor "fuel. type" as the explanatory variable. Recall that this variable identified the type of fuel, diesel or gas, that the car uses. The aim of the analysis is to compare the proportion of cars with four doors between cars that run on diesel and cars that run on gas.

Let us first summarize the data in a 2×2 frequency table. The function "table" may be used in order to produce such a table:

```
cars <- read.csv("_data/cars.csv")
table(cars$fuel.type,cars$num.of.doors)
```

```
##
##          four two
##   diesel   16   3
##   gas      98  86
```

When the function "table" is applied to a combination of two factors then the output is a table of joint frequencies. Each entry in the table contains the frequency in the sample of the combination of levels, one from each variable, that is associated with the entry. For example, there are 16 cars in the data set that have the level "four" for the variable "num.of.doors" and the level "diesel" for the variable "fuel. type". Likewise, there are 3 cars that are associated with the combination "two" and "diesel". The total number of entries to the table is 16+3+98+86=203, which is the number of cars in the data set, minus the two missing values in the variable "num.of.doors".

A graphical representation of the relation between the two factors can be obtained using a mosaic plot. This plot is produced when the input to the function "plot" is a formula where both the response and the explanatory variables are factors:

```
plot(num.of.doors ~ fuel.type,data=cars)
```

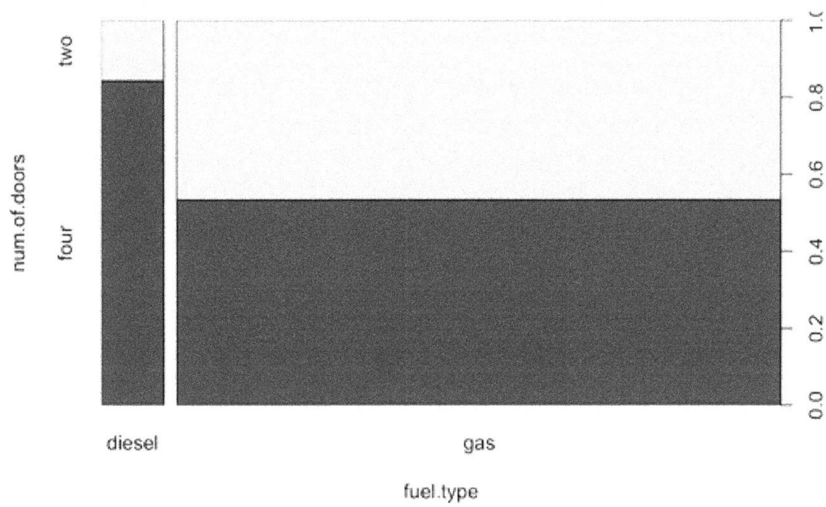

Figure 15.1: Number of Doors versus Fuel Type

The box plot describes the distribution of the explanatory variable and the distribution of the response for each level of the explanatory variable. In the current example the explanatory variable is the factor "fuel" that has 2 levels. The two levels of this variable, "diesel" and "gas", are given at the xx-axis. A vertical rectangle is associated with each level. These 2 rectangles split the total area of the square. The total area of the square represents the total relative frequency (which is equal to 1). Consequently, the area of each rectangle represents the relative frequency of the associated level of the explanatory factor.

A rectangle associated with a given level of the explanatory variable is further divided into horizontal sub-rectangles that are associated with the response factor. In the current example each darker rectangle is associated with the level "four" of the response "num.of.door" and each brighter rectangle is associated with the level "two". The relative area of the horizontal rectangles within each vertical rectangle represent the relative frequency of the levels of the response within each subset associated with the level of the explanatory variable.

Looking at the plot one may appreciate the fact that diesel cars are less frequent than cars that run on gas. The graph also displays the fact that the relative frequency of cars with four doors among diesel cars is larger than the relative frequency of four doors cars among cars that run on gas.

The function "prop.test" may be used in order test the hypothesis that, at the population level, the probability of the level "four" of the response within the sub-population of diesel cars (the height of the leftmost darker rectangle in the theoretic mosaic plot that is produced for the entire population) is equal to the probability of the same level of the response with in the sub-population of cars that run on gas (the height of the rightmost darker rectangle in that theoretic mosaic plot). Specifically, let us test the hypothesis that the two probabilities of the level "four", one for diesel cars and one for cars that run on gas, are equal to each other.

The output of the function "table" may serve as the input to the function "prop. test"[83]. The Bernoulli response variable should be the second variable in the input to the table whereas the explanatory factor is the first variable in the table. When we apply the test to the data we get the report:

```
prop.test(table(cars$fuel.type,cars$num.of.doors))

##
##  2-sample test for equality of proportions with continuity
##  correction
##
## data:  table(cars$fuel.type, cars$num.of.doors)
## X-squared = 5.5021, df = 1, p-value = 0.01899
## alternative hypothesis: two.sided
## 95 percent confidence interval:
##  0.1013542 0.5176389
## sample estimates:
##    prop 1    prop 2
## 0.8421053 0.5326087
```

The two sample proportions of cars with four doors among diesel and gas cars are presented at the bottom of the report and serve as estimates of the sub-populations probabilities. Indeed, the relative frequency of cars with four doors among diesel cars is equal to $\hat{p}_a = 16/(16 + 3) = 16/19 = 0.8421053$. Likewise, the relative frequency of cars with four doors among cars that ran on gas is equal to $\hat{p}_b = 98/(98 + 86) = 98/184 = 0.5326087$. The confidence interval for the difference in the probability of a car with four doors between the two sub-populations, *pa-pb*, is reported under the title "95 percent confidence interval" and is given as [0.1013542,0.5176389].

The null hypothesis, which is the subject of this test, is H_0:*pa=pb*. This hypothesis is tested against the two-sided alternative hypothesis H_1:*pa≠pb*. The test itself is based on a test statistic that obtains the value X-squared = 5.5021. This test statistic corresponds essentially to the deviation between the estimated value of the parameter (the difference in sub-sample proportions of the event) and the theoretical value of the parameter (*pa-pb*=0). This deviation is divided by the estimated standard deviation and the ratio is squared. The statistic itself is produced via a continuity correction that makes its null distribution closer to the limiting chi-square distribution on one degree of freedom. The *p*-value is computed based on this limiting chi-square distribution.

Notice that the computed *p*-value is equal to p-value = 0.01899. This value is smaller than 0.05. Consequently, the null hypothesis is rejected at the 5% significance level in favor of the alternative hypothesis. This alternative hypothesis states that the sub-populations probabilities are different from each other.

15.3 LOGISTIC REGRESSION

In the previous section we considered a Bernoulli response and a factor with two levels as an explanatory variable. In this section we use a numeric variable as the explanatory variable. The discussion in this section is parallel to the discussion in Chapter that presented the topic of linear regression. However, since the response is not of the same form, it is the indicator of a level of a factor and not a regular numeric response, then the tools the are used are different. Instead of using linear regression we use another type of regression that is called *Logistic Regression.*

Recall that linear regression involved fitting a straight line to the scatter plot of data points. This line corresponds to the expectation of the response as a function of the explanatory variable. The estimated coefficients of this line are computed from the data and used for inference.

In logistic regression, instead of the consideration of the expectation of a numerical response, one considers the probability of an event associated with the response. This probability is treated as a function of the explanatory variable. Parameters that determine this function are estimated from the data and are used for inference regarding the relation between the explanatory variable and the response. Again, we do not discuss the theoretical details involved in the derivation of logistic regression. Instead, we apply the method to an example.

We consider the factor "num.of.doors" as the response and the probability of a car with four doors as the probability of the response. The length of the car will serve as the explanatory variable. Measurements of lengths of the cars are stored in the variable "length" in the data frame "cars".

First, let us plot the relation between the response and the explanatory variable:

```
plot(num.of.doors ~ length,data=cars)
```

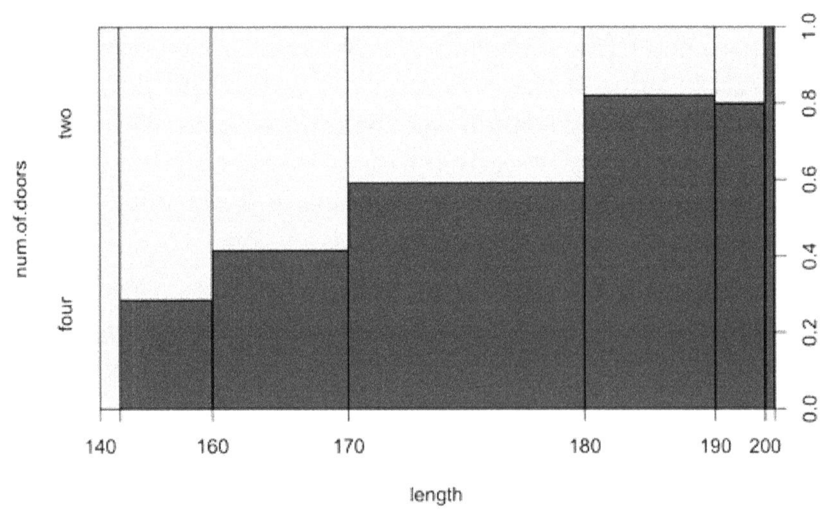

Figure 15.2: Number of Doors versus Fuel Type

The plot is a type of a mosaic plot and it is produced when the input to the function "plot" is a formula with a factor as a response and a numeric variable as the explanatory variable. The plot presents, for interval levels of the explanatory variable, the relative frequencies of each interval. It also presents the relative frequency of the levels of the response within each interval level of the explanatory variable.

In order to get a better understanding of the meaning of the given mosaic plot one may consider the histogram of the explanatory variable.

```
hist(cars$length)
```

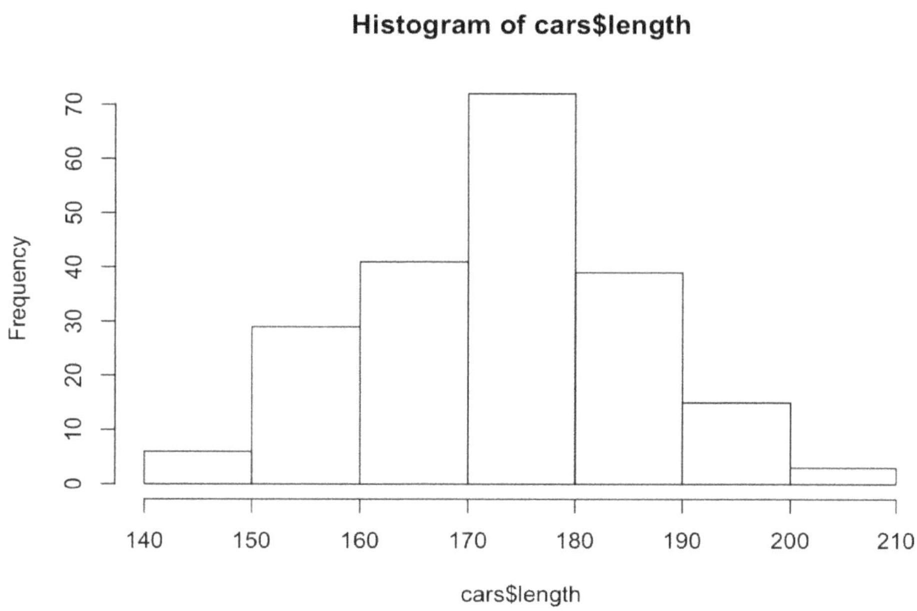

Figure 15.3: Histogram of the Length of Cars

The histogram involves the partition of the range of variable length into intervals. These interval are the basis for rectangles. The height of the rectangles represent the frequency of cars with lengths that fall in the given interval.

The mosaic plot in Figure 15.2 is constructed on the basis of this histogram. The xx-axis in this plot corresponds to the explanatory variable "length". The total area of the square in the plot is divided between 7 vertical rectangles. These vertical rectangles correspond to the 7 rectangles in the histogram of Figure 15.3, turn on their sides. Hence, the width of each rectangle in Figure 15.2 correspond to the hight of the parallel rectangle in the histogram. Consequently, the area of the vertical rectangles in the mosaic plot represents the relative frequency of the associated interval of values of the explanatory variable.

The rectangle that is associated with each interval of values of the explanatory variable is further divided into horizontal sub-rectangles that are associated with the response factor. In the current example each darker rectangle is associated with the level "four" of the response "num.of.door" and each brighter rectangle is associated with the level "two". The relative area of the horizontal rectangles within each vertical rectangle represent the relative frequency of the levels of the response within each interval of values of the explanatory variable.

From the examination of the mosaic plot one may identify relations between the explanatory variable and the relative frequency of an identified level of the response. In the current example one may observe that the relative frequency of the cars with four doors is, overall, increasing with the increase in the length of cars.

Logistic regression is a method for the investigation of relations between the probability of an event and explanatory variables. Specifically, we use it here for making inference on the number of doors as a response and the length of the car as the explanatory variable.

Statistical inference requires a statistical model. The statistical model in logistic regression relates the probability p_i, the probability of the event for observation i, to x_i, the value of the response for that observation. The relation between the two in given by the formula:

$$p_i = \frac{e^{a+b\cdot x_i}}{1+e^{a+b\cdot x_i}} ,$$

where a and b are coefficients common to all observations. Equivalently, one may write the same relation in the form:

$$\log(p_i/[1-p_i]) = a + b \cdot x_i ,$$

that states that the relation between a (function of) the probability of the event and the explanatory variable is a linear trend.

One may fit the logistic regression to the data and test the null hypothesis by the use of the function "glm":

```
fit.doors <- glm(num.of.doors=="four"~length, family=binomial,data=cars)
summary(fit.doors)
```

```
##
## Call:
## glm(formula = num.of.doors == "four" ~ length, family = binomial,
##     data = cars)
##
## Deviance Residuals:
##     Min       1Q   Median       3Q      Max
## -2.1646  -1.1292   0.5688   1.0240   1.6673
##
## Coefficients:
##              Estimate Std. Error z value Pr(>|z|)
## (Intercept) -13.14767    2.58693  -5.082 3.73e-07 ***
## length        0.07726    0.01495   5.168 2.37e-07 ***
## ---
## Signif. codes:  0 '***' 0.001 '**' 0.01 '*' 0.05 '.' 0.1 ' ' 1
##
## (Dispersion parameter for binomial family taken to be 1)
##
##     Null deviance: 278.33  on 202  degrees of freedom
## Residual deviance: 243.96  on 201  degrees of freedom
##   (2 observations deleted due to missingness)
## AIC: 247.96
##
## Number of Fisher Scoring iterations: 3
```

Generally, the function "glm" can be used in order to fit regression models in cases where the distribution of the response has special forms. Specifically, when the argument "family=binomial" is used then the model that is being used in the model of logistic regression. The formula that is used in the function involves a response and an explanatory variable. The response may be a sequence with logical "TRUE" or "FALSE" values as in the example[84]. Alternatively, it may be a sequence with "1" or "0" values, "1" corresponding to the event occurring to the subject and "0" corresponding to the event not occurring. The argument "data=cars" is used in order to inform the function that the variables are located in the given data frame.

The "glm" function is applied to the data and the fitted model is stored in the object "fit.doors".

A report is produced when the function "summary" is applied to the fitted model. Notice the similarities and the differences between the report presented here and the reports for linear regression that are presented in Chapter 14. Both reports contain estimates of the coefficients a and b and tests for the equality of these coefficients to zero. When the coefficient b, the coefficient that represents the slope, is equal to 0 then the probability of the event and the explanatory variable are unrelated. In the current case we may note that the null hypothesis H_0:b=0, the hypothesis that claims that there is no relation between the explanatory variable and the response, is clearly rejected (p-value 2.37×10–7).

The estimated values of the coefficients are -13.14767 for the intercept a and 0.07726 for the slope b. One may produce confidence intervals for these coefficients by the application of the function "confint" to the fitted model:

```
confint(fit.doors)

## Waiting for profiling to be done...

##                     2.5 %     97.5 %
## (Intercept) -18.50384373 -8.3180877
## length        0.04938358  0.1082429
```

15.4 EXERCISES

Exercise 15.1 This exercise deals with a comparison between Mediterranean diet and low-fat diet recommended by the American Heart Association in the context of risks for illness or death among patients that survived a heart attack[85]. This case study is taken from the Rice Virtual Lab in Statistics. More details on this case study can be found in the case study "Mediterranean Diet and Health" that is presented in that site.

The subjects, 605 survivors of a heart attack, were randomly assigned follow either (1) a diet close to the "prudent diet step 1" of the American Heart Association (AHA) or (2) a Mediterranean-type diet consisting of more bread and cereals, more fresh fruit and vegetables, more grains, more fish, fewer delicatessen food, less meat.

The subjects' diet and health condition were monitored over a period of four-year. Information regarding deaths, development of cancer or the development of non-fatal illnesses was collected. The information from this study is stored in the file "diet.csv". The file "diet.csv" contains two factors: "health" that describes the condition of the subject, either healthy, suffering from a non-fatal illness, suffering from cancer, or dead; and the "type" that describes the type of diet, either Mediterranean or the diet recommended by the AHA. The file can be found on the internet at http://pluto.huji.ac.il/~msby/StatThink/Datasets/diet.csv. Answer the following questions based on the data in the file:

1. Produce a frequency table of the two variable. Read off from the table the number of healthy subjects that are using the Mediterranean diet and the number of healthy subjects that are using the diet recommended by the AHA.

2. Test the null hypothesis that the probability of keeping healthy following an heart attack is the same for those that use the Mediterranean diet and for those that use the diet recommended by the AHA. Use a two-sided alternative and a 5% significance level.
3. Compute a 95% confidence interval for the difference between the two probabilities of keeping healthy.

Exercise 15.2 Cushing's syndrome disorder results from a tumor (adenoma) in the pituitary gland that causes the production of high levels of cortisol. The symptoms of the syndrome are the consequence of the elevated levels of this steroid hormone in the blood. The syndrome was first described by Harvey Cushing in 1932.

The file "coshings.csv" contains information on 27 patients that suffer from Cushing's syndrome. The three variables in the file are "tetra", "pregn", and "type". The factor "type" describes the underlying type of syndrome, coded as "a", (adenoma),"b" (bilateral hyperplasia), "c" (carcinoma) or "u" for unknown. The variable "tetra" describe the level of urinary excretion rate (mg/24hr) of Tetrahydrocortisone, a type of steroid, and the variable "pregn" describes urinary excretion rate (mg/24hr) of Pregnanetriol, another type of steroid. The file can be found on the internet at http://pluto.huji.ac.il/~msby/StatThink/Datasets/coshings.csv. Answer the following questions based on the information in this file:

1. Plot the histogram of the variable "tetra" and the mosaic plot that describes the relation between the variable "type" as a response and the variable "tetra". What is the information that is conveyed by the second vertical triangle from the right (the third from the left) in the mosaic plot.
2. Test the null hypothesis that there is no relation between the variable "tetra" as an explanatory variable and the indicator of the type being equal to "b" as a response. Compute a confidence interval for the parameter that describes the relation.
3. Repeat the analysis from 2 using only the observations for which the type is known. (Hint: you may fit the model to the required subset by the inclusion of the argument "subset=(type!=u)" in the function that fits the model.) Which of the analysis do you think is more appropriate?

Chapter 16 CASE STUDIES

16.1 INTRODUCTION: AN OVERVIEW

This chapter marks the end of this book. We begin with a brief recapitulation of the subjects that were examined in the latter portion of the book, specifically the section focused on statistical inference. The focal point of the chapter entails the statistical examination of two case studies. The instruments to be utilized for the analysis are the ones that were previously described in the book. We conclude this chapter and this book with some last thoughts.

16.2 A REVIEW

The second section of the book focused on statistical inference, which is the discipline of drawing general conclusions about an entire population based on data collected from a sample. The statements are grounded on theoretical models that generate the sample distribution. The evaluation of inference procedures is based on their qualities within the context of this sampling distribution. Data is subjected to procedures that possess beneficial qualities. Summaries that describe the theoretical properties of this application can be appended to its output. Specifically, we addressed two methods of drawing conclusions. There were two forms: estimation and hypothesis testing. The objective of estimating is to ascertain the precise value of a parameter within the population. In order to achieve this objective, point estimates or confidence intervals can be utilized. The qualities of point estimators may be evaluated by utilizing the mean square error (MSE), whereas the properties of the confidence interval can be evaluated by considering the confidence level. The objective of hypothesis testing is to make a decision between two competing hypotheses. These theories are expressed in relation to population parameters. A statistical test, known as the decision rule, is created using a test statistic and a rejection zone. If the test statistic falls within the rejection zone, the default hypothesis between the two is rejected. A crucial characteristic that a test must have is a limitation on the likelihood of committing a Type I error, which refers to the possibility of mistakenly rejecting the null hypothesis. The limitation is referred to as the significance level of the test. A test can also be evaluated based on its statistical power, which refers to the probability of correctly rejecting the null hypothesis. Estimation and testing were utilized to analyze individual data and explore the connections between two measurements. We included both numerical variables and categorical variables in our analysis of individual measurements. One can try to perform inference on the mean and/or the variance for numerical variables. When considering factors, we took into account the estimation of the chance of achieving a certain level, or more broadly, the probability of an event happening. We presented statistical models that can be utilized to depict the relationships between variables. One of the variables was assigned the role of the response. The explanatory variable is defined as a variable that has the potential to influence the distribution of the response. More precisely, we examined variables that are numerical and factors that had only two levels. If the explanatory variable is a factor with only two levels, the analysis simplifies to comparing two sub-populations, each associated with one level. If the explanatory variable is numeric, a regression model can be used, either linear or logistic regression, depending on the nature of the response variable. Statistical inference relies on the underlying assumption of statistical models. These models aim to accurately represent reality. Nevertheless, it is recommended to exercise a prudent level of caution when utilizing the models. Prior to proceeding, it is imperative to possess a clear understanding of the underlying assumptions. One should question the reasonableness of these assumptions within the specific context of the analysis. Ultimately, it is crucial to thoroughly examine the soundness of the assumptions based on the available evidence. Plotting the data and comparing it to the model's assumptions can be beneficial.

16.3 CASE STUDIES

Let us apply the methods that were introduced throughout the book to two examples of data analysis. Both examples are taken from the case studies of the Rice Virtual Lab in Statistics can be found in their Case Studies section. The analysis of these case studies may involve any of the tools that were described in the second part of the book (and some from the first part). It may be useful to read again Chapters 9–15 before reading the case studies.

16.3.1 Physicians' Reactions to the Size of a Patient

Overweight and obesity is common in many of the developed contrives. In some cultures, obese individuals face discrimination in employment, education, and relationship contexts. The current research, conducted by Mikki Hebl and Jingping Xu[87], examines physicians' attitude toward overweight and obese patients in comparison to their attitude toward patients who are not overweight.

The experiment included a total of 122 primary care physicians affiliated with one of three major hospitals in the Texas Medical Center of Houston. These physicians were sent a packet containing a medical chart similar to the one they view upon seeing a patient. This chart portrayed a patient who was displaying symptoms of a migraine headache but was otherwise healthy. Two variables (the gender and the weight of the patient) were manipulated across six different versions of the medical charts. The weight of the patient, described in terms of Body Mass Index (BMI), was average (BMI = 23), overweight (BMI = 30), or obese (BMI = 36). Physicians were randomly assigned to receive one of the six charts, and were asked to look over the chart carefully and complete two medical forms. The first form asked physicians which of 42 tests they would recommend giving to the patient. The second form asked physicians to indicate how much time they believed they would spend with the patient, and to describe the reactions that they would have toward this patient.

In this presentation, only the question on how much time the physicians believed they would spend with the patient is analyzed. Although three patient weight conditions were used in the study (average, overweight, and obese) only the average and overweight conditions will be analyzed. Therefore, there are two levels of patient weight (average and overweight) and one dependent variable (time spent).

The data for the given collection of responses from 72 primary care physicians is stored in the file "discriminate.csv". We start by reading the content of the file into a data frame by the name "patient" and presenting the summary of the variables:

```
patient <- read.csv("_data/discriminate.csv")
summary(patient)
```

```
##     weight          time
##  BMI=23:33   Min.   : 5.00
##  BMI=30:38   1st Qu.:20.00
##              Median :30.00
##              Mean   :27.82
##              3rd Qu.:30.00
##              Max.   :60.00
```

Observe that of the 72 "patients", 38 are overweight and 33 have an average weight. The time spend with the patient, as predicted by physicians, is distributed between 5 minutes and 1 hour, with a average of 27.82 minutes and a median of 30 minutes.

It is a good practice to have a look at the data before doing the analysis. In this examination on should see that the numbers make sense and one should identify special features of the data. Even in this very simple example we may want to have a look at the histogram of the variable “time”:

```
hist(patient$time)
```

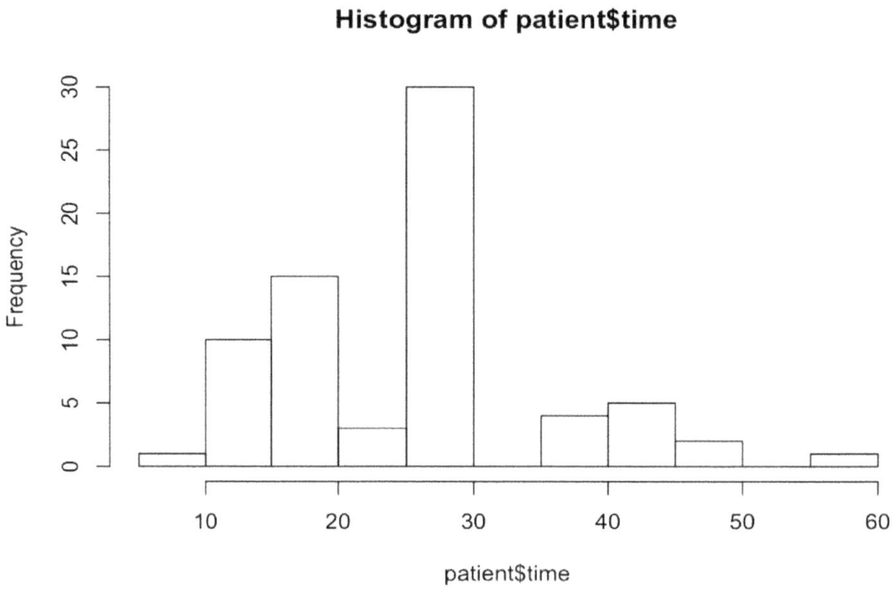

A feature in this plot that catches attention is the fact that there is a high concventration of values in the interval between 25 and 30. Together with the fact that the median is equal to 30, one may suspect that, as a matter of fact, a large numeber of the values are actually equal to 30. Indeed, let us produce a table of the response:

```
table(patient$time)
```

```
##
##   5 15 20 25 30 40 45 50 60
##   1 10 15  3 30  4  5  2  1
```

Notice that 30 of the 72 physicians marked “30” as the time they expect to spend with the patient. This is the middle value in the range, and may just be the default value one marks if one just needs to complete a form and do not really place much importance to the question that was asked.

The goal of the analysis is to examine the relation between overweigh and the Doctor’s response. The explanatory variable is a factor with two levels. The response is numeric. A natural tool to use in order to test this hypothesis is the t-test, which is implemented with the function "t.test".

First we plot the relation between the response and the explanatory variable and then we apply the test:

```
boxplot(time~weight,data=patient)
```

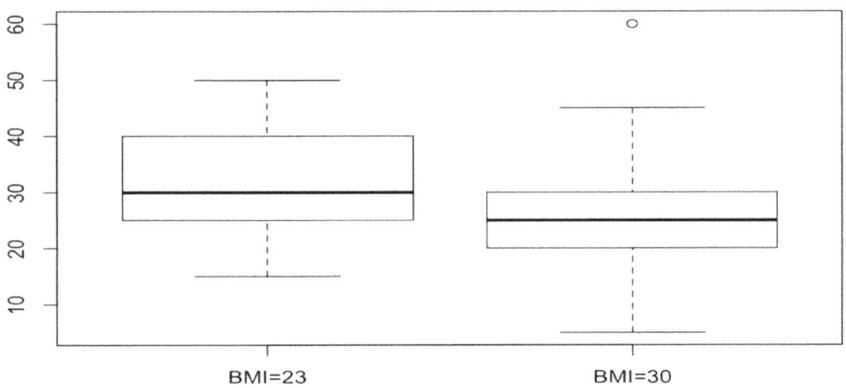


```
t.test(time~weight,data=patient)

##
##  Welch Two Sample t-test
##
## data:  time by weight
## t = 2.8516, df = 67.174, p-value = 0.005774
## alternative hypothesis: true difference in means is not equal to 0
## 95 percent confidence interval:
##   1.988532 11.265056
## sample estimates:
## mean in group BMI=23 mean in group BMI=30
##             31.36364             24.73684
```

Nothing seems problematic in the box plot. The two distributions, as they are reflected in the box plots, look fairly symmetric.

When we consider the report that produced by the function "t.test" we may observe that the p-value is equal to 0.005774. This p-value is computed in testing the null hypothesis that the expectation of the response for both types of patients are equal against the two sided alternative. Since the p-value is less than 0.05 we do reject the null hypothesis.

The estimated value of the difference between the expectation of the response for a patient with BMI=23 and a patient with BMI=30 is 31.36364-24.73684≈6.63 minutes. The confidence interval is (approximately) equal to [1.99,11.27]. Hence, it looks as if the physicians expect to spend more time with the average weight patients.

After analyzing the effect of the explanatory variable on the expectation of the response one may want to examine the presence, or lack thereof, of such effect on the variance of the response. Towards that end, one may use the function "var. test":

```
var.test(time~weight,data=patient)
```

```
##
##  F test to compare two variances
##
## data:  time by weight
## F = 1.0443, num df = 32, denom df = 37, p-value = 0.8931
## alternative hypothesis: true ratio of variances is not equal to 1
## 95 percent confidence interval:
##  0.5333405 2.0797269
## sample estimates:
## ratio of variances
##           1.044316
```

In this test we do not reject the null hypothesis that the two variances of the response are equal since the p-value is larger than 0.05. The sample variances are almost equal to each other (their ratio is 1.044316), with a confidence interval for the ration that essentially ranges between 1/2 and 2.

The production of p-values and confidence intervals is just one aspect in the analysis of data. Another aspect, which typically is much more time consuming and requires experience and healthy skepticism is the examination of the assumptions that are used in order to produce the p-values and the confidence intervals. A clear violation of the assumptions may warn the statistician that perhaps the computed nominal quantities do not represent the actual statistical properties of the tools that were applied.

In this case, we have noticed the high concentration of the response at the value "30". What is the situation when we split the sample between the two levels of the explanatory variable? Let us apply the function "table" once more, this time with the explanatory variable included:

```
table(patient$time,patient$weight)
```

```
##
##       BMI=23 BMI=30
##    5       0      1
##    15      2      8
##    20      6      9
##    25      1      2
##    30     14     16
##    40      4      0
##    45      4      1
##    50      2      0
##    60      0      1
```

Not surprisingly, there is still high concentration at that level "30". But one can see that only 2 of the responses of the "BMI=30" group are above that value in comparison to a much more symmetric distribution of responses for the other group.

The simulations of the significance level of the one-sample t-test for an Exponential response that were conducted in Question may cast some doubt on how trustworthy are nominal p-values of the t-test when the measurements are skewed. The skewness of the response for the group "BMI=30" is a reason to be worry.

We may consider a different test, which is more robust, in order to validate the significance of our findings. For example, we may turn the response into a factor by setting a level for values larger or equal to "30" and a different level for values less than "30". The relation between the new response and the explanatory variable can be examined with the function "prop.test". We first plot and then test:

```
plot(factor(patient$time>=30)~weight,data=patient)
```

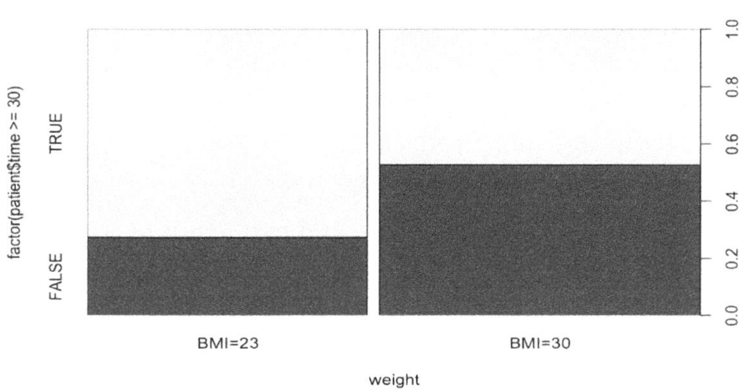

```
prop.test(table(patient$time>=30,patient$weight))

##
##  2-sample test for equality of proportions with continuity
##  correction
##
## data:  table(patient$time >= 30, patient$weight)
## X-squared = 3.7098, df = 1, p-value = 0.05409
## alternative hypothesis: two.sided
## 95 percent confidence interval:
##  -0.515508798 -0.006658689
## sample estimates:
##    prop 1    prop 2
## 0.3103448 0.5714286
```

The mosaic plot presents the relation between the explanatory variable and the new factor. The level "TRUE" is associated with a value of the predicted time spent with the patient being 30 minutes or more. The level "FALSE" is associated with a prediction of less than 30 minutes.

The computed p-value is equal to 0.05409, that almost reaches the significance level of 5%. Notice that the probabilities that are being estimated by the function are the probabilities of the level "FALSE". Overall, one may see the outcome of this test as supporting evidence for the conclusion of the t-test. However, the p-value provided by the t-test may over emphasize the evidence in the data for a significant difference in the physician attitude towards overweight patients.

16.3.2 Physical Strength and Job Performance

The next case study involves an attempt to develop a measure of physical ability that is easy and quick to administer, does not risk injury, and is related to how well a person performs the actual job. The current example is based on study by Blakely et al. [90], published in the journal Personnel Psychology.

There are a number of very important jobs that require, in addition to cognitive skills, a significant amount of strength to be able to perform at a high level. Construction worker, electrician and auto mechanic, all require strength in order to carry out critical components of their job. An interesting applied problem is how to select the best candidates from amongst a group of applicants for physically demanding jobs in a safe and a cost effective way.

The data presented in this case study, and may be used for the development of a method for selection among candidates, were collected from 147 individuals working in physically demanding jobs. Two measures of strength were gathered from each participant. These included grip and arm strength. A piece of equipment known as the Jackson Evaluation System (JES) was used to collect the strength data. The JES can be configured to measure the strength of a number of muscle groups. In this study, grip strength and arm strength were measured. The outcomes of these measurements were summarized in two scores of physical strength called "grip" and "arm".

Two separate measures of job performance are presented in this case study. First, the supervisors for each of the participants were asked to rate how well their employee(s) perform on the physical aspects of their jobs. This measure is summarizes in the variable "ratings". Second, simulations of physically demanding work tasks were developed. The summary score of these simulations are given in the variable "sims". Higher values of either measures of performance indicates better performance.

The data for the 4 variables and 147 observations is stored in "job.csv". We start by reading the content of the file into a data frame by the name "job", presenting a summary of the variables, and their histograms:

```
job <- read.csv("_data/job.csv")
summary(job)
```

```
##       grip            arm             ratings            sims
##  Min.   : 29.0   Min.   : 19.00   Min.   :21.60   Min.   :-4.1700
##  1st Qu.: 94.0   1st Qu.: 64.50   1st Qu.:34.80   1st Qu.:-0.9650
##  Median :111.0   Median : 81.50   Median :41.30   Median : 0.1600
##  Mean   :110.2   Mean   : 78.75   Mean   :41.01   Mean   : 0.2018
##  3rd Qu.:124.5   3rd Qu.: 94.00   3rd Qu.:47.70   3rd Qu.: 1.0700
##  Max.   :189.0   Max.   :132.00   Max.   :57.20   Max.   : 5.1700
```

```
par(mfrow=c(2,2)) # we'll plot a 2x2 grid
hist(job$grip)
hist(job$arm)
hist(job$ratings)
hist(job$sims)
```

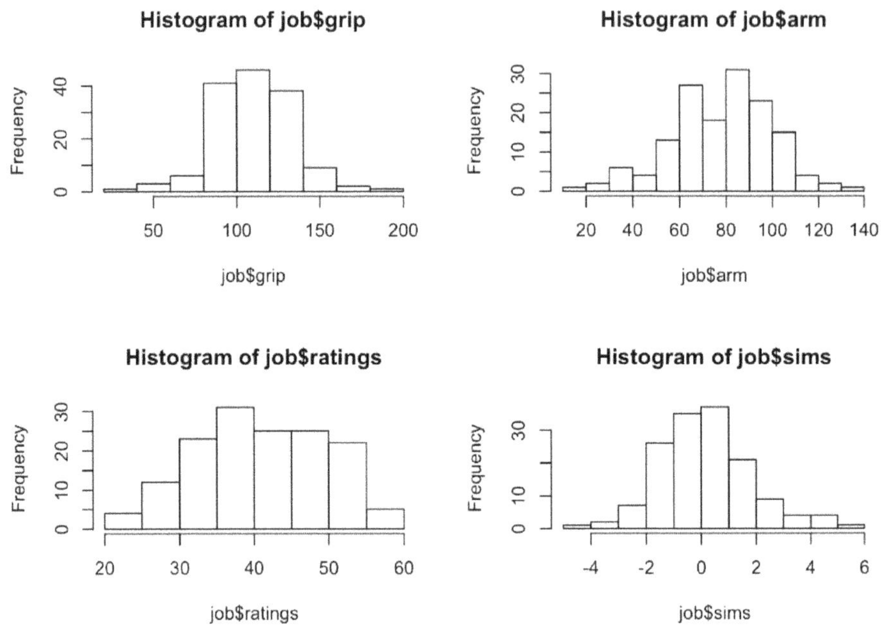

All variables are numeric. Examination of the 4 summaries and histograms does not produce interest findings. All variables are, more or less, symmetric with the distribution of the variable "ratings" tending perhaps to be more uniform then the other three.

The main analyses of interest are attempts to relate the two measures of physical strength "grip" and "arm" with the two measures of job performance, "ratings" and "sims". A natural tool to consider in this context is a linear regression analysis that relates a measure of physical strength as an explanatory variable to a measure of job performance as a response.

```
par(mfrow=c(2,2)) # we'll plot a 2x2 grid

plot(sims~grip,data=job)
sims.grip <- lm(sims~grip,data=job)
abline(sims.grip)

plot(sims~arm,data=job)

sims.arm <- lm(sims~arm,data=job)
abline(sims.arm)

score <- -5.434 + 0.024*job$grip+ 0.037*job$arm
plot(sims~score,data=job)
sims.score <- lm(sims~score,data=job)
abline(sims.score)

plot(grip~arm,data=job)
```

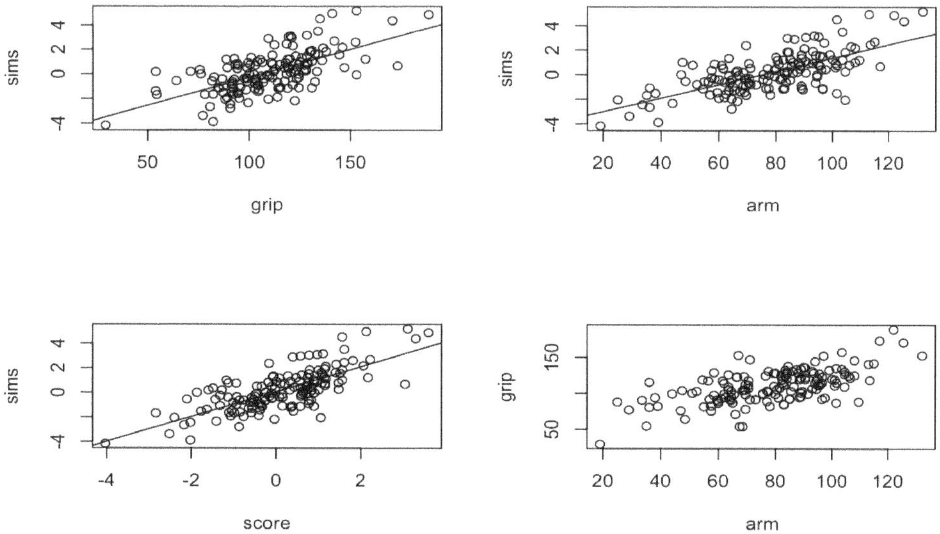

Figure 16.1: Scatter Plots and Regression Lines

Let us consider the variable "sims" as a response. The first step is to plot a scatter plot of the response and explanatory variable, for both explanatory variables. To the scatter plot we add the line of regression. In order to add the regression line we fit the regression model with the function "lm" and then apply the function "abline" to the fitted model. The plot for the relation between the response and the variable "grip" is produced by the code:

```
plot(sims~grip,data=job)
sims.grip <- lm(sims~grip,data=job)
abline(sims.grip)
```

The plot that is produced by this code is presented on the upper-left panel of Figure 16.1.

The plot for the relation between the response and the variable "arm" is produced by this code:

```
plot(sims~arm,data=job)

sims.arm <- lm(sims~arm,data=job)
abline(sims.arm)
```

The plot that is produced by the last code is presented on the upper-right panel of Figure 16.1.

Both plots show similar characteristics. There is an overall linear trend in the relation between the explanatory variable and the response. The value of the response increases with the increase in the value of the explanatory variable (a positive slope). The regression line seems to follow, more or less, the trend that is demonstrated by the scatter plot.

A more detailed analysis of the regression model is possible by the application of the function "summary" to the fitted model. First the case where the explanatory variable is "grip":

```
summary(sims.grip)
```

```
##
## Call:
## lm(formula = sims ~ grip, data = job)
##
## Residuals:
##      Min       1Q   Median       3Q      Max
## -2.9295 -0.8708 -0.1219  0.8039  3.3494
##
## Coefficients:
##             Estimate Std. Error t value Pr(>|t|)
## (Intercept) -4.809675   0.511141   -9.41   <2e-16 ***
## grip         0.045463   0.004535   10.03   <2e-16 ***
## ---
## Signif. codes:  0 '***' 0.001 '**' 0.01 '*' 0.05 '.' 0.1 ' ' 1
##
## Residual standard error: 1.295 on 145 degrees of freedom
## Multiple R-squared:  0.4094, Adjusted R-squared:  0.4053
## F-statistic: 100.5 on 1 and 145 DF,  p-value: < 2.2e-16
```

Examination of the report reviles a clear statistical significance for the effect of the explanatory variable on the distribution of response. The value of R-squared, the ration of the variance of the response explained by the regression is 0.40940.4094. The square root of this quantity, $\sqrt{0.4094} \approx 0.64$, is the proportion of the standard deviation of the response that is explained by the explanatory variable. Hence, about 64% of the variability in the response can be attributed to the measure of the strength of the grip.

For the variable "arm" we get:

```
##
## Call:
## lm(formula = sims ~ arm, data = job)
##
## Residuals:
##      Min       1Q   Median       3Q      Max
## -3.6467 -0.7502 -0.0285  0.6875  3.0770
##
## Coefficients:
##              Estimate Std. Error t value Pr(>|t|)
## (Intercept) -4.095160   0.391745  -10.45   <2e-16 ***
## arm          0.054563   0.004806   11.35   <2e-16 ***
## ---
## Signif. codes:  0 '***' 0.001 '**' 0.01 '*' 0.05 '.' 0.1 ' ' 1
##
## Residual standard error: 1.226 on 145 degrees of freedom
## Multiple R-squared:  0.4706, Adjusted R-squared:  0.467
## F-statistic: 128.9 on 1 and 145 DF,  p-value: < 2.2e-16
```

This variable is also statistically significant. The value of R-squared is 0.47060.4706. The proportion of the standard deviation that is explained by the strength of the are is $\sqrt{0.4706} \approx 0.69$, which is slightly higher than the proportion explained by the grip.

Overall, the explanatory variables do a fine job in the reduction of the variability of the response "sims" and may be used as substitutes of the response in order to select among candidates. A better prediction of the response based on the values of the explanatory variables can be obtained by combining the information in both variables. The production of such combination is not discussed in this book, though it is similar in principle to the methods of linear regression that are presented in Chapter 14. The produced score[92] takes the form:

$$\texttt{score} = -5.434 + 0.024 \cdot \texttt{grip} + 0.037 \cdot \texttt{arm} \,.$$

We use this combined score as an explanatory variable. First we form the score and plot the relation between it and the response:

```
score <- -5.434 + 0.024*job$grip+ 0.037*job$arm
plot(sims~score,data=job)
```

```
sims.score <- lm(sims~score,data=job)
abline(sims.score)
```

The scatter plot that includes the regression line can be found at the lower-left panel of Figure 16.1. Indeed, the linear trend is more pronounced for this scatter plot and the regression line a better description of the relation between the response and the explanatory variable. A summary of the regression model produces the report:

```
summary(sims.score)
```

```
##
## Call:
## lm(formula = sims ~ score, data = job)
##
## Residuals:
##     Min      1Q  Median      3Q     Max
## -3.1890 -0.7390 -0.0698  0.7411  2.8636
##
## Coefficients:
##             Estimate Std. Error t value Pr(>|t|)
## (Intercept)  0.07479    0.09452   0.791     0.43
## score        1.01291    0.07730  13.104   <2e-16 ***
## ---
## Signif. codes:  0 '***' 0.001 '**' 0.01 '*' 0.05 '.' 0.1 ' ' 1
##
## Residual standard error: 1.14 on 145 degrees of freedom
## Multiple R-squared:  0.5422, Adjusted R-squared:  0.539
## F-statistic: 171.7 on 1 and 145 DF,  p-value: < 2.2e-16
```

Indeed, the score is highly significant. More important, the R-squared coefficient that is associated with the score is 0.5422, which corresponds to a ratio of the standard deviation that is explained by the model of $\sqrt{0.5422} \approx 0.74$. Thus, almost 3/4 of the variability is accounted for by the score, so the score is a reasonable mean of guessing what the results of the simulations will be. This guess is based only on the results of the simple tests of strength that is conducted with the JES device.

Before putting the final seal on the results let us examine the assumptions of the statistical model. First, with respect to the two explanatory variables. Does each of them really measure a different property or do they actually measure the same phenomena? In order to examine this question let us look at the scatter plot that describes the relation between the two explanatory variables. This plot is produced using the code:

```
plot(grip~arm,data=job)
```

It is presented in the lower-right panel of Figure 16.1. Indeed, one may see that the two measurements of strength are not independent of each other but tend to produce an increasing linear trend. Hence, it should not be surprising that the relation of each of them with the response produces essentially the same goodness of fit. The computed score gives a slightly improved fit, but still, it basically reflects either of the original explanatory variables.

In light of this observation, one may want to consider other measures of strength that represents features of the strength not captures by these two variable. Namely, measures that show less joint trend than the two considered.

Another element that should be examined are the probabilistic assumptions that underly the regression model. We described the regression model only in terms of the functional relation between the explanatory variable and the expectation of the response. In the case of linear regression, for example, this relation was given in terms of a linear equation. However, another part of the model corresponds to the distribution of the measurements about the line of regression. The assumption that led to the computation of the reported p-values is that this distribution is Normal.

A method that can be used in order to investigate the validity of the Normal assumption is to analyze the residuals from the regression line. Recall that these residuals are computed as the difference between the observed value of the response and its estimated expectation, namely the fitted regression line. The residuals can be computed via the application of the function "residuals" to the fitted regression model.

Specifically, let us look at the residuals from the regression line that uses the score that is combined from the grip and arm measurements of strength. One may plot a histogram of the residuals:

```
par(mfrow=c(2,1))

hist(residuals(sims.score))

qqnorm(residuals(sims.score))
qqline(residuals(sims.score))
```

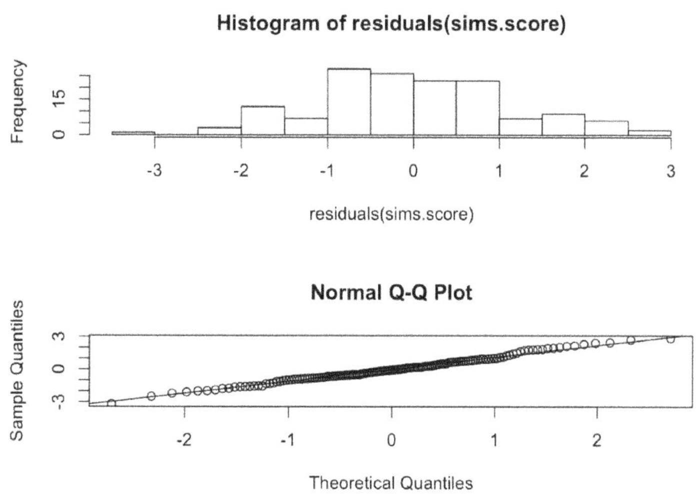

The produced histogram is represented on the upper panel. The histogram portrays a symmetric distribution that my result from Normally distributed observations. A better method to compare the distribution of the residuals to the Normal distribution is to use the *Quantile-Quantile plot.* This plot can be found on the lower panel. We do not discuss here the method by which this plot is produced[93]. However, we do say that any deviation of the points from a straight line is indication of violation of the assumption of Normality. In the current case, the points seem to be on a single line, which is consistent with the assumptions of the regression model.

The next task should be an analysis of the relations between the explanatory variables and the other response "ratings". In principle one may use the same steps that were presented for the investigation of the relations between the explanatory variables and the response "sims". But of course, the conclusion may differ. We leave this part of the investigation as an exercise to the students.

16.4 CONCISE SUMMARY

The book provided a description of certain aspects of statistics that we considered to be sufficiently straightforward to be covered in an introductory statistics course. These concepts are essential for anyone engaged in academic pursuits in any field that involves data analysis. Now that you have completed the book, it is an opportune moment to discuss the statistical aspects that are absent from this book. One component exhibits a higher degree of similarity. The statistical models offered are really basic. A typical application will necessitate more intricate models. Estimation and testing for each of these models may need the use of distinct approaches. The properties of inference, such as significance or confidence levels, are contingent upon the assumptions that the models are presumed to contain. Prior knowledge of computational tools suitable for analyzing intricate models is necessary for the user. Proficiency in understanding the probabilistic assumptions is necessary to interpret the computer output, identify any deviations from these assumptions, and evaluate the impact of such deviations on the validity of the results. Statistical tools have applications beyond estimation and hypothesis testing. For instance, statistics can be utilized for the purpose of making predictions. Assessing the potential values of future observations and determining the range in which they are likely to occur is crucial in numerous applications. Statistical techniques like regression are well-suited for this situation. However, the work at hand does not include testing or estimating the values of parameters. Instead, it requires predicting future values of the response.

A different role of statistics in the design stage. We hinted in that direction when we talked about in Chapter about the selection of a sample size in order to assure a confidence interval with a given accuracy. In most applications, the selection of the sample size emerges in the context of hypothesis testing and the criteria for selection is the minimal power of the test, a minimal probability to detect a true finding. Yet, statistical design is much more than the determination of the sample size. Statistics may have a crucial input in the decision of how to collect the data. With an eye on the requirements for the final analysis, an experienced statistician can make sure that data that is collected is indeed appropriate for that final analysis. Too often is the case where researcher steps into the statistician's office with data that he or she collected and asks, when it is already too late, for help in the analysis of data that cannot provide a satisfactory answer to the research question the researcher tried to address. It may be said, with some exaggeration, that good statisticians are required for the final analysis only in the case where the initial planning was poor.

Last, but not least, is the theoretical mathematical theory of statistics. We tried to introduce as little as possible of the relevant mathematics in this course. However, if one seriously intends to learn and understand statistics then one must become familiar with the relevant mathematical theory. Clearly, deep knowledge in the mathematical theory of probability is required. But apart from that, there is a rich and rapidly growing body of research that deals with the mathematical aspects of data analysis. One cannot be a good statistician unless one becomes familiar with the important aspects of this theory.

I should have started the book with the famous quotation: "Lies, damned lies, and statistics". Instead, I am using it to end the book. Statistics can be used and can be misused. Learning statistics can give you the tools to tell the difference between the two. My goal in writing the book is achieved if reading it will mark for you the beginning of the process of learning statistics and not the end of the process.

EXERCISE SOLUTIONS

CHAPTER 1

Exercise 1.1

1. According to the information in the question the polling was conducted among 500 registered voters. The 500 registered voters corresponds to the sample.
2. The percentage, among all registered voters of the given party, of those that prefer a male candidate is a parameter. This quantity is a characteristic of the population.
3. It is given that 42% of the sample prefer a female candidate. This quantity is a numerical characteristic of the data, of the sample. Hence, it is a statistic.
4. The voters in the state that are registered to the given party is the target population.

Exercise 1.2

One may read the data into R and create a table using the code:

```
n.cost <- c(4,2,1,1,0,2,1,2,4,2,5,3,1,5,1,5,1,2,1,1,3,4,2,4,3)
table(n.cost)
```

```
## n.cost
## 0 1 2 3 4 5
## 1 8 6 3 4 3
```

For convenience, one may also create the bar plot of the data using the code:

```
plot(table(n.cost))
```

The number of days in which 5 costumers where waiting is 3, since the frequency of the value "5" in the data is 3. That can be seen from the table by noticing the number below value "5" is 3. It can also be seen from the bar plot by observing that the hight of the bar above the value "5" is equal to 3.

The number of waiting costumers that occurred the largest number of times is 1. The value “1” occurred 8 times, more than any other value. Notice that the bar above this value is the highest.

The value “0”, which occurred only once, occurred the least number of times.

CHAPTER 2

Exercise 2.1

The relative frequency of direct hits of category 1 is 0.3993. Notice that the cumulative relative frequency of category 1 and 2 hits, the sum of the relative frequency of both categories, is 0.6630. The relative frequency of category 2 hits is 0.2637. Consequently, the relative frequency of direct hits of category 1 is 0.6630 - 0.2637 = 0.3993.

The relative frequency of direct hits of category 4 or more is 0.0769. Observe that the cumulative relative of the value “3” is 0.6630 + 0.2601 = 0.9231. This follows from the fact that the cumulative relative frequency of the value “2” is 0.6630 and the relative frequency of the value “3” is 0.2601. The total cumulative relative frequency is 1.0000. The relative frequency of direct hits of category 4 or more is the difference between the total cumulative relative frequency and cumulative relative frequency of 3 hits: 1.0000 - 0.9231 = 0.0769.

Exercise 2.2

The total number of cows that were involved in this study is 45. The object “freq” contain the table of frequency of the cows, divided according to the number of calves that they had. The cumulative frequency of all the cows that had 7 calves or less, which includes all cows in the study, is reported under the number “7” in the output of the expression “cumsum(freq)”. This number is 45.

The number of cows that gave birth to a total of 4 calves is 10. Indeed, the cumulative frequency of cows that gave birth to 4 calves or less is 28. The cumulative frequency of cows that gave birth to 3 calves or less is 18. The frequency of cows that gave birth to exactly 4 calves is the difference between these two numbers: 28 - 18 = 10.

The relative frequency of cows that gave birth to at least 4 calves is 27/45=0.6. Notice that the cumulative frequency of cows that gave at most 3 calves is 18. The total number of cows is 45. Hence, the number of cows with 4 or more calves is the difference between these two numbers: 45 - 18 = 27. The relative frequency of such cows is the ratio between this number and the total number of cows: 27/45=0.6.

CHAPTER 3

Exercise 3.1

Consider the data "x1". From the summary we see that it is distributed in the range between 0 and slightly below 5. The central 50% of the distribution are located between 2.5 and 3.8. The mean and median are approximately equal to each other, which suggests an approximately symmetric distribution. Consider the histograms in Figure 3.3. Histograms 1 and 3 correspond to a distributions in the appropriate range. However, the distribution in Histogram 3 is concentrated in lower values than suggested by the given first and third quartiles. Consequently, we match the summary of "x1" with Histogram 1.

Consider the data "x2". Again, the distribution is in the range between 0 and slightly below 5. The central 50% of the distribution are located between 0.6 and 1.8. The mean is larger than the median, which suggests a distribution skewed to the right. Therefore, we match the summary of "x2" with Histogram 3.

For the data in "x3" we may note that the distribution is in the range between 2 and 6. The histogram that fits this description is Histograms 2.

The box plot is essentially a graphical representation of the information presented by the function "summary". Following the rational of matching the summary with the histograms we may obtain that Histogram 1 should be matched with Box-plot 2 in Figure 3.4, Histogram 2 matches Box-plot 3, and Histogram 3 matches Box-plot 1. Indeed, it is easier to match the box plots with the summaries. However, it is a good idea to practice the direct matching of histograms with box plots.

The data in "x1" fits Box-plot 2 in Figure 3.4. The value 0.000 is the smallest value in the data and it corresponds to the smallest point in the box plot. Since this point is below the bottom whisker it follows that it is an outlier. More directly, we may note that the inter-quartile range is equal to $IQR=3.840-2.498=1.342$. The lower threshold is equal to $2.498-1.5\times1.342=0.485$, which is larger that the given value. Consequently, the given value 0.000 is an outlier.

Observe that the data in "x3" fits Box-plot 3 in Figure 3.4. The vale 6.414 is the largest value in the data and it corresponds to the endpoint of the upper whisker in the box plot and is not an outlier. Alternatively, we may note that the inter-quartile range is equal to $IQR=4.690-3.391=1.299$. The upper threshold is equal to $4.690+1.5\times1.299=6.6385$, which is larger that the given value. Consequently, the given value 6.414 is not an outlier.

Exercise 3.2

In order to compute the mean of the data we may write the following simple R code:

```
x.val <- c(2,4,6,8,10)
freq <- c(10,6,10,2,2)
rel.freq <- freq/sum(freq)
x.bar <- sum(x.val*rel.freq)
x.bar
```

```
## [1] 4.666667
```

We created an object "x.val" that contains the unique values of the data and an object "freq" that contains the frequencies of the values. The object "rel.freq" contains the relative frequencies, the ratios between the frequencies and the number of observations. The average is computed as the sum of the products of the values with their relative frequencies. It is stored in the objects "x.bar" and obtains the value 4.666667.

An alternative approach is to reconstruct the original data from the frequency table. A simple trick that will do the job is to use the function "rep". The first argument to this function is a sequence of values. If the second argument is a sequence of the same length that contains integers then the output will be composed of a sequence that contains the values of the first sequence, each repeated a number of times indicated by the second argument. Specifically, if we enter to this function the unique value "x.val" and the frequency of the values "freq" then the output will be the sequence of values of the original sequence "x":

```
x <- rep(x.val,freq)
x
```

```
## [1]  2  2  2  2  2  2  2  2  2  2  4  4  4  4  4  4  6  6  6  6  6  6  6
## [24]  6  6  6  8  8 10 10
```

```
mean(x)
```

```
## [1] 4.666667
```

Observe that when we apply the function "mean" to "x" we get again the value 4.666667.

In order to compute the sample standard deviation we may compute first the sample variance and then take the square root of the result:

```
var.x <- sum((x.val-x.bar)^2*freq)/(sum(freq)-1)
sqrt(var.x)
```

```
## [1] 2.425914
```

Notice that the expression "sum((x.val-x.bar)^2*freq)" compute the sum of square deviations. The expression "(sum(freq)-1)" produces the number of observations minus 1 (n-1). The ratio of the two gives the sample variance.

Alternatively, had we produced the object "x" that contains the data, we may apply the function "sd" to get the sample standard deviation:

```
sd(x)
```

```
## [1] 2.425914
```

Observe that in both forms of computation we obtain the same result: 2.425914.

In order to compute the median one may produce the table of cumulative relative frequencies of "x":

```
data.frame(x.val,cumsum(rel.freq))
```

```
##   x.val cumsum.rel.freq.
## 1     2        0.3333333
## 2     4        0.5333333
## 3     6        0.8666667
## 4     8        0.9333333
## 5    10        1.0000000
```

Recall that the object "x.val" contains the unique values of the data. The expression "cumsum(rel.freq)" produces the cumulative relative frequencies. The function "data.frame" puts these two variables into a single data frame and provides a clearer representation of the results.

Notice that more that 50% of the observations have value 4 or less. However, strictly less than 50% of the observations have value 2 or less. Consequently, the median is 4. (If the value of the cumulative relative frequency at 4 would have been exactly 50% then the median would have been the average between 4 and the value larger than 4.)

In the case that we produce the values of the data "x" then we may apply the function "summary" to it and obtain the median this way

```
summary(x)
```

```
##    Min. 1st Qu.  Median    Mean 3rd Qu.    Max.
##   2.000   2.000   4.000   4.667   6.000  10.000
```

As for the inter-quartile range (IQR) notice that the first quartile is 2 and the third quartile is 6. Hence, the inter-quartile range is equal to 6 - 2 = 4. The quartiles can be read directly from the output of the function "summary" or can be obtained from the data frame of the cumulative relative frequencies. For the later observe that more than 25% of the data are less or equal to 2 and more 75% of the data are less or equal to 6 (with strictly less than 75% less or equal to 4).

In order to answer the last question we conduct the computation: (10-4.666 667)/2.425914=2.198484. We conclude that the value 10 is approximately 2.1985 standard deviations above the mean.

CHAPTER 4

Exercise 4.1

Cosult Table 4.4. The probabilities of the different values of Y are $\{p,2p,...,6p\}$. These probabilities sum to 1, consequently

$$p + 2p + 3p + 4p + 5p + 6p = (1 + 2 + 3 + 4 + 5 + 6)p = 21p = 1 \Longrightarrow p = 1/21 .$$

The event $\{Y<3\}$ contains the values 0, 1 and 2. Therefore,

$$\mathrm{P}(Y < 3) = \mathrm{P}(Y = 0) + \mathrm{P}(Y = 1) + \mathrm{P}(Y = 2) = \frac{1}{21} + \frac{2}{21} + \frac{3}{21} = \frac{6}{21} = 0.2857 .$$

The event $\{Y=\text{odd}\}$ contains the values 1, 3 and 5. Therefore,

$$\mathrm{P}(Y = \mathrm{odd}) = \mathrm{P}(Y = 1) + \mathrm{P}(Y = 3) + \mathrm{P}(Y = 5) = \frac{2}{21} + \frac{4}{21} + \frac{6}{21} = \frac{12}{21} = 0.5714 .$$

The event $\{1 \le Y<4\}$ contains the values 1, 2 and 3. Therefore,

$$\mathrm{P}(1 \le Y < 4) = \mathrm{P}(Y = 1) + \mathrm{P}(Y = 2) + \mathrm{P}(Y = 3) = \frac{2}{21} + \frac{3}{21} + \frac{4}{21} = \frac{9}{21} = 0.4286 .$$

The event $\{|Y-3|<1.5\}$ contains the values 2, 3 and 4. Therefore,

$$\mathrm{P}(|Y - 3| < 1.5) = \mathrm{P}(Y = 2) + \mathrm{P}(Y = 3) + \mathrm{P}(Y = 4) = \frac{3}{21} + \frac{4}{21} + \frac{5}{21} = \frac{12}{21} = 0.5714 .$$

The values that the random variable YY obtains are the numbers 0, 1, 2, ..., 5, with probabilities $\{1/21,2/21,...,6/21\}$, respectively. The expectation is obtained by the multiplication of the values by their respective probabilities and the summation of the products. Let us carry out the computation in R:

```
Y.val <- c(0,1,2,3,4,5)
P.val <- c(1,2,3,4,5,6)/21
E <- sum(Y.val*P.val)
E
```

```
## [1] 3.333333
```

We obtain an expectation E (Y)=3.3333.

The values that the random variable YY obtains are the numbers 0, 1, 2, ..., 5, with probabilities {1/21,2/21,...,6/21}, respectively. The expectation is equal to E (Y)=3.333333. The variance is obtained by the multiplication of the squared deviation from the expectation of the values by their respective probabilities and the summation of the products. Let us carry out the computation in R:

```
Var <- sum((Y.val-E)^2*P.val)
```

We obtain a variance V (Y)=2.2222.

The standard deviation is the square root of the variance: $\sqrt{\mathrm{V}(Y)} = \sqrt{2.2222} = 1.4907$.

Exercise 4.2

An outcome of the game of chance may be represented by a sequence of length three composed of the letters “H” and “T”. For example, the sequence “THH“ corresponds to the case where the first toss produced a”Tail“, the second a “Head” and the third a “Head”. With this notation we obtain that the possible outcomes of the game are {HHH,THH,HTH,TTH,HHT,THT,HTT,TTT}. All outcomes are equally likely. There are 8 possible outcomes and only one of which corresponds to winning. Consequently, the probability of winning is 1/8.

Consider the previous solution. One looses if any other of the outcomes occurs. Hence, the probability of loosing is 7/8.

Denote the gain of the player by X. The random variable X may obtain two values: 10-2 = 8 if the player wins and -2 if the player looses. The probabilities of these values are {1/8, 7/8}, respectively. Therefore, the expected gain, the expectation of X is:

$$\mathrm{E}(X) = 8 \times \frac{1}{8} + (-2) \times \frac{7}{8} = -0.75 .$$

CHAPTER 5

Exercise 5.1

The Binomial distribution is a reasonable model for the number of people that develop high fever asion. Let X be the number of people that do so in a give day. Hence, $X \sim$Binomial(500,0.09). According to the formula for the expectation in the Binomial distribution, since n=500 and p=0.09, we get that:

$$\mathrm{E}(X) = np = 500 \times 0.09 = 45 \ .$$

Let $X \sim$Binomial(500,0.09). Using the formula for the variance for the Binomial distribution we get that:

$$\mathrm{V}(X) = np(1-p) = 500 \times 0.09 \times 0.91 = 40.95 \ .$$

Hence, since $\sqrt{Var(X)} = \sqrt{40.95} = 6.3992,$ the standard deviation is 6.3992.

Let $X \sim$Binomial(500,0.09). The probability that more than 40 people will develop a reaction may be computed as the difference between 1 and the probability that 40 people or less will develop a reaction:

$$\mathrm{P}(X > 40) = 1 - \mathrm{P}(X \leq 40) \ .$$

The probability can be computes with the aid of the function "pbinom" that produces the cumulative probability of the Binomial distribution:

```r
1 - pbinom(40,500,0.09)
```

```
## [1] 0.7556474
```

The probability that the number of people that will develop a reaction is between 50 and 45 (inclusive) is the difference between P (X≤50) and P(X≤45)=Prob(X≤44). Apply the function "pbinom" to get:

```
pbinom(50,500,0.09) - pbinom(44,500,0.09)

## [1] 0.3292321
```

Exercise 5.2

The plots can be produced with the following code, which should be run one line at a time:

```
x <- 0:15
plot(x,dnbinom(x,2,0.5),type="h")
```

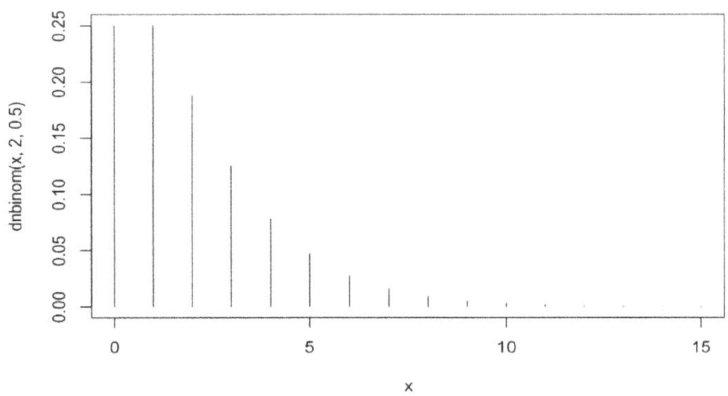


```
plot(x,dnbinom(x,4,0.5),type="h")
```

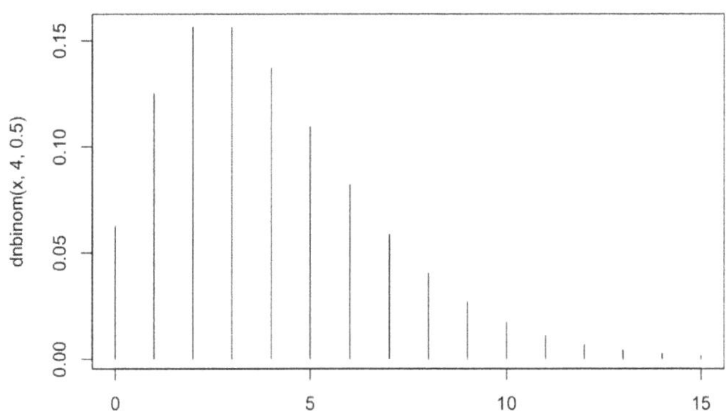


```
plot(x,dnbinom(x,8,0.8),type="h")
```

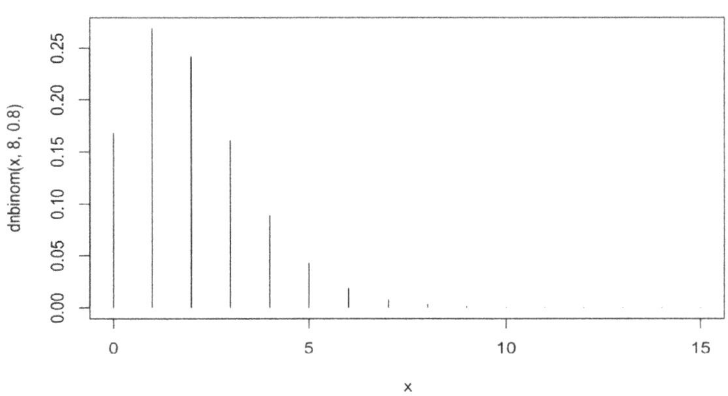

The first plot, that corresponds to X_1~Negative-Binomial(2,0.5), fits Barplot 3. Notice that the distribution tends to obtain smaller values and that the probability of the value "0" is equal to the probability of the value "1".

The second plot, the one that corresponds to X_2~Negative-Binomial(4,0.5), is associated with Barplot 1. Notice that the distribution tends to obtain larger values. For example, the probability of the value "10" is substantially larger than zero, where for the other two plots this is not the case.

The third plot, the one that corresponds to X_3~Negative-Binomial(8,0.8), matches Barplot 2. Observe that this distribution tends to produce smaller probabilities for the small values as well as for the larger values. Overall, it is more concentrated than the other two.

Barplot 1 corresponds to a distribution that tends to obtain larger values than the other two distributions. Consequently, the expectation of this distribution should be larger. The conclusion is that the pair E(X)=4, V(X)=8 should be associated with this distribution.

Barplot 2 describes a distribution that produce smaller probabilities for the small values as well as for the larger values and is more concentrated than the other two. The expectations of the two remaining distributions are equal to each other and the variance of the pair E (X)=2, V (X)=2.5 is smaller. Consequently, this is the pair that should be matched with this box plot.

This leaves only Barplot 3, that should be matched with the pair E (X)=2, V (X)=4.

CHAPTER 6

Exercise 6.1

Let X be the total weight of 8 people. By the assumption, X~Normal(560,572). We are interested in the probability P(X>650). This probability is equal to the difference between 1 and the probability P(X≤650). We use the function "pnorm" in order to carry out the computation:

```
1 - pnorm(650,560,57)
```

```
## [1] 0.05717406
```

We get that the probability that the total weight of 8 people exceeds 650kg is equal to 0.05717406.

Let Y be the total weight of 9 people. By the assumption, Y~Normal(630,61^2). We are interested in the probability P (Y>650). This probability is equal to the difference between 1 and the probability P (Y≤650). We use again the function "pnorm" in order to carry out the computation:

```
1 - pnorm(650,630,61)
```

```
## [1] 0.3715054
```

We get that the probability that the total weight of 9 people exceeds 650kg is much higher and is equal to 0.3715054.

Again, $X \sim \text{Normal}(560,57^2)$, where X is the total weight of 8 people. In order to find the central region that contains 80% of the distribution we need to identify the 10%-percentile and the 90%-percentile of X. We use the function "qnorm" in the code:

```
qnorm(0.1,560,57)
```

```
## [1] 486.9516
```

```
qnorm(0.9,560,57)
```

```
## [1] 633.0484
```

The requested region is the interval

486.9516,633.0484.

As before, $Y \sim \text{Normal}(630,61^2)$, where Y is the total weight of 9 people. In order to find the central region that contains 80% of the distribution we need to identify the 10%-percentile and the 90%-percentile of Y. The computation this time produces:

```
qnorm(0.1,630,61)
```

```
## [1] 551.8254
```

```
qnorm(0.9,630,61)
```

```
## [1] 708.1746
```

and the region is

551.8254,708.1746.

Exercise 6.2

The probability P(X>11) can be computed as the difference between 1 and the probability P (X≤11). The latter probability can be computed with the function "pbinom":

```
1 - pbinom(11,27,0.32)
```

```
## [1] 0.1203926
```

Therefore, P (X>11)=0.1203926.

Refer again to the probability P (X>11). A formal application of the Normal approximation replaces in the computation the Binomial distribution by the Normal distribution with the same mean and variance. Since E (X)=n·p = 27·0.32 = 8.64 and V(X) = n·p· (1−p) = 27·0.32·0.68=5.8752. If we take X~Normal (8.64,5.8752) and use the function "pnorm" we get:

```
1 - pnorm(11,27*0.32,sqrt(27*0.32*0.68))
```

```
## [1] 0.1651164
```

Therefore, the current Normal approximation proposes P (X>11)≈0.1651164.

The continuity correction, that consider interval of range 0.5 about each value, replace P (X>11), that involves the values {12,13,...,27}, by the event P(X>11.5). The Normal approximation uses the Normal distribution with the same mean and variance. Since E (X)=8.64 and V(X)=5.8752. If we take X~Normal(8.64,5.8752) and use the function "pnorm" we get:

```
1 - pnorm(11.5,27*0.32,sqrt(27*0.32*0.68))
```

```
## [1] 0.1190149
```

The Normal approximation with continuity correction proposes Prob(X>11)≈0.1190149.

The Poisson approximation replaces the Binomial distribution by the Poisson distribution with the same expectation. The expectation is E(X)=n·p=27·0.32=8.64. If we take X~Poisson (8.64) and use the function "ppois" we get:

```
1 - ppois(11,27*0.32)
```

```
## [1] 0.1635232
```

Therefore, the Poisson approximation proposes Prob(X>11)≈0.1651164.

CHAPTER 7

Exercise 7.1

After placing the file "pop2.csv" in the working directory one may produce a data frame with the content of the file and compute the average of the variable "bmi" using the code:

```
pop.2 <- read.csv(file="_data/pop2.csv")
mean(pop.2$bmi)
```

```
## [1] 24.98446
```

We obtain that the population average of the variable is equal to 24.98446.

Applying the function "sd" to the sequence of population values produces the population standard deviation:

```
sd(pop.2$bmi)
```

```
## [1] 4.188511
```

In turns out that the standard deviation of the measurement is 4.188511.

In order to compute the expectation under the sampling distribution of the sample average we conduct a simulation. The simulation produces (an approximation) of the sampling distribution of the sample average. The sampling distribution is represented by the content of the sequence "X.bar":

```
X.bar <- rep(0,10^5)
for(i in 1:10^5) {
  X.samp <- sample(pop.2$bmi,150)
  X.bar[i] <- mean(X.samp)
}
mean(X.bar)
```

```
## [1] 24.98484
```

Initially, we produce a vector of zeros of the given lenght (100,000). In each iteration of the "for" loop a random sample of size 150 is selected from the population. The sample average is computed and stored in the sequence "X.bar". At the end of all the iterations all the zeros are replaced by evaluations of the sample average.

The expectation of the sampling distribution of the sample average is computed by the application of the function "mean" to the sequence that represents the sampling distribution of the sample average. The result for the current is 24.98681, which is vary similar[94] to the population average 24.98446.

The standard deviation of the sample average under the sampling distribution is computed using the function "sd":

```
sd(X.bar)
```

```
## [1] 0.3403954
```

The resulting standard deviation is 0.3422717. Recall that the standard deviation of a single measurement is equal to 4.188511 and that the sample size is n=150. The ratio between the standard deviation of the measurement and the square root of 150 is $4.188511/\sqrt{150} = 0.3419905$, which is similar in value to the standard deviation of the sample average[^4].

The central region that contains 80% of the sampling distribution of the sample average can be identified with the aid of the function "quantile":

```
quantile(X.bar,c(0.1,0.9))
```

```
##      10%      90%
## 24.54870 25.42228
```

The value 24.54972 is the 10%-percentile of the sampling distribution. To the left of this value are 10% of the distribution. The value 25.42629 is the 90%-percentile of the sampling distribution. To the right of this value are 10% of the distribution. Between these two values are 80% of the sampling distribution.

The Normal approximation, which is the conclusion of the Central Limit Theorem substitutes the sampling distribution of the sample average by the Normal distribution with the same expectation and standard deviation. The percentiles are computed with the function "qnorm":

```
qnorm(c(0.1,0.9),mean(X.bar),sd(X.bar))
```

```
## [1] 24.54860 25.42107
```

Observe that we used the expectation and the standard deviation of the sample average in the function. The resulting interval is [24.54817,25.42545], which is similar to the interval [24.54972,25.42629] which was obtained via simulations.

Exercise 7.2

Denote by XX the distance from the specified endpoint of a random hit. Observe that $X \sim$Uniform(0,10). The 25 hits form a sample $X_1, X_2, \ldots, X_{25}$ from this distribution and the sample average $\bar{X}$ is the average of these random locations. The expectation of the average is equal to the expectation of a single measurement. Since E $(X)=(a+b)/2=(0+10)/2=5$ we get that E $(\bar{X})=5$.

The variance of the sample average is equal to the variance of a single measurement, divided by the sample size. The variance of the Uniform distribution is V $(X)=(a+b)^2/12=(10-0)^2/12=8.333333$. The standard deviation of the sample average is equal to the standard deviation of the sample average is equal to the standard deviation of a single measurement, divided by the square root of the sample size. The sample size is $n=25$. Consequently, the standard deviation of the average is $\sqrt{8.333333/25} = 0.5773503$.

The left-most third of the detector is the interval to the left of 10/3. The distribution of the sample average, according to the Central Limit Theorem, is Normal. The probability of being less than 10/3 for the Normal distribution may be computed with the function "pnorm":

```
mu <- 5
sig <- sqrt(10^2/(12*25))
pnorm(10/3,mu,sig)
```

```
## [1] 0.001946209
```

The expectation and the standard deviation of the sample average are used in computation of the probability. The probability is 0.001946209, about 0.2%.

The central region in the Normal(μ,σ^2) distribution that contains 99% of the distribution is of the form μ±\texttt{qnorm(0.995)}·σ, where "qnorm(0.995)" is the 99.5%-percentile of the Standard Normal distribution. Therefore,c=\texttt{qnorm(0.995)}·σ:

```
qnorm(0.995)*sig
```

```
## [1] 1.487156
```

We get that c=1.487156.

CHAPTER 9

Exercise 9.1

Let us read the data into a data frame by the name "magnets" and apply the function "summary" to the data frame:

magnets <- **read.csv**("_data/magnets.csv")

```
magnets <- read.csv("_data/magnets.csv")
summary(magnets)
```

```
##      score1          score2          change      active
##  Min.   : 7.00   Min.   : 0.00   Min.   : 0.0   "1":29
##  1st Qu.: 9.25   1st Qu.: 4.00   1st Qu.: 0.0   "2":21
##  Median :10.00   Median : 6.00   Median : 3.5
##  Mean   : 9.58   Mean   : 6.08   Mean   : 3.5
##  3rd Qu.:10.00   3rd Qu.: 9.75   3rd Qu.: 6.0
##  Max.   :10.00   Max.   :10.00   Max.   :10.0
```

The variable "change" contains the difference between the patient's rating before the application of the device and the rating after the application. The sample average of this variable is reported as the "Mean" for this variable and is equal to 3.5.

The variable "active" is a factor. Observe that the summary of this variable lists the two levels of the variable and the frequency of each level. Indeed, the levels are coded with numbers but, nonetheless, the variable is a factor[^12].

Based on the hint we know that the expressions "change[1:29]" and "change[30:50]" produce the values of the variable "change" for the patients that were treated with active magnets and by inactive placebo, respectively. We apply the function "mean" to these sub-sequences:

```
mean(magnets$change[1:29])
```

```
## [1] 5.241379
```

```
mean(magnets$change[30:50])
```

```
## [1] 1.095238
```

The sample average for the patients that were treated with active magnets is 5.241379 and sample average for the patients that were treated with inactive placebo is 1.095238.

We apply the function "sd" to these sub-sequences:

```
sd(magnets$change[1:29])
```

```
## [1] 3.236568
```

```
sd(magnets$change[30:50])
```

```
## [1] 1.578124
```

The sample standard deviation for the patients that were treated with active magnets is 3.236568 and sample standard deviation for the patients that were treated with inactive placebo is 1.578124.

We apply the function "boxplot" to each sub-sequences:

```
boxplot(magnets$change[1:29])
```

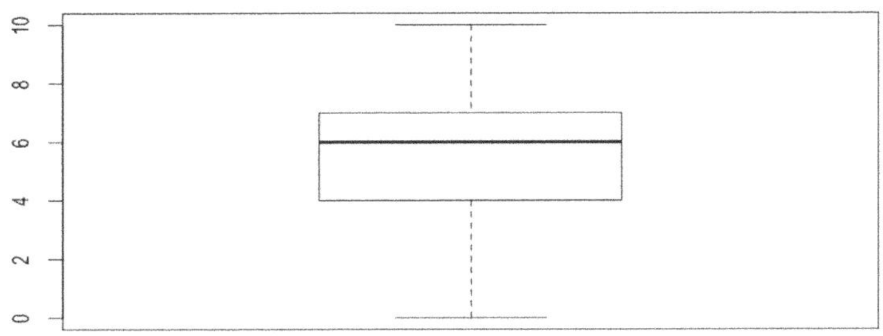


```
boxplot(magnets$change[30:50])
```

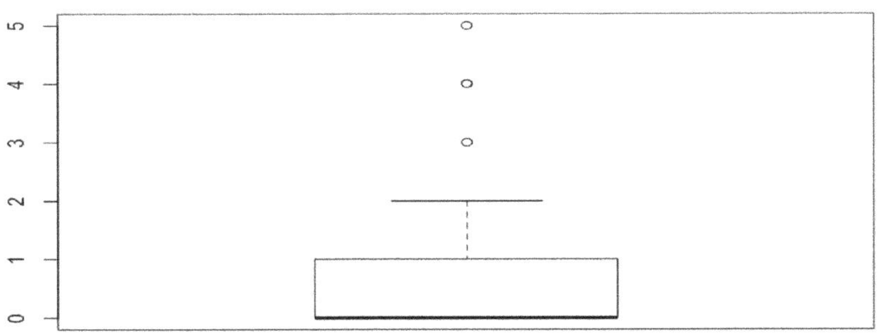

The first box-plot corresponds to the sub-sequence of the patients that received an active magnet. There are no outliers in this plot. The second box-plot corresponds to the sub-sequence of the patients that received an inactive placebo. Three values, the values "3", "4", and "5" are associated with outliers. Let us see what is the total number of observations that receive these values:

```
table(magnets$change[30:50])
```

```
##
## 0 1 2 3 4 5
## 11 5 1 1 2 1
```

One may see that a single observation obtained the value "3", another one obtained the value "5" and 2 observations obtained the value "4", a total of 4 outliers[^13]. Notice that the single point that is associated with the value "4" actually represents 2 observations and not one.

Exercise 9.2

Let us run the following simulation:

```
mu1 <- 3.5
sig1 <- 3
mu2 <- 3.5
sig2 <- 1.5
test.stat <- rep(0,10^5)
for(i in 1:10^5) {
  X1 <- rnorm(29,mu1,sig1)
  X2 <- rnorm(21,mu2,sig2)
  X1.bar <- mean(X1)
  X2.bar <- mean(X2)
  X1.var <- var(X1)
  X2.var <- var(X2)
  test.stat[i] <- (X1.bar-X2.bar)/sqrt(X1.var/29 + X2.var/21)
}
quantile(test.stat,c(0.025,0.975))
```

```
##      2.5%     97.5%
## -2.026201  2.012513
```

Observe that each iteration of the simulation involves the generation of two samples. One sample is of size 29 and it is generated from the Normal(3.5,32) distribution and the other sample is of size 21 and it is generated from the Normal(3.5,1.52) distribution. The sample average and the sample variance are computed for each sample. The test statistic is computed based on these averages and variances and it is stored in the appropriate position of the sequence "test. stat".

The values of the sequence "test.stat" at the end of all the iterations represent the sampling distribution of the static. The application of the function "quantile" to the sequence gives the 0.025-percentiles and the 0.975-percentiles of the sampling distribution, which are -2.014838 and 2.018435. It follows that the interval [-2.014838,2.018435] contains about 95% of the sampling distribution of the statistic.

In order to evaluate the statistic for the given data set we apply the same steps that were used in the simulation for the computation of the statistic:

```
x1.bar <- mean(magnets$change[1:29])
x2.bar <- mean(magnets$change[30:50])
x1.var <- var(magnets$change[1:29])
x2.var <- var(magnets$change[30:50])
(x1.bar-x2.bar)/sqrt(x1.var/29 + x2.var/21)
```

```
## [1] 5.985601
```

In the first line we compute the sample average for the first 29 patients and in the second line we compute it for the last 21 patients. In the third and fourth lines we do the same for the sample variances of the two types of patients. Finally, in the fifth line we evaluate the statistic. The computed value of the statistic turns out to be 5.985601, a value that does not belong to the interval [-2.014838,2.018435].

CHAPTER 10

Exercise 10.1

We simulate the sampling distribution of the average and the median in a sample generated from the Normal distribution. In order to do so we copy the code that was used in Subsection 10.3.2, replacing the object "mid.range" by the object "X.med" and using the function "median" in order to compute the sample median instead of the computation of the mid-range statistic:

```
mu <- 3
sig <- sqrt(2)
X.bar <- rep(0,10^5)
X.med <- rep(0,10^5)
for(i in 1:10^5) {
  X <- rnorm(100,mu,sig)
  X.bar[i] <- mean(X)
  X.med[i] <- median(X)
}
```

The sequence "X.bar" represents the sampling distribution of the sample average and the sequence "X.med" represents the sampling distribution of the sample median. We apply the function "mean" to these sequences in order to obtain the expectations of the estimators:

```
mean(X.bar)
```

```
## [1] 3.000857
```

```
mean(X.med)
```

```
## [1] 3.0007
```

The expectation of the measurement, the parameter of interest is equal to 3. Observe that expectations of the estimators are essentially equal to the expectation[^13]. Consequently, both estimators are unbiased estimators of the expectation of the measurement.

In order to obtain the variances of the estimators we apply the function "var" to the sequences that represent their sampling distributions:

```
var(X.bar)
```

```
## [1] 0.02001728
```

```
var(X.med)
```

```
## [1] 0.03106485
```

Observe that the variance of the sample average is essentially equal to 0.020 and the variance of the sample median is essentially equal to 0.0312. The mean square error of an unbiased estimator is equal to its variance. Hence, these numbers represent the mean square errors of the estimators. It follows that the mean square error of the sample average is less than the mean square error of the sample median in the estimation of the expectation of a Normal measurement.

We repeat the same steps as before for the Uniform distribution. Notice that we use the parameters a=0.5a=0.5 and b=5.5b=5.5 the same way we did in Subsection 10.3.2. These parameters produce an expectation E(X)=3 and a variance V(X)=2.083333:

```
a <- 0.5
b <- 5.5
X.bar <- rep(0,10^5)
X.med <- rep(0,10^5)
for(i in 1:10^5) {
  X <- runif(100,a,b)
  X.bar[i] <- mean(X)
  X.med[i] <- median(X)
}
```

Applying the function "mean" to the sequences that represent the sampling distribution of the estimators we obtain that both estimators are essentially unbiased[^14]:

```
mean(X.bar)
```

```
## [1] 2.999265
```

```
mean(X.med)
```

```
## [1] 2.999101
```

Compute the variances:

```
var(X.bar)
```

```
## [1] 0.02088801
```

```
var(X.med)
```

```
## [1] 0.06065213
```

Observe 0.021 is, essentially, the value of the variance of the sample average[^15]. The variance of the sample median is essentially equal to 0.061. The variance of each of the estimators is equal to it's mean square error. This is the case since the estimators are unbiased. Consequently, we again obtain that the mean square error of the sample average is less than that of the sample median.

Exercise 10.2

Assuming that the file "ex2.csv" is saved in the working directory, one may read the content of the file into a data frame and produce a summary of the content of the data frame using the code:

```
ex2 <- read.csv("_data/ex2.csv")
summary(ex2)
```

```
##        id              sex          age             bmi
##  Min.   :1024982   FEMALE:74   Min.   :26.00   Min.   :15.12
##  1st Qu.:3172782   MALE  :76   1st Qu.:32.00   1st Qu.:22.02
##  Median :5200484               Median :35.00   Median :25.16
##  Mean   :5463304               Mean   :35.09   Mean   :24.76
##  3rd Qu.:7982902               3rd Qu.:37.00   3rd Qu.:27.49
##  Max.   :9934175               Max.   :45.00   Max.   :35.24
##     systolic        diastolic          group
##  Min.   :100.8   Min.   : 51.98   HIGH  : 37
##  1st Qu.:118.1   1st Qu.: 75.02   LOW   :  3
##  Median :124.3   Median : 83.19   NORMAL:110
##  Mean   :125.3   Mean   : 82.44
##  3rd Qu.:132.6   3rd Qu.: 88.83
##  Max.   :154.5   Max.   :112.71
```

Examine the variable “group”. Observe that the sample contains 37 subjects with high levels of blood pressure. Dividing 37 by the sample size we get:

```
37/150
```

```
## [1] 0.2466667
```

Consequently, the sample proportion is 0.2466667.

Alternatively, we compute the sample proportion using the code:

```
mean(ex2$group == "HIGH")
```

```
## [1] 0.2466667
```

Notice that the expression “ex2$group == HIGH” produces a sequence of length 150 with logical entries. The entry is equal to “TRUE” if the equality holds and it is equal to “FALSE” if it dos not[^17]. When the function “mean” is applied to a sequence with logical entries it produces the relative frequeny of the TRUEs in the sequence. This corresponds, in the corrent context, to the sample proportion of the level “HIGH” in the variable “ex2$group”.

Make sure that the file “pop2.csv” is saved in the working directory. In order to compute the proportion in the population we read the content of the file into a data frame and compute the relative frequency of the level “HIGH” in the variable “group”:

```
pop2 <- read.csv("_data/pop2.csv")
mean(pop2$group == "HIGH")
```

```
## [1] 0.28126
```

We get that the proporion in the population is p=0.28126p=0.28126.

The simulation of the sampling distribution involves a selection of a random sample of size 150 from the population and the computation of the proportion of the level "HIGH" in that sample. This procedure is iterated 100,000 times in order to produce an approximation of the distribution:

```
P.hat <- rep(0,10^5)
for(i in 1:10^5) {
  X <- sample(pop2$group,150)
  P.hat[i] <- mean(X == "HIGH")
}
mean(P.hat)
```

Observe that the sampling distribution is stored in the object "P.hat". The function "sample" is used in order to sample 150 observation from the sequence "pop2$group". The sample is stored in the object "X". The expression "mean(X == HIGH)" computes the relative frequency of the level "HIGH" in the sequence "X".

At the last line, after the production of the sequence "P.hat" is completed, the function "mean" is applied to the sequence. The result is the expected value of estimator $\hat{P}$, which is equal to 0.2812307. This expectation is essentially equal to the probability of the event p=0.28126.[^18]

The application of the function "var" to the sequence "P.hat" produces:

```
var(P.hat)
```

```
## [1] 0.001348473
```

Hence, the variance of the estimator is (approximately) equal to 0.00135.

Compute the variance according to the formula that is proposed in Section:

```
p <- mean(pop2$group == "HIGH")
p*(1-p)/150
```

```
## [1] 0.001347685
```

We get that the proposed variance in Section is 0.0013476850, which is in good agreement with the value 0.00135 that was obtained in the simulation[^19].

CHAPTER 11

Exercise 11.1

We read the content of the file "teacher.csv" into a data frame by the name "teacher" and produce a summary of the content of the data frame:

```
teacher <- read.csv("_data/teacher.csv")
summary(teacher)
```

```
## condition      rating
## C:25        Min.   :1.333
## P:24        1st Qu.:2.000
##             Median :2.333
##             Mean   :2.429
##             3rd Qu.:2.667
##             Max.   :4.000
```

There are two variables: The variable "condition" is a factor with two levels, "C" that codes the Charismatic condition and "P" that codes the Punitive condition. The second variable is "rating", which is a numeric variable.

The sample average for the variable "rating" can be obtained from the summary or from the application of the function "mean" to the variable. The standard deviation is obtained from the application of the function "sd" to the variable:

```
mean(teacher$rating)
```

```
## [1] 2.428567
```

```
sd(teacher$rating)
```

```
## [1] 0.5651949
```

Observe that the sample average is equal to 2.428567 and the sample standard deviation is equal to 0.5651949.

The sample average and standard deviation for each sub-sample may be produced with the aid of the function "tapply". We apply the function in the third argument, first "mean" and then "sd" to the variable rating, in the first argument, over each level of the factor "condition" in the second argument:

```
tapply(teacher$rating,teacher$condition,mean)
```

```
##        C        P
## 2.613332 2.236104
```

```
tapply(teacher$rating,teacher$condition,sd)
```

```
##         C         P
## 0.5329833 0.5426667
```

Obtain that average for the condition "C" is 2.613332 and the standard deviation is 0.5329833.

You may note that the rating given by students that were exposed to the description of the lecturer as charismatic is higher on the average than the rating given by students that were exposed to a less favorable description. The box plots of the ratings for the two conditions are presented in Figure 16.2.

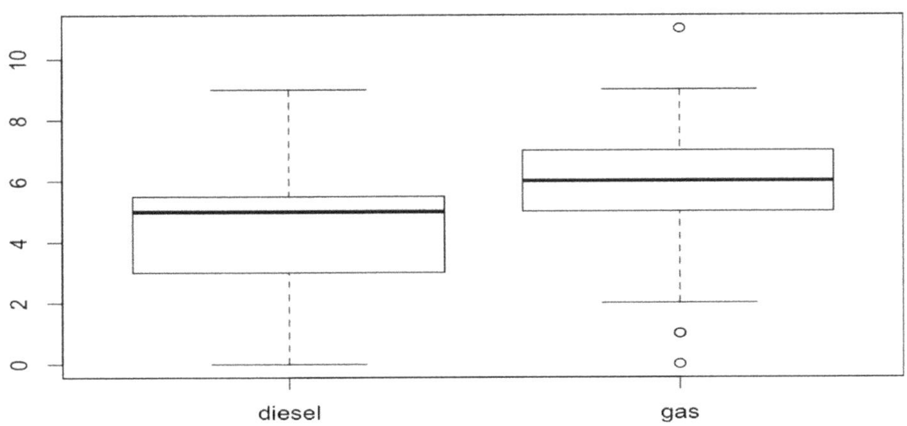

Figure 16.2: Box Plots of Ratings

The 99% confidence interval for the expectation is computed by the formula

$\bar{x} \pm$ `qt(0.995,n-1)` $\cdot\, s/\sqrt{n}$. Only 0.5% of the t-distribution on (n-1)(n-1) degrees of freedom resides above the percentile "qt(0.995,n-1)". Using this percentile leaves out a total of 1% in both tails and keeps 99% of the distribution inside the central interval.

For the students that were exposed to Condition "C", $\bar{x} = 2.613332$, s=0.5329833, and n=25:

```
2.613332 - qt(0.995,24)*0.5329833/sqrt(25)

## [1] 2.315188

2.613332 + qt(0.995,24)*0.5329833/sqrt(25)

## [1] 2.911476
```

The confidence interval for the expectation is [2.315188,2.911476].

The 90% confidence interval for the variance is computed by the formula $\left[\frac{n-1}{\texttt{qchisq(0.95,n-1)}} s^2, \frac{n-1}{\texttt{qchisq(0.05,n-1)}} s^2\right]$.

Observe that 5% of the chi-square distribution on (n-1) degrees of freedom is above the percentile "qchisq(0.95,n-1)" and 5% are below the percentile "qchisq(0.05,n-1)".

For the students that were exposed to Condition "C", s=0.5329833, and n=25:

```
(24/qchisq(0.95,24))*0.5329833^2

## [1] 0.1872224

(24/qchisq(0.05,24))*0.5329833^2

## [1] 0.4923093
```

The point estimate of the variance is s^2=0.53298332=0.2840712. The confidence interval for the variance is [0.18722243,0.4923093].

Exercise 11.2

Let us produce the sampling distribution of the sample average and the sample standard deviation for 20 observations from the Exponential(1/4) distribution:

```
lam <- 1/4
n <- 20
X.bar <- rep(0,10^5)
S <- rep(0,10^5)
for(i in 1:10^5) {
  X <- rexp(n,lam)
  X.bar[i] <- mean(X)
  S[i] <- sd(X)
}
```

We compute the confidence level for a confidence interval with a nominal confidence level of 95%. Observe that using the Normal approximation of the sample average corresponds to the application of the Normal percentile in the construction of the confidence interval.

```
norm.LCL <- X.bar - qnorm(0.975)*S/sqrt(n)
norm.UCL <- X.bar + qnorm(0.975)*S/sqrt(n)
mean((4 >= norm.LCL) & (4 <= norm.UCL))
```

```
## [1] 0.90477
```

The expectation of the measurement is equal to 4. This number belongs to the confidence interval 90.47% of the times. Consequently, the actual confidence level is 90.47%.

Using the same sampling distribution that was produced in the solution to Question 1 we now compute the actual confidence level of a confidence interval that is constructed under the assumption that the measurement has a Normal distribution:

```
t.LCL <- X.bar - qt(0.975,n-1)*S/sqrt(n)
t.UCL <- X.bar + qt(0.975,n-1)*S/sqrt(n)
mean((4 >= t.LCL) & (4 <= t.UCL))
```

```
## [1] 0.91862
```

Based on the assumption we used the percentiles of the t-distribution. The actual significance level is 91.953% ≈≈ 92%, still short of the nominal 95% confidence level.

It would be preferable to use the (incorrect) assumption that the observations have a Normal distribution than to apply the Normal approximation to such a small sample. In the current setting the former produced a confidence level that is closer to the nominal one. In general, using the percentiles of the t-distribution will produce wider and more conservative confidence intervals than those produces under the Normal approximation of the average. To be on the safer size, one typically prefers the more conservative confidence intervals.

Exercise 11.3

The range of the confidence interval with 99% confidence interval is bounded by

$$\texttt{qnorm(0.995)} \cdot \{\hat{P}(1-\hat{P})/n\}^{1/2} \leq 2.575829 \cdot \sqrt{0.25/n} = 1.287915/\sqrt{n}\ ,$$

since qnorm(0.995) = 2.575829 and $\hat{P}(1-\hat{P}) \leq 0.25$. Consequently, the sample size nn should satisfy the inequality:

$$1.287915/\sqrt{n} \leq 0.03 \quad \Longrightarrow \quad \sqrt{n} \geq 1.287915/0.03 = 42.9305$$
$$\Longrightarrow \quad n \geq (42.9305)^2 = 1843.028\ .$$

The smallest integer larger than the lower bound is n=1844.

The 80% confidence interval for the probability is computed by the formula $\hat p \pm \mbox{\texttt{qnorm(0.90)}} \cdot \sqrt{\hat p(1-\hat p)/n}$:

```
```r
n <- 400
p.hat <- 320/400
p.hat - qnorm(0.90)*sqrt(p.hat*(1-p.hat)/n)
```

```
## [1] 0.774369
```

```r
p.hat + qnorm(0.90)*sqrt(p.hat*(1-p.hat)/n)
```

```
## [1] 0.825631
```
```

We obtain a confidence interval of the form $[0.774369, 0.825631]$.

CHAPTER 12

Exercise 12.1

The null hypothesis of no placebo effect corresponds to the expectation of the change equal to 0 (H_0:E(X)=0). The alternative hypothesis may be formulated as the expectation not being equal to 0 (H_1: E(X)≠0). This corresponds to a two sided alternative. Observe that a negative expectation of the change still corresponds to the placebo having an effect.

The observations that can be used in order to test the hypothesis are those associated with patients that were treated with the inactive placebo, i.e. the last 21 observations. We extracts these values from the data frame using the expression "magnets$change[30:50]".

In order to carry out the test we read the data from the file "magnets.csv" into the data frame "magnets". The function "t.test" is applied to the observations extracted from the data frame. Note that the default expectation value of tested by the function is "mu = 0":

```
magnets <- read.csv("_data/magnets.csv")
t.test(magnets$change[30:50])
```

```
##
##  One Sample t-test
##
## data:  magnets$change[30:50]
## t = 3.1804, df = 20, p-value = 0.004702
## alternative hypothesis: true mean is not equal to 0
## 95 percent confidence interval:
##  0.3768845 1.8135916
## sample estimates:
## mean of x
##  1.095238
```

The computed p-value is 0.004702, which is below 0.05. Consequently, we reject the null hypothesis and conclude that a placebo effect seems to be present.

Exercise 12.2

We simulate the sampling distribution of the sample average and standard deviation. The sample is composed of n=20n=20 observations from the given Exponential distribution:

```
lam <- 1/4
n <- 20
X.bar <- rep(0,10^5)
S <- rep(0,10^5)
for(i in 1:10^5) {
  X <- rexp(n,lam)
  X.bar[i] <- mean(X)
  S[i] <- sd(X)
}
T <- (X.bar - 4)/(S/sqrt(n))
mean(abs(T) > qt(0.975,n-1))
```

```
## [1] 0.08017
```

We compute the test statistic "T" from the sample average "X.bar" and the sample standard deviation "S". In the last expression we compute the probability that the absolute value of the test statistic is larger than "qt(0.975,19)", which is the threshold that should be used in order to obtain a significance level of 5% for Normal measurements.

We obtain that the actual significance level of the test is 0.08047, which is substantially larger than the nominal significance level.

We repeat essentially the same simulations as before. We only change the distribution of the sample from the Exponential to the Uniform distribution:

```
a <- 0
b <- 8
n <- 20
X.bar <- rep(0,10^5)
S <- rep(0,10^5)
for(i in 1:10^5) {
  X <- runif(n,a,b)
  X.bar[i] <- mean(X)
  S[i] <- sd(X)
}
T <- (X.bar - 4)/(S/sqrt(n))
mean(abs(T) > qt(0.975,n-1))
```

```
## [1] 0.05177
```

The actual significance level of the test is 0.05163, much closer to the nominal significance level of 5%.

A possible explanation for the difference between the two cases is that the Uniform distribution is symmetric like the Normal distribution, whereas the Exponential is skewed. In any case, for larger sample sizes one may expect the

Central Limit Theorem to kick in and produce more satisfactory results, even for the Exponential case.

Exercise 12.3

We input the data to R and then compute the test statistic and the appropriate percentile of the t-distribution:

```
n <- 55
x.bar <- 22.7
s <- 5.4
t <- (x.bar - 20)/(s/sqrt(n))
abs(t)
```

```
## [1] 3.708099
```

```
qt(0.975,n-1)
```

```
## [1] 2.004879
```

Observe that the absolute value of the statistic (3.708099) is larger than the threshold for rejection (2.004879). Consequently, we reject the null hypothesis.

We recompute the percentile of the t-distribution:

```
qt(0.995,n-1)
```

```
## [1] 2.669985
```

Again, the absolute value of the statistic (3.708099) is larger than the threshold for rejection (2.669985). Consequently, we reject the null hypothesis.

In this question we should recompute the test statistic:

```
t <- (x.bar - 24)/(s/sqrt(n))
abs(t)
```

```
## [1] 1.785381
```

The absolute value of the new statistic (1.785381) is smaller than the threshold for rejection (2.004879). Consequently, we do not reject the null hypothesis.

CHAPTER 13

Exercise 13.1

The score of pain before the application of the device is measured in the variable "score1". This variable is used as the response. We apply the function "t.test" in order to test the equality of the expectation of the response in the two groups. First we read in the data from the file into a data frame and then we apply the test:

```
magnets <- read.csv("_data/magnets.csv")
t.test(magnets$score1 ~ magnets$active)
```

```
##
##  Welch Two Sample t-test
##
## data:  magnets$score1 by magnets$active
## t = 0.41483, df = 38.273, p-value = 0.6806
## alternative hypothesis: true difference in means is not equal to 0
## 95 percent confidence interval:
##  -0.3757896  0.5695498
## sample estimates:
## mean in group "1" mean in group "2"
##           9.62069           9.52381
```

The computed p-value is 0.6806, which is above 0.05. Consequently, we do not reject the null hypothesis that the expectations in the two groups are equal. This should not come as a surprise, since patients were assigned to the groups randomly and without knowledge to which group they belong. Prior to the application of the device, the two groups should look alike.

Again, we use the variable "score1" as the response. Now apply the function "var.test" in order to test the equality of the variances of the response in the two groups:

```
var.test(magnets$score1 ~ magnets$active)
```

```
##
##  F test to compare two variances
##
## data:  magnets$score1 by magnets$active
## F = 0.69504, num df = 28, denom df = 20, p-value = 0.3687
## alternative hypothesis: true ratio of variances is not equal to 1
## 95 percent confidence interval:
##  0.2938038 1.5516218
## sample estimates:
## ratio of variances
##          0.6950431
```

The computed p-value is 0.3687, which is once more above 0.05. Consequently, we do not reject the null hypothesis that the variances in the two groups are equal. This fact is reassuring. Indeed, prior to the application of the device, the two groups have the same characteristics. Therefore, any subsequent difference between the two groups can be attributed to the difference in the treatment.

The difference in score between the treatment and the control groups is measured in the variable "change". This variable is used as the response for the current analysis. We apply the function "t.test" in order to test the equality of the expectation of the response in the two groups:

```
t.test(magnets$change ~ magnets$active)
```

```
##
##  Welch Two Sample t-test
##
## data:  magnets$change by magnets$active
## t = 5.9856, df = 42.926, p-value = 3.86e-07
## alternative hypothesis: true difference in means is not equal to 0
## 95 percent confidence interval:
##  2.749137 5.543145
## sample estimates:
## mean in group "1" mean in group "2"
##          5.241379          1.095238
```

The computed *p*-value is 3.86×10-7, which is much below 0.05. Consequently, we reject the null hypothesis that the expectations in the two groups are equal. The conclusion is that, according to this trial, magnets do have an effect on the expectation of the response[^9].

Once more we consider the variable "change" as the response. We apply the function "var.test" in order to test the equality of the variances of the response in the two groups:

```
var.test(magnets$change ~ magnets$active)
```

```
##
##  F test to compare two variances
##
## data:  magnets$change by magnets$active
## F = 4.2062, num df = 28, denom df = 20, p-value = 0.001535
## alternative hypothesis: true ratio of variances is not equal to 1
## 95 percent confidence interval:
##  1.778003 9.389902
## sample estimates:
## ratio of variances
##           4.206171
```

The computed *p*-value is 0.001535, which is much below 0.05. Consequently, we reject the null hypothesis that the variances in the two groups are equal. Hence, magnets also affect the variance of the response.

Exercise 13.2

We simulate the sampling distribution of the sample standard deviation for two samples, one sample of size na=29 and the other of size nb=21nb=21. Both samples are simulated from the given Normal distribution:

```
mu <- 4
sig <- 4
n.a <- 29
n.b <- 21
S.a <- rep(0,10^5)
S.b <- rep(0,10^5)
for(i in 1:10^5) {
  X.a <- rnorm(n.a,mu,sig)
  X.b <- rnorm(n.b,mu,sig)
  S.a[i] <- sd(X.a)
  S.b[i] <- sd(X.b)
}
F <- S.a^2/S.b^2
mean((F < qf(0.025,n.a-1,n.b-1))|(F > qf(0.975,n.a-1,n.b-1)))
```

```
## [1] 0.05033
```

We compute the test statistic “F” as the ratio of the two sample standard deviations “S.a” and “S.b”. The last expression computes the probability that the test statistic is either less than “qt(0.025,n.a-1,n.b-1)”, or it is larger than “qt(0.975,n.a-1,n.b-1)”. The term “qt(0.025,n.a-1,n.b-1)” is the 0.025-percentile of the FF-distribution on 28 and 20 degrees of freedom and the term “qt(0.975,n.a-1,n.b-1)” is the 0.975-percentile of the same FF-distribution. The result of the last expression is the actual significance level of the test.

We obtain that the actual significance level of the test when the measurements are Normally distributed is 0.05074, which in agreement with the nominal significance level of 5%. Indeed, the nominal significance level is computed under the assumption that the distribution of the measurement is Normal.

We repeat essentially the same simulations as before. We only change the distribution of the samples from the Normal to the Exponential distribution:

```
lam <- 1/4
n.a <- 29
n.b <- 21
S.a <- rep(0,10^5)
S.b <- rep(0,10^5)
for(i in 1:10^5) {
  X.a <- rexp(n.a,lam)
  X.b <- rexp(n.b,lam)
  S.a[i] <- sd(X.a)
  S.b[i] <- sd(X.b)
}
F <- S.a^2/S.b^2
mean((F < qf(0.025,n.a-1,n.b-1))|(F > qf(0.975,n.a-1,n.b-1)))
```

```
## [1] 0.27486
```

The actual significance level of the test is 0.27596, which is much higher than the nominal significance level of 5%.

Through this experiment we may see that the F-test is not robust to the divergence from the assumed Normal distribution of the measurement. If the distribution of the measurement is skewed (the Exponential distribution is an example of such skewed distribution) then the application of the test to the data may produce unreliable conclusions.

Exercise 13.3

We input the data to R and then compute the estimate:

```
s.a <- 13.4
s.b <- 16.7
s.a^2/s.b^2
```

```
## [1] 0.6438381
```

The estimate is equal to the ratio of the sample variances S^2_a/S^2_b. It obtains the value 0.6438381. Notice that the information regarding the sample averages and the sizes of the sub-samples is not relevant for the point estimation of the parameter.

We use the formula:

$$\left[(s_a^2/s_b^2)/\texttt{qf(0.975,14,14)}, (s_a^2/s_b^2)/\texttt{qf(0.025,14,14)}\right]$$

in order to compute the confidence interval:

````
```r
n.a <- 15
n.b <- 15
(s.a^2/s.b^2)/qf(0.975,n.a-1,n.b-1)
```

```
## [1] 0.2161555
```

```r
(s.a^2/s.b^2)/qf(0.025,n.a-1,n.b-1)
```

```
## [1] 1.917728
```
````

The confidence interval we obtain is $[0.2161555, 1.917728]$.

The estimate of the parameter is not affected by the change in the sample sizes and it is still equal to 0.64383810.6438381. For the confidence interval we use now the formula:

$$\left[(s_a^2/s_b^2)/\texttt{qf(0.975,149,149)}, (s_a^2/s_b^2)/\texttt{qf(0.025,149,149)}\right] :$$

```
```r
n.a <- 150
n.b <- 150
(s.a^2/s.b^2)/qf(0.975,n.a-1,n.b-1)
```

```
## [1] 0.466418
```

```r
(s.a^2/s.b^2)/qf(0.025,n.a-1,n.b-1)
```

```
## [1] 0.8887467
```

The corrected confidence interval is $[0.466418, 0.8887467]$.

CHAPTER 14

Exercise 14.1

The line marked in *red* is increasing and at x=0 it seems to obtain the value y=0. An increasing line is associated with a linear equation with a positive slope coefficient (b>0). The only equation with that property is Equation 3, for which b=1. Notice that the intercept of this equation is a=0a=0, which agrees with the fact that the line passes through the origin (x,y)=(0,0). If the x-axis and the yy-axis were on the same scale then one would expect the line to be tilted in the 45 degrees angle. However, here the axes are not on the same scale, so the tilting is different.

The xx-value of the line marked with a *red triangle* is x=-1. The yy-value is below 5. The observation that has an xx-value of -1 is Observation 6. The yy-value of this observation is y=4.3. Notice that there is another observation with the same y-value, Observation 3. However, the xx-value of that observation is x=1.6. Hence it is the point that is on the same level as the marked point, but it is placed to the right of it.
```

Exercise 14.2

The intercept is equal to a=-3.60 and the slope is equal to b=2.13. Notice that the lope is the coefficient that multiplies the explanatory variable and the intercept is the coefficient that does not multiply the explanatory variable.

The value of the explanatory variable for the 3rd observation is $x3$=4.2. When we use this value in the regression formula we obtain that:

$$\mathrm{E}(Y_3) = 2.13 \cdot x_3 - 3.60 = 2.13 \cdot 4.2 - 3.60 = 5.346 \ .$$

In words, the expectation of the response of the 3rd observation is equal to 5.3465.346

Exercise 14.3

After saving the file "aids.csv" in the working directory of R we read it's content into a data frame by the name "aids". We then produce a summary of the fit of the linear regression model of "deaths" as a response and "diagnosed" as the explanatory variable:

```
aids <- read.csv("_data/aids.csv")
fit.deaths <- lm(deaths~diagnosed,data=aids)
summary(fit.deaths)
```

```
##
## Call:
## lm(formula = deaths ~ diagnosed, data = aids)
##
## Residuals:
##      Min      1Q  Median      3Q     Max
## -7988.7  -680.9    23.9  1731.3  7760.7
##
```

```
## Coefficients:
##              Estimate Std. Error t value Pr(>|t|)
## (Intercept)   88.7161  1370.7191   0.065    0.949
## diagnosed      0.6073     0.0312  19.468 1.81e-14 ***
## ---
## Signif. codes:  0 '***' 0.001 '**' 0.01 '*' 0.05 '.' 0.1 ' ' 1
##
## Residual standard error: 3589 on 20 degrees of freedom
## Multiple R-squared:  0.9499, Adjusted R-squared:  0.9474
## F-statistic:   379 on 1 and 20 DF,  p-value: 1.805e-14
```

The estimated value of the slope 0.6073. The computed p-value associated with this slope is 1.81×10−14, which is much smaller than the 5% threshold. Consequently, the slope is statistically significant.

For confidence intervals apply the function "confint" to the fitted model:

```
confint(fit.deaths)
```

```
##                     2.5 %      97.5 %
## (Intercept) -2770.5538947 2947.986092
## diagnosed       0.5422759    0.672427
```

We get that the confidence interval for the slope is [0.5422759,0.672427].

A scatter plot of the two variables is produced by the application of the function "plot" to the formula that involves these two variables. The regression line is added to the plot using the function "abline" with the fitted model as an input:

```
plot(deaths~diagnosed,data=aids)
abline(fit.deaths)
```

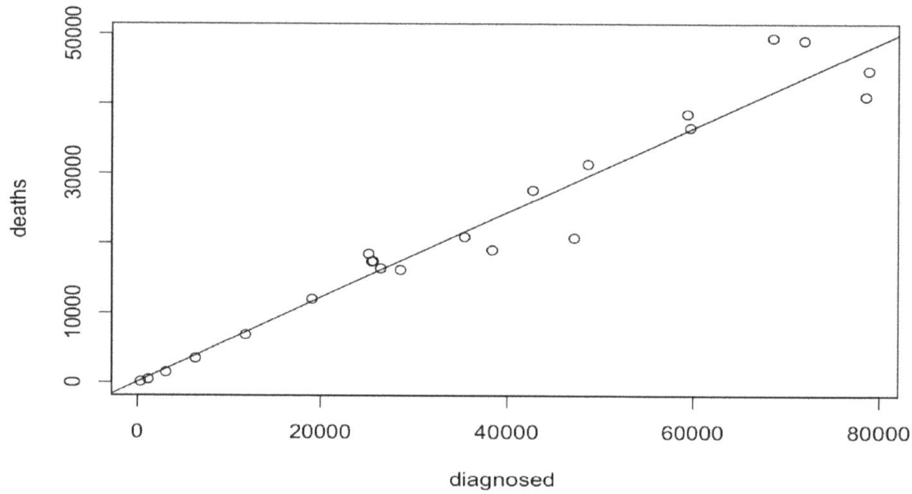

Observe that the points are nicely placed very to a line that characterizes the linear trend of the regression.

We fit a linear regression model of "diagnosed" as a response and "year" as the explanatory variable and save the fit in the object "fit.diagnosed". A summary of the model is produced by the application of the function "summary" to the fit:

```
fit.diagnosed <- lm(diagnosed~year,data=aids)
summary(fit.diagnosed)
```

```
##
## Call:
## lm(formula = diagnosed ~ year, data = aids)
##
## Residuals:
##    Min     1Q Median     3Q    Max
## -28364 -18321  -3909  14964  41199
##
## Coefficients:
##               Estimate Std. Error t value Pr(>|t|)
## (Intercept) -3448225.0  1535037.3  -2.246   0.0361 *
## year            1749.8      770.8   2.270   0.0344 *
## ---
## Signif. codes:  0 '***' 0.001 '**' 0.01 '*' 0.05 '.' 0.1 ' ' 1
##
## Residual standard error: 22940 on 20 degrees of freedom
## Multiple R-squared:  0.2049, Adjusted R-squared:  0.1651
## F-statistic: 5.153 on 1 and 20 DF,  p-value: 0.03441
```

The estimated value of the slope 1749.8. The computed p-value associated with this slope is 0.0344, which is less than the 0.05. Consequently, one may declare the slope to be statistically significant. Confidence intervals are produced using the function "confint":

```
confint(fit.diagnosed)
```

```
##                    2.5 %      97.5 %
## (Intercept) -6650256.665 -246193.429
## year             141.936    3357.618
```

We get that the 95% confidence interval for the slope is [141.9360,3357.618].

A scatter plot of the two variables is produced by the application of the function "plot" and the regression line is added with function "abline":

```
plot(diagnosed~year,data=aids)
abline(fit.diagnosed)
```

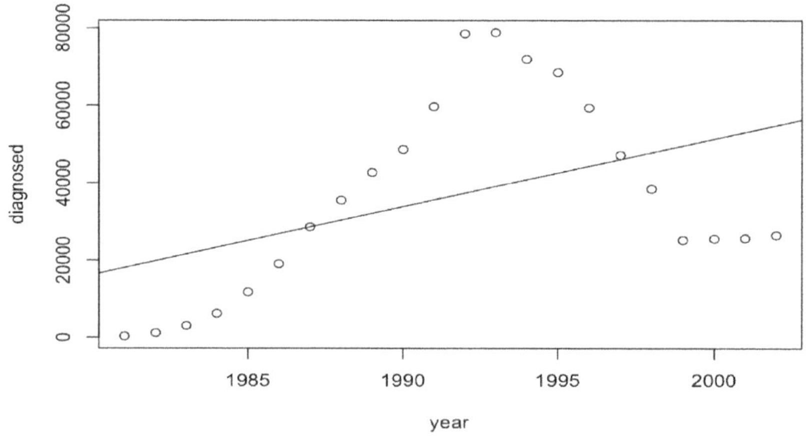

Observe that the points do not follow a linear trend. It seems that the number of diagnosed cases increased in an exponential rate during the first years after Aids was discovered. The trend changed in the mid 90's with a big drop in the number of diagnosed Aids patients. This drop may be associated with the administration of therapies such as AZT to HIV infected subjects that reduced the number of such subjects that developed Aids. In the late 90's there seams to be yet again a change in the trend and the possible increase in numbers. The line of linear regression misses all these changes and is a poor representation of the historical development.

The take home message from this exercise is to not use models blindly. A good advise is to plot the data. An examination of the plot provides a warning that the linear model is probably not a good model for the given problem.

Exercise 14.4

We read the data in the table into R. The variable "year" is the explanatory variable and the variable "percent" is the response. The scatter plot is produced using the function "plot" and the regression line, fitted to the data with the function "lm", is added to the plot using the function "abline":

```
year <- c(1945,1950,1960,1970,1980,1986,1993)
percent <- c(35.5,31.5,31.4,27.3,21.9,17.5,15.8)
plot(percent~year)
abline(lm(percent~year))
```

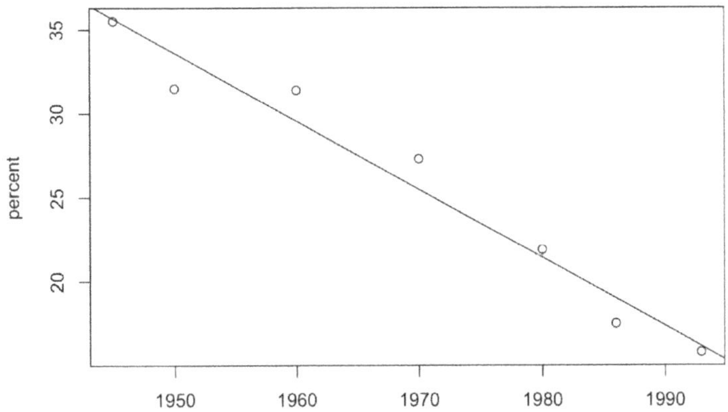

Observe that a linear trend is a reasonable description of the reduction in the percentage of workers that belong to labor unions in the post World War II period.

We compute the averages, standard deviations and the covariance:

```
mean.x <- mean(year)
mean.y <- mean(percent)
sd.x <- sd(year)
sd.y <- sd(percent)
cov.x.y <- cov(year,percent)
mean.x
```

```
## [1] 1969.143
```

```
mean.y
```

```
## [1] 25.84286
```

```
sd.x
```

```
## [1] 18.27957
```

```
sd.y
```

```
## [1] 7.574927
```

```
cov.x.y
```

```
## [1] -135.6738
```

The average of the variable "year" is 1969.143 and the standard deviation is 18.27957. The average of the variable "percent" is 25.84286 and the standard deviation is 7.574927. The covariance between the two variables is -135.6738-135.6738.

The slope of the regression line is the ratio between the covariance and the variance of the explanatory variable. The intercept is the solution of the equation that states that the value of regression line at the average of the explanatory variable is the average of the response:

```
b <- cov.x.y/sd.x^2
a <- mean.y - b*mean.x
a
```

```
## [1] 825.3845
```

```
b
```

```
## [1] -0.4060353
```

We get that the intercept is equal to 825.3845 and the slope is equal to -0.4060353.

In order to validate these figures, let us apply the function "lm" to the data:

```
lm(percent~year)
```

```
##
## Call:
## lm(formula = percent ~ year)
##
## Coefficients:
## (Intercept)          year
##     825.384        -0.406
```

Indeed, we get the same numbers that we got from the manual computation.

Exercise 14.5

The estimate for the expected value for the *i*th observation is obtained by the evaluation of the expression $a+b\cdot xi$, where a and b are the coefficients of the fitted regression model and xixi is the value of the explanatory variable for the iith observation. In our case i=4 and x_4=6.7:

$$a + b \cdot x_4 = 2.5 - 1.13 \cdot x_4 = 2.5 - 1.13 \cdot 6.7 = -5.071 \ .$$

Therefore, the estimate expectation of the response is -5.071.

The residual from the regression line is the difference between the observed value of the response and the estimated expectation of the response. For the 4th observation we have that the observed value of the response is y_4=0.17. The estimated expectation was computed in the previous question. Therefore, the residual from the regression line for the 4th observation is:

$$y_4 - (a + b \cdot x_4) = 0.17 - (-5.071) = 5.241 .$$

Exercise 14.6

We create the response and then fit a model and apply the summarizing function to the model:

```
dif.mpg <- cars$highway.mpg - cars$city.mpg
summary(lm(dif.mpg ~ cars$curb.weight))
```

```
##
## Call:
## lm(formula = dif.mpg ~ cars$curb.weight)
##
## Residuals:
##     Min      1Q  Median      3Q     Max
## -5.4344 -0.7755  0.1633  0.8844  6.3035
##
## Coefficients:
##                    Estimate Std. Error t value Pr(>|t|)
## (Intercept)       8.1653491  0.5460856  14.953  < 2e-16 ***
## cars$curb.weight -0.0010306  0.0002094  -4.921 1.77e-06 ***
## ---
## Signif. codes:  0 '***' 0.001 '**' 0.01 '*' 0.05 '.' 0.1 ' ' 1
##
## Residual standard error: 1.557 on 203 degrees of freedom
## Multiple R-squared:  0.1066, Adjusted R-squared:  0.1022
## F-statistic: 24.22 on 1 and 203 DF,  p-value: 1.775e-06
```

The p-value associated with the slope, 1.77×10-6, is much smaller than the 5% threshold proposing a significant (negative) trend. The value of R-squared, the fraction of the variability of the response that is explained by a regression model, is 0.1066.

The standard deviation is the square root of the variance. It follows that the fraction of the standard deviation of the response that is explained by the regression is $\sqrt{0.1066} = 0.3265$.

Following our own advice, we plot the data and the regression model:

```
plot(dif.mpg ~ cars$curb.weight)
abline(lm(dif.mpg ~ cars$curb.weight))
```

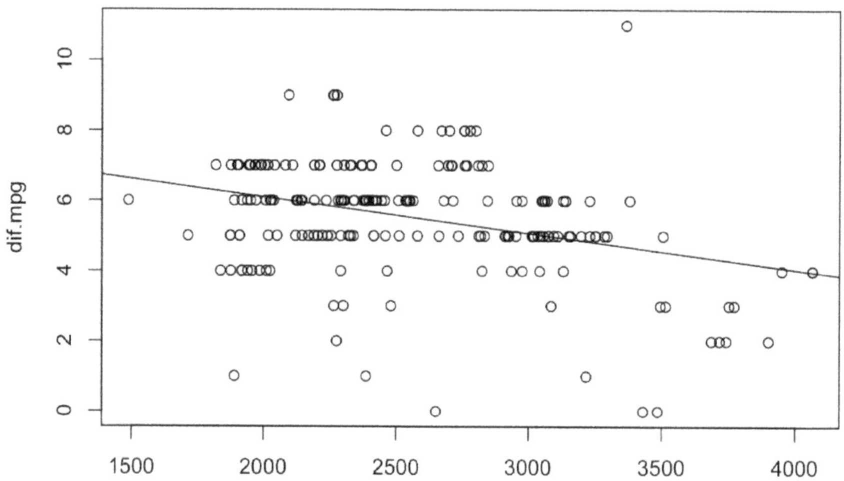

One may observe that although there seems to be an overall downward trend, there is still allot of variability about the line of regression.

We now fit and summarize the regression model with the size of engine as the explanatory variable:

```
summary(lm(dif.mpg ~ cars$engine.size))
```

```
##
## Call:
## lm(formula = dif.mpg ~ cars$engine.size)
##
## Residuals:
##     Min      1Q  Median      3Q     Max
## -5.7083 -0.7083  0.1889  1.1235  6.1792
##
## Coefficients:
##                   Estimate Std. Error t value Pr(>|t|)
## (Intercept)       6.717304   0.359385  18.691  < 2e-16 ***
## cars$engine.size -0.009342   0.002691  -3.471 0.000633 ***
## ---
## Signif. codes:  0 '***' 0.001 '**' 0.01 '*' 0.05 '.' 0.1 ' ' 1
##
## Residual standard error: 1.601 on 203 degrees of freedom
## Multiple R-squared:  0.05603,    Adjusted R-squared:  0.05138
## F-statistic: 12.05 on 1 and 203 DF,  p-value: 0.0006329
```

The regression slope is negative. The *p*-value is 0.000633, which is statistically significant. The value of R-squared is 0.05603. Consequently, the fraction of the standard deviation of the response that is explained by the current regression model is $\sqrt{0.05603} = 0.2367$.

Produce the scatter plot with the line of regression:

```
plot(dif.mpg ~ cars$engine.size)
abline(lm(dif.mpg ~ cars$engine.size))
```

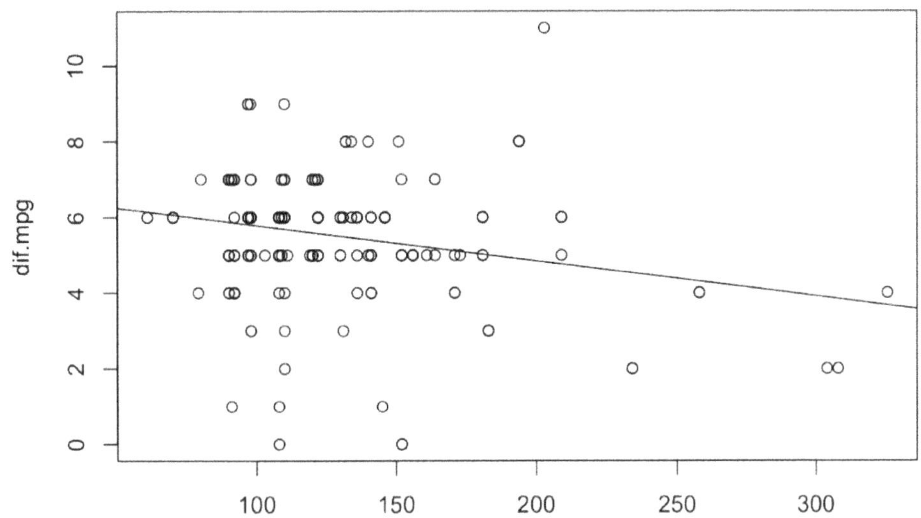

Again, there is variability about the line of regression.

Of the two models, the model that uses the curb weigh as the explanatory variable explains a larger portion of the variability in the response. Hence, unless other criteria tells us otherwise, we will prefer this model over the model that uses the size of engine as an explanatory variable.

CHAPTER 15

Exercise 15.1

First we save the file "diet.csv" in the working directory of R and read it's content. Then we apply the function "table" to the two variables in the file in order to obtain the requested frequency table:

```
diet <- read.csv("_data/diet.csv")
table(diet$health,diet$type)
```

```
##
##            aha med
##   cancer    15   7
##   death     24  14
##   healthy 239 273
##   illness  25   8
```

The resulting table has two columns and 4 rows. The third row corresponds to healthy subjects. Of these, 239 subjects used the AHA recommended diet and 273 used the Mediterranean diet. We may also plot this data using a mosaic plot:

```
plot(health~type,data=diet)
```

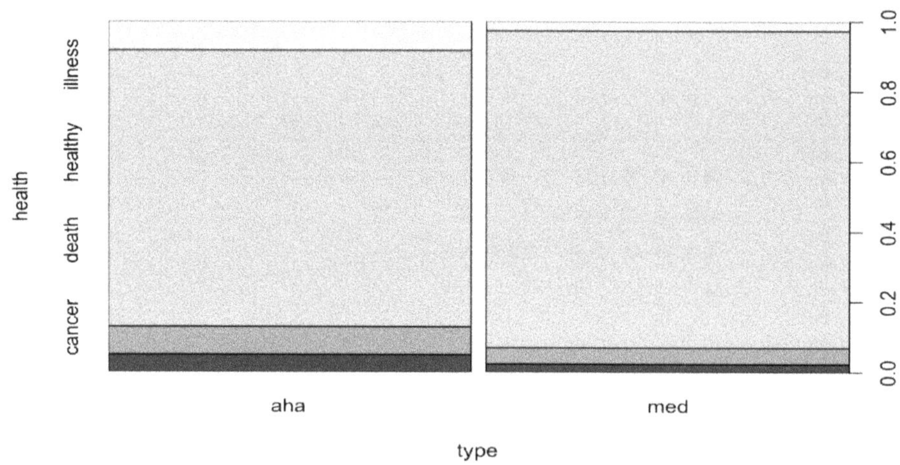

Figure 16.3: Health Condition Versus Type of Diet

Examining this plot one may appreciate the fact that the vast majority of the subjects were healthy and the relative proportion of healthy subjects among users of the Mediterranean diet is higher than the relative proportion among users of the AHA recommended diet.

In order to test the hypothesis that the probability of keeping healthy following an heart attack is the same for those that use the Mediterranean diet and for those that use the diet recommended by the AHA we create a 2×22×2. This table compares the response of being healthy or not to the type of diet as an explanatory variable. A sequence with logical components, "TRUE" for healthy and "FALSE" for not, is used as the response. Such a sequence is produced via the expression "diet$health==healthy". The table may serve as input to the function "prop.test":

```
table(diet$health=="healthy",diet$type)
```

```
##
##         aha med
##   FALSE  64  29
##   TRUE  239 273
```

```
prop.test(table(diet$health=="healthy",diet$type))
```

```
##
##  2-sample test for equality of proportions with continuity
##  correction
##
## data:  table(diet$health == "healthy", diet$type)
## X-squared = 14.555, df = 1, p-value = 0.0001361
## alternative hypothesis: two.sided
## 95 percent confidence interval:
##  0.1114300 0.3313203
## sample estimates:
##    prop 1    prop 2
## 0.6881720 0.4667969
```

The function "prop.test" conducts the test that compares between the probabilities of keeping healthy. In particular, the computed p-value for the test is 0.0001361, which is less than 0.05. Therefore, we reject the null hypothesis that both diets have the same effect on the chances of remaining healthy following an heart attack.

The confidence interval for the difference in probabilities is equal to [0.1114300,0.3313203]. The point estimation of the difference between the probabilities is $\hat{p}_a - \hat{p}_b = 0.6881720 - 0.4667969 \approx 0.22$ in favor of a Mediterranean diet. The confidence interval proposes that a difference as low as 0.11 or as high as 0.33 are not excluded by the data.

Exercise 15.2

We save the data of the file in a data frame by the name "cushings", produce a mosaic plot with the function "plot" and an histogram with the function "hist":

```
cushings <- read.csv("_data/cushings.csv")
plot(type~tetra,data=cushings)
```

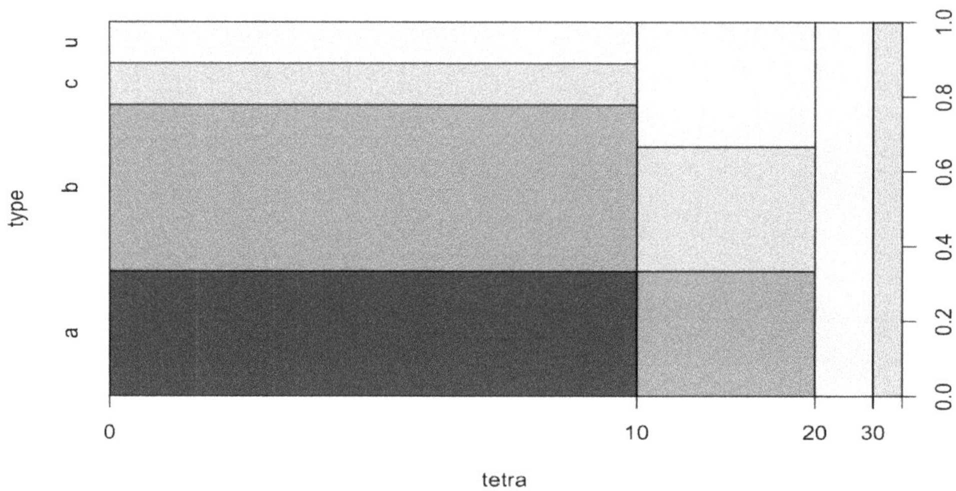

Figure 16.4: Health Condition Versus Type of Diet

```
hist(cushings$tetra)
```

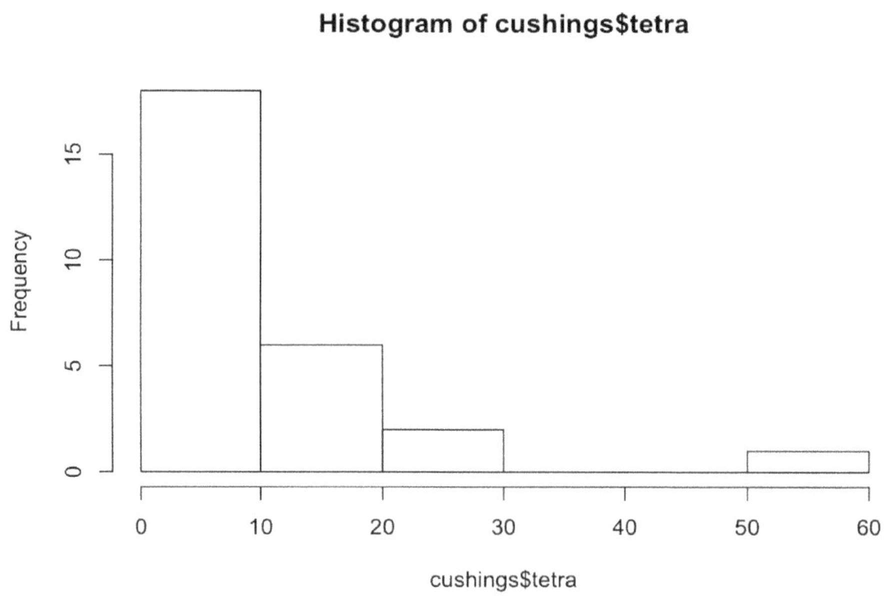

Figure 16.4: Health Condition Versus Type of Diet

The mosaic plot describes the distribution of the 4 levels of the response within the different intervals of values of the explanatory variable. The intervals coincide with the intervals that are used in the construction of the histogram. In particular, the third vertical rectangle from the left in the mosaic is associated with the third interval from the left in the histogram[^6]. This interval is associated with the range of values between 20 and 30. The height of the given interval in the histogram is 2, which is the number of patients with "terta" levels that belong to the interval.

There are 4 shades of *grey* in the first vertical rectangle from the left. Each shade is associated with a different level of the response. The lightest shade of grey, the upmost one, is associated with the level "u". Notice that this is also the shade of grey of the entire third vertical rectangle from the left. The conclusion is that the 2 patients that are associated with this rectangle have Tetrahydrocortisone levels between 2 and 30 and have an unknown type of syndrome.

We fit the logistic regression to the entire data in the data frame "cushings" using the function "glm", with the "family=binomial" argument. The response is the indicator that the type is equal to "b". The fitted model is saved in an object called "cushings.fit.all". The application of the function "summary" to the fitted model produces a report that includes the test of the hypothesis of interest:

```
cushings.fit.all <- glm((type=="b")~tetra,family=binomial, data=cushings)
summary(cushings.fit.all)
```

```
##
## Call:
## glm(formula = (type == "b") ~ tetra, family = binomial, data = cushings)
##
## Deviance Residuals:
##      Min        1Q    Median        3Q       Max
## -1.0924   -1.0460   -0.8652    1.3426    1.5182
##
## Coefficients:
##             Estimate Std. Error z value Pr(>|z|)
## (Intercept) -0.12304    0.61330  -0.201    0.841
## tetra       -0.04220    0.05213  -0.809    0.418
##
## (Dispersion parameter for binomial family taken to be 1)
##
##     Null deviance: 35.594  on 26  degrees of freedom
## Residual deviance: 34.739  on 25  degrees of freedom
## AIC: 38.739
##
## Number of Fisher Scoring iterations: 4
```

The test of interest examines the coefficient that is associated wit the explanatory variable "tetra". The estimated value of this parameter is -0.04220. The *p*-value for testing that the coefficient is 0 is equal to 0.418. Consequently, since the *p*-value is larger than 0.05, we do not reject the null hypothesis that states that the response and the explanatory variable are statistically unrelated.

Confidence intervals may be computed by applying the function "confint" to the fitted model:

```
confint(cushings.fit.all)
```

```
## Waiting for profiling to be done...
```

```
##                    2.5 %     97.5 %
## (Intercept) -1.2955624 1.18118256
## tetra       -0.1776113 0.04016772
```

Specifically, the confidence interval for the coefficient that is associated with the explanatory variable is equal to [-0.1776113,0.04016772]

If we want to fit the logistic model to a partial subset of the data, say all the observations with values of the response other that "u", we may apply the argument "subset"[^7]. Specifically, adding the expression "subset=(type!=u)" would do the job[^8]. We repeat the same analysis as before. The only difference is the addition of the given expression to the function that fits the model to the data. The fitted model is saved in an object we call "cushings.fit.known":

```
cushings.fit.known <- glm((type=="b")~tetra,family=binomial, data=cushings,subset=(type!="u"))
summary(cushings.fit.known)
```

```
##
## Call:
## glm(formula = (type == "b") ~ tetra, family = binomial, data = cushings,
##     subset = (type != "u"))
##
## Deviance Residuals:
##     Min       1Q   Median       3Q      Max
## -1.2079  -1.1865  -0.7548   1.2033   1.2791
##
## Coefficients:
##             Estimate Std. Error z value Pr(>|z|)
## (Intercept)  0.11457    0.59947   0.191    0.848
## tetra       -0.02276    0.04586  -0.496    0.620
##
## (Dispersion parameter for binomial family taken to be 1)
##
##     Null deviance: 29.065  on 20  degrees of freedom
```

```
## Residual deviance: 28.789  on 19  degrees of freedom
## AIC: 32.789
##
## Number of Fisher Scoring iterations: 4
```

The estimated value of the coefficient when considering only subject with a known type of the syndrome is slightly changed to -0.02276. The new p-value, which is equal to 0.620, is larger than 0.05. Hence, yet again, we do not reject the null hypothesis.

```
confint(cushings.fit.known)

## Waiting for profiling to be done...

##                  2.5 %     97.5 %
## (Intercept) -1.0519135 1.40515473
## tetra       -0.1537617 0.06279923
```

For the modified confidence interval we apply the function "confint". We get now [-0.1537617,0.06279923] as a confidence interval for the coefficient of the explanatory variable.

We initiated the process by fitting the model to every single observation. Only observations with known syndrome types are used in this analysis. The practical consequence of using all observations in the fitting process is that it implies that the syndrome type for observations of an unknown type is not type "b". This is not appropriate and may introduce bias, since the type may well be "b". It is more suitable to consider the observations linked to the level "u" as missing data and exclude them from the study. This method is the one that was employed in the subsequent analysis.

INDEX

www.ingramcontent.com/pod-product-compliance
Ingram Content Group UK Ltd.
Pitfield, Milton Keynes, MK11 3LW, UK
UKHW051028041026
15470UKWH00015B/1685

9 781787 153974